SONGBOOK

SONGBOOK

How Lyrics Became Poetry
in Medieval Europe

MARISA GALVEZ

THE UNIVERSITY OF CHICAGO PRESS
Chicago & London

The University of Chicago Press, Chicago 60637
The University of Chicago Press, Ltd., London
© 2012 by The University of Chicago
All rights reserved. Published 2012.
Paperback edition 2015
Printed in the United States of America

24 23 22 21 20 19 18 17 16 15   2 3 4 5 6

ISBN-13: 978-0-226-28051-6 (cloth)
ISBN-13: 978-0-226-27005-0 (paper)
ISBN-13: 978-0-226-28052-3 (e-book)
10.7208/chicago/9780226280523.001.0001

The University of Chicago Press gratefully acknowledges
the generous support of Stanford University toward the
publication of this book.

Library of Congress Cataloging-in-Publication Data

Galvez, Marisa.
Songbook : how lyrics became poetry in medieval Europe / Marisa Galvez.
pages : illustrations ; cm
Includes bibliographical references and index.
ISBN-13: 978-0-226-28051-6 (cloth : alkaline paper)
ISBN-10: 0-226-28051-9 (cloth : alkaline paper)
1. Songbooks, Medieval — Europe. 2. Poetry, Medieval — History and criticism.
3. Lyric poetry — History and criticism. 4. Illumination of books and manuscripts,
Medieval — Europe. 5. Art and literature. I. Title.
PN688.G35 2012
809.1'02 — dc23
2011046238

♾ This paper meets the requirements of
ANSI/NISO Z39.48-1992 (Permanence of Paper).

To Roland Greene,
and to the memory of my father,
Alberto Icarangal Galvez
(1944–1992)

Contents

List of Illustrations / ix

Acknowledgments / xi

INTRODUCTION
The Medieval Songbook as Emergent Genre / 1

CHAPTER ONE
Paradigms: The *Carmina Burana* and the *Libro de buen amor* / 17

CHAPTER TWO
Producing Opaque Coherence: Lyric Presence
and Names / 57

CHAPTER THREE
Shifting Mediality: Visualizing Lyric Texts / 99

CHAPTER FOUR
Cancioneros and the Art of the Songbook / 167

CONCLUSION
Songbook Medievalisms / 203

Notes / 219

Bibliography / 253

Index / 269

Illustrations

COLOR PLATES *(following page 148)*

1–3. Historiated initials from *Chansonnier R*

4. Marginalia from *Chansonnier N*

5. Christ's Capture from *Donaueschinger Psalter*

6. Johannes Hadlaub miniature from *Codex Manesse*

7. Reinmar von Brennenberg miniature from *Codex Manesse*

FIGURES

1. *Nummus versus* from *Carmina Burana* / 28

2. Example of endline configuration from *Carmina Burana* / 30

3. Dido miniature from *Carmina Burana* / 32

4. Nature miniature from *Carmina Burana* / 33

5. Evangelist from *Gospels of Saint Médard of Soissons* / 101

6. Holy Face from *Indulgence for Königsfelden* / 106

7. Holy Face from Church of the Assumption, Bohemia / 107

8. Pilgrims miniature from *Cantigas de Santa María* / 109

9. Saint Francis receiving the stigmata from Gradual / 115

10–12. Alfonso X miniatures from *Cantigas de Santa María* / 117–119

13. Frederick II from a fresco in the Palazzo Finco, Bassano del Grappa / 120

14. Emperor Henry miniature from *Codex Manesse* / 131

15. King David from *Topographia Christiana* / 132

16. King Solomon from *Weltchronik des Rudolf von Ems* / 133

17. Frederick II from *De arte venandi cum avibus* / 134

18. Frederick II from *Exultet* / 135

19. Walther von der Vogelweide miniature from *Codex Manesse* / 138

20–22. Privilege images from *Kopialbuch* / 139–141

23. Cicero as "Orator" from Ms. Lat. f. 252, f. IV / 142

24. Frauenlob miniature from *Codex Manesse* / 145

25. Pfeffel miniature from *Codex Manesse* / 146

26. Alram von Gresten miniature from *Codex Manesse* / 147

27. Ulrich von Lichtenstein miniature from *Codex Manesse* / 148

28, von Buchein miniature from *Codex Manesse* / 149

29. Wachsmut von Künzigen miniature from *Codex Manesse* / 152

30. Tannhäuser miniature from *Codex Manesse* / 153

31. Hartmann von Aue miniature from *Codex Manesse* / 155

32. Rudolf von Neuenburg miniature from *Codex Manesse* / 157

33. Klingsor von Ungerlant miniature from *Codex Manesse* / 159

Acknowledgments

THIS BOOK RESULTS from delightful conversations with friends, colleagues, and mentors. I want to express my thanks to Sepp Gumbrecht, Jennifer Summit, Cécile Alduy, Orrin Robinson, Sarah Kay, and Bill Tronzo. I am thankful to the late Brigitte Cazelles, whose creativity remains at the core of this book. I am grateful for Vincent Barletta's help in the editorial process, and the indispensable friendship of Nicole Lopez Stengel, Eliza Zingesser, John Bullock, Alec Bemis, Stephanie Choi, and Paul Levine through the years. Thanks to the Stanford Humanities Center, and especially Theodore H. and Frances K. Geballe for making my productive year at the center possible, and to the Stanford Presidential Research Grant for Junior Faculty. The energy and vitality of the students who have attended my seminars, as well as my colleagues in the Junior Faculty workshop, have been an invaluable intellectual and moral resource. Margaret Tompkins, Christine Onorato, and Marco Aresu have also been there when I most needed them. I also want to express my gratitude to the readers from *Modern Philology*, to the two anonymous readers who read this book in manuscript for the University of Chicago Press and offered invaluable suggestions, and to the staff at the Press for guiding this first-book author through the publishing process. A special thank you is due to Randy Petilos, whose support from the earliest stages and professionalism have made working with him a privilege and a pleasure. I also thank Margaret Mahan, for her wonderful copyediting, and the archivists and librarians who allowed me access to the materials from their collections that I cite and reproduce in this book. For a view of the Frederick II fresco, I am grateful to Gianni Bizzotto. My family has been a constant source of spiritual assistance over the years: Marietta, Dom, Paul, and Christina. I believe my father, Alberto Galvez, would have been happy that I am doing something I love. From early on he encouraged me to see beauty and possibility. And finally to Roland: an inspirational model of intellect, my best friend, whose daily support and conversation enriches my life in countless ways.

San Francisco, California
June 2011

xi

Introduction

THE MEDIEVAL SONGBOOK AS EMERGENT GENRE

WHEN WE PEER BACK at the origins of poetry in the European ver-
naculars, often we can go no further than poems collected into codices that
are called songbooks: these are known in French as *chansonniers*, in German
as *Liederhandschriften*, and in Spanish as *cancioneros*. Songbooks embody the
beginnings of these great lyric traditions, and the choices made in gathering them into codices undoubtedly shaped the history of later poetry in
these languages. And yet it has never been asked, in a comprehensive study,
whether songbooks of different national traditions have common properties, or how songbooks enable us to understand the process that sees a song
made permanent in manuscript or print, allows a series of songs to tell a
story in a book, and creates productive tensions within these changes. In the
spirit of songbook studies that have focused on vernacular lyric anthologies
in the separate languages, this project charts the rise and persistence of the
genre in the Occitan troubadour, the Middle High German *Minnesang*, and
the Iberian *cancionero* traditions from the high to late medieval period, circa
1200 to 1500. I address the nature and purposes of songbooks, the *what* and
why of this foundational genre, but I am chiefly concerned with the *how*,
namely how songbooks establish expectations of the poem, the poet, and
lyric poetry itself. Superficial similarities aside, a careful comparative study
that draws from medieval and modern theorists reveals the songbook not
only as a product of historical forces but as a living entity—a concrete, communal object that establishes a system of values for medieval lyric, including
rhetorical, bibliographical, and phenomenological horizons. For example,
how is "Bernart de Ventadorn" (fl. 1147–70), perhaps the most famous trou-

badour of the period when lyric poetry flourished in southern France (ca. 1100–1300)—a name governing a corpus of texts, memorialized for future generations through a written medium, and thus assigned cultural status— an invention of the songbook? How is "Walther von der Vogelweide" (ca. 1170–1227), the most celebrated Middle High German poet—a name associated with a certain meditative portrait and with a group of other named poets collectively known as *Minnesänger* (or minnesingers)—a product of a songbook? These are the kinds of questions that animate this study.

I primarily use the term *songbook* to mean a multiauthor and anonymous lyric anthology contained in a manuscript codex or volume of parchment leaves bound together in book form (in contrast to a scroll or roll, leaves sewn together with horizontal or vertical orientation) that displays an intention to gather and organize different vernacular lyric texts as an overall collection. Yet throughout this study, songbooks also range from anthologies occupying only a few folios within a larger volume to large compilations coextensive with the entire codex or bound volume that includes them. In this sense I bring Seth Lerer's "idea of the anthology" to bear, since the key concept of a "songbook" is that a "controlling literary intelligence" governs a collection of lyric texts,[1] and more often than not the anthology displays the editorial intention to collect representative specimens of various lyric genres for artistic preservation. Given that all short medieval texts are transmitted either in miscellanies (ranging from haphazard or practical incorporation to collections put together on commission or speculation by a patron) or anthologies (items brought together according to some intelligible governing principle), these songbooks were literary objects that collated individual nonnarrative poetry in stanzaic form. Following this idea of heterogeneity, I exclude single-author anthologies, narrative anthologies in octosyllabic couplets (such as the Old French romance or *dit*), and prose works that share thematic similarities with the courtly love song from this study. The songbooks most relevant to the development of Western poetry, in terms of their typical qualities and conscious intention to establish literary traditions, are the monumental manuscripts compiled from the thirteenth century onward, such as the chansonniers of troubadour and *trouvère* poetry and *Liederhandschriften* of German *Minnesänger*.

In treating various songbooks as a genre, I do not assert that each of the works that I will examine possesses a number of unchanging characteristics. On the contrary, in the Middle Ages before the age of printing, every "work" in a codex, whether transmitted on a manuscript folio or a flyleaf, is contained in a unique, material object with its own history of compilation, production, transmission, and reception. The conscious application of the word "genre" is essential to my methodology of viewing the medieval songbook as a phenomenon: can we track the songbook genre as it comes into being? In other words, if we take the editorial intention of manuscript books such as Italian chansonniers of Occitan lyric as a generic baseline, where the organization articulates an overall idea of the book as greater than the sum of its similar or dissimilar parts (including lyric and nonlyric texts), how do other works converge or depart from that intention? My methodology is a heuristic application that came about with a simple observation: the remembering of medieval lyrics, that is to say songs, through the physical and conceptual book undergirded the transformation of ephemeral, anonymous lyrics into modern conceptions of poetry and the poet. These modern conceptions, such as poetry as capturing the most essential qualities of human nature through language, depend on the antecedent genre of the songbook as a place in which to work out these ideas.

This approach builds on the diversity of theoretical reflections that have come to bear on medieval studies in the last forty years, in particular on the works of Hans Robert Jauss, who in his assertion of the "alterity and modernity" of medieval genres argues for an aesthetic pleasure that arises from an understanding of the concrete, "experiential horizons" of the traditions and conventions of a distant past. To appreciate the social function of medieval texts as a medium that, once reconstructed, anticipates or compensates for forms of life — ceremonial repetition of salvation history, happiness in marriage à la Chrétien de Troyes — modern readers must reorient themselves to a single work that neither possesses formal or temporal limits nor exists as the discrete, self-enclosed production of an author.[2] Together with Hugo Kuhn, Jauss views literary evolution — the rise and alteration of such forms as expressions of changing horizons of possibilities or social modes of behavior — as the history of audience expectations and reception, rather than the aesthetic innovation of authors and works.[3] As a material locus where personal and collective values, conventions, and interests are played out in the interpretation and codification of lyric texts, my own study explains how the songbook genre forms itself within certain conditions, and how social, cultural, and historical contexts shape a cohesive structure out of these conditions, creating a genre as an autonomous and self-sustaining form.

This goal of describing the songbook genre as an emergent process is different from describing historically ossified objects from a diachronic perspective, or a genre constituted in imitation of a classical tradition such as tragedy in the early modern period. My approach tracks the trajectory of the songbook as genre, its process of change without a preconceived end-point of work or author, by historically delimiting and describing certain medieval manuscripts that share familial resemblances as lyric anthologies in form and structure. I am concerned with textual, semantic, and visual properties of these books, not with the music usually associated with them. While such music can be understood as a stratum of meaning comparable to the editorial and visual meanings I pursue, it is beyond the scope of this study. Most codices I examine preserve lyric texts rather than musical nota-tion, include prose texts, and are large-format, costly objects of parchment rather than performance manuals of traveling singers. In this sense, my goal is not to empirically define what a songbook is,[4] nor to offer hypotheses of manuscript transmission in the separate vernacular traditions.[5] Rather, given that a medieval songbook contains heterogeneous lyric texts and the quality of an overall corpus, how and why does a compiler structure and ordinate this textual material to form a coherent overall collection? This study sets out to construe typologies from these resemblances and devia-tions among songbooks, typologies that tell us much about the historical and cultural contexts of the compilers and their public, and the evolving reception of medieval vernacular lyric. The advantage of this approach, as I see it, is that it allows one to see how collecting and ordering lyric texts in a codex was a fluid, often ad hoc process, shaped by immediate and local-ized valuations of vernacular lyric, elementary needs for the embodiment of universal order and ritual, and the shifting horizons of the songbook's medieval public. In time this process of lyric reception became a monu-ment and foundation of vernacular traditions. Yet even from this apparent end-point perspective, modern-day critics and editors of the songbook as artifact bring their own aesthetic values to an object that in its very nature invites multiple interpretations. Thus in considering the songbook as an emergent genre, I seek to trace how a collection of lyric texts came into being from performance practices that were at origin openly mediated acts of memorial transmission, and became a form that medieval people began to use consciously as an aesthetic means — poetry existing for and because of the book. Moreover, to understand the evolving structure of songbooks over time, I examine the conditions in which a songbook becomes visible as genre: how do structural alterations transform a songbook's social function from a local medium of preservation to a literary object that shapes lyric production? Or seen otherwise, at what point is a songbook as genre visible to a later audience, for whom the original context of songbook production must be reconstructed?

Throughout this book, I tackle questions of this kind by studying song-books from several vernacular traditions and by applying ideas central to the disciplines of literary studies, art history, and philology. Posed from a comparative perspective, many of these theoretical questions are empirically unanswerable. Yet by analyzing concrete situations from the evidence available, we may advance the discussion of the way songbooks shaped modern concepts of poetry and the development of literary consciousness. In my efforts to historically document the life and evolution of the medieval songbook, I build on studies of the songbook both as material anthology and as literary object, and more generally on studies of *compilatio* and the idea of a single manuscript as historical artifact: since the rise of New Historicism and New Philology in premodern literary studies, all of these critical perspectives have been productive explorations.[6] Seminal work using this approach include Sylvia Huot's and Stephen G. Nichols's studies on *trouvère* and troubadour chansonniers;[7] the ongoing empirical and theoretical work on the cancioneros by Vicenç Beltran Pepió and Michel Garcia, based on Brian Dutton's foundational compilation and bibliographical assessment;[8] and the interdisciplinary and methodological perspectives in the German tradition as seen in the recent work of Jan-Dirk Müller, Horst Wenzel, and Kathryn Starkey.[9] Finally, the comparative and phenomenological approach expands the scholarly consensus about a songbook as a unifying principle greater than the sum of its parts—a "silloge"—whether a tonal unity that reflects a social-cultural reality or a pragmatic unity that reflects a compiler's intention mediated by external material conditions.[10] By considering social and material contexts, assessing aspects of compilers' choice, and posing new hypotheses regarding different reception situations of medieval lyric through the songbook—on this last point John Dagenais's emphasis on medieval reading as an ethical activity has been especially influential[11]—*Songbook* shows how lyrics were communally produced and received. This portrayal of the genre may challenge the rarely acknowledged application of modern concepts to the medieval context of lyric poetry—such as the often implicit assumption that a poem is composed by a poet rather than by a network of poets and readers.

This book argues that what we consider "poetry" is built on the remains of lyrics seen in the material formation of the songbook. Before the thirteenth century, the terms "poem," "poet," and "poetry" were reserved for classical authors; contemporary vernacular versifiers designated their lyrics and art with different terms—*trobadors* skilled in *trobar* or *chantar*, or skilled in the art of combining "moz e sons" or "vers e·l so" (words and melodies, or *vers* [the song] and the melody; see chapter two). These terms are consistent with those used by the middle-Latin versifiers of the *Carmina Burana* (ca. 1230) who designated their songs as *rhythmi, versus,* or *carmina.* An examination of songbooks shows how secular vernacular lyric was in the process of achieving the same status as classical poetry without being designated as such. This lyric was preserved in writing as an "art"—in the Latin sense of the deployment of skill or craft in rhetoric and grammar—and archival strategies conferred value on genres such as the *canso* (love poem).

Transmitted both orally and by the written word, this lyric came out of aristocratic courts and was both outside of and in dialogue with the official Latin culture of the Church and schools. One of the goals of this book is to use representative examples from the different traditions to show the diverse ways in which lyrics were received, despite being organized in books and memorialized as the monument of a certain audience. In other words, by studying how the songs were compiled, we can go back to the original hybrid nature of medieval lyric before it was "poetry": the book as embodying overlapping cultural and historical perspectives, as showing the formation of genres and the act of reading through visual and verbal texts, and as displaying the fluidity between prose and verse. *Songbook* shows how lyric came into being as a communal phenomenon, even if seen only through its written transmission years later. My research compels us to revise our modern idea of individual, subjective introspection directly translated to a written publication.

Why did I choose such disparate songbook traditions (Latin Goliardic verse, troubadour lyric, *Minnesang,* examples from the Iberian tradition) for my comparative study? While I would have liked to incorporate as many traditions as possible, my choices serve as points of a compass, the examples forming a constellation of the genre rather than a linear narrative: they possess enough dissimilar qualities to challenge the historical view of songbooks, held since the Renaissance, as leading to the unified *poet* and *book* most often embodied in the work of figures such as Dante (d. 1321), Petrarch (d. 1374), and Guillaume de Machaut (d. 1377). Because the majority of troubadour and *trouvère* chansonniers, as well as Italian *canzonieri* such as the late thirteenth-century Florentine Canzoniere palatino (BNC, Banco Rari 217), share overlapping qualities as anthologies keyed to authors and lyric genres, I thought it would be productive to compare the troubadours' chansonniers to the *Minnesang Liederhandschriften,* so as to see how the portraits in the latter represent a new development in this author principle. The *Carmina Burana* and the fourteenth-century *Libro de buen amor,* as a clerical songbook and an autobiographical lyrico-narrative that is anthological in nature, may be read as songbooks in a different sense from the chansonniers and *Liederhandschriften*. The Castilian cancioneros show the full development of the genre as operative: the cancionero as a literary object deployed by lettered men. Throughout, I refer to Alfonso X's *Cantigas de Santa María* (ca. 1270–90), a songbook associated with a Davidic king figure as patron, poet, and compiler of songs. As a counterpoint to the secular lyric songbooks, it shows a transformation of that tradition. For instance, it resembles the near contemporary Galician-Portuguese *Cancioneiro da Ajuda* (ca. 1280), a collection of secular *cantigas*, by including miniatures that show musical performance and transmitting notation (as the *Ajuda* intended to); but as a collection of songs devoted to the miracles of the Virgin Mary and treating the life of a kingdom, it departs from the *cancioneiro,* which, like the Italian troubadour chansonniers, organizes by author corpora.[12] The *Cantigas* definitively shapes the Iberian tradition as a reference for later poets and for its promotion of a songbook embodying a collectivity. In this sense, it is noteworthy that this period of Iberian songbook production succeeds the military, political, and cultural consolidation of the territorial gains of the Reconquest, culminating in the taking of Seville in 1248. My secular examples reflect collections that articulate a tradition or literary consciousness, yet do so in ways that, first, lack an overarching poet figure as the interpretive principle (even in the case of the *Libro de buen amor*, when seen as a communal songbook) and, second, are illuminating from a comparative perspective for expressing how diverse audiences interpreted lyric through songbooks.

This comparative study of the songbook in several vernacular traditions thus offers a pluralistic and dynamic view of medieval lyric seen from the material situation of the songbook. Such a view enhances our understanding of vernacular lyric poetry — both secular and religious — through preservation practices that incorporate various contemporary media to form a tradition, a practice seen, for example, in the visual commentary of songbooks (chapter three). The emergence of the songbook, then, should not be taken as simply an organic narrative of an increasing secularization toward early modern humanism—for instance, the appreciation of erotic love lyric as a celebration of the humanist individual. Rather, the preservation of lyric means creative spiritual edification for lay readers and the promotion of lyric as a ritualized, communal craft — a process we see in the visual pilgrimage of the fourteenth-century chansonnier R (Paris, Bibl. Nat. fr. 22543)[13] or the involution of cancionero poetry as a serial repetition of forms or increasingly euphemistic lyric genres (chapter four). What develops from the thirteenth century onward is a rising consciousness of the songbook as genre on the part of poets, compilers, and readers, even as it continues to be a medium of disparate texts and scribal idiosyncrasies that blur distinctions between author, compiler, and lyric persona.

Throughout this book I will refer to the ways in which Dante and Petrarch shaped the modern understanding of the lyric tradition through songbooks, but I will also elaborate on how their readings and works allude to the nature of songbooks without getting at what they were about. By placing the troubadours by association under the rubric of "poeta" in *De vulgari eloquentia* (ca. 1303), Dante's reading of the troubadours as poets definitively shaped the Romance lyric tradition.[14] Rather than viewing the songbooks as a collection of canonized poets from this traditional perspective, my book aims to read the songbook qua songbook, sui generis: as embodying myriad localized perspectives of coherence—authorship, book, lyric corpus, proper name, coterie. This approach reconsiders directed narratives within the traditional literary histories, such as narratives of song to book, and of multiauthored lyric anthology to single-authored songbook.[15] Further, from the thirteenth century one sees lyrics depicted as multiauthorial from different historical vantage points (singer, scribe), and modular, available to be interpreted with different media and other kinds of lyric or prose. We can consider Petrarch's *Rime sparse* (ca. 1342–74) as alluding to this very idea of lyrics as scattered over time, multivocal and inchoate before they were gathered and memorialized in his authorial songbook as an eternal, subjective unity, what John Freccero describes as the autoreflexive sign of the laurel becoming a neutral emblem that laureates the poet.[16] While Petrarch alludes to the troubadours in his new tradition of poetry, songbooks manifest this reflexivity in its protean form. The circular model of *Lauro-laura* can be found in songbooks by way of discrete and localized moments: for example, in chapter two I will describe how the name of a troubadour in a *canso* is neutralized and then reinterpreted by an anonymous author (performer, compiler, scribe) as a rubric in order to reify the presence of the lyric texts contextualized by that name. Certainly songbooks constitute memorial archives that fix lyrics against the passage of time. Yet how and what they go about memorializing embodies a plurality of processes that include reproducing performative elements as well as reifying lyrics as self-contained textual objects. These processes represent a situation in which lyrics truly are scattered and memorialized as such, a situation before Petrarch's self-reflexive poetics of presence.

Thus *Songbook* does not seek to answer the persistent "subjectivity" question of the medieval lyric "I," seen in the debates around Paul

Zumthor's view of medieval lyric as nonreferential in his seminal *Essai de poétique médiévale* (1972). Rather, by building on pioneering studies of the intersection of orality, performance, and written text, as well as critical appraisals of medieval texts as cultural knowledge,[17] my study applies a phenomenological and comparative perspective to reorient the investigation: in the case of the lyric anthologies, how can we enhance our description of the lyric persona as a product of various readerships — copyists, troubadours, and readers/editors — both synchronically and diachronically? Or in the case of the fifteenth-century cancioneros, how did what we might call a cancionero consciousness enable or limit the composition of different kinds of lyric poetry? As the historian Jacques Le Goff writes, "the medieval mind was inclined toward the universal at the same time as it subscribed to the here and now, to what was embodied in a single person or place."[18] *Songbook* strives to describe how and why the songbook embodies both the universal and the singularity of the here and now in its articulation of lyric poetry: whether in the thirteenth century or the nineteenth, the songbook invites us to see a lyric persona as a particular engagement between reader and text in a material context (what Nichols would call a "manuscript matrix").[19] It thus maintains different social narratives of cultural, historical, and professional preoccupations through the ages, even as it transmits — and gains prestige as a result of transmitting — singular authorial identities and lyrics of indelible historical situations, such as Marcabru's (fl. 1130–49) crusading song, "Pax in nomine Domini" (Peace in the name of the Lord [PC 293.35]) discussed in chapters two and three.[20] Examined closely as literary objects and transmitters of lyric texts, these anthologies decisively form concepts of the poet and literary tradition as archive, following the occurrence of what Jacques Derrida calls the "pathology of the archive"; that is to say, when the archive acts against itself as the destruction of "live" memory by making a "word or figure stabilized so as to take on a signification."[21] Yet this project illuminates points of tension between lyric as performed event (through both oral and written transmission) and the translation of this lyric into knowledge; such tension occurs through a cultural economy of the songbook made possible through rubrics, names, ordination, and verbal and visual commentary.

THE FLUIDITY OF THE SONGBOOK AS PRODUCING CULTURAL AND SOCIAL MEANING

In the course of this book, several themes are foundational for the emergence of the genre. The first is the dual quality of the songbook as a coherent corpus and a collection of discrete units. This duality facilitates a creative process of compiling new canons while endowing the songbook with the prestige of older ones. Through strategies of organization, compilers and patrons of songbooks create narratives that attribute cultural or social value to lyric in a certain manner, yet this attribution of value never overtakes the heterogeneous nature of the songbook. This aspect holds because of the ad hoc historical situation of compilation, based on pragmatic concerns such as the availability of exemplars. Further, while this attribution of value through the order in which contents appear and through rubrics or marginalia informs our understanding of lyric reception, the dual nature of the songbook maintains competing interests of a community of readers, and becomes a work space for the negotiation of values from different moments of lyric reception. Thus the songbook can retain heterogeneity while endorsing certain social or moral values. For example, the major thirteenth- and fourteenth-century troubadour Italian chansonniers preserve Occitan lyric, a generation after the original performance environment, according to the idea of the individual poet represented through biographies (*vidas*) and author portraits; they also transmit lyric without musical notation and organize lyric by genre. These compilers and their aristocratic patrons employed these elements to create a written tradition of a by then prestigious, yet nonnative lyric tradition.[22] On the other hand, the *Carmina Burana,* which preserves Latin and German lyrics, and the fifteenth-century cancioneros, which preserve Spanish lyric, demonstrate communal values through certain poetic topics or forms of lyric favored by the poets they represent, such as clerical students or a coterie associated with a particular court.

A second thematic concern is the way the songbook enables the assimilation and convergence of various vernacular cultures — such as orally transmitted popular lyric (e.g., refrain lyric), ritual lay activities, or court pageantry — with classical or clerical literate cultures or the aristocratic *canso.* The songbook genre allows us to see the manner in which this convergence becomes a framework for a particular public. I discuss such formal frameworks with regard to the refrain lyrics in the *Carmina* and the *Libro de buen amor* as a particular songbook phenomenon (chapter one) that accommodates different kinds of lyric while maintaining a lyrico-narrative, or to the visual citation of sacred imagery in the heraldic rhetoric of the large Heidelberg manuscript of Middle High German lyric, Codex Palatinus Germanicus 848, known as Manuscript C or the *Codex Manesse* (ca. 1300–1340, chapter three).

A third thematic concern that I apply to the songbook in different contexts and traditions is the condensation of lyric material into forms of knowledge. As compilers memorialized lyric texts and made them archival by placing them in prosaic constellations of rubrics and glosses, they also reflected and commented upon lyrics through other visual media such as marginalia and historiated initials. Citational through these forms, poets and texts became available for appropriation and translation into other discourses, such as religious, political, or personal narratives. In chapters two and three, for example, I discuss the cultural currency that Marcabru's name acquires seen in light of his nominal self-invocations in his lyrics and the transmission of this name both as a rubric and as an attachment to visual commentary such as an image of Christ's face in a songbook.

FROM ARCHAEOLOGICAL PREHISTORY TO LITERARY OBJECT: THE PATH OF EMERGENCE

In my first chapter, I venture to describe as songbooks two works—the middle Latin compendium the *Carmina Burana*, and the Castilian *Libro de buen amor*—not conventionally regarded as lyric anthologies in the same sense as the monumental lyric anthologies such as the troubadour chansonniers. As these works were compiled near the time when many of the lyrics they contain were composed and performed, I analyze their function as songbooks in terms of their textual properties that allow for audience participation and reader interpolation. In imagining how a songbook may have emerged from certain kinds of textual material and performance and compiler practices, I cast light on the formal and hermeneutic structure that enables a work to be engaged to a community of readers, and oral and literate traditions to be assimilated to one another.

In my second chapter I analyze the phenomenon of the songbook through the transformation of the proper name from a lyric presence to a name as rubric, which functions as a metonymy for the poet and his or her corpus of lyric texts. This analysis is concerned with lyric self-invocation, a name in a poem being different from a name in a narrative or drama, and addresses notions of communality and poetic identity as mediated by the songbook. Long before the existence of printing, troubadours had notions of publication—in the literal sense of making public—that were based on performance. How do the material properties of a songbook shape this concept of publication based on oral transmission? Furthermore, how do chansonniers translate the lyric presence of a proper name through *vidas* and editorial arrangements of author corpuses? In that chapter I describe what I call the effect of "hermeneutic opacity," the accumulation of archival knowledge that emerges once names are placed in songbooks. This opacity results not in a consolidation of a unified meaning regarding the identity of a poet but in a condensation of numerous interpretations made legible through the disposition of lyric texts as both rubric and trace of singular bodily performance. By presenting this phenomenon as one that resists attributing value or agency to any single situation of reception or reader, I show how the proper name serves as a vehicle for a process of translation that ultimately maintains different occasions and engagements between lyric texts and an evolving community of readers.

My third chapter treats the visualization of lyric texts in songbooks by examining marginalia, historiated initials, and full-page miniatures from Occitan and Middle High German songbooks. Such images are essential for understanding not only how readers understood lyric texts, but the relation of vernacular lyric to medieval visual culture. Like the proper name as rubric, images condense lyric material to make it memorable and to supplement the lyric performance, but they serve other functions as well, such as expanding lyric metaphors, acting as moralizing glosses, or creating a visual narrative among different lyric texts. I also discuss how visual media were essential to rising secular institutions such as the imperial ambitions of Alfonso X and Frederick II. By depicting themselves as troubadour-kings, these thirteenth-century rulers appropriated a troubadour culture shaped by songbooks as part of an imperial program of legitimacy; their portraits demonstrate the wider significance of songbooks for understanding the politics of cultural production during this period. Finally, in my analysis of the *Codex Manesse*, I show how emblematic author portraits function rhetorically as readings of lyric texts in conjunction with other images both intrinsic and external to the book. Unlike the images in troubadour chansonniers and the images of secular rulers, the *Codex* miniatures reflect the urban milieu of fourteenth-century Zürich and the rise of lay literacy through the compilers' use of local visual media of heraldry and illustrated books to form a visually cohesive cultural monument. The *Codex* miniatures collectively form playful relations between different lyric texts and miniatures throughout the songbook.

In asking how the *Codex Manesse*'s miniatures emblematize a poet's identity and individuality within a paradigm of the communal book, generations after the original performance environment, and how this process reveals a changing courtly imaginary, I argue that much that we consider fundamental to poetry—poets as discrete agents, poems as overtures to a particular public — is negotiated through a user's interaction with the song-book. In chapters two and three, which treat lyric personae and the inter-mediality of images and lyric texts, I show how the consultation of a ma-terial object may invest authority and exclusivity in a group of poets, and how a collection may impart a range of tones through bibliographical means or otherwise. Further, visual marginalia, historiated initials, heraldry, and author portraits may create a moralizing or playful dialogue with the lyric texts. In other words, a songbook teaches everyone involved in the transac-tion, poets and readers alike, how to fulfill their roles, and bestows status on certain constructs (the poem, the poet). Likewise, by inviting readers to engage the text through various visual and bibliographical apparatuses, the songbook imparts a cultural and social memory that is materially and historically specific. Even though a songbook may memorialize the motives and symbols of the courtly world, the complex legibility of the songbook reveals the process of adaptation required to maintain this world's power in changing historical and social situations. To take one example, the min-iature of Reinmar von Brennenberg in the *Codex* cites sacred iconography available in contemporary religious manuscripts to reinforce the image of a sacrificial lover in Reinmar's lyrics (chapter three); it possibly draws upon other legendary or historical material concerning this poet's murder in order to create a myth — ironic or serious — about this poet.

Compared to other illuminated manuscripts (Books of Hours, *Le Roman de la Rose,* for example), the relative paucity of miniatures in even the most luxurious Occitan chansonniers highlights the particular situation of the songbook as an anthology of lyric texts.[23] To some degree, all medieval ver-nacular genres, including epics and romances, share the editorial problem of reconstructing oral production and an authorial voice from written texts. Songbooks transmit verbal texts that are generally transcripts of improvised performance of a remembered text with a speculative history of transmis-sion from composition to script. Since no individual pages have come down to us before the earliest dated songbook in the chansonnier tradition (1254), critics have proposed theories involving both oral and written transmission that acknowledge a sophisticated oral-musical memorial culture.[24] Further, as Amelia Van Vleck has shown, the authority of a troubadour song and no-tions of literary property are independent of written transmission, and the instability of songs is reflected in manuscript variants.[25] When comparing the transmission of lyric texts and author corpuses to that of a romance by Chrétien de Troyes, for example, it is useful to recall his clerkly refer-ences to his art of "bele conjunture" (beautifully ordered composition),[26] or to the concept of *translatio imperii et studii* in his prologue to *Cligès*. These references suggest that the matter and meaning of a romance may be understood in a different sense from a troubadour *canso* and its textual and musical properties. All of these qualities of the songbook manuscript tradition, its specific "orality and literality,"[27] influence the way chansonniers idealize lyric song through generic or idealized individual portraits, or alternatively provide visual analogs or mimetic commentary.

In the fourth chapter I contrast these earlier songbook traditions with the cancioneros from the Iberian kingdoms of Aragon and Castile. Like the works of the Occitan and Middle High German traditions, cancioneros are collections of texts in metrical form; until the last quarter of the fifteenth century they were copied into handwritten codices, and later appeared in printed versions. The texts in these anthologies show the changing status of "poetry" and its reception, thanks to the evidence of rubrics, treatises, and texts themselves. These lyric texts—mostly transmitted without music—were likely read privately as well as sung or set to music, and are often labeled *decires*, referring to an early fifteenth-century interest in rhetorical composition in the classical sense, *ars dicendi*, with the discovery of new texts of Cicero and Quintilian.[28] Following the rise of lay literacy and vernacular humanism, the compilation of cancioneros and the composition of courtly verse in Castilian became a medium for justifying one's social status for aristocrats and rising poets alike. As a form of communal poetic production among court poets, the production of cancioneros as literary objects representative of distinct coteries embodied an important social ritual. Further, as poets composed poetry with the cancionero as genre in mind, this kind of songbook served as a platform for literary intertextuality, which sustained the production of and experimentation among different lyric forms. I examine the cancionero in terms of other fifteenth-century courtly rituals, such as Enrique de Villena's description of the Barcelona Consistory in *El arte de trovar* and Pedro Carrillo de Huete's description of the Fiesta of 1428 held in Valladolid, in order to demonstrate how much the display of competition, pageantry, codification of rules, and purification of communal values in certain court activities converged with the ritualized production of cancioneros. Certain operations of the cancionero—the juxtaposition of canonical poets with contemporary ones, the creation of intertextual dialogues, as well as other orderings and collations of lyric texts and poets—grant the recognition of both individuality and collectivity, as well as deviations and consolidations of lyric forms through serialized production. Thus, these cancioneros enable a kind of social and literary hybridity within a stable material container by means of innovative groupings of fixed forms or performances of literary rituals that accommodate rather than exclude new variants.

This last chapter examines the process by which preserving a corpus of masters is gradually overtaken by the idea of storing poetry as an *ars,* a craft. In other words, when does the act of minting a song or a poet as a material display of courtly competence or adherence to social values become no less important than the song or poet being preserved? I address this question by comparing the serial production of cancioneros with the other European traditions. To what extent do the earlier traditions of the songbook reflect a closed monumental past, and the cancioneros a shifting, historically and socially determined display of courtly competence? Certainly these two aspects of songbooks are not mutually exclusive; chapter four describes the dual identity of the songbook as both literary monument and bibliographic technology through a comparative analysis of chansonnier and cancionero rubrics. I also address the limits of the genre by looking at poetry contained in a cancionero that first appears in the first quarter of the sixteenth century, the *Cancionero general de Hernando del Castillo.* Rather than trying to see the extent to which this poetry begins to imitate the Italian tradition, which would eventually dominate the poetry of the early modern period, I take poems by Antón de Montoro, Costana, and Caravajal, and refer to the development of lyric genres produced in the coterie of the Catholic Monarchs (*invençiones, canciones*) in order to speculate about how we might perceive the gradual transformation of aesthetic value occurring within the genre of the cancionero rather than externally imposed. I hypothesize that the communal expectations of court poets to create more situational and performance-related poetry based on visual and verbal cues, the intrusion of the autobiographical within a typical mode of poetry seen from the historically unique position of a Cordobese poet such as Montoro, or the increasingly theatrical quality of Costana's object poetry in which the poet creates ambivalent modes of address — all these developments occur as a result of the cancionero, which enables an inward and localized poetic activity among a network of poets.

In this chapter, I stress the extent to which, as a literary genre, the functionality of the cancionero as literary object results in a proliferation of citation — of poets, themes, and poems — constituting a network of intertextuality through a material apparatus. Textual associations of this kind, made possible through these poets' awareness of the cancionero as a platform of social and textual performance, allow for a discursiveness that eventually causes the cancionero to implode. Shaping a literary consciousness of communal poetic production, the cancionero embodies par excellence the goal of this project, which is to show the songbook as at once a hermeneutic and a material apparatus in which one sees a poet, a poem, and poetry within a shifting constellation of the one and the many.

In the conclusion to this book, by historicizing how the songbook has been regarded as a philological object in various literary traditions, I discuss the intimate ties of the songbook genre to national and aesthetic interests. From the early modern period to the present, songbook scholarship has shaped literary canons and cultural traditions. Yet scholars have approached the dual aspect of the songbook as source and container for heterogeneous material in a manner that reflects the mediation of philology by dominant ideologies, aesthetic values, or personal interests. For example, although romantic discourse has been associated with the empirical practice of philology in the quest for origins and the reconstruction of an *Urtext*, little attention has been given to the way philological approaches to the songbook have differed in the national traditions, such as the canon of Middle High German poets created by the *Des Minnesangs Frühling* tradition as compared to individual troubadour editions. Nor have these national projects been placed in relation to regional Renaissance, Enlightenment, and eighteenth-century studies of songbooks, all of which had their own hermeneutic agendas before notions of "scholarship" became institutionalized. For example, I will take up the eighteenth-century cultural mythologies that influenced the studies of lyric manuscripts by Jakob Bodmer and Jean Baptiste de La Curne Sainte-Palaye in order to show how their philological practices differed from those of the more familiar late medieval period or the nineteenth century. Finally, the history of scholarship regarding cancioneros indicates how much a national medievalism influenced the view of a cancionero as an active practice rather than an archival object, and as representative of mediocre court poetry that preceded the Golden Age. From the moment of their compilation to their use as sources for modern critical editions, songbooks have been crucial to the discussion of periodization and creation of literary canons. The collection of vernacular song in particular, in a poetic, at times nonnative or historically distant language from that of the compiler or reader, evokes an irrecoverable past and a sense of cultural origins rooted in orally transmitted social practices. The encounter with vernacular songbooks, especially ones that seem to border the traditionally defined periods of the Middle Ages and the Renaissance — such as the cancioneros or the Italian chansonniers of Occitan poetry as formative models for an Italian Renaissance — has evolved throughout history according to intellectual or political dispositions.

Chapter One

cᛆᚱ cᛆᚱ

PARADIGMS: THE *CARMINA BURANA* AND THE *LIBRO DE BUEN AMOR*

UPON HEARING THE term *medieval songbook* a modern reader usually imagines a manual with musical notation and lyric texts for a performance. While many such manuals exist, most songbooks that are at the origin of European lyric traditions are actually large format manuscripts written in court hand on parchment. These are luxurious artifacts of the aristocracy — far from props for orally circulated lyric used by traveling minstrels. Though likely based on paper exemplars of the manuals we imagine, the great Occitan chansonniers transmit lyrics without music, and were probably compiled at least a generation after the lyrics were last performed. If we lack such manuals, what might a songbook look like that documents lyric texts being composed, performed, glossed, and compiled contemporaneously? In other words, how can we reconstruct a songbook that both accounts for the performance of lyric and is itself a literary object? Considering these questions in this chapter, I will analyze two works that are not conventionally considered songbooks in the manner of, for example, the Italian troubadour chansonniers or the Castilian cancioneros discussed in the later chapters. Yet, in treating them as "songbooks," I apply the term as a descriptive experiment: Does the term pertain when the editorial intention typical of a chansonnier is not explicitly present, and the characterization of the work as songbook can be deduced from the work's functional openness rather than from a single moment of reception? It is a truism, with few exceptions, that almost all lyric of the Middle Ages was composed to be sung or recited. Exploring how we can read a unified medieval "work" as a collection of separate lyric texts, and the value of reading a work as such, is the goal of this first chapter.

My analysis treats two codices containing songs that were being performed close to the time of their compilation. (As my later chapters will show, this is not the case in most troubadour or *Minnesang* manuscripts.) Together, these codices offer a paradigmatic contrast of the songbook mode: both show uses of scholastic and theological *ordinatio* (the ordering of texts) and *compilatio* (compiling glosses on texts),[1] but they deploy these practices differently according to subject matter of lyric performance, moral-satirical lessons, or the agency of a first-person narrator. These works show polarities in their manner of participatory emendation and compilation, and as such provide a basis for understanding the songbook as a kind of heterogeneous work space.

Although it is impossible to determine with any certainty how a work was used by a medieval reader, the two works that I treat in this chapter — the *Carmina Burana*, circa 1230 (*Carmina*),[2] and the *Libro de buen amor*, circa 1330–43 (*Libro*)[3]—contain texts whose nature suggests that these codices were understood as autonomous books even if read, sung, or consulted in fragments. Like an anthology or a miscellany, each work may have been read as a moral encyclopedia, a collection of lyric or fables, or a musical repertory. The *Carmina* contains anonymous clerical student songs, mostly middle Latin but including macaronic and bilingual verse, that reflect the influence of liturgical song and treat various secular topics such as springtime, satirical diatribes against the church, or drinking and gambling. The latest manuscript of the *Libro*, the Salamanca or S manuscript, is a heterometric codex containing fables, love stories in *cuaderna vía*, a variety of lyric verse, and a scholastic prose sermon. The erotic autobiographical narrative, which includes doctrinal excurses, tales, and songs, treats the central theme of *buen amor* or good love. Displaying Hispano-Arabic, Hispano-Hebraic, and European literary influences, its theme is elusive due to the variety of sources on which the composition is based (*exempla*, learned and popular sermons, fabliaux, Goliard poetry, Ovid, Latin drama, and religious and popular lyric) as well as the enigmatic narrator. Recent studies regarding the author's intentions and hermeneutic strategies and the work's deliberate ambiguity have focused on Augustinian readings of the author's truth claims and the influence of Semitic literary traditions. While this study is not the first to view the *Libro* as a songbook or "Cancionero," its comparison with the *Carmina* aims to expand upon former analyses by Ramón Menéndez Pidal, Leo Spitzer, and others of this work as at once a humorous, ironic, and didactic text. Furthermore, the analysis advances an interpretive account of the *Libro* that maintains its aspect as intended for a learned, clerical audience of individual readers while not eliminating the possibility of other kinds of audience and delivery in the long history of the work's reception.[4]

In the case of the *Carmina*, the *versus*, or quantitative verse or verses (the plural of this Latin word is the same as the singular), structures the codex into thematic subgroups and offer moral gloss. In the *Libro*, the narrator-protagonist Archpriest of Hita unifies the disparate elements of the *Libro* without promoting any one moral interpretation. Indeed, *buen amor* can mean both divine and sexual love, and the Archpriest seems to want to undermine a reader's desire to gloss the text for its meaning. In the way that the Archpriest merges into different characters, and different parts of the *Libro* resist becoming a unified narrative, his role converges with the compilers and annotators of the *Carmina*. In both the *Carmina* and the *Libro*, a compiler brings together a heterogeneous variety of songs and verse. Yet such a unifying presence, while joining diverse elements to form a book, does not eliminate the integrity of autonomous texts or text groups. Further, even as the *Carmina* elements such as the *versus* and the Archpriest's *yo* (I) are the tissue that unites the songs into a book, the codices always retain the a priori quality of having to be interpreted by their users. We can deduce from the evidence of the manuscripts that these codices are open enough for readers to use as they see fit: performed aloud or studied silently from any point and through one's own moral lens. Whether sung or used as a mnemonic aid, the codex invites an evolving interaction between composer, compiler, and audience.

Examining the formal structure and content of these works, I will describe how songbooks entail a kind of *ordinatio* and *compilatio* that takes into account these activities in a secular performance and literary environment. I have chosen the *Carmina* and the *Libro* because, although they are very different, they document a fluid translation and adaptation of scholastic, secular, and liturgical cultures, as well as Latin and vernacular composition and performance of lyric. In the way their organization tends toward a coherent narrative unity while retaining distinct subgroups, these codices reflect the gathering of diverse material into a protean text in relation to a particular performance-oriented environment.[5] A songbook resembles a form made of building blocks that never merge into a seamless, autonomous whole: it reflects the reception of song clusters toward a platonic ideal or form — the book, the Archpriest as *auctor*, the seven sins. While the *Carmina* and the *Libro* document a process of lyric reception between audience, singers, composers, and scribes, such a reception does not preclude the ordering of texts by means of scribal and literary processes.

HISTORICAL AND SOCIAL
CONTEXTS: THE ENVIRONMENT OF
THE *CLERICUS* AND GOLIARD

Both the *Carmina* and the *Libro*, as codices compiled near the time of their songs' production, reflect the adaptation of several traditions within a student milieu. While several historical and social factors that I describe below shape each of these milieus, the songbook itself, as a sort of work space, reinforces the student practices of translating established musical and literary forms into local, orally transmitted ones.

The Carmina Burana

A diverse collection of monolingual medieval Latin poems and bilingual poems (Latin/German, Latin/Romance), the *Carmina* is exceptional as the single witness of secular lyric composition in the twelfth and thirteenth centuries other than hymns and poetry for ecclesiastical feasts. Although most of the poems are anonymous, including secular and a few sacred Latin lyrics, liturgical plays and a Latin Gamblers' Mass, many poets are known from other manuscripts such as the Saint Martial and Notre-Dame repertories.[6] While the *versus* and many poems treating antique material are in quantitative meter, all of the secular and religious songs (hymns, tropes, sequences) use stress-syllabic or rhythmical meters meant to accompany melodies. As I will discuss later on in this chapter, in the *Carmina* the appearance of the quantitative verse differs from the rhythmical. Such diversity of lyric in the *Carmina* corresponds to the idea of this period as a kind of Renaissance: there is an emerging interest in newly translated writings of Plato and other philosophers; universities in Chartres, Paris, and Bologna flourish; and Latin culture attains a wider reach from Spain to Scandinavia. A Latin poetry emerges from this student world of the nascent universities—a poetry, since labeled "Goliard,"[7] often critical of political and social conditions, influenced by the vernacular lyric of the troubadours/*trouvères*, and merging sacred and secular traditions.[8]

The *Carmina* was compiled in Bavaria, and associated with the abbey of Benedictbeuern and a wealthy or important patron schooled in both clerical and courtly love poetry.[9] It documents a local milieu over a span of time and serves as witness to an international phenomenon. Through a process of textual adaptation and bibliographic groupings, the codex represents a clerical community's experimenting with discrete traditions—ecclesiastical and secular song traditions, liturgical *conductus* and hymn forms, and love songs inspired by Ovid, *Minnesänger*, and the *trivium* taught in the schools.

The Libro de buen amor

Although in many respects unlike a collection of Goliard poetry, the *Libro* also emerges from a milieu in which more established literate forms are in the process of being adapted to native or popular traditions. The dating of its manuscripts,[10] along with what we can deduce from Juan Ruiz, the Archpriest of Hita, the supposed composer of the *Libro*,[11] situates the *Libro* in terms of its audience and historical context. Similar to the *Carmina*, the *Libro* exhibits a milieu conversant in Ovid, Romance genres, and Catholic didacticism. Yet the work also represents the culture of the Iberian peninsula during the reign of Alfonso XI (1312–50). A confluence of Jewish, Muslim, and Christian traditions, Spain at this time experienced social changes due to a flourishing maritime and wool trade, and literary developments after the founding of new universities and expansion of the church's pedagogical activities.[12] A university-educated Archpriest of Hita (whether or not he really existed) would have been involved in the local affairs of his synod, knowledgeable about canon law, and well traveled: an excellent conduit of church, university, and lay culture in a town historically known to have been populated by Jews and Mozarabs (Spanish Christians who adopted Muslim dress and spoke Arabic). Although many scholars are convinced that the *Libro*'s intended audience was exclusively clerics familiar with its scholastic references, the work also clearly aims to serve as popular entertainment by including minstrel song and folk tales.[13] Moreover, like the *Carmina*, the *Libro*'s changes of register and diversity of content speak to a work adapted to the needs and tastes of its audience.

During this period in Spanish literary history, monastic *cuaderna vía* poems of religious and didactic subjects gave way to a form of verse as social criticism. The *Libro* is cast as a *cuaderna vía* composition, but it incorporates such a variety of metrical texts and a prose sermon that it escapes simple classification. Much of its complexity is due to its autobiographical aspect mixed with didactic materials—for instance an *exemplum* after the narrator's rejection by his lady is offered as a means of interpreting the rejection. Religious and popular lyric elaborate on the love affairs of the narrator, but it is most likely that these texts circulated orally before being incorporated into the composition. The scholarly consensus tends toward the idea that the *Libro* was composed or assembled over a long chronological period, the disparate materials brought together by a university student as a unified composition. Dagenais has argued for the *Libro* to encompass the medieval text (in all the different forms of its manuscripts, fragments, and quotations) and its readers' glosses during the fourteenth to sixteenth centuries. I build on Dagenais's treatment of reading practices rather than of an author and his work: what I will try to describe in this chapter is how the songbook aspect of the *Libro* — illuminated through a comparison of the *Libro* with the *Carmina* — constitutes its character as a book to the extent that it overrides the questionable authorial intention of the Archpriest.

THE PLACE OF THE *CARMINA* AND THE *LIBRO* IN THE HISTORY OF THE BOOK AND THE HISTORY OF SONG

Despite their differences, both collections may have been used in various student performance environments. The dance songs of the *Carmina* may have been performed for large festive gatherings,[14] while the *Libro*'s lyric works were likely musically staged, especially in the case of the lyric using the *estribote* form of rhyming couplets with refrains. The *Carmina*'s poems with musical notation, rhythmical poetry, and quantitative *versus* suggest songs sung aloud and read, as well as studied for their content; the Archpriest likewise indicates various modes of performing his *Libro* in other ways, inviting his audience to play his book like an instrument (stanza 70). These books allow multiple modes of interpretation because readers can consult lyric texts as separate performance pieces or as parts of a literary or moral narrative.

The *Carmina* and the *Libro* reflect the influence of scholastic material culture as well as the importance of song — liturgical and secular — in the life of the cleric. Since the physical modification of the Bible at the end of the fourth century from scroll to codex, participants in literary culture and especially the scholastic culture of the high Middle Ages depended more on indexed codices for the storing of information than on memory. Given the value of codices in general and the notion of medieval man as an "organizer, a codifier, a builder of systems,"[15] the prevalence of heterogeneous compiled materials in manuscripts is hardly surprising, especially during the flourishing of the universities. The *Carmina* and the *Libro* emerge from a manuscript environment where the dominant works include Gratian's *Decretum*, the *Glosa Ordinaria*, and Peter Lombard's *Sententiae* — the common books of scholastic research.[16] Peter compiles the *Sententiae* "ut non sit necesse quaerenti librorum numerositatem evolvere, cui brevitas collecta quod quaeritur offert sine labore" (to escape the need for the researcher to search numerous books, since without effort a compact collection offers him what is sought, PL 192.522).[17] Such compilations, as a natural progression of the Bible Codex, enable encyclopedic comparison and cross-referencing, and facilitate the research of specific information.

While these works share some of these physical aspects of the scholastic codex, they remain distinctive as lyric anthologies. Although these codices would have been consulted as an archive, they also represent the confluence of orally transmitted vernacular song and student literary activity: they document lyric composition, performance, and compilation — quite possibly a reception situation that includes a public recital from (or with the help of) a written text but does not preclude the occasional private reader. They may also document literary composition as inflected by nonliterary lay performance practices. In the *Carmina*, many lyrics were probably written from memory, or at the dictation of those who sang them; this would account for the better versions of these poems in other repertories where there exists a longstanding literary transmission of a song. Like other medieval books, songbooks bestow symbolic, cultural, and canonical value on a collection of songs — whether for a patron or a community of users. Although what I describe as songbooks certainly share many characteristics with other medieval texts such as scholastic *florilegia*, these codices both reflect the strong influence of oral traditions and performance communities and maintain the literary qualities of these texts.

As I will describe in detail the songbook aspects of the *Libro* in the second half of this chapter, in discussing the *Carmina* I will focus on the *versus* and vernacular stanzas in several senses: the *versus* are the "unique contribution of the *Carmina* compilers,"[18] and are literary-historical *unica* unattested elsewhere,[19] while the vernacular stanzas, though not always original compositions, are unique in the way they supplement or complement the Latin poems that precede them. Both play a significant role in helping us imagine how the *Carmina* was compiled as well how it may have been received and consulted as a codex.

THE CONTENT AND STRUCTURE OF THE *CARMINA*: HETEROGENEITY AND ORDER

The *Carmina*, or *Codex latinus Monacensis* (Clm 4660), consists of one hundred and twelve leaves with an additional seven called the *Fragmenta Burana*

(Clm 4660a);[20] it has four main sections: moral and satirical poems; love songs; songs of drinkers, gamblers, and goliards; and religious plays.[21] The compilers collated the texts according to subject matter and other internal thematic groupings,[22] yet the organizational principles allowed for the inclusion of songs according to the practical availability of sources and preferences of the moment.

The annotative *versus* integrate heterogeneous material by building on the theme of a subgroup (e.g., in the moral section, a section on simony) or elaborating on a specific motif of one text. Bernhard Bischoff, Günther Bernt, Benedikt Konrad Vollmann, and Burghart Wachinger view the *versus* as supporting thematic groups within the sections of poems marked by the miniatures that end them.[23] It is mainly because of the *versus* that scholars have been able to determine that the *Carmina* is not only a musical manuscript but a didactic text collection similar to other moral encyclopedias such as the *Distinctiones monasticae et morales* and the earlier *Summa recreatorum*.[24] These moral and didactic annotations in metrical verse function to organize text groups as commentary, as well as providing moral glosses to particular subgroups or poems.[25] For example, appended explanatory stanzas such as *versus* CB 64 and CB 66 are metrical poems composed of hexameters and distichs of a didactic nature that gloss the poem or poems preceding them. These *versus* are frequent in the moral-didactic section as framing commentary for the rhythmical poetry, often consisting of classical *sententiae* or proverbs from Otloh von Sankst Emmeram's (ca. 1010–70) *Liber proverbiorum*. Thus through such groupings and annotations, various readings and uses of the *Carmina* are possible: students could enjoy the entertainment of secular love songs (CB 89–102) and spring dance songs; but through the presence of the *versus* they could also reflect on the moral lessons offered as annotations to songs.[26]

In addition to creating a moral commentary and encyclopedia, *versus* facilitated ad hoc compilation. Bischoff suggests that "whenever the compiler of the songs came across something suitable, he included it," resulting, Bischoff claims, "in a collection of songs with moral and didactic annotations." The compilation of the codex most likely involved Otto Schumann's principle of organization based on the *Carmina*'s groupings as well as Bischoff's idea of active accommodation of available anthologies using the *versus*. These various groupings and annotations, including the special case of the German supplemental stanzas, a series of love and dance songs to which a German stanza has been added ad hoc in order to appeal to a wider audience,[27] best represent the communal use of this codex.[28]

As stated earlier, while including poetry of well-known middle Latin poets found in other sources,[29] and attested *Minnesang* lyric,[30] the collection is mainly anonymous and compiled from several collections. The intention to accommodate contemporaneous or earlier smaller collections available on a limited basis is clear, for example, in the great number of German lyrics in the love song section: the fact that some are not what one would normally categorize as love songs perhaps indicates the availability of one collection at a certain time (for example, the *planctus* or lamentation series within the love section). In addition we find the arbitrary separation of German stanzas from a poem by Walther von der Vogelweide, such as 151a and 169a. These particularities suggest that compilers did not hesitate to use the collections according to their own groupings of themes or motifs, as well as pragmatic considerations of using available texts.

Despite the inclusion of the didactic and literary *versus*, the *Carmina* is certainly a songbook in the strict sense because of the inclusion of musical notation in many of the texts, as well as the choice of the rhythmical poems whose melodies may be reconstructed from other musical repertories.[31] The *versus* and supplemental vernacular stanzas represent two overlapping functions and interests of the *Carmina*—literary and musical; clerical and popular entertainment. For example, texts headed "versus" may include ancient and early medieval pieces that would have been learned in the schools; however, the Latin love songs with supplemental vernacular stanzas cater to the entertainment interests of a wider audience. Thus as the starting point for our study of songbooks, we can see that the *Carmina* enables divergent paths of consultation for its audience and users through not only its content but specifically through its form and structure as a codex. Before showing convergences of the *Carmina* with the *Libro*, I will describe in detail how we can distinguish the *Carmina Burana* as a work space that, through the *versus*, various principles of groupings, and the vernacular stanzas composed or added by the compilers, allows diverse approaches to the collection within certain parameters.

THE *VERSUS*: LITERARY AND MUSICAL FUNCTIONS

For the compilers and readers of the *Carmina*, the formal term *versus* could have been applied to several contexts — literary, musical, and liturgical. The functions of the *versus* in these contexts may have inflected the bibliographic and literary ones of the *Carmina*.

There are three contexts of the Latin *versus* as detailed by Richard Crocker. The first refers to metrics: Augustine in *De musica* (V.I)[32] describes the *versus* as a metric unit with a proper ratio of division and a definite end; a *versus* is therefore "a line of metric poetry or a poem using a pattern of such lines."[33] From the early Middle Ages the *versus* often refers to a particular kind of pattern, one in which a classical quantitative model existed, such as a dactylic hexameter. The second context is the Latin Psalter, where the Psalms are divided into verses; in the third context, the *versus* designates a second section, or bridge, and applies to an episodic musical function. This third context applies to the liturgy: for example, as Crocker explains, the incorporation of the Matins versicle *Benedicamus Domino* makes such a piece a *Benedicamus-versus*.

In the *Benedicamus-versus*, one perceives possible convergences with the literary *versus* of the *Carmina*. The liturgical or musical *versus* incorporates song, ritual performance, and books: the *versus* may have been surmised either from a tag at the end of a stanza, "or from the assignment of such in an antiphoner or gradual (either by rubric or position in the series), or by position in an analogous book."[34] In the *Carmina* the *versus* not only are visually and metrically distinctive, but similar to the liturgical/musical *versus*, they act as bridges from one text to another. Perhaps the metrical regularity and identifiable phrasing of the *versus* in the *Carmina* encouraged a relation between different kind of texts. One realizes the literary properties of the *versus* by contrasting them with the unique preludes of an earlier middle Latin songbook of devotional and secular matter, the eleventh-century *Cambridge Songs*.[35] In this collection, the compiler used these preludes to inform readers of the musical or performative qualities of the texts that follow. Considering the didactic function of the *versus*, and despite the *Carmina* sporadically providing melodies, these texts emphasizing musical theory and practice demonstrate the musical quality of this collection compared to the later *Carmina*.[36]

The Rhetoric of the Versus: The Moral-Satirical Section

Through their visual organization and rhetorical efficiency, the *versus* of the moral, satirical and religious poems clarify and condense the themes or subject matter of the poems they follow. Often they play a complementary role, adding a corrective gloss to a poem of youthful exuberance. In general, the *versus* represent the many ways a reader could rhetorically reflect on a poem, whether through proverbs, schematic visual orientation, or extended commentary on a particular moral theme.

Versus can gloss texts as visual or rhetorical repetitions. In one example, the octosyllabic rhythmical verse CB 6, a world-upside-down poem with an apocalyptic tone about the fall of virtue to vice and the idleness of youth, finds its corrective in the repetition of "Nobilitas hominis" (Nobility of man) in the *versus* of CB 7: the rhymed hexameters repeat an emphatic declaration for rectitude and reform. Rather than dispatching the theme briefly,[37] these *versus* tend to amplify the themes by repeating "Nobilitas" or "Nummus" (Money) (CB 11) in the same first position line after line.

Other *versus*, such as the invocation of *auctores* seen in Juvenal and Ot-loh's *Proverbia*,[38] are efficient metrical citations, *sententiae*, serial verses, or *exempla* for quick recollection by means of condensed forms.[39] These *versus* interspersed within the lyrics lend the codex its authority as both lyric collection and didactic encyclopedia, while imposing a moral order on the available lyric texts. Through the complementary dimension of proverbial wisdom, didacticism, and learning distinct from the rhythmical poetry, these *versus* compound the quality of the *Carmina* as a communal songbook used for what we might call moral training.

The Amatory Section

The *versus* of the second and largest section, poems about love and nature, also form poetic groupings through their instructive and supplementary character. The *versus* in this section may act as instructive appendixes or thematic bridges, the latter a way to include different songs in a book. Examples of appendixes are both CB 64 and CB 66: the former lists Hercules' twelve major tasks in reference to the previous poem about the singer as a new Hercules who renounces love for reason. CB 66 is an instructive appendix for 65 2a, describing the different steeds of Apollo for the different parts of the day. One sees instructive *versus* glossed interlinearly with the vernacular—such is the case with the poem that lists the names of birds ("Nomina avium," CB 133) and one of animals ("De nominibus ferarum," CB 134). As for the second function, CB 119a thematically bridges two categories of complaints, one about women and the other about the love of friends and homeland. The poet of 119 frames the sorrow of his affair through a synaktikon, a speech about a reluctant departure, celebrating his homeland and comrades. CB 119a responds to the poet of 119, who is about to die from the madness of love ("periturus amoris rabie" l. 4), by promoting "mensura" (correct proportion) instead. This stoic shift applies well to the next section about love and politics, where an elegy for Richard I, King of England (CB 122) and a rhymed hexameter about Marbod von Rennes (122a) emphasize

1. *Nummus versus* from *Carmina Burana* (Clm 46660, f. 46v) (thirteenth century). Photograph: Bayerische Staatsbibliothek, Munich.

the fleeting nature of life. Both types of *versus* bring out the extemporaneous nature of student glossing, as well as the deliberate attempt to organize different sections through artful transitions.

The Visual Appearance of the Versus

As we have seen, the *versus* are set apart not only in their moralizing function, metrical form that lacks musical notation like rhythmic verse, and mnemonic phrasing, but in their parallel visual configurations in the manuscript. Other visual poetics are further evident in the reductive display of derivative endings for two lines for CB 6 and 7 (f. 44v–45), which seems to impart a graphic answer of order in response to the poem about the world-upside-down. In CB 7 for example, most lines emphasize "Nobilitas" through anaphora: the scribe represents graphically the anaphora of each initial half-line and the rhyme at the end of each succeeding half-line. Such a visual display emphasizes how much the grammatical quality of the verse accords with its derivative moral message and the need to declaim "nobilitas" as a rhetorical effect, the central value from which each line develops. Besides the clear rubrication of "versus," the visual display of the texts themselves is an essential element of their mnemonic functions. These visual representations of order or alphabetical listing of proverbs (CB 28) allow a compiler or reader to memorize moral hierarchies among interrelated texts.

One final pair (26 and 27 [3] and *versus* 28 [3v]) also emphasizes the visual difference between a rhythmical song and its *versus*. The proverbs of *versus* 28 follow two poems on "De correctione hominum" (On the improvement of men). Numbers 26 and 27 are both admonitions of vice (26) and exhortations to trust in God (27). Each contains phrases and words that would have been sung in a liturgical context.[40] On 3v, the last line of number 27 ("pane tuo vescere!" you should eat your bread!) contains space between the syllables and one long red line between "ve" and "scere," indicating a melisma, a group of five or six notes sung to one syllable. In contrast to this musical representation, the following *versus* 28 is clearly a literary gloss: the capitalized red initials of the proverbs are alphabetized, and there are red lines following each proverb to indicate that each should be allotted one line for emphasis. The proverbs, a compact lesson per line, indicate a step-by-step process of correction as they allude to and affirm the subject of the previous poems: the eyes commit no sin, if the heart rules, one should not hesitate to convert someone, what cares hour by hour the heart makes! With each

2. Example of endline configuration from *Carmina Burana* (Clm 46660, f. 45) (thirteenth century). Photograph: Bayerische Staatsbibliothek, Munich.

proverb occupying one line, there is an emphasis on daily, hourly correction and efforts to improve in the face of God: "peccans cottidie studeat mox se reparare." In such a way *versus* 28 formally refers to the practice of Christian moral discipline. In this pair, one sees such visual representation as indicators of the codex's performance and scholastic contexts.[41]

Miniature Versus?

Although not *versus* in the formal sense, miniatures visually mark and bridge separate sections of the codex. The miniature that narrates Aeneas's departure and the suicide of Dido corresponds with the previous Troy poems (98–102), but it also introduces the different section of love complaints. The beginning two stanzas of sequence 103, although building upon conventional topics of love (healing/sickness, death/sadness), do not directly treat the story of Dido and Aeneas. However, the lover's complaint directly below the Dido miniature corresponds to the miniature's portrayal of Dido's anguish (in the codex, Dido is pictured on fire, throwing herself headlong from her tower) in seeing her departed lover, as 103 begins: "Eia Dolor! / nunc me solor / velut olor / albus neci proximus / abiectus lugeo, / despectus pereo, / exclusus langueo" (Eia sadness! / Now I comfort myself / like the / white swan dying. / Abject I grieve / despised, I die / cut off, I pine).[42] The miniature, by vividly depicting Dido's lament, connects the Troy material to the love complaints.

One striking miniature within the love poetry section, the nature scene (f. 64v), seems merely decorative at first glance; yet it reflects the work space quality of the *Carmina* as it invites numerous textual and visual interpretations with the surrounding texts. The nature image occurs within two love song sections: springtime and summer love songs without German supplementary stanzas (CB 156–60), and songs with German stanzas treating love and Venus (161–75). Perhaps inspired by creation cycles depicting a variety of animals and plants together on the fifth or sixth day, Adam naming the animals, or bestiaries depicting animals in a natural setting, the subjectless landscape miniature joins *topoi* of the two sections: spring openings, summer, and Venus. Furthermore the stylized, bulbous plants echo the historiated initials.[43] In its content and *versus* role, the miniature alludes to the spirit of linguistic inclusion and supplementation seen in the German stanzas appended to springtime round dances; and in a figural sense it alludes to the act of procreation through communal and diverse participation in a codex.

3. Dido miniature from *Carmina Burana* (Clm 46660, f. 77v) (thirteenth century). Photograph: Bayerische Staatsbibliothek, Munich.

4. Nature miniature from *Carmina Burana* (Clm 46660, f. 64v) (thirteenth century). Photograph: Bayerische Staatsbibliothek, Munich.

GERMAN STANZAS:
REFLECTION AND COMPOSITION

Troubadour Supplemental Stanzas

In contrast to the *versus*, the German stanzas attached to Latin poems in
the amatory section have more ambivalent relations to their accompanying
texts.[44] While the *versus* are separate poems (indicated by "Versus" and their
format), the German stanzas are indicated by an initial intermediate in size
between the beginning initial of a song and the stanza initials, and are visually continuous with the Latin text. Thus although not distinguished with a
separate line or title, they have a special status. In many ways they are similar
to the *versus* in reinforcing certain themes and motifs within a text group,
but as poetic texts (at times stanzas of known German *Minnesang* poems)
they are in dialogue with their Latin poems in a more complex manner.

The German material varies in terms of lyric type, and may correspond
with the preceding Latin poems through form (Latin or German) or content. Sometimes the German stanzas have no relation at all to the Latin
poem to which they are attached. In an example of formal rather than thematic similarity, CB 113a is a German stanza that is formally similar to the
Latin poem to which it is attached in its refrain structure, but contrasts in
subject matter. CB 113a, a *Wechsel* by Dietmar von Aist, is a woman's response
to a refrain of 113: "Temporis nos ammonet lascivia" (The playfulness of the
season urges us). While 113 is a male lover's complaint, in an interesting turn
113a contains the woman's complaint for her lover: "an ein ende ih des wol
chome, wan div hûte; / selten sin vergezzen wirt in minem mûte" (in this affair I might succeed, / with enough discretion; / rarely is that man not on my
mind). Whereas in 113 there is a more abstract dialogue between the male
lover and his thoughts about love, the concreteness of the *Wechsel* jumps out
at us for its dialogic vernacular interjection of the lady's voice and desire.
In general, the German stanzas attested elsewhere often have strong formal correspondence with the Latin, suggesting that perhaps the compilers'
first priority was to use an available collection of German poetry despite a
minimal interpretive association between the Latin poem and a German
stanza.[45] Yet their presence, like the *versus*, may link a group of poems into
relation with each other through textual correspondences with other poems
in proximity to them in the manuscript. This is most evident in the series
of dancing songs, where, for example, a German stanza at the end of a Latin
poem (167a) prompts the placement of a song that describes a dance in the

first stanza (168). Here, like the *versus*, such German stanzas serve in a general way to coordinate the poems, demonstrating textual groupings based on general themes and practical considerations.

German Stanzas Sung to Dances

As mentioned previously, the German supplemental stanzas of Latin songs sung to the round dances of *clerici* may have served the practical function of including a nonliterate lay audience. This bilingual poetic activity creates paratactical relations between different texts rather than unambiguous hierarchies of song and gloss (as is often the case with the *versus*), Latin and vernacular texts, or entire poem and supplement.

In some cases it is difficult to ascertain whether the Latin or German text served as the model of composition in this series, and many scenarios of bilingual composition have been proposed.[46] Perhaps when the compiler found ready-made parallels, he made use of them, but in other instances composed original songs;[47] perhaps the poet simultaneously composed both parts of one song.[48] Another possibility is that the composition of parallel stanzas was an activity among friends.[49] It is now accepted that only a few forms, such as the German *Vagantenstrophe* (four thirteen-syllable lines divided by a caesura, with monorhyme), are derived from the Latin;[50] but when the *Carmina* was first being examined as an early source of *Minnesang*, many scholars believed that most of the German stanzas were derived from the Latin, and thus focused on attested *Minnesang* stanzas, rather than on a local vernacular imitating middle Latin lyric. However, it is the varied composition of the stanzas that demonstrates how the *Carmina* could be used for original compositions and as a compilation of different lyric texts.

These philological speculations help us imagine this uninterrupted series as a songbook among student circles; current melodies may have been added to the manuscript during its circulation.[51] Given the closeness of the songbook to a current performance environment and the practice of bilingual composition in the codex, a two-way reception may have occurred naturally, German melodies based on Latin ones, and vice versa.[52] However, these songs were by no means necessarily performed as they appear in the codex, and so the bilingual composition is probably a strictly literary phenomenon. Nevertheless, the appearance of the supplemental stanzas and bilingual texts in the *Carmina* speaks to the nonhierarchical interchange between Latin and vernacular cultures and the interest, for whatever reason, in compiling bilingual texts.

More than simple translations or glosses of Latin, the stanzas of the dance series respond to the content of the Latin text while corresponding metrically. Let us look closely at a pair of *Vagantenstrophe* that includes Latin and German stanzas: 136 and 136a. CB 136 describes a conventional theme of faraway love and the renewal of spring and love. In 136a the speaker imagines bodily closeness, supplementing the contentment of 136 with a more erotic wish fulfillment: "mohtih si hand holde" (if I could but take her tenderly, 6). Although the German stanza is most likely based on the Latin, 136a effectively eroticizes 136 by disrupting the serene balance of its three stanzas. In 136 the lover pledges fidelity, loving unlike 'those who are whirled around the wheel.' In 136a, the lover is in movement, torn between erotic desire and faithfulness: "min herçe mûz nah ir streben; / mohtih si han holde, / so wolde ih in wunne sweben, / swere ih nimmer dolde" (my heart yearns and only for her; / if I could but take her tenderly, / then would I bask in ecstasy / and grief would never more be mine, 5–8). The shorter stanza and the status of the vernacular tradition in this student circle creates poetic possibilities and indeterminacy through the use of languages and the supplementary character of the German stanza; the latter both is integral to the entire text and remains separate from it, and can often unbalance a conventional love trope of Goliard poetry by introducing direct language or a more vivid erotic discourse. Thus instead of coordinating different genre subgroups, these German stanzas produce a subtle poetics of German-Latin texts.

OTHER STUDENT POETRY IN THE *CARMINA*

While the practice of composing *versus* and vernacular stanzas is significant for understanding the *Carmina* as a product of its clerical and lay environment, other texts indicate its nature as a student anthology of diverse material and uses: black magic poetry and treatments of antique material. In the former, two texts suggest students envisioned the songbook as a kind of charm, while the latter documents school exercises common to any cleric in the cathedral schools at this time.

The texts of black magic, CB 54 and 55, suggest that students regarded the *Carmina* as more than a lyric collection or moral encyclopedia; perhaps they also saw it as a book of spells or charms in the same way that in certain places today people put a charm or cross above their door to drive away evil spirits.[53] CB 54 is an incantation of evil spirits in rhythmical verse of different lengths and includes some prose; it names the spirits as an act of exorcism, and ends by calling on God to protect mankind from them. In 55, there is a leonine hexameter of what one might call "devil speech," apparently circulating in various manuscripts at this time.[54] Almost nonsensical, these lines have been interpreted as an incantation of a student calling upon the devil so that he can help the student compose verse and avoid being punished by his teacher. It is also possible that, like 54, 55 is an exorcism. In contrast to the moralizing *versus* that often visually suggest spoken contrition, these two poems encourage an entirely different kind of performance: in CB 55 the student may have used the songbook as a role-playing game, a play on words, or both. A lazy or uninspired student may have fantasized about talking to the devil after reading the incantation of 54. Moreover, the visual placement of the two lines of devil speech occurs at the top of f. 18v, acting almost like a door charm in that they directly precede the heading that announces the love song section: "Incipunt Jubili."

The treatment of antique material in the *Carmina* documents brevity in quantitative verse and the evolving adaptation of this material to different forms. Moreover, the performance environment is conducive to the compilation of both musical-lyrical and rhetorical treatments. CB 99a and b and 101 are examples of a particular "condensation of antique material" during the twelfth century.[55] The hexameter epigrams of 99a and 99b and the elegiac distichs of *versus* 101 represent the eloquent brevity favored by poets of the *Carmina*. The form of 101 was commonly applied in school treatments of epic material, and similar forms gained in popularity for vernacular versions of the fall of Troy as well. The epic material in 97–102 reflects the diversity of antique poetry as rhetorically condensed or musically inflected. While distichs 99a and b are condensed enough to fit in the margins of fols. 74r and 75r, the previous folio, 73v, contains 98, a lay sequence in which the first four words have neumes, musically portraying Aeneas's happy encounter with Dido's realm. A clear indication of musical performance, a melisma appears in the first line between c and i in "excidium," representing the melodic extension of a vowel for emotional emphasis: "Troie post excidium" (after Troy's destruction). These versions of epic material—whether abbreviated summary judgments or lyrical episodes—show how a topic may receive various treatments in the *Carmina*. Readers favored both compact *exempla* (99a and b) and performance-oriented treatments of Troy material. The *Carmina* visually displays the diversity of poetic treatments and scholastic material: form (quantitative and rhythmical lyric) and subject matter (revelry, love, appetites, epic). It portrays experimentation by students with school exercises they are currently learning and practicing, as well as common treatments of Latin poetry during the twelfth and early thirteenth centuries.

In conclusion, the *versus,* the German stanzas, and the diversity of poetic material in these sections attest to the varied ways readers interpreted the material of this student anthology: they studied, read, or composed lyrics. Composing lyrics may have meant a compiler's putting vernacular stanzas together with Latin ones, or adding a moralizing gloss. The *versus* and the inclusion of supplemental stanzas in the vernacular allow the formation of either textual or visual relations between discrete lyric texts: for these readers, poetry resulted from different relations occurring between stanzas, rhythmical poetry, quantitative verse, or miniature and lyric genre. As we have seen from the first section of the *Carmina,* *versus* texts encompass a range of gloss — commentary, appendix, and elaboration in various forms including *sententia* (120a) and proverb (121a, 122a, 125–Otloh's *Proverbia* again). Both the moral dimension of the *versus* and the sometimes ambivalent quality of the German stanzas do not reduce the singable quality of the Latin rhythmical texts. On the contrary, they expand the possibilities (recalling Crocker's *Benedicamus-versus* situation) by which one could interpret different texts in the codex. *Versus* and the miniatures may bridge two different sections (from complaints about love to those about politics and homeland) or simply offer emphatic moral glosses or appendixes to a previous lyric. German stanzas may emphasize correspondences between neighboring texts in the codex, or may form dialogic textual relations to the previous Latin text. These elements demonstrate how compilers and readers reflected on themes and forms of a text group or expanded on an individual song to produce their own ideas of poetry.

FROM THE *CARMINA* TO THE *LIBRO*: CONVERGENCES

By bringing the *Libro de buen amor* into this discussion, I aim to expand the conception of this work described by E. Michael Gerli as "charged with discursive and rhetorical ambiguity as it stages a struggle between secular and sacred meaning."[56] Since Anthony N. Zahareas's study of 1965 on the art and ambiguity of Juan Ruiz as the Archpriest of Hita,[57] scholars have pursued "more nuanced views of the *Libro*'s didacticism, informed by a deeper understanding of the many ways in which medieval didactic ideas differed from modern ones."[58] While building on these views, and recognizing the differences between the *Carmina* and the *Libro* as outlined at the beginning of this chapter, I apply the issue of ambiguity to the notion of the *Libro* as a songbook. Like the *Carmina*, the *Libro* offers various modes of consultation, and documents a fluid exchange between scholastic, secular, and vernacular cultures. Moreover, both codices may be perceived as texts adaptable to the needs of their audiences: just as we saw the *Carmina* as both a singable repertory and codex for literary activities such as the moralizing *versus*, the *Libro* reflects a performance context as well as a literary one if read as a narrative love poem or moral encyclopedia. Thus by using the comparison with the *Carmina* to propose a particular way of imagining various contexts of a medieval text, my analysis provides an interpretive framework that may account for a songbook's dual nature as a heterogeneous and unified work.

Because of the beguiling presence of the Archpriest, it is tempting to read the *Libro* by trying to guess the composer's intentions. Yet interpreting the work in this way runs the danger of obscuring it as a plurality of works. There are many arguments for reading the *Libro* through the Archpriest, and such perspectives offer striking contrasts to the *Carmina*. The Archpriest, like the narrator of the *Frauendienst* of Ulrich von Lichtenstein (ca. 1255), Dante in his autobiographical *Vita Nuova* (ca. 1295), or the narrator of the *Voir-Dit* of Guillaume de Machaut (ca. 1363–65), presents himself as a lover in a lyrico-narrative, linking stories under the ambiguous theme of "buen amor," which he hints can mean worldly or spiritual love.[59] Where in the *Carmina* we can infer the motivations of the compilers by interpreting textual relations formed by *versus* or the vernacular stanzas, the Archpriest explicitly identifies himself as the compiler of these songs and tales, and comments often ironically and ambiguously on how one should read his *Libro* ("avré algunas burlas aquí a enxerir; / cada que las oyeres non quieras comedir / salvo en la manera del trobar e del dezir," I have included some humorous tales, when you hear them do not reflect upon them, except in the way they are invented and composed, 45b–d). He explicitly invites people to make emendations ("añadir e enmendar si quisiere," add to it and emend if he wants, 1629b), whereas in the *Carmina* we assume that the codex represents students communally adding lyrics, annotative *versus*, and German stanzas through two scribes. Furthermore, unlike the *Carmina,* which is compiled from other preexisting lyric repertories, the texts of the *Libro* seem to be mainly the original creation of the Archpriest. He effectively adapts texts that would have been recognized by his readers, such as the Latin elegiac comedy of Pamphilus and Galatea, Aesop's fables, proverbs, fabliaux, visions of the soul and body after death, and other traditions.[60]

FROM *VERSUS* TO ARCHPRIEST:
THE PROLOGUE AS HERMENEUTIC CHALLENGE

Just as in the *Carmina,* in the *Libro* we find songs celebrating spring and the joys of youth, and glosses warning the reader that such joys never last, as the Archpriest teasingly tells us in his prose prologue:

> e conpuse este nuevo libro, en que son escriptas algunas maneras
> e maestrías e sotilezas engañosas del loco amor del mundo, que
> usan algunos para pecar. Las quales, leyendo las e oyendo las omne
> o muger de buen entendimiento, que se quiera salvar, descogerá e
> obrar lo ha. . . . enpero, por que es umanal cosa el pecar, si algunos,
> lo que non los conssejo, quisieren usar del loco amor, aquí fallarán
> algunas maneras para ello.

> I composed this new book, in which some of the techniques, skills,
> and deceiving subtleties of foolish worldly love are written, which
> some use to sin. If any man or woman of good understanding reads
> or hears them and wishes to be saved, he or she will choose and
> act upon it. . . . however, because it is human to sin, if some people
> want to partake of foolish love, which I do not advise, here they will
> find various ways to do so.

Here the Archpriest stages his *Libro* as a hermeneutic challenge to his read-ers— "descogerá e obrar lo ha." Whether interpreted as serious or ironic, the prologue emphasizes the vagaries of interpretation rather than a unitary meaning of the book. By offering readers a choice to read the book morally or as an example of "loco Amor," the Archpriest encourages readers to use it as a source of many experiences, one from which they can master the art of choosing between bad and good. Readers must learn to interpret the *Libro* well (*entender el bien*) so that they can apply its lessons throughout their lives. With good memory, understanding, and will, the soul chooses the love of God and good works (Prologue).

Varied interpretations of the Prologue—as ironic or parodic, joyous-playful, learned-meditative, or a "private joke"[61]—emphasize its deliberately provocative nature. It has even been posited that someone else wrote it, as the prologue appears only in the Salamanca manuscript and the Latin is significantly different from the other sections of the *Libro* that contain Latin.[62] An address that includes women also suggests that the Archpriest sees love as a situation that involves the good judgment and reflection of both sexes. However, one can also read this as a joke among a select group of clerical male students in the manner of the early twelfth-century Occitan troubadour Guilhem IX's "companho" boasting songs, or drinking songs in the Mozarabic tradition.

Affirming the Archpriest's invitation to interpret his book in various ways, late medieval citations of the *Libro* suggests its reception as *auctor*, miscellany of proverbs or fables, or repertory of verse. In his universal history *Libro de Bienandanzas y fortunas* (ca. 1471–76), the Vizcayan nobleman Lope García de Salazar (1399–1476) uses the *Libro*'s prologue as a source of authorities and as a guide to writing prologues;[63] he never mentions that the Archpriest is the source of his material. In his discussion of Salazar, Dagenais argues that he "uses 'the Archpriest' as a convenient lens through which to view still more ancient authorities: Cato, Aristotle, David, Solomon."[64] In his *Prohemio e carta al Condestable de Portugal* (ca. 1446–49), Iñigo López de Mendoza, the Marqués de Santillana (1398–1458), cites the "Libro del Arçipreste de Hita" as one example of a text in a literary tradition that contains works of various meters ("el metro en asaz formas").[65] Clearly, Salazar and Santillana view the *Libro* as both a formal *exemplum* and an *auctor*. In the case of the prologue and these examples of reception, one imagines that the *Libro* could be read as a scholastic reference (such as the sermon or religious verses), as a historical sourcebook, and finally as a guide for a parodic group performance (such as the burlesque lyrics and Pamphilus adaptation). A coterie of students may have read the *Libro* aloud to each other and, playing with various tones, created nuanced degrees of now lost irony[66] in the relation between reader, text, and Archpriest.

Even as the insertion of sentences and proverbs throughout the *Libro* suggests that it served, like the *Carmina*, as a moral encyclopedia, there is no single, overriding message imposed, but a recurrent moral conundrum. It is in this shared, persistent indeterminacy that we may view the *Libro* and the *Carmina* as distinct in content, yet similar in function. The prologue and other commentary function like the *versus* in that they suggest a reading of lyric texts or narrative passages (such as the Pamphilus episode) without making the interpretation of these passages contingent upon the gloss. Given the confusion between *yos* (Archpriest or lover/narrator) and often contradictory tales about *buen amor*, marginalia indicate that readers were perfectly happy to read a few stanzas out of context — whether for a certain proverb,[67] or perhaps merely as a mnemonic aid to bawdy songs such as the *serranillas* or *troba caçurra*. Such fragmentary reading (or, as Dagenais calls it, "florilecture") is the kind of consultation that vernacular songbooks like the *Carmina* and the *Libro* invite as rich, heterogeneous repositories of both moral and entertaining material.

THE TENSION BETWEEN PERFORMANCE AND READING: THE EXAMPLE OF THE BAD TROUBADOUR

While both the *Carmina* and the *Libro* contain material for musical performance and literary study, the *Libro* foregrounds the tension between creative performance of a song and reflective, interpretive reading of a book. The Archpriest invites his audience to take on the role of *mester de joglaría,* just as he and his characters (such as Trotaconventos, the go-between) do. The *joglar*, as minstrel, sings a song but is not responsible for its subject matter since in the traditional sense he does not compose it (e.g., "far esta troba" 114a). One can see this theme of *joglaría* playing out in the scene with Ferret (1618–25), who as a bad messenger acts in place of the sender and botches the songs (1625). In another instance a lady who refuses the Archpriest ends up singing the song as the better "trobador" (92d). The bad messenger or bad troubadour encapsulates the idea that a song's reception depends on the person embodying it and the situation of its execution. Likewise, songs in the *Libro* may be interpreted differently according to context through a narrative framework that maintains the autonomous and open quality of lyrical verses. This idea is significant, since it is likely that different people performed the *Libro* aloud.

In his commentary, the Archpriest often recognizes that his lyric insertions may be openly interpreted as performance and only later reflected upon morally in the context of the book. For example, he introduces a *cantica de serrana* by saying: "Desta burla passada fiz un cantar atal: / non es mucho fermoso, creo, nin comunal; / fasta que el libro entiendas, dél bien non digas nin mal, / ca tú entenderás uno e el libro dize ál" (I wrote a song about this escapade, I don't think it is very lavish, or base; until you understand the book, don't judge it as good or bad for you will think one thing and the book will say something else, 986). By saying that his song is not *comunal,* a word also used by Occitan troubadours to debate the reception of their songs,[68] the Archpriest means that although his songs may please a wide audience (the popular *canticas de serranas* evoke local landscapes and traditions), they are also intended for a learned audience who recognize the *canticas* as a burlesque of the *pastourelle*.[69] Further, as he says in other interpolations such as stanzas 68 and 69, one may judge his *Libro* and its parts differently.

In another use of the word *comunal,* he mentions that he writes melodies "de comunales maneras" so beautiful that they appeal to many people (stanzas 1513–14). A song that is "comunal," lively, pleasurable entertainment for a wide audience, also has the possibility of merging with the didactic purposes of the book in creative ways. The Archpriest advises the audience to judge sections only retrospectively in light of understanding the entire book and on the context of each case ("por puntos la juzgat," 69c).

This tension between performing or composing the song as entertainment and interpreting the book also appears in the Archpriest's invitations to emendation: "emiende la todo omne, e quien buen amor pecha, / que yerro e mal fecho emienda non desecha" (anyone can emend it who pays tribute to good love, since error and wrongdoing do not preclude emendment, 1507cd). The performance of a song assumes the immediate context: one's feelings at a certain moment ("con el mucho quebranto fiz aquesta endecha," in great sorrow I wrote this lament, 1507a) influence the performance, whether for good or for ill. Therefore anyone who follows good love is justified in emending the song after it is set down. While one might wonder whether the Archpriest's claim to send a song is an empty formula when the song does not appear in the text—as in line 80a, "Enbié le esta cantiga que es de yuso puesta" (I sent her this song, written below)—such claims support the idea that the book serves as prompt for a potential text or performance.[70]

Just as we can imagine the compilers of the *Carmina* annotating songs, the learned sermon and the *cuaderna vía* of the *Libro* sections were probably later interpolations alongside recited material.[71] By focusing on the discontinuities of the separate sections where the Archpriest plays only a marginal role of didactic interpolator, could we instead look upon the *Libro* as what R. B. Tate calls a "transcript" similar to the *Carmina,* where the lyrics are autonomous units and the Archpriest acts more like the *versus,* inviting interpretation without undermining freedom of performance?[72] The Archpriest's commentaries, along with the communication of good and bad messengers, suggest that meaning happens in the moment of performance ("ande de mano en mano a quien quier quel pidiere; / como pella a las dueñas, tome lo quien podiere," may it pass from hand to hand, to whoever asks for it, like a ball in a women's game, take it who will, 1629cd). Tate suggests the invitation to emend is like adding an introit and an epilogue to a fixed form. This idea of musical performance (a possible context of the *Libro,* especially regarding the lyric sections), coupled with the Archpriest's comments about audience participation, helps us imagine the transcriptive quality of the *Libro.*

Similar to the context of the *Carmina,* various songs and episodes of the

Libro may have evolved according to its close relation to an entertainment context and as a communal text among Juan Ruiz and his "comarca" group.[73] In María Rosa Lida de Malkiel and Raymond Willis's idea of the *Libro* as a performance piece that welcomes spontaneous interjections while maintaining a basic open structure, we see a songbook that, rather than relying on rigid literary forms, is in a state of becoming, or active as a "potential" book, through the presence of the Archpriest.[74]

Finally, as Américo Castro argues, we may do well to imagine the production and reception of the *Libro* through the context of its *mudéjar* culture, particularly its architecture. Castro sees the *Libro* as a "cancionero," and compares it to a fifteenth-century *mudéjar puerta* of the Baeza Cathedral, where Gothic columns frame a Moorish decoration that blurs the distinction between "dentros" and "fueras."[75] Like the *puerta*, the *Libro* invites the viewer to meditate on the shifting ambiguity of *amor* as at once "bueno" and "loco." Another example we can turn to is the Alhambra, that surviving testimony to the Peninsula's Moorish past; similar to other medieval Islamic palaces, many rooms of the Alhambra are not an end in themselves but, like the stage of a theater, may be modified according to the activity and need of the moment.[76] In a similar way the structure of the *Libro* provides rooms and stages for the audience's needs of the moment.

"YO LIBRO": THE ARCHPRIEST AS BOOK AND INSTRUMENT

At one point, the Archpriest identifies himself with the book as an instrument that needs to be played: "De todos instrumentos yo, libro, só pariente: / bien o mal, qual puntares, tal te dirá çiertamente. / Qual tú dezir quisieres, ý faz punto, ý ten te; / si me puntar sopieres, sienpre me avrás en miente" (I, the book, am ancestor of all instruments, I can tell how well or badly you pluck my strings. What you desire to find you will choose and find; if you know how to play me, I shall stay in your mind, 70a–d). While inviting the audience to play the book and find moral meaning, the Archpriest suggests that what one finds depends on how one plays. He essentially invites the reader or listener to imitate his role as adaptor and translator by adapting or playing the *Libro*.[77]

The Archpriest assumes the roles of commentator, compiler, and protagonist in various instances. In the Doña Endrina episode, for example, an adaptation of the Pamphilus story, the narrative *yo* merges with the Don Melon de la Huerta character, and it is only at the very end of the episode (909b) that he says he is not the protagonist of the story. In the *serrana* episodes, the Archpriest interpolates a narrative context, "bridge passages," around four different *canticas de serrana*; the narrative framing texts are consistent in tone while one can imagine the lyrics as independent insertions.[78] The Archpriest plays the role of commentator who frames his *Libro* as an instrument to be played: playing a troubadour in the mountains (the narrative), he also compiles a mini-anthology of mountain songs of which he is the commentator.

In this *serrana* section, the Archpriest in his "yo libro" role converges with the compiler-composers of the *Carmina,* as he structures groups of lyrics without imposing a single moral perspective. While possessing moral judgments and a tone consistent with the rest of the *cuaderna vía* sections, the *serrana* narratives do not create a unified progressive sequence with the lyrics (950–1042), nor do they duplicate the content of the lyric. Rather the narrative describes particular elements of the *serrana* situation (being lost, the encounter with the mountain girls, the requirements of marriage, the enumeration of ugly qualities) or sets up the plot. Clearly, these elements complement or are contrasted to each other in diverse ways.[79] The narratives contain sentences and proverbs that, rather than moralize, often enhance the comic effect of the story, thus offering different points of reference for the audience to judge the lyrics. For example, an inserted *sententia* in one of the narratives is a warning given to the mountain girl not to "leave what you have got for what you have to get" (996), a warning against rashness and bad judgment; yet in the following lyric we do not know whether the girl is given false promises or the lyric anticipates a successful marriage. The frame narratives in the *Libro* create not only intertextual relationships like the *versus* or vernacular stanzas of the *Carmina* but links to the entire *Libro* and narrative of the Archpriest (the narrative sections possess the same tone as the other *cuaderna vía* sections), all the while emphasizing the relatively similar genre and structural elements that unite the episode. Building our anticipation for each encounter between the protagonist and the mountain girl by directing our attention to the lyrics' possible climaxes (shelter, passage, coitus, or marriage), the frame narratives in the *serrana* sections produce a rhythm of expectation and unity within the episodes and relate to the *Libro* at large, even as the lyrics remain autonomous from them.

REFRAIN POETRY IN
THE *CARMINA* AND THE *LIBRO*

Después fiz muchas cantigas de dança e troteras,
para judías e moras e para entenderas;

para en instrumentos de comunales maneras;
el cantar que non sabes, oy lo a cantaderas.

Cantaras fiz algunos de los que disen los çiegos
e para escolares que andan nocherniegos,
e para muchos otros por puertas andariegos,
caçurros e de bulrras, non cabrian en diez pliegos.

After this I wrote a lot of songs for dancing and traveling,
for Jewesses and Moorish girls, and for lovers,
for the instruments with beautiful melodic phrasing.
If you don't know these songs, listen to the women who sing them.

I wrote some songs for blind men
and for students who go out at night,
and for many others who beg from door to door,
minstrel songs and mocking songs, well over ten sheets' worth.

(1513–14)

The composition of vernacular stanzas in the *Carmina* represents the desire to appeal to an audience beyond the reaches of a literary, clerical environment; likewise the employment of the *estribote*, or *zéjel*, in the lyric texts of the *Libro* suggests the composition of songs for many purposes and people. The presence of the *estribote*, with the metrical structure *AA//bbb/aa/AA* (the AA as the refrain, or *estribillo*),[80] employed here for the first time in Castilian,[81] brings together religious and secular verse through a common flexible metrical form, as well as clerical and popular indigenous cultures.[82]

In contrast to the courtly *canso/chanson/canzone*, the *estribote*, cultivated under different names from the twelfth century—the Occitan *dansa*, the French *virelai*, the Spanish and Portuguese *cantiga*, and the Italian *lauda*—originated as a form of low style. Dante, in defining the *canzone*, the most excellent of genres in his opinion, specifically cites one of its distinguishing features as the absence of a refrain (*sine responsorio*).[83] The popularity of this form is clear in the Occitan treatise *Doctrina de compondre dictats* (ca. 1290), which identifies the *dansa* as a melody that is danced to, has a pleasing melody, and is accompanied by instruments.[84] Although Dante accords supremacy to the *canzone*, the description of the *dansa* in the *Doctrina* suggests the popularity of this lower style in Romance lyric.

The cultivation of the peninsular *estribote* is rooted in a confluence of these aforementioned popular continental forms and local cultures. To what extent the Arabic *zéjel* or medieval Latin prototypes influenced the formation of the Spanish *estribote* is difficult to ascertain.[85] The earlier Galician-Portuguese repertory the *Cantigas de Santa María*, compiled during the reign of Alfonso X El Sabio (r. 1252–84),[86] is a clear influence in the *Libro*. The collection represents contemporary tastes for refrain poetry as opposed to retrospective or antiquarian interests, such as the troubadour chansonniers that contain *cansos* and record a tradition in its final stages a generation later. Until the fourteenth century, this lyric form took many variations while maintaining its popular metrical form of *AAbbba*. In the *Cantigas*, the refrains accommodate not only instrumental and dance performance but hybridization of musical genres and contrafacta of secular songs. They are also distinct from the *canso/chanson* in that they are lyrico-narrative (*cantigas de miagre*) rather than strophic courtly love songs. By the time Santillana mentions them in his *Prohemio,* he refers to the musical setting of this verse as *estrambotes* (from the Italian *strambotto* or Old French *estrabot*), and the lyrics alone with numerous variations as *villancicos*.

The refrain of the *estribote*, the *estribillo*, produces a lyric mode distinct from the narrative *cuaderna vía* parts of the *Libro*. In a manner similar to the spring dance songs of the *Carmina*, these lyrics help us imagine the performance potential of the *Libro* in its clerical context. Although it is hard to know whether the *estribillo* served as a refrain for an audience in response to a soloist in the *Libro* (as compared to the *Cantigas,* where we have notation and miniatures suggesting the manner of execution), each stanza of the *estribote* could occur in relation to the rhymed *estribillo*, producing echoing effects of either close parody or a religious subtext requiring stanza-by-stanza reflection. Such effects would have made these lyrics conducive to a performance between audience and soloist, and to indefinite continuation of the song as long as each stanza returns to the refrain. The interactive character of the *estribillo* is such that we can imagine why it has had a longstanding tradition in Iberian literature as a popular lyric form. The nature of refrain songs also increases the possibility that these, as well as other invisible songs that the Archpriest claims to have composed,[87] may have been added extemporaneously, similar to the composition or inclusion of vernacular stanzas in the *Carmina*.[88] Moreover, as in the earlier codex, one could emend the *Libro* according to circumstances and audience.[89]

As the *cuaderna vía* occurs in the narrative sections of the *Libro* and structures the practice of forward reading (that is, the fourteen-syllable lines are grouped into monorhymed quatrains), the *estribote*, on the other hand, in its rhythmic, choral musicality, facilitates the interaction between a (possibly changing) protagonist-soloist and audience (the chorus), and the return to the refrain. The structure of the *estribote* perhaps encourages a different kind of emendation and participation of the audience with the refrain as the center of the lyric sequence. It has been suggested that the narrative sections, if seen as introducing the lyric, are like a minstrel introducing a song, or a director in a dancehall.[90] One must ask to what degree the *cuaderna vía* context mediates the performance conditions of the refrain lyric: do the *estribotes* record an oral performance, or, as Ardis Butterfield in her discussion of thirteenth-century lyric puts it, do they exemplify a "writing which imitates an oral performance style"?[91] The dependent and independent nature of the *estribote* suggests two possibilities: either the lyrics were used for performance, or they represented a poet's idea of a performance and an audience's reception of these lyrics written into a narrative. Whether fragmentary or stylized representations of such a performance, these refrain lyrics document a complex process of interaction between oral and written traditions specific to the clerical environment in which the *Libro* has been created.

Finally, by comparing the use of the *estribillo* to the German refrain stanzas of the *Carmina*, one can imagine that the *Carmina* compilers, like the Archpriest, might consider structural and metrical similarities over subject matter in their appended stanzas to Latin dance songs. Through the refrain, literary and popular entertainment contexts converge, signifying the role this type of lyric plays in forming the musical and poetic character of these works. A close reading of examples from both of these works demonstrates the advantages of imagining them as platforms for various modes of performance.

The Estribillo *in the* Libro

Both the parallel vernacular stanzas in the *Carmina* and the *estribote* in the *Libro* may be seen as products of local performance environments. In the *estribote*, emendation can occur when the audience interacts with the joglar through the refrain, or *estribillo*. As the *estribote* was executed in a dance and music context,[92] the audience may have emended these lyrics to the *Libro* "transcript" according to different performance situations. Three different examples demonstrate the adaptation of this lyric form to different subject matters and tonal registers: the burlesque of the *troba caçurra*, the religious earnestness of the *Gozos*, and the theatrical *serranillas*.

Although one can imagine various hypothetical performance situations involving the *estribillo* in the *Libro*, it is difficult to determine with any certainty from the manuscript evidence just how the *estribote* was executed during the fourteenth and fifteenth centuries. D. McMillan notes "the scribes of the S and G manuscripts — especially the former — have not always transcribed their texts in such a way as to make the structure self-evident . . . ; they offer virtually no evidence, viz., on the use of the *estribillo* as a refrain rather than as a mere prelude."[93] Yet if the *estribote* in the *Libro* was still performed as a chorus in the traditional manner (as Pierre Le Gentil suggests is a possibility in the *Libro*), then that at least distinguishes these lyrics from the *cuaderna vía*. The strongest example of the *estribillo* as a possible repeating refrain occurs in the *troba caçurra*, or satirical minstrel's song:

Mis ojos non verán luz
pues perdido he a Cruz.

Cruz cruzada, panadera
tomé por entendedera,
tomé senda por carrera
commo faze el andaluz.

Coidando que la avría,
dixié lo a Ferrand Garçía
que troxiese la pletesía
e fuese pleités e duz.

My eyes shall see no light
since I have lost my Cross.

Cross crusaded, the baker girl,
I took her for my lover,
I mistook a pathway for a highway
like the Andalusian Moor.

Thinking I should have her soon
I asked Ferrand García
to put my case before her,
as negotiator and guide.

(115–17)

On a literary level, the use of the *estribote* is essential for hitting the right notes of religious parody, bawdy verse, and learned irony. On the one hand, the theme of returning to the refrain taps all the potential nuances of the *estribillo*: the association of each stanzaic end rhyme (*vuelta*) with the refrain ("Mis ojos . . .") shifts the *estribillo*'s meaning after each stanza according to the new progression of the narrative. For instance, 117d introduces the biblical link of Judas with his go-between friend who betrays him; 118d combines the figure of the *panadera* with the idea of the Eucharist; the two images are certainly linked to the *estribillo* image of *cruz* as worldly and spiritual love. The *estribillo* balances all these meanings of *cruz* because each stanza, building up to its last line, activates a new potential meaning for the *estribillo*'s metaphors by referring back to the refrain.

On the other hand, the musical quality of an *estribote* song, well established by the famous *Cantigas de Santa María,* and common to circulating local romance or low minstrel verse, provides a suitable vehicle for a conflation of religious ritual (the Passion, stations of the Cross) with worldly love. The burlesque and *joglar* quality of the song derives not only from its content but also from the particular jingle and tune of its constant refrain.

On a macroscopic level, the *estribote* creates parody by relating songs of vastly different subject matter but similar form. In the Salamanca manuscript (which contains the most religious lyrics), the parody of the *troba caçurra* musically and thematically echoes other serious religious lyrics (although they could also be parodied depending on the performance) of *estribote* form: the *Gozos de Santa María,* the *Pasión,* the *Ave María* and the second *Cantica de loores de Santa María.* To a certain extent, the two begging songs (*De commo los scolares demandan por dios,* 1650–55, 1656–60) also belong in this category although they are distinctive as Goliard verse. In the *Gozos* (20–32) and *Pasión* (1046–58, 1059–66), the *estribillo* serves as a reflective refrain or as a prelude to a prayer (*Pasión* 1046). In the begging songs it is a plea (1650, 1656). As the prayers enumerate the *Gozos* or the steps of the Passion, each stanza metrically and musically returns to the refrains. These serious verses, which reflect upon the joys of the Virgin Mary and the death of Christ, like the *troba caçurra* "Cruz" refrain, can also become a self-conscious parody of the protagonist's suffering. Alternatively, although the refrain of the *troba caçurra* accentuates the pun of *cruz,* the reflective refrain of the other lyrics emphasizes the act of a meditative return to the *cruz,* one appropriate for such a song of prayer.

While the *estribillo* of the *caçurra* and religious lyrics produce an effect that is essential to its parody or meditation, the *estribote* of the *serranillas* functions in another sense. Two of the four *canticas de serrana* are *estribotes*: 987–92 (*Cantica* II) and 1022–42 (*Cantica* IV). As discussed earlier, the *cantica* lyrics may be seen as autonomous units ("indivisible wholes")[94] apart from the *cuaderna vía* frame narrative. The *canticas* in *estribote* forms, however, are further distinguished as their lyrical structure shapes the theatrical exchange between the protagonist and the mountain girl.

Cantica IV, the longer of the two *estribote canticas*, uses a complex form with an *estribillo* of four rhyming hexasyllables and double rhyming *mundanza* couplets.[95] The *estribillo* economically announces the theme of the song:

> Çerca la Tablada
> la sierra passada,
> fallé me con Alda,
> a la madrugada.

> Around the Tablada Pass
> beyond the mountain range,
> I came across Alda
> in the early morning.

>   (1022)

The *estribillo* begins with elements resembling a *pastourelle*: the nature setting ("cerca la Tablada / la sierra passada") and the peasant girl (Alda). Compared to stanza 997, the first stanza of *Cantica* III, which elaborates on these details and ends with a greeting ("dixe le yo: 'Dios te salve, hermana!'" I said to her, God save you, sister!), the *estribillo* of "Çerca la Tablada" does not enter into the narrative but announces the song as a remembered experience invoked lyrically. The economy of words in keeping with the hexameter and rhyme encapsulates an entirely different kind of poetic event for its listeners. Likewise in *Cantica* II:

> Sienpre se me verná miente
> desta serrana valiente,
> Gadea de Río Frío.

> I shall always remember
> that lusty mountain girl,
> Gadea of Riofrío.

>   (987)

"Sienpre se me verná miente" explicitly evokes a memory translated to a song about Gadea, "Gadea Río Frio." Perhaps these *estribillos* were like hearing the beginning of a well-known tune. In any event, the musical return to the *estribillo* at each stanza enacts the unity of a performance piece with rhythmic continuity and variation.

The refrain structure reinforces a call and response dialogue between the *serrana* and the protagonist essential to the courtship song and its burlesque qualities. For while the other lyrics may repeat a rhyme within a stanza (such as in *Cantica* I, where there is a rhyme between first and last line, and *Cantica* II, with monorhyming stanzas), the *estribillo* emphasizes what happens (or perhaps could happen) in the song between *serrana* and protagonist by effectively arbitrating a poetic center within the course of the song. Thus it stages the dialogue between the two characters and prevents the song's being governed by a narrator's voice. On another level, if this song was performed to a participatory audience, the *estribillo* creates a center between singer(s) and audience, as the refrain directs the listener's attention to the dialogic relation between a courtship song and the actual participation in the singing of the *estribillo*. Considering that these *Canticas*, like the Galician-Portuguese *cantigas*, may have been danced to, the burlesque effect may have been even greater.

The *capfinadas* stanzas of the second *Cantica*, the last word of the *vuelta* recurring as the first of the following stanza, also reassert the give-and-take effect of the *estribillo* throughout the lyric. For example, the protagonist repeats the words of the *serrana*: "'e andas commo rradío.' / 'Radío ando, serrana, / en esta grand espessura'" (and you are quite lost. Quite lost am I, mountain girl, amidst this great mass of bushes, 988d and 989a). Perhaps the repeated words also would have enabled the staging of comic gestures and actions between the two characters:

"Sí la cayada te enbío."

Enbió me la cayada
aqui tras el pastorejo;
fizo me ir la cuesto lada . . .

Watch that I give you my crook.

She threw the crook at me,
here, behind my ear,
and I fell sideways . . .

(990i, 991abc)

From these examples one can see how the *estribillo* variations produce dynamic relations between different voices, and between singer and audience.

The German Stanzas and the Refrain Lyrics of the Libro: Two Views of Songbook Participation

We can think of the flexibility of the *Libro*'s refrain poetry in the same light as the *Carmina* compilers' practice of composing German stanzas: both incorporate local traditions and available exemplars within a structurally consistent set of refrain poems. Similar to the tonal exchanges within and among different *estribote* lyrics, the ad hoc composition of original vernacular refrains to Latin songs enables relations between texts in the book and multiple readings of an individual song. Likewise the metrical and musical flexibility of the *estribote* accommodates various subject matters as it supplements and reinforces a coherent narrative.

One can imagine different scenarios of compilation for the refrain series of the *Carmina* due to contemporary performance revisions, availability of repertories, or simply ad hoc composition. It is likely that the composer desired to build a series around refrains. Subordinating the particularities of individual songs to the concept of a refrain collection, he may have composed the Latin and German at the same time with a similar refrain structure in mind, or he may have had access to a songbook with refrains he wanted to use. For example, in the refrain song series with German stanzas, CB 179–83, 179a is not thematically related to its Latin counterpart, yet it derives its structure from it. The six- and four-syllable lines at the beginning of the Latin stanza have been translated into two- or three- beat lines in the German one. Thematically the German refrain stanza relates more to 180 which treats the same topic of love correspondence ("brief," 179a line 1, and "littera" 180, line 4). CB 180 contains an original German refrain — perhaps composed because of its location in a refrain series, as it bears no relation to the Latin lyrics. This refrain is an isometric couplet associated with a four-beat, four-line strophe. CB 180a is metrically similar to 180, suggesting that we have the composition of a German stanza parallel to the Latin poem. Although there is a strong formal similarity, there are no obvious textual similarities except the common refrain. The "Mandaliet" of 180, like "lodircundeia" of 163, also marks the stanza as a nonce word common in refrains.[96] The following Latin songs in the series, 181 and 182, are also similar in form with their simple rhythmic structures with couplet refrains. Another German refrain to a Latin round dance consists of two stanzas of thrice-repeated dance calls that correlate with thrice-repeated liturgical acclamations such as *Laudes regiae* (148a).[97] Such treatment demonstrates that this stanza was composed in a milieu conversant with Latin and German song traditions.

Similarity of refrain structure rather than content suggests a practice of composing dance songs for which there are no definitive models. The series displays an adaptation of traditions (popular, *Minnesang*) to create similarities ad hoc in the codex. The instances of archaic meters (only final vowels rhyming, four-beat couplet refrains with no anacrusis), strong accentual rhythms, and onomatopoeic formation and nonce words, follow what must have been popular dance interjections, rhythms, and sounds adaptable to both German and Latin lyric.[98] Although we can never know whether the students actually danced to these songs, this practice of adding German stanzas to Latin poems or adapting Latin poems to German refrains represents the reciprocal influence of the two traditions and a milieu willing to experiment in a fluid and expedient manner.

In the final analysis, the *Libro*'s evolving state as a "transcript" with invitations for the audience to emend ad libitum resembles the close textual process of emendation and compilation in the *Carmina*, as compilers or composers create a series based on the refrain. Whereas we can often only imagine (in the case of the missing lyrics) how an audience emended or performed today's existing codices of the *Libro*, in the *Carmina* we see a documentation of these activities, which are more than likely the result of both popular traditions and literary practices.

CONCLUSION

In describing these two works as songbooks, I have presented three different ways of approaching these medieval texts:

First, from my perspective as a modern reader, I have described these medieval codices (whose texts can often be traced to multiple sources) as both lyric collections with autonomous texts and as unified books. This view considers the books as transcripts or platforms for potential activity around a consistent structure. In the case of the *Carmina* this structure may be the *versus* or the correspondences made by the German stanzas. In the case of the *Libro*, the ambivalent figure of the Archpriest allows creative participation by the audience while also acting as sort of stage director, controlling the activity through his interpolations.

Second, I have stressed the importance of imagining the contemporary practice of making a songbook; both these codices accommodate and assimilate contemporary and popular tastes specific to their environments. Both are work spaces adapting different kinds of lyric and texts while allowing for extemporaneous emendation. The *estribote* accommodates different lyric types as well as performance situations. In the *Carmina*, the German stanza refrains are efficient tools for songbook compilation, providing a structuring element for a fluid bilingual exchange of Latin and popular vernacular traditions.

Third, by taking into account both synchronic and diachronic perspectives of songbooks, we can better imagine how readers used the songbook in certain situations, as well as how an open songbook structure can become a unified text. As part of the active situation of these books, it is important to view their reception as unfolding in time. A songbook makes possible creative reception situations for various participants within its circle of influence. Some of these receptions are partially documented, and others spring from the open-ended state of the songbook itself.

Chapter Two

PRODUCING OPAQUE
COHERENCE: LYRIC PRESENCE
AND NAMES

Aqui son escrig li noms dels trobadors qui/son ena*qu*est livre que
ant trobadors laç ca*n*/sos lun apres lautre.[1]

Here are written the names of the troubadours who are in this
book who have composed *cansos* one after another.

> Rubric from chansonnier I, Paris, Bibl. Nat. fr. 854, thirteenth-century
> Italian chansonnier of troubadours, f. 1

THE CHANSONNIER, PROPER NAMES,
AND HERMENEUTIC OPACITY

In the previous chapter I sought to explain how participatory emendation
and compilation constitute the songbook mode. As we will see, this mode
proves crucial for the formation of literary histories, because songbooks
invite multiple vantage points for interpreting the authorial voice. In this
chapter I shift to the Italian chansonniers of Occitan lyric, among the earliest known anthologies of lyric poetry in a European vernacular. I will elaborate upon the notion that the lyric persona, as a product of the songbook,
depends upon its presentation of lyrics under the claim of historical and
cultural authenticity. In the case of the Italian chansonniers, the claim is
based on these volumes' creation of what appears to be a stable identity for
the poet: compiled in northern Italy from the mid-thirteenth century on,
and representing the earliest efforts to create a written literary tradition of

the troubadours,[2] these songbooks celebrate discrete poets through *vidas* and illuminated portraits, and organize songs like the rubric of the chansonnier cited at the head of this chapter: songs under names ("li noms dels trobadors") and by genre, *cansos*, *sirventes* (political or satirical songs), and *tensos* (debate songs). The organization of lyrics by the troubadour's name, often reinforced in this instance by *vidas* preceding the lyric corpus and the portraits, shows the extent to which the idea of the troubadour corpus — the poetic subject ("trobador"), and his work ("cansos") — is manifested by the cohesive book or chansonnier ("livre").

Famously, troubadours rarely invoke their proper names in their lyrics, preferring a *senhal* or secret name. But what happens when they invoke their true names? This chapter explores these invocations that belong to the phenomenon of the songbook, and argues that rather than creating stable identities as metonymic headings for lyric corpuses, these names reveal a particular troubadour as a multiauthored, fluid assemblage arising from the hermeneutic position of the songbook reader. Far from fixing an identity behind the "I" of a song, the proper name in the songbook belongs within what a scholarly consensus now understands as the medieval lyric first person. According to that consensus, the proper name can entail fictitious, authorial self-representation, poetic activity at times merging with historical selfhood and references, and a dialogic engagement with an implied audience.[3] What is remarkable and counterintuitive about the songbook genre is that compilers' attempts to extrinsically stabilize a lyric voice as an author through prosaic commentaries and generic classifications only complicate what Olivia Holmes has called "the implied author" as "an aggregate of inferences based on the text, primarily on the use of the first person."[4] How, precisely, does the songbook accumulate these "inferences," or, seen otherwise, how can the reader engage with the proper names in the songbook as dynamic rather than stable markers? I contend that the bodily envoicement of the troubadour proper name within lyric texts continues through the material body of the songbook, the songs themselves as well as the apparatus around them. In my specific examples, the voice of the proper name can take on many forms and modalities through the medium of the chansonnier, which makes them cohere. As a case study, proper names in chansonniers function as indexes of how songbooks work from a phenomenological perspective: how lyrics accrue value as "poetry" through a specific material situation.

The study of chansonniers takes for granted that all troubadour songs transmitted in writing were copied from written sources now lost. Although, since Gustav Gröber's work on the *Liedersammlungen,* many hypotheses have been advanced, it is impossible to say with certainty how much troubadours or *joglars* relied on memory or performance manuals to work out their verses. What is certain is that during the twelfth and thirteenth centuries, oral transmission of this poetry was significant for its preservation; that oral and written traditions coexisted; and that by the thirteenth century, source collections (in other words, songbooks before they appeared in the bound volumes that survive today) served as the foundation of the earliest attested chansonniers.[5] Certainly the study of chansonniers aligns itself with the study of medieval *compilatio*, the examination of the historical and material conditions in which texts were assembled in miscellanies or compendia (an arbitrary or casual collection of texts), or in more cohesive books with corresponding parts, which tells us about the reception of authors at the moment of their compilation.[6] For the northern Italian copyist of chansonnier I, the practice of organizing lyrics by authors follows theological and university manuscript traditions common by the thirteenth century, such as illustrating psalters with evangelist portraits and including indexes, running titles, and rubricated chapters. The practice of collecting varied texts or *recueils*, and by extension the organization of texts under proper names, draw from earlier medieval collections of sacred writings such as the *pandect*, traditions of saints' lives, and Saint Jerome's *De viris illustribus*—an encyclopedia of famous authors and their works.[7] By adapting these traditions for lyric anthologies that include prose commentaries, illuminated portraits, and genre and poet sections set forth by rubrication and careful indexes, compilers of the Italian chansonniers created prestigious cultural objects for their aristocratic patrons that anticipate modern editions.[8]

Chansonniers represent certain developments in vernacular medieval texts at this time (the compilation of songbooks in professional scriptoria ordered by aristocratic patrons, the bibliographical authorization of secular poets using biblical and classical models),[9] and a close observation of them reveals multiple functions of a name in relation to its subject matter. A name may appear as an organizational principle or possess a specific meaning within a lyric; as such, names indicate how songbooks work as anthologies of lyrics, music, *vidas*, and *razos* (prose commentaries). They offer a site from which to examine the songbook as a dynamic collocation of diverse texts that retain their autonomy as discrete units while converging thematically. For thirteenth-century Italian compilers of chansonniers and nineteenth-century philologists alike, then, names provide a memorial structure for an archive and grant authority to this corpus of lyric poetry. Although modern scholarship no longer supposes that *vidas* unambiguously transmit the historical identities of these poets, there has been productive study of troubadour proper names within the context of the Christian Middle Ages: for instance, the way in which a proper name authorizes the namer by empowering a person to reveal a thing's nature and establishes the truth between *nomen* and *res,* following the account of Adam's act of naming in Genesis or Isidore of Seville's etymologies.[10] My analysis of names bears on troubadour proper names in two contexts I can only mention here: in the fourteenth-century Occitan *ars poetria* called the *Leys d'Amors,* a treatise for poetic competitions in Toulouse; and in the prose texts where the names serve as citational metonymies for lyric corpuses.[11] Judging from the instrumental work a proper name can do in these prose texts — the grammatical function of proper names in the *Leys,* the troubadour name as sign for his work and life — we should see the proper name as an important factor in shaping the transmission of the lyric tradition. As conspicuous indexes of both oral and written transmission of lyric texts in the songbook, proper names facilitate the bi-directional flow between lyric and prose, voice and letter, live performance and manuscript performance.

In the songbook, one sees the tension between two versions of the name: as a voiced event and as a rubric identical to a lyric corpus — and, in extension, to the rubric, the *vidas* and portraits, as representations of discrete identities. The copyist attributes meaning to a proper name — through the association with that name with a patron in a rubric, for instance — even as this attribution coincides with a lyric text that eludes fixed meaning. While we might expect chansonniers to make the reception of the troubadours more consistent, narrowing the possibilities of interpretation, this encounter between the name within the lyric text and the same name as absorbing diverse cultural meanings makes the proper name in a songbook a vehicle for multiple interpretations. From the perspective of the songbook, the proper name cannot be separated from its particular context of transmission in each chansonnier; yet we must also recognize the poetics of nominal self-invocation by the troubadour — a lyrical gesture in which the troubadour names him- or herself as maker of a song. This gesture is an assertion of authority and an affirmation of bodily desire in an individual voice, an envoicement of the proper name lying between the poet as maker of a *vers* and a finished text as *auctor.*[12] From the bodily performance of this invocation to its transmission in chansonniers, organization by proper names and generic classifications attempts to create an interpretive protocol for the reader: from desiring poet to authoritative text governed by the principle of a proper name. Yet the phenomenon of the songbook allows these two points to be available simultaneously as well as in this protocol; the proper name acts as metonymy both for the troubadour in the process of singing and for the lyric corpus of his or her texts. For example, in chansonniers we see the name as phenomenon of *vox corporis* inherent in the troubadours' thematization of the body as instrument of both singing and composition, as when Bernart says at the end of a *canso*, "Bernartz de Ventadorn l'enten" (Bernart de Ventadorn [who externalizes his desire through song] understands it [the song that he made, which he now dispatches]). At the same time, we also see the name as head of a lyric corpus.

Considering that several written versions of a song may exist and no one lyric text can be considered authoritative,[13] the proper name both as deictic particle within a lyric and as rubric for a body of songs may represent heterogeneous functions from oral to written context. It is through this built-up residue of multiple functions that one may view the songbook from the thirteenth century forward not as unambiguously assigning value to the troubadours and their lyrics, but as producing what we might call a phenomenon — gradually and intermittently attributing meaning to inchoate texts. The proper name as vehicle for pluralistic hermeneutics, a way of reading that allows for multiple interpretations, is an important part of this phenomenon. Although copyists place a body of lyric under "Bernart de Ventadorn," or memorialize his lyrics through the *vidas*, what the name signifies cannot be separated from the event of "Bernart de Ventadorn" as mediated by the songbook. That is to say, how a reader interprets that name as both lyric text and rubric will be determined by the perspective of the reader, the contextualization of the name in a particular songbook, its placement on the page, and the reader's own understanding of the lyric text — for example, as a remembered performance during the late Middle Ages, or as an archival encounter in the modern age influenced by Dante and Petrarch's readings of troubadours. As I will show, attribution of meaning through the proper name in songbooks produces a second-order anonymity. We return to the troubadours' original refusal to signify themselves and their song, not through the absence of names, but through the activity of naming, which produces multiple meanings. In this process, a hermeneutic opacity develops: that is, an interpretive effect of the songbook's materiality from which we can deduce how names function from various vantage points without attributing agency to any one standpoint, such as poet or scribe, or value to any one situation of reception. An accumulation of archival knowledge results when a deictic phenomenon of voice, such as a proper name during an oral performance, becomes embedded into networks of knowledge.

For example, the songbook as archive may transmit the genealogy of a lyric text, as the external authorization of a poet's biography does before a lyric corpus. It may determine analogous relations of value, like the cultural value of troubadours granting prestige to Lord Alberico da Romano, patron of chansonnier D (Modena, Biblioteca Estense α, R. 4. 4); or the sacred and secular authority of Marcabru as visually presented through a rubric and Christ image in chansonnier R. These localized events and interpretive situations constitute an opacity in the sense that they may be read as attempts to render certain aspects of lyric texts as purely aesthetic objects, especially through the reification of proper names. More than just polysemous, which would imply a relation between a text and multiple meanings, these events and situations are accretive, parallel, and fluid amalgamations of interpretive modes between lyric text(s) and prosaic indexes or surrogates, manifested through the material phenomenon of the songbook. They represent the coming into being of interpretive strategies between verbal or visual texts. As a locus for several historical and phenomenal positions of a reader, the songbook embodies these networks of knowledge consisting of fluid and shifting interpretations between lyric texts and aspects of the songbook. This hermeneutic opacity does not compromise the songbook. It *is* the songbook.

HERMENEUTIC OPACITY IN PEIRE D'ALVERNHE'S "CANTARAI D'AQESTZ TROBADORS"

First, let us see how hermeneutic opacity works in a song about naming, Peire d'Alvernhe's famous satirical gallery of troubadours, "Cantarai d'aqestz trobadors" (PC 323.11), where he parodies his contemporaries at a festive gathering at Puivert between 1165 and 1173:[14]

Cantarai d'aqestz trobadors
que canton de maintas colors
e·l pieier cuida dir mout gen;
mas a cantar lor er aillors
q'entrametre · n vei cen pastors
c'us non sap qe · s mont'o · s dissen.

D'aisso mer mal Peire Rotgiers,
per qe n'er encolpatz primiers,

car chanta d'amor a presen;
e valgra li mais us sautiers
en la glieis'o us candeliers
tener ab gran candel'arden.

E · l segonz, Girautz de Borneill,
qe sembl'oire sec al soleill
ab son chantar magre dolen,
q'es chans de viella porta – seill;
que si · s mirava en espeill,
no · s prezari'un aiguilen.

I shall sing of those troubadours
who sing in many fashions, and all praise
their own verses, even the most appalling;
but they shall have to sing elsewhere,
for a hundred competing shepherds I [see],
and not one knows whether the melody's rising or falling.

In this Peire Rogier is guilty,
thus he shall be the first accused,
for he carries tunes of love in public right now,
and he would do better to carry
a psalter in church, or a candlestick
with a great big burning candle.

And the second: Giraut de Bornelh,
who looks like a goatskin dried out in the sun,
with that meager voice of his, and that whine,
it is the song of an old lady bearing buckets of water;
if he saw himself in a mirror,
he would think himself less than an eglantine.[15]

Before the compilation of songbooks, troubadours probably heard about one another through their songs and through the close networks of people and places in the courtly environment of medieval Occitania. In such an environment, the sense of a troubadour's name may have included familiarity not only with his or her lyrics but with the troubadour's theatrical gestures, quality of voice, and stature. We can imagine that troubadours encountered each other in courtly gatherings and there learned their counterparts' origins, patrons and travels, enemies and friends.[16] Such intimacy is conveyed in Peire's song. It appears that "Cantarai" anticipates the conventional understanding of troubadour proper names in songbooks as fixing the identity of a poet or creating canons of poets in its serial listing of troubadours with caricatural descriptions. Yet the song also represents how much the performance tradition of this lyric poetry thrives upon unstated referential codes within a community of troubadours rather than proper names as indicators of status and fixed individual identities. Walter Pattison has noted that for the humor of this piece to be fully developed, the troubadours themselves must have been present.[17] While we can ascertain that these troubadours were active around the same time, the satirical portraits depend as much on conventional traditions of burlesque and satires of the troubadours' lyric texts (for example the stanza about Bernart de Ventadorn takes the rhyme schemes of one of Bernart's *cansos*) as on any historical portraits of these poets that one might deduce. In any case, as Peire continues naming fellow troubadours, some well represented in the chansonniers and others about whom we know very little, he ridicules his friends in a way that creates an intimate knowledge of their appearance, background, and lyrics: Peire Rogier should go back to a career in the church ("e valgra li mais us sautiers/en la glieis'o us candeliers tener ab gran candel'arden"); Giraut de Bornelh looks like a dried-out goatskin ("qe sembl'oire sec al soleill") and has a weak voice like an old woman carrying a water bucket ("ab son chantar magre dolen,/q'es chans de vieilla porta – seill").

Chansonniers appear to replace the intimate performance context of troubadour names here—a case of creating lyric identities through the performance environment, lyric texts, and other references lost to us today—with editorial interventions. Certainly we would assume that these archival apparatuses cannot render the presence evoked by a troubadour name that was a mixture of stage performance, lyric personae, and historical existences. Yet the resistance and fascination that the troubadour name offers, an untranslatable deictic specificity of which we see traces in this song, is a line of inquiry into the phenomenological function of the medieval songbook. The transmission of "Cantarai d'aqestz trobadors" in the *Liber Alberici* section (D^a) of chansonnier D embodies the process of hermeneutic opacity: that is to say, how value—cultural, economic, or otherwise—may be attributed to Peire's song and the names within it. Once a phenomenon of the songbook, the name attracts heterogeneous interpretations rather than a consolidation of meaning. Let us see how it works.

First, this songbook belongs to a tradition of chansonniers compiled in northern Italy that begins with Peire d'Alvernhe, thus giving him high rank among the troubadours. This honor accords with *vidas* that state that Peire "era tengutz per lo meillor trobador del mon, tro que venc Guirautz de Borneill"[18] (was the best troubadour in the world until Giraut de Bornelh came along). In fact the *Liber Alberici* of songbook D was most likely a smaller version of the luxurious chansonniers of this tradition, AIK, since it lacks their *vidas*. The *Liber* is also one songbook within a greater songbook (manuscript D) that collates different works; D also contains a French songbook, a florilegium of quotations, and a didactic text (Arnaut de Maruelh's *Ensenhamen*). Because the index preserves the distinctions among these sections, we can be sure that D was to be taken as a collection that includes three distinct songbooks as well as other nonlyric texts.[19] Scholars agree that the *Liber* was the work of Uc de Saint Circ, resident poet of the powerful baron Alberico da Romano (d. 1260). Uc's name was added by a later hand in the index on f. 8r, at the end of the *Liber*'s index, and it is thus possible that he was responsible for the original compilation of Alberico's book.

Whether the *Liber Alberici* belonged to Alberico, or was a copy of the original songbook, or was the work of the compiler-poet Uc, Peire's celebrated song is already placed in a context of a songbook and later a larger collection (D^a, D), associated with a certain patron, compiler-poet, and northern Italian tradition (ADIK) that ranks Peire as the first troubadour. Furthermore, the notation on f. 6 that attributes chansonnier D^a to Lord Alberico in the index uses language similar to the opening rubric of I, but is in Latin and names the book:

> Hec sunt inceptiones cantionum de libro qui fuit domini Alberici et nomina repertorum eorundem cantionum

> Here are the beginnings of the songs of Lord Alberico's book and the names of the authors of these songs

This colophon associates the patron's name with the prestige of the troubadour names ("nomina repertorum"), and affirms this authority through attribution of the book ("Liber Alberici"). As indexes of cultural value, the listing and collection of names constitute a kind of economic transfer: the viability of names grows by being compiled in an expensive manuscript book, and the patron acquires their aggregate increasing value through the identification of prestigious names with his personalized monument.

Second, the manuscript tradition of Peire's gallery reflects variants based on the Monk of Montaudon's imitation circa 1195 of Peire's song, a song that also appears in the *Liber Alberici* ("Pos Peire d'Alvergn'a chantat," Since Peire d'Alvernhe has sung [PC 305.16]). Indeed, the structure of "Cantarai d'aqestz trobadors," is particularly conducive to substitution of other names and stanzaic variation, but the Monk's imitation seemingly influenced an alternate version of Peire's song, which appears in *Liber*'s "Cantarai." Following the Monk's gallery song, the eighth stanza of "Cantarai" substitutes "Peire de Monzo" in chansonnier *a* and "Peire Bremon" in CR — two relatively unknown troubadours — with the stanza of Arnaut Daniel, an important troubadour in the Italian tradition reflected in Dante's citation of him in works such as *De vulgari eloquentia*.[20] With this interpolation of the Arnaut stanza from the Monk's version, we cannot know whether this variant occurs due to written transmission, as both Peire and the Monk's songs appear in the collection of D^a, or to an orally transmitted revised version of "Cantarai d'aqestz trobadors" circulated at the time of this chansonnier's compilation. Most important, it is easy to imagine names of authors and names within a song as interchangeable, both synchronically in an easily adaptable gallery song, and diachronically through interpolations from now cohesive songs by troubadours of different moments in the songbook stage of transmission. Given this indeterminacy, one could also simply imagine a protean gallery open to variants and attributions.

The songbook appears to set fixed versions of songs in order under authors, but this examination of "Cantarai" in D^a shows how troubadour names in chansonniers are framed within overlapping traditions of other names to produce heterogeneous cultural valuations of troubadour and song, since names mean and do different things in these instances: the performance context of a gallery song, a chansonnier that highly ranks Peire d'Alvernhe, or Lord Alberico da Romano's book. For readers of a songbook, naming creates hierarchies, but these names may also provide a platform for nominal valuation to migrate and carry meaning with them, such as the instance of the later troubadour Arnaut's name in Peire's "Cantarai d'aqestz trobadors." As another example of this practice, it has been noted how Bernart de Ventadorn's *vida* possibly borrows from the caricature in "Cantarai d'aqestz trobadors," an example of how names occur in lyric and prose texts and thus have different functions within the structure of the songbook.[21]

ARISTOCRATIC NAMING: GUILHEM DE PEITIEU AND RAIMBAUT D'AURENGA

Turning to troubadours' nominal self-invocations and their transmission in the chansonniers, it is compelling to begin with the feudal lords Guilhem de

Peitieu, seventh count of Poitou and ninth duke of Aquitaine (1071–1127), and Raimbaut d'Aurenga, count of Orange (fl. 1147–73),[22] concerning whom historical documents exist. The social reality signified, implicitly or explicitly, by the proper names of Guilhem and Raimbaut in their lyric texts grants their invocations a particular referential quality. What I call the incantatory quality of these invocations refers to the historical meaning and power an aristocratic name had in medieval Occitania, from which these troubadours deliberately distance themselves through the creation of a fictive lyrical identity.[23] For example, Guilhem, a powerful lord in his day, often refers in his songs to the possession (and dispossession) of women as property when telling his knights or comrades ("cavalier" or "companho") about his horses, a deliberately playful and bawdy allusion to his mistresses.[24] The ritualized ludic affirmation of an implied social status in these boasting songs — sexual, poetic, and chivalric prowess conflated as part of Guilhem's aristocratic gaming with a group of peers — becomes explicit in a nominal self-invocation in his *planh* or funeral lament "Pos de chantar m'es pres talenz" (Since I have been taken with a desire to sing [PC 183.10] Pasero 277–82), where he leaves his lands to his son as he prepares to leave for the crusades. The incantatory effect of the first instance, where an externalized bodily performance of song questions and affirms the presupposition of a historical body, contrasts with the different phenomenon in the *planh*. As a lamentation, the song includes historical references to Guilhem's position as a lord going on crusades and invites the reinscription of an incantatory presence through proper name as metonymy of the troubadour. Reinforced by a chansonnier's nominal rubric and the *vida*, the lyric identity gains a different purchase as it becomes attached to a determination of biographical, historical, and political agency at once part and parcel of poetic play. The manuscript transmission of such instances, whether as scribal interpolations or as evidence of a popular song, demonstrates that compilers supplement the incantatory effect of a poetic voice in Guilhem's outward bodily expression of performance with the memorial incantation of an extralyrical proper name, even if in tension with the troubadour's lyrical ambivalence over it.

With respect to this translation of the incantatory quality of the name, it is important to note how the material documentation and transmission of the name (or no name) facilitates an appropriation and reappropriation of the voice in different forms: hermeneutic opacity constitutes an aggregation of multiple meanings of the proper name and its poetic textuality, and supplements a "lost voice" through the memorial devices of the songbook. Voice and writing coexist, even as the significance of the proper name multiplies as a function of the material context of the songbook. As we will see in the examples of Guilhem and Raimbaut, readers render the proper name within new textual bodies, and these new forms cohere as cumulative arts of interpretation—building upon each other, appearing in conflict with each other—and lack absolute determination, or authorial historicity, even as they are made up of determinant gestures (the *vida*, the rubric). In short, the songbook manifests a multiauthorial, fluid lyric presence as a function of the material archive.

Both Guilhem and Raimbaut avoid naming themselves, and thematize naming as a game and a form of aristocratic posturing. In the case of Guilhem, he composes a song ostensibly about nothing, "Farai un vers de dreit nien" (I shall make a *vers* about absolutely [or exactly] nothing [PC 183.7], 92, line 1). In this song, his general refusal of nominal self-invocation, and the assumption that he does not need to invoke his name in a performance situation, are consistent with his crude humor and paradoxical knowledge of sense and folly ("Eu conosc ben sen e folor," I know sense and foolishness well [183.2], 165, line 8). Famous as the inventor of the *gap* or boasting song, Guilhem frequently brags about what he can do, deliberately conflating his verbal, chivalric, and sexual "equipment" ("garnimen") as a self-named "sure master" ("maistre serta") ("Companho farai un vers [qu'er] covinen," Comrades, I shall do a *vers* that's well made [PC 183.3], 16, line 11; "Ben vueill que sapchon," I want everyone to know [PC 183.2], 167, line 36). Thus, his stance of not knowing or naming himself within a performance of negation is a double provocation. By emphasizing what he will not sing about, or what he is not, he aggrandizes what he has and what he is, and amplifies his aristocratic bragging about his women, horses, or castles ("Companho farai un vers [qu'er] covinen," 16, line 1). Guilhem knows that the present historical and social context will supply what is missing.

Guilhem's denial of nominal self-invocation represents a will to vex the social identity defined by his feudal world, determined at the moment of his birth and outside of his agency. Correspondence between Guilhem and religious officials demonstrates the importance of his name in political relations. In letters to Guilhem, the abbot of Vendôme (d. 1132) addresses him honorably as "Guillelmo omnium militum magistro, et nobilissimo duci Aquitanorum" (To William, master of all knights and most noble duke of Aquitaine).[25] Likewise Pope Urban II (d. 1099) addresses "dilecto filio Guillelmo Pictaviensium comiti" (his beloved son William, count of the Poitevins).[26] In the daily social and political life of Guilhem, proper names indicate the count's social rank, responsibilities as feudal lord, and obligations to others. Moreover, the address indicates the hierarchical relationship between addresser and addressee.

The Occitan paraphrase of Boethius's *Consolation of Philosophy* (*Boeci* fragment, ca. 1000),[27] from a period slightly earlier than that of Guilhem's activity, contextualizes Guilhem's deliberate avoidance of his name. Based on the medieval adaptation of Boethius as a Christian author, the *Boeci* invokes names and titles in a hierarchical fashion, thus demonstrating the importance of these markers in a vernacular religious text. In one stanza we learn that Boethius was a count of Rome ("Cóms fo de Roma" line 34) and that he was lord of the entire empire ("de tót l'emperi·l tenien per senor," line 37); but his nobility is more renowned for another reason ("Mas d'una causa nom avia genzor," line 38), namely that they called him teacher of wisdom ("de sapiencia l'apellaven doctor," line 39). Here we see Christian principles played out through the name: Boethius has a social identity ("Cóms de Roma, senor de tót l'emperi"), but this is contrasted to his greater spiritual title as a teacher of wisdom. His "nom" represents his true essence or nature as 'doctor de sapiencia,' which transcends his worldly title.[28]

In contrast to the spiritual significance of the name in the *Boeci*, Guilhem's identity is based on vernacular performance, on a discursive activity of *trobar*. His identity, or rather nonidentity, emerges through vernacular performance, an incantation as nominal negation that plays on the pretext of his worldly titles of count or duke. This lyric identity, often expressed through bawdy humor, frees him from both official Latin culture and the moral Christian sphere of the *Boeci*, granting him an imaginative agency over his titles as secular lord.

Like Guilhem, Raimbaut rarely invokes his proper name. But when he does, the incantatory effect of his name is clear, especially when he associates it with the conflated values of the worthy lover and the social rank of lord. Raimbaut seems to have an obsession with naming and names, and protects his right of self-naming as a poetic act. As Elizabeth Poe has argued, the Occitan *nova* or narrative poem "So fo el tems" (ca. 1199–1213, attributed to Raimon Vidal [PC 411.II]) confirms Raimbaut's obsession by thematizing names as a courtly game. For the audience of this *nova*, "Raimbaut" has special significance and relates to his lyrics about naming. Poe points out, for example, that they would have known of his *tenso* with Peire Rogier ("Peire Rotgier, a trassaillir," Peire Rotgier, I shall transgress [PC 389.34]), in which he hints at wanting to be called "drut" or worthy lover: "Per me voletz mon nom auzir. Cals sons?—o drutz . . . Er clau las dens! (You wish to hear my [love] title from me. What am I—an accepted lover or . . . ? Now I say no more!)²⁹ Raimbaut wants to protect his right of self-naming over Peire's assignment, even as a *drut*. Further, he engages with the idea of naming his poem in "Escotatz, mas no say que s'es" (Listen, gentlemen, but I don't know what [PC 389.28]), where he jokes that he does not know how to name his song ("It is not a *vers*, *estribot*, or *sirventes*, nor can I find a name for it," 152, line 3). From these examples, Raimbaut shows how names of love, lover, or song are ever shifting in the world of lyric poetry, and he wants to claim the right to name these things and himself as he sees fit. A name in poetry ostensibly signifies deeds and reflects the established values of the same name in the world: "For true worth is not revealed in speech but is made known in action, and because of the deeds the accounts come afterward" (88, lines 19–21). But while he claims names come from deeds, his poetry enacts the power of appellation. He thus constantly rewrites the value of a "nom" that depends upon the true worth resulting from speech and deed.

Given this obsession with the value of a name in a lover's discourse, Raimbaut invokes his proper name in a manner that merges his social and lyric identities. An example of his proper name as incantation is in "Ben s'eschai q'en bona cort" (It is indeed fitting in a good court [PC 389.20]). In this song, Raimbaut says that if not deemed worthy by his beloved lady, he is merely a Raimbaut: "Et agra nom Raembaut" (138, line 35). In other words, if he does not please his lady, he is, as Pattison suggests, merely a commoner ("a" Raimbaut) and not worthy of the noble title "en Raimbaut" ("Lord" Raimbaut), as sometimes stated in indexes such as that of chansonnier I.³⁰ In a series of songs about naming, Raimbaut indicates that true love goes beyond a mere "nom"; he says, "pos malgrat lor n'ai mai del nom" (in spite of them [his enemies] I have more than the name [of lover], 111, line 18). His "nom," similar to the definition in the *Boeci* of a spiritual rather than secular title, but now applied to the religion of love, signifies his potential as a lover. The actual value has no name, as it lies beyond being called a mere *drut* or "nom": a love beyond a name. Yet when Love calls him by his proper name, as in "Apres mon vers vueilh sempr'ordre" (After my *vers* I wish immediately [PC 389.10]), another song that thematizes naming, it reminds him of his pledge as lover through the act of invoking his proper name:

Viatz m'assajer'a volvre
S'Amors me volges absolvre;
    Mas, pres en loc de colom,
Me fai de seschas envolvre,
      Qe no·m gic penr'un sol tom,
      E m'apella per mon nom.

I should try promptly to turn my love elsewhere if Love would free
me from my pledge; but, like a captured dove, he has wrapped me
in rushes (for I do not avoid taking a single fall) and he calls me by
my proper name.

(79, lines 31–36)

Calling him by his "nom," Love holds him to his status as lover even though
he often wants to break free of these bonds, or create his own beyond nominal assignment. His "nom" is a moral and ethical bind, one defined by his behavior as a lover in conquest: he admits that he has a crazy desire ("fol talan,"
line 45) because he pursues love despite feeling harmed (lines 43–48). He is
at the mercy of his lady and Love to call him by his name, in other words
to recognize his nobility and value as a lover. In this example, Raimbaut
transfigures the feudal meaning of "nom" as a lord to one that guarantees his
claim as nameless lover. When Love calls out his proper name, it transfers
the ethical bind of Lord Raimbaut to one as lover, a worth that in turn he
hopes his Lady will recognize. When Raimbaut invokes his own name or a
secret "nom" as an act of self-preservation, his self-invocations represent an
effort to signify his own name against other nominal assignments that might
demean him as troubadour and lover.

How does the chansonnier adapt and transform these instances of
aristocratic incantation? Although chansonniers often supply official titles
that indicate social background in the *vidas* and indexes, aristocratic troubadours such as Guilhem and Raimbaut, despite their social position, are
not valued more than other troubadours.[31] Rubrics rank troubadours, not
according to feudal society, but by other criteria. Ranking may be based on
a regional preference of a particular audience, a copyist's personal preference, or the availability of an existing collection—for example, Italian chansonniers placing Peire d'Alvernhe as the first poet, or chansonnier R giving priority to Marcabru. As François Zufferey has pointed out, in the case
of chansonnier M (Paris, Bibl. Nat. fr. 12474), Marcabru's songs may have
been misattributed to Raimbaut due to an organization that gives priority to certain troubadours while filling out the rest of their space with less
important ones.[32]

Despite the absence of a hierarchy based on social rank, however, variants of written transmission suggest that an aristocratic proper name held
a compelling presence for compilers, copyists, and readers of troubadour
lyrics. An example of where we can still discern the incantatory power of
an aristocratic name in the manuscript context is in the popularity of Guil-

hem's "Pos de chantar m'es pres talenz."[33] In this song of penitence, Guilhem renounces his former courtly life and states his identity when he declares his departure from the lordship of Poitiers: "La departirs m'es aitan greus / del seignorage de Peiteius" (Departing from the lordship of Poitiers is so hard for me, 277, lines 9–10). It seems appropriate that Guilhem's only nominal self-invocation is in a renunciation of his formal courtly self, a self that denied or played with the idea of predetermined or moral nominal identities in the feudal or Christian sense. Contrite, he now rejects his boasting, as he says "Mout ai estat cuendes e gais, / mas Nostre Seigner no·l vol mais" (I was very charming and gay / but our Lord no longer permits that, 279, lines 29–30). Not only does its dissemination in many of the manuscripts attest to its popularity and prestige (in chansonnier I, it is the only transmitted song of "lo coms de peitieus"), but its melody is found in the manuscript of a fourteenth-century Occitan religious play, *Jeu de sainte Agnès*, now held in the Vatican Library. A stage direction accompanying the song even cites the melody using Guilhem's name: "Modo surgunt omnes et tendunt in medio campi et faciunt omnes simul planctum in sonu del comte de peytieu" (Now all rise and go to the middle of the field and all at once perform a lament to the melody of the count of Poitou).[34]

Like a *vida* that, though mostly derived from the lyric texts, presents the troubadour as a figure external to his lyric, Guilhem in the *planh* presents himself in the past tense as the count of Poitiers. Indeed, Guilhem uses the same preterite tense ("De proeza e de joi fui / mais ara partem ambedui," I was a man of prowess and joy / but now we part from each other, 279, lines 25–26) as the *vidas* ("Lo coms de Peitieus si fo," The count of Poitiers was). He speaks as if that former self were already dead as he goes off into spiritual exile ("non serai obedienz" and "Qu'era m'en irai en eisil," I will no longer be obeisant to men as a count, Now I shall go into exile, 277, lines 3, 5) and worries about his son, the inheritor of his name. Thus his invocation plays an important role in the enduring popularity of this song. By distancing his "I," the *planh* provides a historical context for the future rubric of "lo coms de peitieus." In contrast to the incantation of nonnaming in defiance of feudal norms, his invocation in the *planh* carries an incantatory quality because it maintains a spiritual and feudal obeisance to God and the king of France (line 14) while memorializing an external existence as troubadour and count.[35] Songbooks such as Languedoc chansonnier C (Paris, Bibl. Nat. fr. 856), in which Guilhem's *planh* and "Farai un vers de dreit nien" are transmitted, documents the absence and reinscription of the name as lyrical incantation, rendering the proper name a vehicle for hermeneutic opacity.

Similarly, scribal interpolations of Raimbaut's name as nominal self-invocation suggest copyists' interests in asserting the social authority of his proper name. The *tornada* of "Cars, douz e fenhz" (Dear, sweet and fictitious [PC 389.22], 66, lines 68–71), the final shorter stanza that addresses a patron, friend, or lady, includes a political tag: "Raimbautz" sends out his song to "comte Barselones," representing the alliance of Lord Raimbaut with the family of Barcelona.[36] Since this stanza is missing in three manuscripts and perhaps apocryphal or a scribal interpolation,[37] its presence suggests that the Italian copyist of the early fourteenth-century chansonnier M, a chansonnier whose arrangement ranks Raimbaut as one of the most important troubadours, wanted to imprint Raimbaut's lyric corpus with his social identity—perhaps also a specific interest of the Neapolitan court of Charles d'Anjou II, under whom the chansonnier was compiled.[38]

Further, in a variant of Raimbaut's song "Escotatz, mas no say que s'es," Raimbaut's name curiously appears in a way that seems contrary to his play on naming unknown subjects ("no say que s'es"). The copyist undoes the *gap* and the theme of nonnaming by having the poet reveal himself at the end. In "Escotatz," the social and poetic bond between Guilhem and Raimbaut appears evident: their interest in creating a poetic "something" out of "nothing" or "I don't know what this is." They deliberately thumb their noses at the importance of their own names and delight in revealing their poetic identities through a performance of thematic nominal negation. Part of the joke of the *gap* is the implied true subject of the poem: the troubadour is the subject of the "subjectless" or "nameless" song. Thus not disclosing one's proper name would seem to be consistent with the joke. In chansonnier M, however, the copyist includes "en Rainbaut" as part of the prose line. Here is Pattison's edition of the last stanza of "Escotatz" using chansonnier R as the base:

> Er fenisc mo no-say-que-s'es,
> C'aisi l'ay volgut batejar;
> Pus mays d'aital non auzi jes
> Be·l dey enaysi apelar;
> E diga·l, can l'aura apres,
> Qui que s'en vuelha azautar.
> E si hom li demanda qui l'a fag, pot
> dir que sel que sap be far totas
> fazendas can se vol.

Now I finish my "I don't know what it is," for thus I have baptized it; since I never heard of such a thing before I ought indeed to name it so; and let anyone who wishes to enjoy it recite it when he has learned it. And if they ask him who made it, he can say one who knows how to do all deeds well when he wants to.

(153, lines 36–44)

The variant in M is as follows:

Uai ses nom e qit dem[an]da qita fag digas li den rainbaut qe sap ben far una balla de foudat qan si uol;

Go without a name and whoever asks who made it tell him Lord Raimbaut who knows well to make a ball of nonsense when he wants.

(My trans., 153, line 42)

The variant changes the song from showing the poet's confidence in his audience's knowledge of his persona to explicitly endorsing "Lord Raimbaut."[39] It discloses the troubadour making a nameless *vers*. Whether the M copyist misread the poem (the nameless version retains the *gap* spirit by flaunting the troubadour's ability not to name himself, as in, 'I don't have to tell you my name, my boasting speaks for itself'), or deliberately wanted to disclose the identity of Lord Raimbaut as the key to understanding this *gap*—the *tornada* as *razo* or *vida*—he might also have wanted to affirm the identity of Raimbaut that appears in the *tornada* of "Cars, douz e fenhz" of the same section. For the M copyist, the absence of the performance context requires the supplementation of the incantatory and authoritative written proper name to definitively end the game.

NAMES AS LYRICAL GESTURE AND AUTHORIZING MARK: BERNART DE VENTADORN AND MARCABRU

In contrast to the nonnaming/naming of the aristocratic troubadours, the transmission of the names of Bernart de Ventadorn and Marcabru represents a different example of hermeneutic opacity. These troubadours invoke their proper names explicitly as lyrical gesture and authorizing mark, and the songbook translates the inherent tension of proper names situated between performed song and literary object. For these poets, their names are a synecdoche for the experience of their songs; through nominal self-invocation they configure different performative relations between their lyric personae and their audiences. Bernart's name as a speech act of transmission through the *tornada*, and Marcabru's name as a self-sufficient and textualized mark outside of his frequent caricatures and mysterious disguises,[40] anticipate the use of the proper name by readers of troubadour lyric. In other words, the songbook provides the material structure for a proper name to be metonymically deployed in a manner that builds upon the troubadours' own synecdochic use of their names.

In contrast to what we know about Guilhem IX and Raimbaut D'Aurenga, most of our information about Bernart de Ventadorn and Marcabru comes from allusions in their own lyrics and the *vidas*. Both *vidas* relate that they were of humble origins: Bernart was the son of a baker, and there are two accounts for Marcabru: the *vida* in K relates that he was the son of a poor woman called Marcabruna, while the one from A states that he was a foundling brought up by Lord Aldric de Vilar.[41] From lyrics and the *vidas* we can surmise that Bernart's patron was most likely Lord Eble, that he was associated with the court of Ventadour, and that he visited England. Both poets invoke their (most likely stage) names in a way that reflects the images they promote of themselves: for Bernart his sincerity as an earnest lover, and for Marcabru his identity as preacher and moralist. While Marcabru invokes his name to emphasize his often polemical, cryptic style, his name appearing in different places of his songs as quasi-auctorial citations, Bernart's rare invocations suggest a disavowal of identity as a gesture of transparency. Such a disavowal of apparent sincerity accords with his recognizable easy and simple style, which is known as *trobar leu*.

The chansonniers transmit two *cansos* in which Bernart de Ventadorn invokes his proper name, and "Chantars no pot gaire valer" (Singing cannot be worth it [PC 70.15]) is the only one that contains his entire name. The transmission of "Chantars" makes it unlikely that the *tornada* with Bernart's name is apocryphal or a scribal addition. With uniform stanza order in all manuscripts, the song possesses two *tornadas* that were probably used interchangeably. Despite the rare occurrences of Bernart's name in his corpus, nominal self-invocation in "Chantars" represents an emphatic closure to a *canso* that refers to an external world of possibility. For Bernart, this world is one that is affected by his song, a world where his lady returns his love and grants him joy:

Bernartz de Ventadorn l'enten
e·l di e·l fai, e·l joi n'aten.

Bernart de Ventadorn understands it,
says it, makes it, and hopes for joy from it.

(My trans., 81, lines 53–54)

In "Chantars," Bernart formally conveys his sincerity in singing as coming from the heart. He uses the rhyme scheme *abaccdd* to explore and then emphasize his convictions, for in each stanza there is a movement toward a semantic and metrical turn followed by an affirmation in the couplets (*ccdd*); through singing, he demonstrates the worthiness of his love and heart. The turning point emerges in the open end rhyme "*-aus*" of the first couplet, which is followed by the closed end rhyme "*-en*" of the closing couplet. For Bernart, loving is an act of singing that is both dynamic and composed; while his true love springs from the heart, he maintains a careful balance of rhythms and rhymes in each stanza to express these free-flowing feelings.

In the third stanza, Bernart sings of a love that is "comunaus," common or vulgar, which is not true love but has only the "nom" of love:

Amor blasmen per no-saber
fola gens; mas leis no·n es dans,
c'amors no·n pot ges dechazer,
si no es amors comunaus.
aisso non es amors; aitaus
no·n a mas lo nom e·l parven,
que re non ama si no pren.

Foolish people criticize love out of ignorance; but there is no harm done, for love cannot be destroyed as long as it is not vulgar love. That is not love; it has nothing but the name and appearance of it and is not interested in anything it cannot profit from.

(80, lines 15–21)

Bernart's true, nameless love can be expressed and understood by his audience through listening to his superior singing ("cabaus," 80, line 5) and the progression of his *canso*. The *canso* formally plays out the careful balance of "en agradar et en voler" (81, line 29), or pleasing and desiring, through the stanzaic structure of alternating rhymes that become sustaining couplets. The stanzaic movement embodies both the balance between poet and lady and the poet's own efforts to modulate his self-reproachful yearning with affirmation of the worthiness of his desire.

This oscillating motion of doubt and desire resolves itself in the *tornadas*. The *tornada* that includes his invocation takes us to a liminal space both inside and outside of the *canso*. The effect of Bernart's enunciation of his "nom" coincides with the ambiguity of "l'enten." The word could mean anything from "conceives it" (Nichols's translation) to "understands it," suggesting the simultaneity of making and understanding a *canso*. The present tense emphasizes this temporal ambiguity of the singer's position regarding the lyric text: while he may finish and understand his text, it also seems to be in an incomplete state. With "l'enten" and the other actions of which Bernart is the subject, "e·l di, e·l fai, e·l joi n'aten," the poet merges these present verbs that are continuing—he awaits joy as he sings and makes the song—within a *tornada* that paradoxically signals the close of these actions, a song as being dispatched (this would be closer to Nichols's "conceives it"). In short, "Bernartz de Ventadorn" is inseparable from the song in its potential and completed state. The deictic quality of the proper name is the culmination of a *canso* that celebrates a love demonstrated through song rather than simply a "nom" of "amors." Thus the *tornada*, as a nominal gesture, continues the progression of the song while being a receipt of transmission. Bernart's understanding ("l'enten") of his song places a completed *canso* in the future space of expectation ("joi n'aten"): he awaits joy from his song as he sends out himself in it.

A close examination of "Chantars no pot gaire valer" in chansonnier D portrays the translation of a nominal self-invocation to a proper name as substitute for the lyric act. Where Bernart's invocation acts as synecdoche, or the compact reduction of the lyric "I" sending out at once himself and his song to a certain someone, and encompassing the liminal space of singing and physically transmitted song, the chansonnier through its rubrication and organization now places the name outside a *canso*. Although certainly related to the boasting and authorial practices of self-naming as noted by Ernst Robert Curtius in Latin works since the twelfth century, the vernacular, secular, and lyrical occurrence of names and naming in troubadour songbooks is a phenomenon distinct from what Mary Carruthers has called the indexing convention of the medieval signature as *auctor*.[42]

For example, the *Liber Alberici* transmits "Chantars" in the rubricated section of Bernart de Ventadorn as indicated in the index with the colophon of Lord Alberico, placing Bernart's name in relation to a patron and among a canon of troubadours. Bernart's name no longer has the same purchase within the context of the chansonnier as it has in a single lyric, for the attributive function of the proper name places it categorically outside the poetic activity of the song. Whether it appears in the index, at the beginning of a section, or before a lyric (as it does in the first section of chansonnier D), the proper name directs the reader in how to read groups of texts in relation to each other. Like the attribution of cultural value to troubadour names through the colophon of *Liber Alberici*, names as rubrics facilitate economic and cultural transactions: the bibliographical efficiency of the metonymic proper name presents a cultural history in indexical form. For Alberico, lord of Treviso, power would have been justified less through personal loyalty than through legal documentation and other government records, and exercised less through force than through documents that attested to claims, taxes, or royal decrees. This interest in documentation as a drive to record a cultural legacy can be extended to the chansonniers. Costly Italian chansonniers attest to a practical literate culture in which written sources and archives were replacing oral testimony; records of quotidian affairs and cultural legacy directly shape human experience by establishing the credibility of their owners.[43] Within an institutional program of cultural documentation, a nominal self-invocation whose value depends on an immediate performance context becomes an archived name that acquires a transmissible, cumulative value. Appearing prominently outside the *canso* in Alberico's index as "Bernart de Ventedor," a name signifies the power of a lord overseeing the production of a chansonnier.

But to return to the production of hermeneutic opacity: a contiguity exists between Bernart's proper name in his *canso* (synecdoche) and the metonymy of his name for his lyric corpus in the chansonnier. The mutual dwelling of these two phenomena in the songbook illustrates how the performative proper name, which points back to the speaker in a particular instance, can also serve as a universal sign for a textual community. For instance, in chansonnier I, "Bernartz del Ventedorn" (f. 1) may be interpreted within "Chantars" while being under the more general category of "trobador" as indicated by the index. The paradoxical quality of lyric specificity coexisting with general reference produces opaque coherence, in which a gesture of clarity such as the making of a rubric in turn produces multiple readings of a name. In another example, Bernart's nominal self-invocation in chansonnier C coincides with the practical and authoritative presence of the rubric. Here the *tornada* appears with the rubric "B. de Ventadorn" over it, strikingly unlike the conventional practice of the rubric appearing between the last line of a *canso* and before the first line of the next. Although this may have resulted from space limitations on the page, the close doubling of the lyrical gesture and rubric, and a manicula pointing to both in the margin, suggest a copyist's acute awareness of nominal self-invocation coinciding with the rubric as metonymy in the songbook.

Bernart's signature in the *tornada* of C, the sending out of his song and himself, understood ("l'enten") in the moment of the song, translates into a pivotal point for understanding "Bernat de ventadorn" (index, f. 2v). The manicula (literally a deictic proper name attached with a sign that says "here") implies, "understand this, as you want," while the rubric facilitates a comparison with a song of Bernart's or another troubadour's. This place in chansonnier C acts as a locus for determining the value of Bernart and his *canso*. One can refer to Roman Jakobson's idea of the proper name as a unique speech event in order to understand why this locus comes about. Nominal self-invocation constitutes a communicative act in which the addresser and addressee (here, troubadour and audience) must know the reference code of the proper name, as the name "means anyone to whom this name is assigned."[44] Once in the songbook, the proper name can be placed under many categories of value while maintaining its intrinsic nominal quality. For any given situation of a songbook, as within the limits of a *canso* or a troubadour's lyric corpus, the addresser and addressee of a proper name—here, copyist and readers of the chansonnier—give a general reference code to that name while maintaining the singular identity.[45] The copyist or reader of a chansonnier recognizes the specificity of Bernart's nominal self-invocation and the general nature of the rubric "Bernat de Ventedorn" as a corpus of songs worthy of chansonnier C. In other words, while the proper name as both lyrical gesture and rubric in the chansonnier authorizes the singularity of Bernart's *tornada*, as a metonymy for his lyric corpus his name also enables membership in a prestigious vernacular tradition worth transmitting in a luxurious songbook. This is the productive framework of hermeneutic opacity: the material situation of chansonnier C enables the repositioning and reinterpretation of the proper name by troubadour, copyist, and patron, even as the songbook attributes general meaning to the proper name as sign—the name of "Bernat de Ventedorn" as rubric in C, or the name placed under the headings of "repertor" in the *Liber Alberici*, or "trobador" in I.

If Bernart's rare invocation creates a paradoxical effect of distance and intimacy by insisting on a continuing presence through the formal closure of the *tornada*, Marcabru's frequent self-referencing creates a different kind of distance between himself and his listeners. As he associates his name with his "entensa pura" (pure understanding or meaning, 134, line 2), the name functions as a cipher for his reason (*razo*) and particular style as a poet. In the song "Auias de chan com enans' e meillura" (Hear how this song progresses and improves [PC 293.9]), the troubadour not only binds the theme and progression of the song to his hidden intention, but uses his name to signify and authorize its bounded quality: "Marcabru, segon s'entensa pura, / sap la razo del vers lasar e faire" (Marcabru, according to his pure intention [*or* flawless judgment], knows how to make and bind up the theme of the *vers*, 134, lines 1–4). Famous for his harsh condemnations of moral corruption and spiritual decay, and for making up compound names to criticize his enemies, Marcabru uses his name as cipher and mark of an *auctor*, and demands that his public be attentive and faithful interpreters of his messages, as in this *tornada* of "Lo vers comenssa" (The *vers* begins [PC 293.32]):

D'aqest flagel
Marcabrus si coreilla
ses compaigno.

Marcabru is alone to complain about this plague.

(408, lines 91–93)

Here Marcabru invokes his name as moral authority or proverbial voice in the desert, and invites his audience to gloss his name for its *intentio*. His self-referencing distances him morally from the false and base lovers he criticizes. Not only does Marcabru have *entensa pura* and the skill to compose a song perfectly according to the theme, but the constant connection of his name with these two qualities invests it with the moral currency of a biblical *auctor*.[46] In such a way, Marcabru's frequent invocations of his proper name lay the foundation for the chansonnier's transformation of the proper name from a lyrical invocation to a metonymy for the poet. Just as his name literally means "making a brown mark" or, alternatively, is an abbreviated version of "Marcus Brunus" ("Mark Brown," "the brown one"),[47] the poet audibly brands — brown marks — his audience with moralizing songs in which he often exploits courtly language for the description of vulgar acts (for example his use of the key to the lady's lock or *clau segonda* to refer to sexual organs and acts).[48] Further, his name itself is an opaque mark that embodies his lyric product as *vers*, bound up so well that "even if you search through it with a fine-tooth comb, you won't be able to find a rusty word in it."[49]

As much as Marcabru attempts to fix his proper name as moral authority and seal of the Law, it remains inseparable from the ambivalence of lyrical self-invocation: in a self-serving and circular move, the invocation of his own name as an external authority binds his *vers* and authorizes his song and name. Songbook transmission of his name embodies and expands upon the circularity of this ambivalence and of a name as textual cipher. In "Pax in nomine Domini" in chansonnier R (Peace in the name of the Lord! [PC 293.35]), this famous crusading song's transmission builds upon the contradictions of Marcabru's efforts to constitute his nominal self-invocation as both internal and external to the *vers*. This chansonnier not only gives prominence to Marcabru by being the only chansonnier to begin the lyric section with the troubadour — his songs are introduced with a rubric that designates him as the first troubadour ("aisi come*n*sa so de marc e bru q*e* fo lo premier trobador q*e* fos") — but emphasizes his moral authority by having the first song accompanied by a historiated initial of Christ's face:

> Pax in no*m*ine Do*m*in*i*!
> Fes marc e brus lo vers e·l so.
>   Auiaz q*e* di:

> Peace in the name of the Lord! Marcabru made the *vers* and the tune. Hear what he says.

>   (lines 1–3, version of R)

Marcabru's nominal invocation is embodied in the "vers e·l so," the *vers* and the tune: a song (*vers* can include both words and melody, or the measure) embodying the word as God's authority, and the *vox corporis* of Marcabru as speaking subject in which the word first emerges.[50] He calls upon his audience to listen to his song (the tune, "so") inscribed with his proper name as Christian authority. Thus, the voicing of "Marcabru" and the listening to the sound of "Pax in nomine Domini" engender the spiritual meaning of the image of Christ and crusade. The name of "Marcebru" as a rubric and his self-invocation coincide with the invocation of the Lord's name, "nomine Domini," in a *versus cum auctoritate*, a figure from the *artes praedicandi* in which a preacher inserts a biblical or liturgical phrase during a sermon.[51]

This coincidence conflates Marcabru's words and sound with the act of making, "far": is "he" God, or Marcabru as the Lord's spokesman? "He" is the maker of the *vers*, proposing Augustinian contemplation through the frontal image of Christ and the rubric. At the same time "he" makes the tune that embraces the corporeal senses as he tells the audience to listen, "Auiaz!" While it is common for nonlyric texts to begin with an invocation to Christ, this is something different. The compilers and illuminators consider Marcabru's name an invitation to associate his self-created authority as troubadour with the authority of Christ.[52]

In the final analysis, the first lines of "Pax in nomine Domini," the rubric, and the Christic initial establish the proper name as a *res* or spiritual and figurative sign, and as a form that memorializes the troubadours and the meaning of "Marcabru." Yet once again this quality is contiguous with the authorial ambivalence and corporeal voice-word continuum of "Fes marc e brus lo vers e·l so / Auiaz qe di." This hermeneutic configuration — the productive opacity through the name — invites readers to attribute cultural value to "Marcabru" in harmony with the lyrical ambiguity of Marcabru's mark. This occurrence recalls Michelle Bolduc's analysis of the "distortion" of medieval author portraits (pagan authors as saints, etc.) as the manuscript page invests vernacular authors with the "iconography of exegetical and scholastic texts."[53] Therefore, while we would expect the proper name to represent the songbook's function of transforming lyric poetry into prosaic knowledge, the songbook resists the transformation of lyric into spiritual, solitary contemplation. Rather, in chansonnier R, the proper name serves as the proving ground in which a textual community of early fourteenth-century southern France reinvents the lyrics for its own secular and religious interests, investing the voiced proper name in lyric with the material corporeality of the songbook — including musical notation. The material apparatus of the songbook supplements an earlier generation's performance and reception of these lyrics.

TRANSMISSION OF NAMES AS CONDITIONED BY SONGBOOKS: MATFRE ERMENGAUD DE BÉZIERS'S *BREVIARI D'AMOR*

Matfre Ermengaud de Béziers's citation of Marcabru in his *Breviari d'amor* (ca. 1288) illustrates how the proper name, once mediated through the songbook, functions as a site of interpretation and attribution of value. In the *Breviari*, Matfre quotes more than sixty troubadours in his treatise about love (the "Perilhos tractat"), and one of his comments about Marcabru summarizes his songs in this way:

D'En Marcabru non ai auzit
ni en lunh sieu cantar legit
quez ell lunh tems se penedes
en sa vida, ni coffesses
ni reconogues sa error
del mal qu'avia dig d'amor.

Concerning Sir Marcabru, I have not heard or read in any of his songs that at any time in his life he repented, or confessed or recognised his fault in the evil that he spoke of love.

(Trans. Harvey, 5.78, lines 28366–71)[54]

In keeping with Matfre's intent to establish troubadours as *auctores* in a theological *summa* (even as he criticizes Marcabru, he still considers him an authority),[55] he uses *legir*, a verb that appears primarily in Occitan didactic or religious texts referring to clerical activities.[56] Moreover, Matfre's use of the verb indicates troubadour lyric as heard and read ("auzit" coupled with "legit"). However Matfre receives Marcabru, whether transmitted orally or as a legendary figure and written authority imagined mainly through the songbooks, he understands "Marcabru" as a lyric corpus — the "vida" of "En Marcabru." Does Matfre base his summarizing judgment on reading and studying Marcabru in a chansonnier? If so, he evaluates Marcabru's intentions and moral progression through his lyric persona as embodied through his corpus. Where in the performance context Marcabru says "Marcabru" and thus controls his name as a game of role-playing or as *auctor*, the lyric corpus, *sa vida*, allows a reader such as Matfre to begin with the written authority of a proper name greater than the collected lyric texts and to define the entirety of "Marcabru" according to his interpretive reading.

While readers of songbooks such as Matfre may have understood Marcabru by reading intertextually among collated songs, near-contemporary and later troubadours often connected him to his famous "Vers del Lavador," as "Pax in nomine Domini" came to be known according to their references. The mid-twelfth-century troubadour Bernard Marti cites Marcabru and the "lavador" song as he condemns slanderous "lauzengiers" (slanderers or gossips) who will never attain the washing place or *lavador*:

Mas si Dieus vol far mon coman,
Ja us non er al Lavador,
Cel c'auzis a Marcabru dir,
Qu'en enfer sufriran gran fais.

But if God answers my prayer, not one of them will ever enjoy the *Lavador*, the one you heard Marcabru talk about, for they will suffer great torment in hell.

(Trans. Harvey, 31, lines 25–28)[57]

Marti's reference to Marcabru's metaphor for a spiritual washing place in "Pax in nomine Domini" assumes his public's familiarity with the song. In another reference, the thirteenth-century troubadour Guillem Magret implies the cultural value of Marcabru and his crusading song when he complains about the declining morals of his time. Money is worth more than songs, he says; he can win the love of the innkeeper's wife with four coins rather than with the "Vers del Lavador": "e dels quatre tenrai l'ost'en amor / meilz no fera pel Vers del Lavador."[58] Another prominent example of Marcabru as linked to the crusading song is in the wedding feast scene in the anonymous Occitan verse romance, the *Roman de Flamenca* (ca. 1250), in which within a long list of works performed, Marcabru is the only author named, and someone performs "lo vers de Marcabru," most likely referring to "Pax in nomine Domini."[59] Whether as "lo vers del lavador" or "lo vers de Marcabru," the song gains a citational title, further valorizing the poet's name as enduring mark with a currency associated with the title.

This examination of troubadour names suggests a confluence and accretion of values and references attributed to the translation of the proper name, the effect of hermeneutic opacity specific to the phenomenological situation of the songbook. In Guilhem's *planh* and the interpolations of chansonnier M, the name supplements a fragmentary awareness of an aristocratic person, acquiring value by signifying a life and a narrative, and extending this value to the poet's corpus. Through the marking textuality of Marcabru's nominal self-invocation, his name comes to signify a predetermined state of morality even as it exists in both the "*vers* and the tune" of chansonnier R. The songbook provides a means for studying the troubadour name as a repository of cultural knowledge that both stabilizes signification and acts as a performed signifier. As a loose framework of organization and classification, it allows us to regard the translation of the proper name not as part of a narrative history tending toward authorial unity but as the residue of discrete occasions, involving networks of readers and cultural influences.

ARNAUT DANIEL: TRANSFORMATION OF THE DEICTIC *TORNADA* INTO SIGNATURE

In this last section of chapter 2, I will consider the development of Arnaut Daniel's (fl. 1180–95) name as signature—a certain mode of nominal self-invocation where the proper name confers the worth of a poet in a qualitatively different way from the previous examples. Dante and Petrarch's adaptation and translation of "Arnaut Daniel" grant that name an independence from the songbook context. Laureating their names through his, they adapt Arnaut's name to their authorial visions and self-created literary tradition.

In the last lines of the *canso* "En cest sonet coind'e leri" (In this little song, playful and pretty [PC 29.10]),[60] Arnaut closes with a *tornada* that has become known as one of his signatures:

Ieu suis Arnautz q'amas l'aura
e chatz la lebre ab lo bou
e nadi contra suberna.

I am Arnaut who gathers the wind
and hunts the hare using the ox
and swims against the tide.

(274, lines 43–45)

The writer of Arnaut's *vida* cites this *tornada* directly, as do Dante and Petrarch in their own works such as the *Commedia* and *Rime sparse*. Where nominal invocation is concerned, one recognizes an immediate difference between Arnaut's *tornada* and those of other troubadours I have discussed. Arnaut states not only his name "Arnautz" but "Ieu suis Arnautz"; with a first-person invocation, he insists on his proper name. Second, the *tornada* is an example of adynaton, or a confession of an impossibility using a proverbial description of the world upside down, "chatz la lebre ab lo bou / e nadi contra suberna." Arnaut's use of this classical *topos* to describe his poetic mission corresponds to the functionality of this signature by later writers as a metonymy for his lyric corpus. As Curtius suggests in his discussion of the medieval usages of the *topos*, Arnaut's adynata achieve a new "psychological function" in that instead of having a pejorative sense, they demonstrate his "artistic mastery."[61] Thus Arnaut's invocation embodies his lyric persona as signature: his impossible erotic mission and self-authorized poetic mastery. We will see how Arnaut's signature explicitly associates his name with distinct qualities of his lyric craftsmanship, as well as how the writer of his *vida* and a contemporary poet may have understood his signature in relation to his lyric corpus. Finally we will see how Dante and Petrarch transform this signature in their own works to show their debt to, and surpassing of, their common poetic master. A comparison of these different perspectives suggests that Arnaut's signature forms a reference point for readers of his lyrics to imagine his poetic corpus, and shapes the reception of his lyric independent of the songbook.

Arnaut's Nominal Self-Invocation as Signature — "Ieu suis Arnautz"

Out of eighteen songs attributed to Arnaut Daniel in Gianluigi Toja's edition, only three are transmitted without his name. His frequent invocations in *tornadas* represent a desire to establish his name as a testament to his poetic craftsmanship, as well as to memorialize his lyric persona and textual corpus through his name. While most of Arnaut's *tornadas* follow the conventions of addressing, using a *senhal*, an unknown lady or a specific person and of repeating the rhymes of the penultimate stanza,[62] Arnaut's signature *tornadas* (songs X, XVI, XVIII in Toja's edition [PC 29.10, 29.3, 29.14]) distinguish themselves from the other troubadour *tornadas* because two are marked by an intransitive phrase in the first person: "Ieu suis Arnaut" (274, line 43) and "Sieus es Arnautz" (351, line 43). Like other troubadours, Arnaut's invocations include boasts about his superiority in loving ("ses parsonier, Arnaut," without a partner, Arnaut, 259, line 107), but they are best known for his signatures depicting the futile pursuit of his erotic obsession ("nadi contra suberna") and his desire to enter the inaccessible "cambra" (bedroom, XVIII) of his lady. Arnaut's insertion of his name in *tornadas* resembles Bernart's calling upon the audience to remember the poet's name; but unlike the other troubadour, Arnaut completes his song by merging his act of "being" with his "making": "Ieu suis Arnautz." Whereas others use their names in the act of doing something like transmitting a song, the phrase emphasizes the poet's self-consciousness in the act of nominal invocation. More explicitly, Arnaut sets up a self-reflexive condition of identity: not only does he say who he is, but he makes us aware that he is naming himself. Indeed, when used by other poets, "Ieu suis" is often followed by a pronomial or adjectival qualifier, the most common being "I am hers" or "I am [adjective]."[63] Even when Peire Vidal says, "Ieu suis senher dels genoes" (I am Lord of the Genoese), it is part of his act of telling tall tales to impress his lady.[64] The "I am Arnaut" directs us to the question "who is Arnaut?" rather than "what does Arnaut do?" or "whom or what is this song for?" Rather than emphasizing the "far" (making), he foregrounds himself as subject: "Ieu suis."

The rarity of such a phrase in troubadour *tornadas* suggests that Arnaut deliberately situates his nominal invocation within the greater context of proper names and naming in Christian universal history. In God's universe, there is an adequation between word and things. Only God has the power to create *ex nihilo*, and God's creation is successive and accordingly hierarchical. In addition to creating man in his image, God inscribed his works with names whose meaning would be revealed at the proper time in the history of mankind. As Howard Bloch summarizes Augustine: "Names, as signs, bear prospectively the mark both of their meaning and of their historical effects; understood through time, they fulfill the promise — complete the genealogy — that they contain."[65] This is clearest in the New Testament doctrine of Incarnation: the Word of God is revealed through the Son, who is the Word made flesh. As Tertullian writes, Moses had been told that "the Son is the Father's new name" (*Filius novum Patris nomen est*) because the name of God the Father was revealed to us in the Son.[66] Surely we can assume that Arnaut, having some clerical background,[67] would have been familiar with the ideas of major Christian figures such as Jerome, Augustine, and Isidore of Seville, who affirm importance of names for determining the universal truth. Even in his signature *tornada*, we know that the reference to one who "hunts the hare with the ox" is borrowed from a proverb similar in content to one in *Ecclesiastes* 34.2: "the man that giveth heed to lying visions, is like to him that catcheth at a shadow, and followeth after the wind." Following a convention of secular medieval literature, Arnaut applies a biblical proverb about vanity to a virtuous, even if futile, amatory pursuit.[68]

Not only does Arnaut name himself in a way that echoes the response of the Lord to Moses, "Ergo sum qui sum," but just as Yahweh's response implies the divine freedom and eternal mystery of an everpresent God, Arnaut's "Ieu suis" implies a confidence in the originality and superiority of his craft, and the self-reflexivity of his mode of desire. Moreover, his particular mode of nominal self-invocation imitates the revelation of the Son as the Father's new name, as in the signature Arnaut claims to reveal himself through his *canso*. Arnaut's "Ieu suis" says: "I produce my *canso* and am revealed through it," just as in Augustinian terms the "uncreated Word produces its signifier and is in turn made manifest by it . . . , the redemptive process as tautology."[69] Thus in using the prominent "Ieu suis," Arnaut invokes the Christian concepts of both revelation and proper name identity in the doctrine of Incarnation. As the name of the Father is revealed in the Son, so Arnaut's proper name is manifested through song production. Arnaut strives to achieve a parallel identity of Love and art as the essence of *fin' amor*, an identity that is humanly insatiable and ends in the "I" of his finished *canso*.

"q'amas l'aura"

The signature phrase "q'amas l'aura" encapsulates Arnaut's orchestration of rare rhymes ("caras rimas" in his *vida*),[70] complex metrical structures, and surprising diction. Through his efforts to mold the end rhyme and word *aura* in "L'aur'amara" (The bitter wind [PC 29.13]) and "En cest sonet coind'e leri" (songs IX and X), we are made aware of Arnaut's "planing" ("qan n'aurai passat la lima," 272, line 4) of words. As a master of *trobar ric*,[71] Arnaut uses *aura* to demonstrate his technical mastery of physical images.[72]

Both "L'aur'amara" and "En cest sonet coind'e leri" are *cansos* composed of *coblas unissonans* (rhymes kept throughout the poem). "L'aur'amara" (The bitter wind) has been cited as an example of Arnaut's virtuosity in *rimas caras* and *dissolutas*[73] as it combines more than three types of meters, including one- and two-syllable verses:

L'aur'amara
fa·ls bruoills brancutz
clarzir
qe·l dous'espeis'ab fuoills,
el·s letz
becs
dels auzels ramencs
ten balps e mutz,
pars
e non pars;
per q'eu m'esfortz
de far e dir
plazers
a mains, per liei

que m'a virat bas d'aut,
don tem morir
si·ls afans no m'asoma.

The rough wind
traces out the ramify-
ing trees
that the sweet breeze weights with leaves,
and makes the joyful
beaks
of the birds in the branches
stammering and mute,
the paired
and the unpaired.
And so I force myself
in word and deed to bring
pleasures
to many, for the one
who has made me come down from the heights,
and now I fear death
if she does not end the sum of my afflictions.

(Trans. Goldin; 254, lines 1–17)[74]

It is possible that Arnaut's use of *l'aura* in IX, *-aura* in X, and the *laurs* in XVI suggests a conscious use of the single rhyme *-aura* in his corpus. Yet Arnaut's play on *aura/l'aura* in his works demonstrates a poetic craftsmanship that trumps any higher symbol or thematics of *l'aura*.[75] In these poems he uses the physical *l'aura* to express a range of contradictory feelings about being in love.

In the opening lines of "L'aur'amara," and throughout "En cest sonet coind'e leri," Arnaut embeds *aura/l'aura* within a series of dissonant and condensed oppositions. "L'aur'amara" is the insinuating force of a nature opening dense with alliteration and harsh consonant fricative clusters ("bruoills brancutz"), and contrasting images of audiovisual density, clarity, and silence ("dous'espeis ab fuoills/clarzir; letz becs/balps e mutz"). In "En cest sonet coind'e leri," Arnaut employs the end rhyme *-aura* as a poetic substance through which to shape a series of opposites, the main image being:

Sieus sui del pe tro q'en cima,
e si tot venta·ill freid'aura,
l'amors q'inz el cor mi plou
mi ten chaut on plus iverna.

I belong to her from my foot to the top of my head;
and let the cold wind blow,
love raining in my heart
keeps me warm when it winters most.

(Trans. Goldin; 272, lines 11–14)[76]

Just as in "L'aur'amara," in which Arnaut uses the formal metrical verticality of *rimas dissolutas* and tonal horizontal density to create complex lyrical oppositions, here he contrasts the verticality of the image "sieus sui del pe tro q'en cima" with the interior/exterior, hot/cold of the "freid'aura" that rains in his heart but keeps him warm when it winters most. Another oppositional configuration of *-aura* in "En cest sonet" occurs when the lady submerges him and then ideally restores him after his heart chafes itself ("s'eisaura," "lo cors e·m rima," "restaura," 273–74, lines 26, 32, 33).

The use of *-aura* in "En cest sonet" demonstrates how the signature phrase "Ieu suis Arnautz q'amas l'*aura*" associates his proper name with the identity of lover-artisan. Arnaut modestly labors ("laura," one who works the earth 274, line 40) and Love aureates his finished song ("daura," 272, line 5). In the *-aura* passage in which his lady submerges his heart (273, lines 22–28), Arnaut couples a powerful water image of being submerged ("sobtretracima" 273, line 25) with an image of his lady as usurer ("tant a de ver fait renou / c'obrador n'a e taverna," her demand is so usurious / she gets both craftsman and workshop, 273, lines 27–28). By implying that he is an "obrador" in a "taverna," he undercuts his lady's power over him by reminding us that he is a master craftsman.[77] Through this song, we can see how the "q'amas l'aura" of the signature encapsulates Arnaut's production of naturalistic images to show his artisanal control.

Thus Arnaut displays his virtuosity through *-aura*, a *cara* rhyme employed to describe the opposing forces that figure desire. The ambivalent phrase "q'amas l'aura," is apt: it suggests both control over and chasing after the wind. Likewise, "nadi contra suberna" epitomizes Arnaut's dogged pursuit of the impossible. The degree to which he sees this signature as integral to his lyric persona is clear in the way he refers to its images or sound in songs XIV and XVI of his corpus, "Amors e iois e liocs e tems" ("can cassava·l lebr' ab lo bou," when I have hunted the hare on an ox, 328, line 4) and "Ans qe·l cim reston de branchas" ("e mos bous es pro plus correns que lebres," and my ox is faster than a hare; and "anz per s'amor sia laurs o genebres," for love of her I would be a laurel or juniper, 348, lines 7 and 14). Through the signature he aureates his name with a certain moral regard concerning his technical virtuosity: a *trobar ric* and ethic of *fin' amor* whose meaning resides in the quest, rather than conquest, of the lady. In his "Ieu suis," he claims that a poet who goes against the tide or challenges the hierarchical order of things (Logos) proves his worth as lover.

Arnaut's signature asserts his lyric persona by making a clear connection between his statement of adynaton and his particular transgression of Christian logocentrism. His self-conscious use of invocation shapes the hermeneutic opacity that occurs as a function of his signature. Judging from the references to his signature by his *vida* and a near-contemporary, the troubadour Monk of Montaudon (fl. 1193–1210), it was not long before Arnaut's signature referred to his persona and lyrical style. Thus like Marcabru's name, Arnaut's signature as metonymy for his lyric corpus gains a citational value that anticipates autonomy from the phenomenological vagaries of the songbook.

The *vida* cites the signature while adapting the rhetorical performance of adynaton and first-person "Ieu suis" to the conventions of the *vida* genre. This is clear from the very first line: "Arnautz Daniels si fo d'aquella encontrada don fo N'Arnautz de Meruoill, de levesquat de Peiregors, d'un castel que a nom Ribairac, e fo gentils hom" (Arnaut Daniel was of the same region as Lord Arnaut de Maruelh, of the bishopric of Perigord, from a castle named Ribérac, and he was a noble man).[78] While the rhetorical performance of nominal invocation is deflated through the association of Arnaut's name with another "Arnaut," the geographic names of "Peiregors" and the castle "Ribairac" become equally important, as the name "Arnaut" is now in a quasi-historical stabilizing context rather than a discursive one. This first line announces: there exists a world from which Arnaut emerges, and this is where he acquires his name. The conventional style of all *vidas* places Arnaut categorically among other troubadours, like the other "Arnaut." His name is certainly not his own making, he does not claim it as his own, and the names of places and people belong to a sphere of received knowledge outside of lyric discourse. From the *vida* we learn that Arnaut was probably schooled as a cleric ("Et amparet ben letras e delectet se en trobar," He defended letters well and delighted in *trobar*, line 2). After describing how he invented a manner of *trobar* in *caras rimas* ("una maniera de trobar en caras rimas") that are not easy to understand or to learn ("no son leus ad entendre ni ad aprendre," line 3), the *vida* states that he loved the high-born wife of Lord Guillem de Bouvilla. As no record exists of this couple, it is highly probable that the writer of the *vida* invented "Bouvilla" from Arnaut's signature cited at the end, "E chatz la lebre ab lo bou," the "bou" and "Bouvilla" understood as a *senhal* for his lady.[79] Moreover, the *vida* rationalizes the poetics of Arnaut's signature by placing his name within a context of other names which deflate the tension of his secret love, such as the name of his lady. This may seem a matter of course with the *vidas*, but as one point in the reception of Arnaut's signature his name changes from a nominal performative discourse to a nominal historical identity.

Another example—like the *vida*, still in the songbook context—in which Arnaut's signature acts as a receptacle of determinant interpretation and value is the reference by the Monk of Montaudon, the song to which I referred in the beginning of this chapter. The Monk makes fun of Arnaut with his signature:

> Ab Arnaut Daniel son set
> Qu'a sa vida be no chantet,
> Mas us fols motz e'on non enten:
> Pos la lebre ab lo bou chasset
> E contra subern nadet,
> No val sos chans un aguillen.

> With Arnaut Daniel makes seven
> that in his life he didn't sing well
> except with stupid words that one doesn't understand:
> since he hunted the hare on an ox
> and swam against the current,
> his songs are not worth an eglantine.[80]

The Monk's employment of Arnaut's signature to cast his negative judgment—he pokes fun at Arnaut's adynaton—suggests that at this time the poet is already well known for a certain style of poetry, *caras rimas*, and that his signature in particular conveys his notoriety among his peers.[81] Embodying the contradictory sense of Arnaut through its images and mode of adynaton, the signature in the Monk citation and the *vida* demonstrates its role in the transmission history of Arnaut's lyric. One can imagine the signifying

function of Arnaut's signature drawing the attention of later songbook readers with a particular interest in Arnaut: Dante and Petrarch.

"Arnaut Daniel" to Dante and Petrarch: From l'aura *to* Laura

By consulting chansonniers, Dante and Petrarch reconsider Arnaut's signature in relation to the poet's corpus and to other troubadours. They interpret
his name independent of the songbook context and adapt the meaning of
his lyric corpus into their own works.[82] In the *Commedia* and the *Rime sparse*,
Dante and Petrarch not only cite Arnaut as poetic forebear, but separate
the technical skill of Arnaut as poetic craftsman from the moral ambivalence of his lyrics, thus adapting Arnaut's poetry of desire — chasing the hare
and swimming against the tide — into their own self-authorized symbolic
systems. In *Purgatorio*, Dante makes a memorial context (a "grazïoso loco,"
gracious place, 26.138) for Arnaut's signature by recasting it as the voice of
a contrite penitent. Petrarch also contextualizes aspects of Arnaut's signature, particularly the "l'aura," and transforms the word from a poetic material of shifting meanings into a closed hermeneutic system that symbolizes
his love for Laura and his self-crowning (*lauro*) as poet laureate.

In the passage in which the pilgrim meets Arnaut in *Purgatorio* 26,
Dante shows his reverence for Arnaut by writing in *lingua d'oc* (26.139–47)
and making him the last speaking shade before he enters the earthly para-
dise.[83] Even before he speaks, Arnaut's placement in the *Commedia* indicates
Dante's admiration for him as the "miglior fabbro del parlar materno" (a
better fashioner of the mother tongue, 26.117). Moreover, Arnaut's signature
as confessional recantation is a prologue to the unique moment when Dante
gains the name "Dante" through Beatrice's address in *Purgatorio* 30 — a moment of proper name appellation that James Nohrnberg suggests is crucial
to understanding Dante's personal salvation in the *Commedia*.[84]

Dante purposefully frames Arnaut's signature with the opening phrase
"Tan m'abellis" (So pleasing to me, 26.140); already these words indicate
the surpassing of the troubadour tradition and the future accession of the
pilgrim's soul through his spiritual journey. The words recall the lustful
Francesca in *Inferno* 5, and the incipits of Sordello and Folquet de Marseille
(the latter troubadour appearing in *Paradiso*).[85] Instead of a first-person self-
naming that performs an identity manifested and revealed through the production of song, the "Ieu suis" of Arnaut in purgatory now disavows his former life and embodies the gradual conversion (Francesca–Arnaut–Folquet)
of secular love and literature in the *Commedia*. As a penitent, he is no longer

in a constant state of desire swimming against the tide. Like the others in purgatory, he looks at once back at his past folly and forward to the joy he hopes for; he constantly moves forward, weeping and singing (26.142). Whereas in his lyrics Arnaut makes us aware of his artistry that creates pleasures through "word and deed" ("far e dir" 254, lines 11–12), whether through the alliteration and dissonant consonants of "l'aur'amara," or through images of effort ("per q'eu m'esfortz"), in Dante's purgatory he is stripped of that power of artifice. He cannot cover himself through song ("qu'ieu no me puesc ni voill a vos cobrire," that I cannot nor will not hide myself from you, 26.141) since he has submitted himself to God's power. In "L'aur'amara," Arnaut associates the single-mindedness of his love with covering truths ("q'ieu soi fis drutz / cars / e non vars / ma·l cors ferms fortz / mi fai cobrir / mains vers," I'm a true lover, / dear, / and faithful, / but my firm and strong heart / makes me hide / many truths, 256, lines 42–47), whereas Dante makes him hide himself in the purgatorial fire: "Poi s'ascose nel foco che li affina" (Then he hid himself in the fire that refines them, 26.148).

This last symbolic image of refining oneself as an act of contrition contradicts Arnaut's craftsmanship, where the aureation of words manifests and perpetuates the fire of desire. He builds "aura" into a trademark craft of oppositions (the "freid'aura" that makes him warm, 272, lines 12–14), one that sustains a hot heart in need of the lady's cooling balsam ("al chaut cor," "refrezir," 256, lines 49–51). Meanwhile, Dante's refinement of Arnaut seeks to restore allegorical order by insisting on the true meaning of fire through Arnaut's particular "name place" ("al suo nome il mio disire / apparecchiava grazïoso loco," my desire was preparing a / gracious place for his name, 26.137–38) in purgatory and thus in God's cosmology. "Consiros" or contrite, first and foremost (26.143), Arnaut must subordinate his skill in planing words to the refining fires. His song proceeds not from his Lady (272, line 6) but from a higher Power (26.145–46).

Like Dante, Petrarch was influenced by Arnaut's technical brilliance, yet he changes Arnaut's boasting into a lover's words of distant contemplation. Petrarch separates the signature from the persona and transforms Arnaut's signature into a proper name that serves his own autonomous creation: Laura.[86]

Through the structure of the *Rime sparse*, Petrarch uses time to figure love as introspection and meditation, including feelings of frustration and melancholy. The sensuality of love emerges through the collected texts, replacing Arnaut's lyrical concretization of desire. Petrarch adapts the "aura" of Arnaut's signature to his self-reflexive cosmology of *laura-lauro-l'aura*, making it an evolving textual figure for his subjective experience of love through the immortalization of Laura.

In sonnet 212 ("Beato in sogno," Blessed in sleep) and sestina 239 ("Là ver l'aurora," At the time near dawn),[87] Petrarch transforms the impossible lyrical moment of Arnaut's signature into a study of desire. Far from resolving Arnaut's contradictions, he places such feelings into the *canzoniere*'s context of duration and integration: different versions of the "aura" build into a synthesis of Laura. In 212, Petrarch deflates the signature's erotic tension by framing it with contentment and languidness: "Beato in sogno et di languir contento" (Blessed in sleep and satisfied to languish, line 1). The lover's struggle lacks the effort of Arnaut's adynaton: Petrarch alludes to the troubadour's signature of swimming and gathering wind ("nuoto per mar che non à fondo o riva," I swim through the sea that has no floor or shore, 3, and "abbracciar l'ombre et seguir l'aura estiva," to embrace shadows, and to pursue the summer breeze, 2) only to depict a lover plowing through the waves of a sea with "no floor or shore" rather than swimming against a tide; he is content to embrace shadows in pursuit of the summer breeze. Petrarch transforms Arnaut's craftsmanship of honing opposites into a languid notation of nature. The poet concedes to nature and tries to embrace it as he writes on the wind: "scrivo in vento" (4). Rather than crafting a poetics of carnal resistance, Petrarch tries to overcome the ephemeral nature of desire through a spiritualized poetics. Similar to Arnaut, he pursues a wandering, fleeing doe with a lame, slow ox ("et una cerva errante et fugitiva / caccio con un bue zoppo e 'nfermo et lento," 8), but his quest is metaphysical as he gazes yearning at the sun, becoming blind ("e 'l sol vagheggio si ch'elli à già spento / col suo splendor la mia vertù visiva," and I gaze yearning at the sun so that he has already put out with / his brightness my power of sight, 6). Petrarch indicates that his quest is for an intellectual knowledge superior to Arnaut's lyrical physicality; it is one that avoids what Augustine would identify as the trap of a merely erotic love—an unfulfilled love that Arnaut admits "never reaches an end" (259.109). Resigned in his blindness, he is "beato and contento" in his faith in love. The lover's twenty years of labor ("affanno," 12) resolves Arnaut's "eroica volonte di lottare" (heroic will to struggle) by integrating conflicting feelings into an enduring love for Laura embodied in the *Rime sparse*.[88]

In "Là ver l'aurora," Petrarch imitates the Arnauldian sestina (XVIII) and incorporates Arnaut's signature only to reject the sestina's revolving form and circular stasis of time and *eros*.[89] Arnaut is famous for inventing the sestina, the lyric form where rhyme words recur in every possible posi-

tion. In Petrarch's sestina, there is clearly a spiritual development of "aura."
In the springtime opening of the first stanza, the breeze is sweet, "l'aura" is
"dolce" (1), inspiring him to return to his notes, "note" (6). In the next stanza,
the "l'aura" is "Laura" (8): Petrarch makes an explicit equivalence between
the sweet breeze that inspires and the object he wishes he could inspire,
Laura. In the third stanza, he plays on this idea more, as Laura is resistant to
the sweet breeze: "Ella si sta pur com' aspr' alpe e l'aura / dolce" (She stands
there, a harsh mountain to the sweet breeze, 16). Thus we have "l'aura" as a
source of inspiration, as an object of his affections, and as one resistant to his
verses. Yet the naming of Laura in lines 27–28 surpasses Arnaut's artistry by
replacing an erotic desire embodied in the reflexive "l'aura" that constantly
returns to its physical character as sound (and thus fragmentary meaning),
with the integrated "Laura" and *versi*—"l'aura" as part of "Laura," "Laura" as
part of the *Rime sparse*: "né 'l pianger mio, né i preghi pon far Laura / trarre
o di vita o di martir quest'alma" (nor my weeping nor my prayers can cause
Laura / to free either from life or from torment this soul). At this turning
point, Petrarch relinquishes a worldly love of "Laura" for a spiritual love that
the poet anticipates in lines 13–14: "Quante lagrime, lasso, et quanti versi /
ò già sparti al mio tempo" (How many tears, alas, and how many verses /
have I already scattered in my time!) After the naming of Laura in line 27,
the poet extols the virtue of his *versi,* which conquer time and thus redeem
his impossible quest for the cold Laura: "Nulla al mondo è che non possano
i versi" (There is nothing in the world that cannot be done by verses, 28). In
this new vision, Laura's "angelica alma" will not be deaf to his amorous notes
(33), for now the recasting of Dante's contrite Arnaut appears in lines 35–36
as a lover's melancholy resignation contextualized in the faith of *versi* (28).
Petrarch's new reading of Arnaut's signature testifies at once to the immor-
tality of his verses and to his love for "Laura." In such a way, the poet replaces
the proper name of Arnaut and his signature of "l'aura" with the spiritualized Laura who laureates the lover. The Petrarchan "l'aura" disperses into
different meanings, only to become reintegrated into the figure of Laura
and the laureate poet.

CONCLUSION: HERMENEUTIC OPACITY
AS RESISTANCE TO AUTHORIAL UNITY

Much scholarship on songbooks presupposes Petrarch's *Rime sparse* or *Canzoniere* as the culmination of the troubadour songbook tradition.[90] From this
starting point, one looks back retrospectively in order to trace a path from

medieval vernacular lyric anthologies toward this poet's unified collection of poems. The translation of the voiced proper name in the chansonnier is by no means teleological, the endpoint being the adaptation of the troubadours by Dante and Petrarch. Dante and Petrarch's treatment of "Arnaut Daniel" may be considered as two songbook readings among many potential readings. Anticipated by Arnaut's self-reflexive signature, they succeed in adapting Arnaut's name to a literary situation external to the communal phenomenological songbook situation, since they place troubadour names within their own authorial songbooks. Nevertheless, one must consider their readings as in dialogue with — and even consciously resistant to — the hermeneutic opacity integral to the phenomenon of the proper name in the songbook.

Chapter Three

⚜

SHIFTING MEDIALITY:
VISUALIZING LYRIC TEXTS

WHEN MODERN READERS imagine a close relation between poem and image in premodern culture, they often think of Renaissance emblems,[1] in which an image represents a present or implied text — and nearly always, as in most early modern examples, text dominates image. Whereas early modern emblems are closed, images in medieval manuscripts such as historiated initials and marginalia are open; whereas Renaissance images serve a text, the miniatures and author portraits of songbooks — the landscape in the *Carmina Burana*, the Christic image next to Marcabru's name — are often indissolubly linked to their texts. They helped medieval readers make sense of poems and poets, and, in ways that modern readers might find strange, they *were* those poems and poets — that is, before those poems and poets became reified as what we know today. In this chapter I will show how images of several kinds serve as commentaries, analogs, or emblems before the emergence of a modern covenant between text and image. Visual connections between songbooks and other media affirm common metaphors about love or scripture that were often visually apprehended in a nonliterate era and immediately recognizable to the reader in their significance. In songbook illustration, one sees the medieval phenomenon of what Barbara Newman describes as "crossover," "the intentional borrowing and adaptation of courtly themes in devotional art and vice versa,"[2] a concept related to the *contrafactum* in literary studies. We might go so far as to say that songbook images often thematize the process of sublimating corporeal or worldly love through devotional references; that is, they confirmed to readers that they were interpreting properly, becoming another layer of discourse to comple-

ment the lyrics themselves. For every reader who was familiar with learning through pictures about things that could not be read in books, such
images offered a radical, challenging way to contemplate ideas of love in
the lyrics.[3]

Although songbook images might seem meager compared to illuminated psalters, Books of Hours, or moralized Bibles, not to mention famous
vernacular works such as the manuscripts of the popular *Roman de la Rose*,
they are equally invested in ways of seeing applied to religious iconography: the physical, material image as a gateway to a spiritual, hidden world.[4]
Readers expanded upon these ways of seeing by applying them to vernacular
poetry and secular culture. The songbook provided an opportunity for readers to think about how, for instance, Augustine's discussion of seeing God
described in his *De Genesi ad litteram*,[5] a type of vision elevated by the grace
of God and fundamentally different from corporeal vision, might apply to
courtly vernacular literature and the visual culture of European courts. A
milieu where power and social status were expressed through visual signs
(heraldry, falconry) and where love was often based upon a theory of tangible
vision (a lover is struck by his lady's glance, or is struck in the eye by Love's
arrows), secular visual culture might have been influenced by Augustine's
distinctions of corporeal and spiritual faculties of viewing.[6]

While authors' portraits that I will analyze in this chapter may cite the
religious authority of sacred iconography, they represent the emergence of
a separate vernacular and secular tradition. For instance, the visualization
of the secular poet with respect to concepts of vernacular song and the depiction of an oral rather than written *auctoritas* differ from portraits of the
evangelists, perhaps one of the most important author portrait traditions
during the Middle Ages. Haloed evangelists are typically depicted sitting
at a desk, writing instrument in hand and parchment before them.[7] Often
accompanied by an animal attribute or an angel, the evangelist possesses
auctoritas, veracity worthy of belief, by virtue of God's permitting him to
write for all Christians. As earthly transmitters of the Word, the evangelists
are merely instruments of the divine author. These portraits underline the
direct correspondence between the Word and the production of the scribe.

The troubadour portraits in the chansonniers lack this direct correspondence to the Word of God. As they idealize vernacular song rather than
the written word, they also demonstrate what Alistair Minnis has shown
as an important shift occurring in the thirteenth century: the shift from a
distant religious or classical *auctoritas* figure to an *auctor* (producer) deriv-
ing authority from a life lived, guaranteeing the text or events he or she

5. Evangelist from *Gospels of Saint Médard of Soissons* (Bibl. Nat. lat. 8850, f. 8lv) (ninth century). Photograph: Bibliothèque nationale de France.

produces (*auctor* being associated with the Greek *authentin*, authority as authenticity).[8] Laura Kendrick has pointed out that even when illuminators represent troubadours as author figures in the Italian chansonniers, they represent them not in the act of writing, an activity reserved for a scribe, but reading from or holding a codex, for example.[9] The compilers and artists of these chansonniers aim to valorize these troubadours according to their historical attributes — their knowledge, courtliness, or religious piety.[10] When considering troubadour portraits in the different songbook traditions as distinct from the sacred image of the scriptural scribe-author, or from canonical authority, one views a developing conception of the secular poet's *auctoritas* — a secular value or guarantee of a troubadour corpus as affirmed by the author portrait and *vida* — through various typical or symbolic depictions. The chansonnier provides a flexible structure for shaping the vernacular *auctoritas* of a lyric tradition — and, by extension, a readership's self-legitimacy — and author portraits often refer to various iconographic traditions from antiquity to the Middle Ages. These images mediate between an oral tradition of vernacular song now transmitted in books, and a written tradition having been reserved only recently for sacred texts in Latin alone. They demonstrate a complex broadening of perspectives with respect to concepts of authority and vernacular lyric traditions.

For modern readers, images in songbooks reveal the competing authorities available for interpreting lyric. The rise of lay literacy and urban society as well as the competing claims of powerful secular rulers and ecclesiastical authorities in the twelfth to fourteenth centuries result in not a "secularization of society" but, rather, as Michael Camille argues, "a demand for ever more intimate involvement in spiritual matters among lay folk, much of it using images."[11] When a songbook contained images, readers could tend to spiritual matters by interpreting secular lyrics as a means to reflect upon the divinity, or by visualizing erotic love in relation to spiritual love. A Christic frontal gaze, for example (discussed below), might implicate or challenge the viewer to internalize a troubadour's call to crusade, while a chansonnier's marginalia might act as a mimetic representation and gloss on a lyric text. These images, as textual analogs, constitute the interpretive potential of songbooks for building cultural traditions from lyric: images being at once allegorical gloss, narrative, and mimicry, they incorporate and provoke reader responses, therefore significantly shaping a reader's memory of lyric. This shifting mediality in songbooks challenges us to reconsider how texts and images lend meaning to one another to constitute poetry in a specific material context.

TROUBADOUR CHANSONNIERS R AND N:
VISUALIZING TROUBADOUR TEXTS IN
LANGUEDOC AND NORTHERN ITALY

In the chansonniers, miniatures or illuminations generally come in three different categories: historiated initials or miniatures that precede lyric texts, often as portraits of a troubadour; historiated initials of generic or decorative images, depicting a man or a woman, an animal or a beast, and similar ornamentation; and marginalia. Building upon past scholarship on the troubadour miniatures and illumination,[12] my study of the late thirteenth-century Paduan chansonnier N (New York, Pierpont Morgan Library Ms. 819) and fourteenth-century Languedoc R reveals how certain images in these chansonniers provide visual strategies for reading troubadour lyric in the late Middle Ages by furnishing moral contexts or analogs.

In addition to the noteworthy images that I will discuss, chansonniers R and N contain typical author portraits seen in Italian chansonniers A, I, and K that individualize the troubadour and his or her lyric corpus as *vidas* do. These images usually depict the troubadour with clothing appropriate to his or her rank or profession according to the *vida*, or as a generic nobleman or clergyman; they may also depict the figure making a conventional rhetorical gesture, such as a declamatory gesture with an arm. These qualities belong to a generic vocabulary of clothing and rhetorical gestures recognizable to the chansonniers' readers. In contrast, the historiated initials of chansonnier R (see plates 1–3), and the marginalia of chansonnier N (see plate 4) are categorically different in the way they work with the lyric text and songbook. Not only do they embody the troubadour and his lyric texts, but as visual images they structure a process of thought in which the reader understands and spiritually interprets lyric material. These images are instructive as well as meditative, representing the medieval idea of memory as a pictorial image being imprinted on the mind.[13] As a visual concretization of verbal metaphors, images of N and R act upon the reader, enabling a spiritual understanding of a courtly imaginary made possible through the medium of the songbook.

In the first songbook I will examine, chansonnier R, the three main initials of its lyric section by the same artist — the image of Christ's face on f. 5, the portrait of Saint James of Compostela on f. 67, and the portrait of a crowned Virgin Mary on f. 103v — guide the reader to visualize a proper love by suggesting at once the insufficiency of troubadour lyric and its potential for a greater good through Marian devotion. As visual analogs to the texts of Marcabru, Peire Cardenal (fl. 1205–72), and Guiraut Riquier (fl. 1254–92), these images form a pilgrimage within chansonnier R that directs readers to reflect historically on the changing context of the lyrics, and spiritually meditate on the lyrics as a kind of prayerbook toward reconciliation. Readers are drafted as pilgrims, and the initials serve as stations as they progress through the songbook. Each initial instructs them in how to read the author corpus, and cumulatively in how to read these corpuses in relation to each other. Further, together the initials offer a reading of the troubadour lyric tradition. Beginning with Marcabru's crusade song, and proceeding to the criticism and hypocrisy of the clergy addressed by Peire Cardenal, the pilgrimage ends with Guiraut Riquier as an ideal troubadour who reinscribes troubadour lyric within a new religious context of southern France and the changing realities of courtly culture in Languedoc and Castile.

Philological and iconographical analyses of chansonnier R by Geneviève Brunel-Lobrichon and Zufferey have established the political and religious context of early fourteenth-century Toulouse reflected in this chansonnier[14]: the history of the crusades in both the East and West, the progressive dominance of ecclesiastical powers in this region after the Albigensian Crusade in 1229, and disputes concerning the papacy before the Great Schism (1378–1417). The visual religious tone accords with the didactic and devotional texts contained in the chansonnier such as a Dominican debate; the enumeration of sacraments, sins, and virtues; and Marian poems.[15] Further, Brunel-Lobrichon and Zufferey speculate that the chansonnier may have been associated with the Consistori de la sobregaia companhia del gai saber (or the Jeux Floraux), an institution founded in 1323 by layman poets to preserve the Occitan troubadour tradition, as it perhaps belonged to Peire de Lunel de Montech, member of the Jeux Floraux.[16] Members of this company sought to preserve the troubadour tradition by inscribing it within a cult dedicated to the Virgin Mary and the art of speaking well, modeling their activities after university procedures and producing an *ars poetria*, the *Leys d'Amors*.[17] Thus the chansonnier reflects the orthodox religious environment of Toulouse, as well as civic interests to preserve a vernacular tradition during a period of growing French influence.[18]

As the first step of the pilgrimage through the songbook, the Christic image appears in the historiated initial that begins Marcabru's "Pax in nomine Domini," which alludes to the failed Second Crusade around the 1140s in the East and the Reconquest led by Ramon Berenguer IV of Barcelona (r. 1131–62). Through the use of particular religious iconography, the initial directs the reader to interpret Marcabru's lyric and image together and to collectively read the other pilgrimage initials with their lyric texts in order to morally progress through the songbook. In the frontal portrait, the Holy Face gazes out of the initial, with blue eyes, finely detailed blond hair, and delicate red cheeks against a red and gold leaf background. This image honors the "first troubadour" ("lo premier trobador," as the rubric states) and calls attention to the ideology of his crusading lyric: the Holy Face reminds its viewers of the last image of Christ that was beheld, the Veronica, a sight one cannot experience until the Day of Judgment. An encouragement for crusading, the face of Christ points back to itself as merely an image, reminding living Christians that they must fulfill their duties on earth in order to see God face to face after death, when he comes to judge the world. Moreover, as the initial that begins a collection of both profane and devotional lyric texts, the frontal gaze directly engages its readers, reminding them not only of the invisible presence of Christ but of the responsibility to interpret troubadour lyric as a form of contemplation of divinity. Opening the chansonnier, the small portrait promotes spiritual vision in order to illuminate how Marcabru's crusading lyric preaches the right kind of love for Christ.

We might expect this visual knowledge to moralize Marcabru's text unequivocally. However, the choice of Christ's face acts as a locus of discursive readings rather than a univocal sign of authority. At first the visual image appears to reinscribe the verbal and performative instability (since this song was certainly adopted for political expediency) of Marcabru's *lavador* — the song's key metaphor of a washing place used for baptism, spiritual cleansing, and the remission of sins associated with crusade[19] — within a universe that is now logocentric, speculative, and symbolic: "cum nos a fait per sa dousor / lo seignorius celestius (lo senhor rey in R), probet de nos, un lavador" (how the heavenly Lord [or lord king], in His loving-kindness has created for us, in our vicinity, a washing-place, 438, lines 4–6). Although the word is used in various contexts throughout the song, here the judgment of Christ invokes the Spanish Crusade ("probet de nos") as a *lavador*. However, the poetic analog of image and *vers* translates the polysemous quality of the *lavador* by allowing different interpretations of crusade and secular lyric: does Christ's face authorize crusade, or Marcabru and the Occitan tradition? Both are possible; the analog opens an imaginative space for meditating on the lyrics by enacting what David Freedberg calls a "constitutive verisimilitude,"[20] reproducing rather than representing the lyric presence of Marcabru's song. The image in the songbook affirms what Jeffrey Hamburger has recognized as the innovative nature of Western theological art developing in a "variety

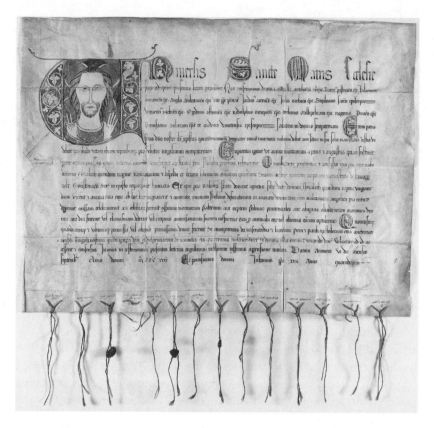

6. Holy Face from *Indulgence for Königsfelden, Avignon 1329* (Cod. 814). Photograph: Burgerbibliothek, Bern.

of imaginative spaces," such as images used as "instruments of devotion, didactic devices, or prompts to memory."[21]

Moreover, the Christic face of R resonates with the use of the Veronica and the Holy Face as a visual experience associated with pilgrimage and popular piety in religious practice or decoration.[22] It resembles a Holy Face that appears on an indulgence issued in 1329 in Avignon, but illuminated in Germany for a convent, and one of an early panel painting dated circa 1304–6 from a church in Bohemia.[23] The image of Christ's face in these instances and chansonnier R speak not only to the late medieval popularity of the Veronica and the Holy Face in Western Europe but to their use for penitence and remission of sins.

Given this connection to the remission of sins through the metaphor of

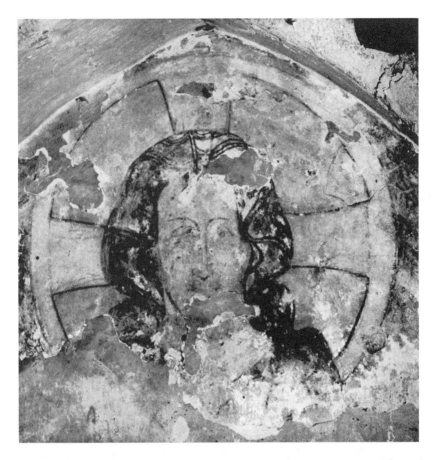

7. Holy Face from Church of the Assumption of the Bendectine Monastery at Police nad Metují (ca. 1304–6). Photograph: Vlasta Dvořáková et al., *Gothic Mural Painting in Bohemia and Moravia, 1300–1378* (London: Oxford University Press, 1964).

the *lavador* and papal indulgences, the analog between the Christic face and "Pax in nomine Domini" offers the songbook as a practice for the spiritual cleansing of sins, the songbook as *lavador.* In other words, while the initials collectively form a spiritual progression through the songbook, the overall effect of this pilgrimage anticipates the *lavador*'s metaphorical meaning, to which the opening Christ initial and Marcabru's crusading song analog alludes. During this period in the Midi, therefore, we can see chansonnier R as a *lavador* for past violences. Whether this songbook belonged to aristocrats or a fraternity of mercantile bourgeois, such a poetic analog indicates a desire to come to terms with the events of the past, preserve a vernacular heritage, and reactivate a lyric tradition in the present. The songbook as *lavador* not only grants religious legitimacy to the Occitan tradition. It establishes Marcabru and the Occitan lyric tradition as a spiritual "washing place," which situates a past lyric tradition in a devotional present.

While reasons for beginning the lyric collection and Marcabru's corpus with the Christic face may seem fairly clear, more ambiguous is the initial that heads Peire Cardenal's corpus, which could be a pilgrim, Saint James, or a portrait of the troubadour.[24] The image resembles pilgrims in the slightly earlier Escorial T.I.1 codex of the *Cantigas de Santa María*,[25] and features a man's head in three-quarter profile with a large red hat, characteristic of a pilgrim or Saint James. Like the Christ initial, a gold leaf background highlights the importance of the Peire initial. The initial heads the lyrics of a troubadour famous for his moral *sirventes*, and what one scholar has called his "tortured soul" as a devout Christian living among and dependent upon corrupt clergymen and nobility of his day.[26] Although Peire is well known for his moralizing invectives, one must view them as part of a long tradition of anticlerical satire independent of the particular context of fourteenth-century Toulouse, even as we consider how the compilers and artists of R would have perceived or interpreted him in such a context.[27]

Peire's initial — distinguished in its style and careful detail with fine hair and red cheeks — serves as the second step in the pilgrimage between the Christ and the Virgin Mary initials; like the Christ initial, it offers various readings as a visual analog to Peire's corpus. One plausible reading is that the artist is trying to allude to Peire's mention of Compostela in a personal invective against Esteve de Belmon, a corrupt clergyman. Belonging to a series of *sirventes* attributed to Peire that accuse Esteve of *infamia* and demanding that he do penance,[28] in "Un sirventes trametrai per messatge" (I will send a *sirventes* by messenger [PC 335.68]; the first stanza with the reference appears on f. 70 of R), Peire reproaches Esteve, saying he will sing his song until his servant ("l'enfan," a virtuous chevalier), of whom Esteve has taken advantage, goes to Compostela as a penitent for his sins:

> L'enfan
> De que fes guavèla
> [lacuna] ema
> iers chantan
> Tro en Compostèla,

8. Pilgrims miniature (Escorial T.I.1, f. 224) from the *Cantigas de Santa María* (ca. 1270–90). Photograph: Facsimile edition, *El 'Códice Rico' de las Cantigas de Alfonso el Sabio: Ms. T.I.1 de la Biblioteca de El Escorial* (Madrid: Edilán, 1979).

Pes del [lacuna] ploram
S'en an,
Qu'en questa rudèla
A fag trop de mazan.[29]

The child that he has brought down, I will send him with my song,
all the way to Compostela, his feet [bare], and crying, he will go
away for on this mean route he has made scandalous commotion.

While this textual allusion is possible, especially since the song calls attention to itself by appearing split in two different places—likely because of the
insertion of a quaternion after a series of quinions for the lyric section[30]—
there is another reason that may link this initial to the Christic face of Marcabru's corpus. As Saint James is associated with the pilgrimage of Compostela, a pilgrimage to honor the sepulcher of Saint James, which became one
of the most important destinations in the world during the Middle Ages,
perhaps the artist views Peire as a pilgrim in search of meaning in a fallen
world in which he feels an exile. In another *sirventes* in R, "Las amairitz, qui
encolpar las vòl" (Lovers, if someone wants to accuse them [PC 335.30]),
which appears on the same folio as "Un sirventes trametrai per messatge,"
he laments that nobody understands him, as he is the only one who has
God's sense:

A mos ops chant e a mos ops flaujol,
car homs mas ieu non enten mon lati;
atretan pauc com fa d'un rossinhol
entent la gent de mon chant que se di.
Ez ieu non ai lengua fiza ni breta,
ni sai parlar flamenc ni angevi,
mas malvestatz que los escalafeta
lor tol vezer que es fals ni es fi.

A mi non cal que crois hom s'entrameta
de mon chantar pos siei fag son porsi.[31]

For myself alone I sing, and toot my horn, because nobody but
me understands my language; just as a crowd understands little of
a nightingale, so it understands my chant and what I want to say.
However, I do not have a meager or Breton tongue, nor do I know

how to speak Flemish or Angevin. But viciousness seals them and
puts in view those who are false and those who are true.

I don't care that a crude man bothers with my song because his
acts are of a pig.

In "Las amairitz," Peire speaks the truth in the language that only he understands, being the only one to have the sense of God in a mad city (as in
another song, "Que·l sens de Dieu lor par folía. . . . Car lo sen de Dieu an
perdut," For the wisdom of God is madness to them . . . For they have lost
the sense of God).[32] The initial further emphasizes this moral righteousness
already seen in the pilgrimage/penitence message of "Un sirventes trametrai
per messatge." Furthermore, the truth he conveys as a pilgrim/troubadour
coincides with the idea of Saint James as the patron saint of the Spanish
crusades: it was under the banner of Saint James that the Galician Christians fought the Muslims to drive them out of Spain, beginning in the ninth
century. As a progression from the Holy Face of Marcabru's song, the Saint
James / pilgrim initial inscribes and continues the energetic evangelicalism
of Marcabru by evoking and justifying the Eastern and Spanish crusades:
the Holy Face, although appropriated by French Gothic artists by the thirteenth century, is associated with the Byzantine East (the mandylion) and
the relic of the sudarium in Rome after the twelfth century, while the iconography of Saint James is closely related to the Spanish Reconquest. Just
as the initial of Marcabru emphasizes the troubadour's self-fashioning as
scriptural authority (see chapter 2), so the initial of Peire positions him as
the true voice of moral and Christian righteousness in the aftermath of the
Albigensian Crusade through his *sirventes* of specific political and historical
disputes of the thirteenth century.[33]

Judging from the song that heads his corpus next to the pilgrim initial,
"De sirventes faire no·m tuelh" (I won't stop making *sirventes* [PC 335.17]),
in which he proclaims that "he detests Injustice, and loves Righteousness"
("car azir tort . . . am dreg," lines 3–4),[34] and from the song that originally
ended his corpus in R but is now missing, "Vera vergena, María" (True virgin,
Mary [PC 335.70]),[35] as the midpoint of the songbook pilgrimage, the initial
of Peire directs a reading of his corpus from a position of righteousness to
bitter invectives against the injust and to reconciliation through Mary. She
serves as mediator for his reconciliation with God, and the corpus appropriately ends with the song that contains the words "Vera vida, vera fés, / vera
vertatz, *vera vía*" (True life, true faith, true truth, *truth path*, my emphasis).[36]

Peire as troubadour is literally a finder of the "vera vía": the initial reveals how he is a pilgrim or Saint James who attempts to reconcile "l'idéal évangelique et l'idéal courtois"[37] in his moral invectives, satires of courtly love, and Marian hymns. Mary is his "estela que guía,"[38] the "guiding star" that shows the pilgrim the right path. Consistent with the function of the songbook as *lavador*, the initial of Peire directs its readers to seek spiritual redemption by honoring Peire's pursuit of the truth and reconciliation through Mary. The Christic and Marian themes and the idea of pilgrimage represented in the initials also suggest the East-West *translatio* of the crusades and of the seat of the papacy from Rome to Avignon in the fourteenth century, as well as the migrating circulation of the Holy Face and the rising popularity of local cults to the Virgin Mary seen in religious art and lyric poetry.[39]

If Peire represents one stage of the pilgrimage of the "vera vía," Guiraut Riquier's corpus in this chansonnier understands the end point of the progression toward Mary and the emergence of a new kind of troubadour. While the Peire analog emphasizes his isolating tactic as preacher and moralist, the initial of the Virgin Mary that begins the lyric collection of Guiraut Riquier represents the troubadour's calling on Mary as an advocate for secular institutions.[40] One song transmitted in C, and Guiraut's dated and annotated songbook transmitted in C and R,[41] display his perceived historical awareness of a late stage of troubadour culture. Guiraut sings of his belatedness in one of his last songs, "Be·m degra de chantar tener"[42] (I ought to stop my singing, [PC 248.17]). He regrets that he has come too late ("mas trop suy vengutz als derriers") and that he is one of the few people who can still appreciate the "belh saber / de trobar" (the beautiful knowledge of *trobar*). Although he invokes a common rhetorical topic, one could argue that his pessimism matches his situation as a professional poet. For example, in nonlyric texts Guiraut addresses his position as a poet. In a *supplicatio* written in 1274 to Alfonso X that is transmitted only in R,[43] Guiraut complains that those who have true poetic talent and whose poetry possesses moral value, that is, troubadours, should be distinguished from mere entertainers or *jongleurs*.[44] After the death of his patron the Vicomte Amalric I in 1270, Guiraut spent the next ten years at the court of Alfonso X; in his epistle, in which he tries to affirm the moral and artistic superiority of troubadours, and in his religious lyrics, Guiraut angles for a new role for the troubadour distinct from a common minstrel. Although one sees this same spiritual superiority in the polemics of Peire Cardenal, in Guiraut's songs of religious matter and love lyrics to the Virgin Mary as *senhal*, he envisions the troubadour as moral herald and spiritual adviser to his patron through

Marian song. Like Peire Cardenal's eschewal of the *canso*, many of Guiraut's songs celebrate the Virgin Mary as the true *domna*, as illustrated in this song composed at the court of Alfonso X in 1273 and transmitted with music in R: "Humils, forfaitz, repres e penedens . . . vos clam merce, Dona, Verges plazens, maires de Crist" (Humbled, guilty, mortified and repentant . . . I beg you for mercy, Lady, gracious virgin, mother of Christ).[45]

The artist recognized Guiraut's belated self-fashioning and his position in relation to Peire Cardenal and Marcabru because the initial that heads the collection indicates the subject matter of his Marian verses and Guiraut's place as the "last poet," the opposite of Marcabru, the "first poet." Reinforcing this opposition between Marcabru and Guiraut is the variant unique to chansonniers CR in line 5 of the "Vers del Lavador": "lo senhor rey." Perhaps the image of a crowned Virgin relates back to this line. From the first troubadour (Marcabru) to the last (Guiraut Riquier), with the midway point of Peire Cardenal as a troubadour who struggles to find his way toward reconciliation, the artist of these initials charts a spiritual path for a reader's reception of vernacular lyric, offering images as analogs to show how these lyrics can be morally instructive and spiritually uplifting, especially in terms of the recent past.[46]

Finally, it must be emphasized that these poetic analogs between texts and images, as markers of the songbook pilgrimage, form potential readings rather than a single, closed narrative imposed upon the texts. To summarize: the analog between Christ and "Pax in nomine Domini" stages the songbook as a *lavador*, in that the progressive reading of lyric texts through the coordinates of the pilgrimage initials can enact the metaphorical meaning of the *lavador* as historical reflection, penitence, and spiritual cleansing. The pilgrim image next to Peire's satirical invectives encourages moral righteousness and reconciliation with the past through Marian song, while also continuing to advocate the crusade ideology seen with Marcabru. Guiraut Riquier heralds the new role of the troubadour by establishing authoritative control over his lyrics in his own annotated songbook, and by emphasizing the moral necessity of the professional troubadour in his letters to Alfonso X and songs to the Virgin Mary. This pilgrimage through the songbook as *lavador* embodies the *renovatio* of a vernacular lyric tradition through the medium of the chansonnier. By referring to circulating media such as the Veronica or images of pilgrims, the pilgrimage allows a textual community to participate in these lyrics on its own terms, as cultural history or personal devotion, much as the musical performance of these lyrics may have invigorated this troubadour tradition in a new urban environment of Toulouse.

While the religious authority of the initials in R establishes an open framework to read secular lyric in terms of devotional piety, the "crossover" image of the six-winged seraph that occurs predominantly in the Folquet de Marseille (fl. 1178–95; d. 1231) section of chansonnier N — an image with various connotations in a religious context, now applied to Love as an abstract concept — functions differently as a visual analog due to its marginal placement and recurrence keyed to a sequence of texts. Besides the section of *cansos* and *coblas* (stanzas) organized by author corpora (f. 55–274), the first fifty-two folios of chansonnier N contain nonlyric works: two didactic *ensenhamens* (codes of courtly conduct) of Arnaut de Maruel, a fragment of the *Roman de Jaufré*, a novella of Raimon Vidal, and an anonymous "Court of Love" narrative. The manuscript's final section (f. 275–93) transmits *partimens* or debate poems on a chosen topic (unattributed, but the genre itself names the poet being addressed). Although there are portraits in the historiated initials in the first section of the manuscript, the various *bas-de-page* and marginal pictures occur only in the section of author corpora. Framed by didactic sections, the illustrations of the lyric section of this chansonnier — the section in which the seraph occurs — are influenced by the expositions of self-governance treated in the nonlyric genres or rhetorical debate of the *partimens*. In this way the images perhaps represent a didactic mode — whether as narrative gloss or as dialogic text-image interpretation of a chosen topic within the lyric — translated into a different medium. As a visual analog of Love as both erotic and spiritual, the seraph offers different opportunities to explore what Newman, Carruthers, and Caroline Walker Bynum have shown to be an image's function as a "flexible matrix, open to a range of meanings and formulations, amidst a range of responses that reach from high church doctrine to popular piety."[47]

In the marginal sequence of f. 56 that accompanies Folquet de Marseille's canso "Ben an mort mi e lor" (They have killed me and themselves [PC 155.5]; see plate 4),[48] the seraph is cued to the word "Amors," and appears next to a lover fleeing what pursues him (*Amors*), and pursuing she who flees him (his lady). While I agree with the conclusions that Newman, Huot, and Nichols have proposed—that the closed- and then open-winged seraph, as the god of Love, suggests the "psychic disturbance" of the lover or a depiction of the paradoxical experience of love depicted in "Ben an mort mi e lor"; that the three faces and six wings suggest the Trinity and sacred iconography of the cherubim and seraph; and that the five instances of the seraph in the Folquet corpus seem to imply a "coexistence of worldly and spiritual love as a Plotinus-like continuum of experience"[49]—I would briefly like to add to these interpretations by reflecting upon this mode of visual commentary in contrast to the R initials.

As Huot and Nichols[50] have rightly noted, the seraphic *Amors* is an ambivalent image that could signify either a critique of an *Amors* that masquerades as a sacred love, or a true veneration of *Amors*. It is an apt figure for lovers agonizing about the ethics of their behavior — the lover, as marionette or wounded by Love's lance, concedes to the psychic control of the seraph.[51] Embodying the dynamic process of reflection through its fluttering movement, seraphic Love stages the conflict between following spiritual virtue or submitting to *Amors*. Nichols has suggested the seraph in the Folquet corpus could also be read as moving from this moral conflict to a narrative of conversion, the image of seraphic Love corresponding to Folquet's *vida*, which states that he renounced his worldly life, became a Cistercian monk, and wound up as bishop of Toulouse.[52] While this narrative is certainly plausible, the multiplicity of the seraph's form seems to suggest multiple readings of *Amors*. In contrast to the way the initials in R provide keys to understanding a lyric corpus in relation to the poet as well as to the entire lyric section of the chansonnier, the winged seraph of N acts as a mediating tool that glosses *Amors*

9. Saint Francis receiving the stigmata from Gradual (Ms. 5, f. 181v) (second half of the thirteenth century). Photograph: Archivio Comunale, Montalcino, Ospedale S. Maria della Croce.

or acts as a typological correlative to Folquet's life. The seraph may suggest the confusion of the lover desirous for his *domna*, or the spiritual clarity of Folquet's path from troubadour to bishop, allowing the reader to reflect on two kinds of love, rather than dictating one as overpowering the other. N's marginalia and initials offer discrete interpretive analogs between lyric and text as well as a cumulative narrative of the seraph in Folquet's corpus.

Like the circulating religious images that may have influenced the artists of R, the use of the seraph to analyze troubadour lyric may have been influenced by Italian depictions of Saint Francis, dating from the second half of the thirteenth century, in which God appears in the form of a crucified seraph and wounds his lover's body through the eyes.[53] The citation of seraphic Love in the courtly context draws a reader to reflect on the wounds of a lover versus the stigmata of a true vision as seen by Saint Francis, lover of Christ; it attests to the cross-fertilization of troubadour lyric and other forms of religious and vernacular art. As analogs to verbal texts, these images offer not a singular interpretive key but an imaginative platform for readers to think about love both in individual lyrics and in a narrative within and among corpuses of troubadours; further, they are in dialogue with a visual culture extrinsic to the songbook.

TWO IMAGES OF TROUBADOUR-KINGS: ALFONSO X IN THE *CANTIGAS DE SANTA MARÍA* AND FREDERICK II IN THE FRESCO OF BASSANO DEL GRAPPA

Chansonnier N and R's lack of definite affiliation with an institution or patron reinforces the uncodified relations between their images and texts. Despite the influence of courtly and devotional traditions, these images, as another layer of the lyrics, create frameworks indefinite enough for readers to build their own conceptions of poetry and literary traditions. To widen the context around songbooks, I will now look at contemporary institutional images of troubadour lyric, such as the famous miniatures of the *Cantigas de Santa María* (figs. 10–12) and the fresco at the Palazzo Finco in Bassano del Grappa dating from the first third of the thirteenth century that depicts the Hohenstaufen Emperor Frederick II in a courtly mise-en-scène (fig. 13).[54]

10. Alfonso X miniature (Escorial T.I.1, f. 5) from the *Cantigas de Santa María* (ca. 1270–90). Photograph: Facsimile edition, *El 'Códice Rico' de las Cantigas de Alfonso el Sabio: Ms. T.I.1 de la Biblioteca de El Escorial* (Madrid: Edilán, 1979).

11. Alfonso X miniature (Escorial T.I.1, f. 157v) from the *Cantigas de Santa María* (ca. 1270–90). Photograph: Facsimile edition, *El 'Códice Rico' de las Cantigas de Alfonso el Sabio: Ms. T.I.1 de la Biblioteca de El Escorial* (Madrid: Edilán, 1979).

12. Alfonso X miniature (Escorial T.I.1, f. 170v) from the *Cantigas de Santa María* (ca. 1270–90). Photograph: Facsimile edition, *El 'Códice Rico' de las Cantigas de Alfonso el Sabio: Ms. T.I.1 de la Biblioteca de El Escorial* (Madrid: Edilán, 1979).

13. Frederick II from a fresco in the Palazzo Finco, Bassano del Grappa (first half of the thirteenth century). Photograph: Marisa Galvez.

Unlike the typical images of troubadours in the chansonniers, or the images of R and N that function as textual glosses or analogs, these images represent imperial agendas: they explicitly link the political ambition of the kings with the ideal aspirations of courtly culture. As part of an institutional program of self-authorization, the Bassano fresco and the *Cantigas* are notable in two ways: first, they represent these rulers' efforts to adopt troubadour culture by visually inserting themselves into particular scenes of courtly love — a new development of the biblical iconography of King David; and second, as opposed to other institutional portraits in which Alfonso and Frederick present themselves solely in the iconography of the classical emperor or in divine regalia independent of ecclesiastical authority (the depictions of Frederick in *De arte venandi cum avibus* and the *Exultet* roll, and Alfonso's portrait in the opening of the *Cantigas*, for example),[55] the fresco and the miniatures present personal, naturalized scenes of the troubadour-kings interacting with their subjects. Such self-portraiture promotes authority in parallel with classical and ecclesiastical models but also appeals to their subjects on a vernacular and secular level through troubadour song.[56] While these works have been studied in terms of the cultural production associated with the reigns of Frederick II and Alfonso X, it has never been asked what the Bassano fresco and the *Cantigas* together might have to do with the broader interrelation of visual art and troubadour reception in medieval Europe. In particular, these works offer a wider context to understand the images in chansonniers by directly linking troubadour memorial culture to two important rulers of the thirteenth century. The fresco and the *Cantigas* represent the centrality of troubadour culture to these rulers' programs of secular self-authorization, and generally the growing importance of troubadour lyric and its memorialization in songbooks in the context of the century's international politics. Frederick's and Alfonso's concern to create an imperial legitimacy that would link the people of their disparate territories in their evolving kingdoms made sense during a period of contentious rivalry between secular rulers, the papacy, and local lords.[57]

The Bassano Fresco: Frederick II as Troubadour-King Signifies the Spiritualized Love of His Curia

The Bassano fresco dates from the period before Frederick's second excommunication in 1239, when he was trying to reestablish order in his kingdom, especially the axis of the Swabian-Alpine-Lombard crown possessions. Throughout his reign as Holy Roman Emperor (1220–50), Frederick struggled to consolidate his power in his claimed territories, in present-day Germany, Italy, and the Sicilian Kingdom, in opposition to the people and territories loyal to the papacy (Welfs). By employing *ministeriales* on the local level, he attempted to establish an imperial rule of law within an itinerant kingship. The Bassano fresco probably dates to the years 1235–39, when Frederick celebrated his wedding to Isabella, the sister of Henry III of England. The image, rare for the medium of monumental fresco painting, appears in what was one of the baronial households of Alberico and Ezzelino da Romano. It is likely that the fresco was commissioned exclusively in honor of Frederick's extended visit to Padua in 1239.[58] The fresco depicts a youthful king presenting a rose to a frontally facing queen, who holds a sparrow hawk on her gloved left hand. It is unclear whether they share the same regal bench, but the equal position of their heads suggests that they do so. The expressive details of Frederick's portrait — the wrinkles around his eyes, the detail of the crown, and the hair emerging from his bonnet — and the inclined movement of his gesture suggest a naturalistic Gothic style of France or Germany.[59] The other characters in the scene share this style and realistic details. To his farthest right is a troubadour playing a viol; between this figure and the king is a young man standing with his arms folded, watching the interaction between the king and the queen. Maria Elisa Avagnina first identified these figures as Frederick II, his third wife Isabella of England, and Alberico da Romano. Maria Luisa Meneghetti argues that the dress of the figures in the fresco corresponds to the northern Italian troubadour chansonniers, reflecting the Ghibelline culture of Frederick's circle at the time.[60] Moreover, she views the image as a a mise-en-scène of the Italian troubadour Pier della Vigna's *quaestio de rosa et viola*, and sees the figure playing the viol as Uc de Saint Circ, or some other high-ranking troubadour close to Frederick's circle.[61] Pier rose from a troubadour of modest means to a notary in the imperial chancery, and was an influential member of Frederick's circle.

A visual synthesis of the troubadour tradition transmitted by the northern Italian chansonniers through the court of Frederick II, the Bassano fresco promotes Frederick as the ultimate protagonist in the secular religion of love. As part of his political program of depicting himself as a Roman emperor and establishing his rule as a form of "sacralità alternativa,"[62] the fresco expresses the emperor's legitimacy through the courtly ideals of *fin' amor.* The sparrow hawk on Queen Isabella's hand and Frederick's wooing of her with a rose belong to the courtly images of the falcon and the hunt, both used as metaphors for the lady who controls her lover.[63] Frederick offers his spiritual, not physical, love embodied in the rose. While belonging to the courtly topic of falconry and its symbolic language of love, the image of the bird also embodies Frederick's interest in natural science seen in the treatise *De arte venandi cum avibus* and its ornithological illustrations and images of falconry. Both *De arte venandi* and the Bassano fresco represent these interests in a distinct curial style. This visual vernacular creates an elevated imperial culture that rises above hierarchical realities between emperor and subjects and above the local cultures of his itinerant court. Frederick establishes an official style invested with cultural prestige and historical distance, expressed in the northern "natural realism"[64] evident in *De arte venandi* and the fresco. Far from being a minor exception to his monumental works, the fresco reveals how Frederick's reception of the troubadours is essential to understanding his agenda of establishing a "secular truth"[65] independent of everyday realities and the Christian ethos that we will see embraced by Alfonso X in his *Cantigas.*

The survival of a troubadouresque fresco, rather than a curial songbook, reflects Frederick's desire to both appropriate and distance himself from the Occitan troubadour tradition. Frederick seems to have possessed what Meneghetti calls "an antiquarian spirit," an interest in a secular lyric distant from contemporary matters, likely cultivated from the archival study of chansonniers such as the one belonging to Alberico da Romano, chanson-nier D[a], discussed in chapter 2.[66] Perhaps in consulting chansonniers like the *Liber Alberici* rather than creating a curial songbook, and having himself visually depicted as a troubadour-king in the fresco, Frederick developed a hermetic culture of troubadour study easily shaped for ideological purposes, a stable court culture for an itinerant court.[67] Meanwhile, the promotion of poetic activity in the vernacular and adoption of the themes and formal elements of the troubadour tradition into a new poetic koine were in them-selves political statements. The "Sicilian school" of poetry associated with Frederick's curia between 1230 and 1250, including works by Jacopo Mostacci and Giacomo da Lentini, reflects this hermetic culture: while their poetry includes the themes and forms of *fin' amor*, the political or satirical *sirventes* is unknown, the rhetorical address of the *tornada* and *senhal* is unattested, and songs were not sung to melodies.[68] These poets also favored lyrics by troubadours such as Pier della Vigna and Folquet de Marseille, who dwell on abstract love topics and foreground formal and rhetorical complexity. The Sicilian school under Frederick did not favor the themes of "militanza politica" common in the songs of contemporary troubadours, and his curia deliberately encouraged lyric that went against popular tastes.[69]

The mise-en-scène quality of the fresco demonstrates this politiciza-tion of love as spiritualized ideal. Despite the detailed Ghibelline clothing and nuanced intimate gestures, the empty background frames an idealized scene rather than a specific genre, and there is a general lack of hierarchi-cal markers besides the crown of Frederick and the enthroned Isabella, the beloved *domna*. The image represents both the performance of the song (the troubadour playing) and the subject matter of the song (Frederick giving the rose to Isabella) with an enigmatic mediator (Lord Alberico listening or reflecting on the idea of the song?). By staging a troubadour song with real figures of Frederick's intimate circle, the fresco succeeds in what C. Jean Campbell calls "transforming history into song" as a "representation of po-etic diplomacy."[70] As a troubadour-king, Frederick performs as a love pro-tagonist in an incarnation of *fin' amor* and its ethical values.

The Cantigas de Santa María: *Alfonso as Troubadour-King Unifies the Religious Devotion of his Kingdom*

Alfonso X belonged to a group of able European statesmen vying for the throne of the Holy Roman Empire during the interregnum after Freder-ick's death in 1250 and the decline of the Hohenstaufen dynasty. Despite being connected dynastically to the Hohenstaufen and particularly interested in the imperial-Italian nexus of the German crown, Alfonso was unable to fulfill his imperial ambitions of expanding the borders of his peninsular kingdom because of domestic affairs. Such problems included the rebellion of the noblemen in 1270, Castilian defeats in Andalusia by North African invaders in 1275, and the disputed struggle for succession. Yet these are the years from which the greatest cultural achievements of Alfonso's court emerge, such as the *Cantigas de Santa María* and his treatises on astronomy and astrology. Under his direction, the *Cantigas* was compiled in three closely related codices written between 1270 and 1290. A collection of over four hundred songs in Galician-Portuguese dedicated to the Virgin Mary and the first major anthology of lyric indigenous to the Iberian peninsula, the *Cantigas* depicts the quotidian life of Alfonso's kingdom in songs and miniatures concerning miracles performed by the Blessed Virgin, and inculcates divine grace into the life of his court. The miniatures in two of the codices (Escorial T.I.1 and B.1.2) depict scenes of everyday medieval life in comic-strip style (local anecdotes, European legends, pilgrims journeying to shrines, a Jewish moneylender hoarding his profits, crusades, musicians with instruments) in which the Virgin regularly appears to dispense mercy and justice. In the opening panel of the *Cantiga de loor* 1 in the T.I.1 codex (see fig. 10), an enthroned young Alfonso appears in a tripartite panel depicting the king in his courtly world and kingdom, represented by the elaborate architecture of arches and cathedral spires in the background. In his role as supervisor or instructor to scribes in the process of compiling the *Cantigas*, Alfonso is flanked by his clerks, who take his dictation or orders on parchment rolls, while to the side of these clerks musicians tune up and wait, and courtiers read from a codex, perhaps preparing to sing the *Cantigas*.[71]

A comparison of the opening miniature of the *Cantigas* and the Bassano fresco suggests that Frederick and Alfonso, as patrons of vernacular song, envisioned themselves as troubadour-kings in different ways. Alfonso's centrality to the religious *Cantigas* represents him as the supervisor — "maker" in a universal sense — of religious vernacular verse that would convey the everyday reality of divine grace in his kingdom. Throughout the *Cantigas*, Alfonso appears among his people in the court as supervisor of his songbook (*Cantiga de loor* 1), or a troubadour discovering the Virgin Mary for his court (*Cantiga de loor* 110 and 120 [see figs. 11 and 12]). Finally, the *Cantigas* miniatures depict the details of everyday life and of song production: musicians tuning up, scribes writing, common people on pilgrimages to cities in Alfonso's kingdom, and architecture marking shrines, cities, and landscapes throughout his kingdom. Maricel Presilla has argued that part of the political program of the *Cantigas* was "territorial and political integration." It was in Alfonso's interest to establish pilgrimage sites dedicated to the Virgin to centralize his empire.[72] Through the making of the *Cantigas*, Alfonso encourages a dynamic culture of troubadour poetry, not only the translation of secular verse into Marian verse and vice versa, but a songbook that reflects Galician-Portuguese song as a popular tradition that can unite his kingdom and consolidate his power through ritualized Marian worship.

In contrast to the antiquarian interest of Frederick's court, the *Cantigas* was produced over a significant span of time, involving many artisans with the king as supervisor; these songs would have been performed regularly, according to Alfonso's will that the *Cantigas* be circulated after his death and sung on Marian feast days.[73] We know that the *Cantigas de loor* were sung, as a note to *cantiga* 418 in the Toledo codex states clearly that the songs were performed for the festivals of the Virgin during the month of August.[74] The performances probably took place in the Seville Cathedral, involving the musicians, dancers, and goliards depicted in the miniatures. The large-scale technical representation of the production, subject matter, and performance of the *Cantigas*, involving all of Alfonso's subjects throughout the kingdom, contrasts with the intimate, idealized representation of song in the fresco.

THE *CODEX MANESSE*: CULMINATION OF THE THIRTEENTH-CENTURY SONGBOOK TRADITION?

As secular rulers, Frederick and Alfonso's appropriation of vernacular song into their imperial political programs corroborates Ernst Kantorowicz's analysis of the complicated history of kingship during the Middle Ages, in that both the fresco and the *Cantigas* represent "a spiritualization and sanctification of the secular."[75] Through an apparatus of images, laws, and secular texts, the emperors sanctify their sovereignty by positioning their court and selves in the center of the cult of the *domna* or Virgin. Informed by this use of vernacular song as a means of cultural legitimization, the compilers and artists of the later Middle High German songbook tradition construct a visual vernacular, which integrates the universal language of sacred iconography and local secular traditions.

Compiled between 1300 and 1340 in Zürich, the *Codex Manesse* or *Große Heidelberger Liederhandschrift*, is a distinct product of its urban environment. Containing almost 6,000 verses from 140 poets dating from the midtwelfth century onward, and 137 full-page color miniatures, it is the most comprehensive collection of Middle High German secular verse, conveying a variety of genres and forms without musical notation. The large collection of Middle High German lyrics belonging to the patrician Rüdiger Manesse (1252–1304) and son Johannes (d. 1297) is considered to be the main source of the Heidelberg manuscript. In a lyric that appears in the *Codex* on f. 372, "Wa vunde man sament so manig liet?" (Where would one find so many songs together?), Johannes Hadlaub (fl. 1302–1340?) praises the Manesse family for their patronage of *Minnesang* and their compilation of songbooks in Zürich.[76] The literary circle to which the Manesse family belonged included secular aristocrats (upper nobility and ministerials), and prominent lay and clerical individuals who supported the patronage of art objects and literature in a city known as a thriving center of manuscript production. Scholars have compared this environment of civic self-consciousness, political autonomy, and lay cultural development to the situation of the Italian city-states in the same period.[77] Religious and secular works emerging from scriptoria in the region of Lake Constance, including the *Codex Manesse*, share stylistic and iconographical similarities characteristic of the *Kunstlandschaft*.[78]

Thus, like our earlier songbooks, though of a different milieu, the *Codex* authorizes and sanctifies its lyric for its urban readers through pictorial and organizational strategies that cite sacred and secular texts to constitute a self-sustaining myth of *Minnesang*. At least four illuminators were involved in making the miniatures of the *Codex*, and 110 miniatures are attributed to the *Grundstock-Maler* or foundation painter. In a workshop environment, artists worked in cooperation with the master compiler and scribes, and one can see that different stages were involved in composing the images, such as the preliminary draft, application of colors to figures, application of heraldry, red accents on lips, and so forth.[79] The large-scale idealized author portraits play a crucial role in this process of mythmaking, as they evoke the sacred iconography of the evangelists and other common scenes from psalters, and function as the visual equivalent of the *vidas* of the chansonniers; like these prosaic biographies they provide an extralyrical framework for the texts they introduce. The *Codex* ennobles its public by conflating social rank and the secular religion of courtly love through an emblematic vernacular of local heraldry.

The Performance of the Codex as Book and Its Emblematic Mode

The preservation of Johannes Hadlaub's panegyric about the Manesse family and their patronage of "liederbuoch" in Zürich[80] demonstrates a historical and artistic consciousness made possible through the rise of lay literacy in the cities of fourteenth-century Europe. The poetics of the *Codex* emerges from a manuscript book culture in which illuminators had several sources of visual authorities available for citation, most likely circulating in pattern or model books.[81] Significant studies have treated the complex manner in which images participate in the authority of the "I" in secular narrative texts and lyric collections; the author persona and the work could be visualized in a generic courtly scene, as an authority drawn from legal or religious visual discourses, or as a product of the patron's generosity in a dedication scene.[82] While these studies have made productive contributions to our understanding of how manuscript images construct lyric and narrative personae, I am mainly interested in the way a songbook such as the *Codex* enables readings of lyric from several perspectives of assemblage: lyric text and miniature, author corpus and miniature, and miniatures and the songbook in its entirety. For the patrons of *Minnesang*, the *Codex* allows a flexible system of self-authorization as a collection of discrete lyric texts and authors, the miniatures adding another layer of paratextual and intrinsic references. Thus rather than focusing solely on the construction of an author though its miniatures — which, as Ursula Peters has shown, ought to be studied in light of other illustrated narrative works in addition to lyric anthologies — I am concerned with what the *Codex* miniatures make available, namely, occasional rather than determinant situations of reading lyric texts.

The meaning of the *Codex* derives not from the imperial agendas of secular rulers and contemporary courtly activity, but from the productive rhetorical interaction between the songbook's visual composition and lyric texts. This rhetoric includes the formation of complex analogs between full-page author portraits and lyric corpuses, and these relations within the songbook. Such analogs make reference to local religious and secular illustrated books, sculpture, and baronial houses.[83] Through this historical distance from the authoritative role of religious or courtly iconography seen in the fresco and the *Cantigas*, the artists of the *Codex* develop what I call an emblematic mode of the book, characterized by a uniform style of monumentality and codification of courtly images played out in different ways (intertextually, intrinsically) according to the subject matter. As another layer to the open interaction of texts and images in songbooks, this craft of courtliness, particular to the urban milieu of the *Codex* and forming an integrative memorial vernacular of *Minnesang*, was an efficient mode of cultural self-stylization; another version of this stylization can be seen in the related decorative heraldry in houses of the same period in Zürich and

Basel.[84] Collectively, the full-page illustrations of the *Codex Manesse* present a unified authoritative claim different from the images of the earlier works — they are given status equal to, if not greater than, the lyric texts they introduce. Readers of the *Codex* could interpret the rhetoric of its miniatures and lyrics, and the adaptation of pictorial traditions in diverse ways, all while recognizing the emblematic vernacular as a commemoration of *Minnesang*.

The Codex *as Related to Heraldic (Verbal and Visual) Arts*

The *Codex* adapts classical and medieval heraldic traditions into a visual system that authorizes a lyric anthology of diverse poets and lyrics.[85] No fewer than 116 of the 137 miniatures in the *Codex* contain shields accompanying the poet, in addition to other knightly attributes such as crest and sword. But the fact that these miniatures contain heraldry is not what makes them heraldic; it is rather the formal organization of repeated postures or gestures, the balanced two-dimensional organization of images within the frame of blank parchment background for exaggerated abstraction, that lends the *Codex* miniatures what many scholars have called their "heraldic mode."[86] In them one can see two aspects of heraldic verbal description. First, the verbal translation of a material object encapsulates and clearly communicates a character's status as knight errant but without explicitly alluding to a symbolic realm. Second, this same translation of heraldic plastic arts bears symbolic meaning (shields with the cross of the crusaders or the goddess of love, for example). The shields within the *Codex* miniatures contain the canonized tinctures of heraldry (gold or yellow, silver or white, red, blue, black or brown, and green) and both historically correct and imaginative arms, such as the imperial black eagle on a gold background of the opening miniature of Emperor Henry VI (d. 1197), the imperial shield insignia used since King Rudolf I of Habsburg (d. 1291), and a bird in a cage to signify Walther von der Vogelweide, an attribute taken from the poet's name. The heraldic authority of the miniatures derives not only from the symbolic value of arms alone but from the frequency of the shields in the book, giving the *Codex* as a whole a heraldic character. In other words, there is a clear visual organization within each miniature frame, as the arms are often visually repeated on the body of the poet as a stylistic effect, and possess a signifying relation to verbal texts either within or external to the *Codex*. This heraldic mode, therefore, visually communicates the status — social or poetic — of the poets. In parallel with literary texts, and clearly as a pictorial phenomenon, the poetic function of heraldry in the *Codex Manesse* produces a formal organization that invites the reader to engage with constitutive elements in each frame and to recognize their correspondence to other miniatures.

While borrowing pictorial authority from the heraldic arts, the *Codex* expands upon their translation of literary texts. Like the rose in Jean Renart's thirteenth-century *Roman de la rose ou de Guillaume de la Dole*, the compilation and placement of heraldic images in the *Codex* allow for multiple narratives of authority. A rose, shield, or cart, as extensions of the body, may act as a poetic screen "deflecting determinate readings of the proposed narrative."[87] The poetic screen of the *Codex* occurs on the level of its collected images, which form discourses of citation among different verbal and visual texts and visual conventions. In my analysis of the *Codex*'s songbook poetics, I will first show how the opening miniature of Emperor Henry acts as a metonymy for the emblematic and lyric mode of this work. I will then show how certain miniatures in the *Codex* function rhetorically to create a self-authorizing discourse of *Minnesang*.

"Ich grüeze mit gesange die süezen" and the Empty Roll: The Kaiser Heinrich Image as Shield for the Codex

The *Codex* begins with Frederick II's father, Emperor Henry VI, son of Frederick I (Barbarossa), the first Hohenstaufen and German emperor, and continues in hierarchical order according to social rank. As the opening portrait, Henry endows the poets of the *Codex* with the religious and secular nobility of Christian wisdom contained in the citation of the biblical King David and classical emperor. Here we see a precise example of how lyrics become poetry in songbooks: in this case, through the interpretation of an iconographical tradition applied to a body of lyric texts and to the entire songbook. Hugo Steger, in his analysis of the opening miniature, argues that Emperor Henry, as a *rex et propheta* figure, appears as the Davidic king who prefigures the noble poets of *Minnesang*. The portrait thus belongs to the biblical tradition that presents the king as *princeps litteratus*, model of noble poets.[88] Henry sits frontally on his throne in the ceremonial garb of a purple mantle, brown shoulder-length curly hair emerging from his crown of golden leaves, holding a lilied scepter in his right hand. Instead of David's harp or an orb, he holds an empty parchment roll (*rotulus*)—an attribute of poets. A sword appears on the left-hand side of the frame, dangling in space unattached to the king, and in the top corners appear a gold shield with the black imperial eagle of German kings and a crowned element with another black eagle attached. The Henry image also directly resembles an image of the crowning of King Solomon in an illustrated book stylistically, geographically, and historically close to the *Codex Manesse*, the *Weltchronik des Rudolf von Ems* (ca. 1270–75, f. 195). Moreover, Ewald Jammers argues that this portrait is representative of the idealized world of the *Codex*, since kings in the early Middle Ages styled themselves in the tradition of Christ in Majesty, the frontal portrait of the enthroned Christ with a mandorla.[89] Except for the roll in his left hand, Henry belongs to the iconographical tradition seen in the imperial portraits of Alfonso X in his *Cantigas* and of Frederick II in the miniatures of the *De arte venandi cum avibus* and the *Exultet*.[90] The portrait of Henry, however, combines the *princeps litteratus*–Davidic king as noble poet with the image of the classical imperial ruler.

The opening portrait differs significantly from previous troubadour-king portraits. Although Henry appears as the classical emperor like Frederick and Alfonso, the equal pictorial emphasis on secular rank and aspect as poet indicates that the poets of the *Codex* are noble because of their poetic ability rather than their membership in a court. A key indicator of this poetic nobility is that Henry holds a prominent empty roll rather than an orb: his nobility as a poet — the roll signifying the open space of orality and invention — equals or is worth more than his dominion as Hohenstaufen emperor. By way of comparison, the seated Alfonso in the opening miniature holds the *Cantigas* and points to it with his left hand, authorizing the work being done by the scribes that surround him. Frederick acts out a lyrical scene with real members of his court. Thus Henry, while embodying a *princeps litteratus*, communicates this tradition hermeneutically outward, adumbrating all the poets of the *Codex* and the concept of poetry itself.

Further, Henry's portrait alludes to pictorial conventions of sacred and secular orders without the *Codex*'s actually following a strict social ordination.[91] The *Codex* begins with an ordering of noblemen, but after the first poets there is no ranking between various classes of society such as land-holders, ministerials, and clergy.[92] The lack of strict ordering reflects social ambiguity among lesser nobility in the dynamic urban context in which the *Codex* was most likely compiled, as well as pragmatic considerations of the compiler.[93] Moreover, when comparing the heraldry of the *Codex* with a local heraldry book, the *Züricher Wappenrolle* (ca. 1335–45), the *Codex* heraldry is consistent with that source only for the first part of the songbook (the section on nobility). This further suggests that although the *Codex* artists may have used such books as a reference, they did not feel obliged to follow them consistently. Instead, they were a starting point for imaginative attributes. While none of the other portraits contains the same level of prestigious

14. Emperor Henry miniature from Codex Palatinus Germanicus 848, f. 6 (*Codex Manesse*) (ca. 1300–1340). Photograph: Universitätsbibliothek Heidelberg.

15. King David from Cosmas Indicopleustes, *Topographia Christiana* (Vat. Graec. 699, f. 63) (ninth century). Photograph: © 2012 Biblioteca Apostolica Vaticana.

attributes or iconography as Henry, many miniatures are fanciful and unmotivated by historical authenticity or even iconographical similitude. Finally, if we compare the miniatures of the related *Weingartner Liederhandschrift* (produced at the beginning of the fourteenth century in Constance), a collection that most likely shares a common exemplar with the *Codex Manesse*, we see that the *Weingartner*, though beginning with Henry, is even more loosely ordered by rank than the larger collection. In the case of both codices, then, the compilers apparently found it unnecessary to adhere to a strict social ranking of poets.[94]

Wc schalhs ist nu inder star
Dw mere er un do sagen bar
Er spich da ist Salomon
Gewihre schone in Geon
Z ekynge vbir elliv lant
Do in diz mere wart erchant

lj on welhte wurdin sin mein
Ds alle fluhin widir hein
Do o floch advni
lh in da gons alter w.
v si druhte sere sich daran
mir welhte furhten er began

16. King Solomon from *Weltchronik des Rudolf von Ems* (VadSlg Ms. 302, f. 195) (first half of the fourteenth century). Photograph: Kantonsbibliothek Vadiana, Sankt Gallen, Switzerland.

17. Frederick II from *De arte venandi cum avibus* (Pal. Lat. 1071, f. 1v) (ca. 1240). Photograph: © 2012 Biblioteca Apostolica Vaticana.

18. Frederick II from *Commendato Regis* from the *Exultet* of the Diocesan Museum "S. Matteo" of Salerno (thirteenth century). Photograph: Calò Mariani et al., *Federico II: Immagine e potere* (Venice: Marsilio, 1995).

The loose hierarchical ordering of the *Codex* and the pictorial variety of the other miniatures suggest that the portrait of Henry should be considered representative of the heraldic style or motive that encompasses the entire *Codex*. On a blank parchment background, the king sits in the middle of the frame, a quadrant divided into four spaces. This division of the miniature frame into four quadrants is consistent for most of the portraits; these quadrants are easily recognizable by virtue of the fact that most miniatures contain heraldic attributes in the upper two quadrants of the frame. The sword's unconventional placement in the frame reinforces the impression that the object is placed there not only for narrative or descriptive purposes but to formally balance out the space so that the viewer sees all the various attributes surrounding the enthroned king as equally significant — an important quality of the visual emblematic mode.[95] In its two-dimensional quality as *Wappensymbol*, Henry's image effectively conveys, as a sort of shield to the entire *Codex*, a courtly style of a unified pictorial vernacular. Both sacred and secular pictorial traditions are balanced out in the quadrants and songbook according to different combinations of intrinsic or intertextual sources.

Finally, the empty roll that fills out the space to the right of the king is a typical image symbolizing the poetic production of the *princeps litteratus* and *Minnesang*, and is crucial for our interpretation of King Henry as shield to the *Codex*. Michael Curschmann argues that the king's roll, different from a *Spruchband* or speaking banner, fits into a secular iconography of the *Codex* that suggests a near coexistence of oral and written communication in cultural and historical terms: such blank rolls may suggest either oral performance of lyric texts or written texts.[96] Throughout the *Codex*, blank rolls of varying sizes have different functions in the miniatures.[97] A smaller roll may represent a love letter or song in the miniature of Graf Konrad von Kirchberg (24r). In the miniature of Reinmar von Zweter (323r), the blind poet is seen deep in thought but apparently dictating one of his songs to a girl, who is writing on a roll, and a scribe is copying on a diptych filled with wax. A roll represents lyric production and enables spiritual *conversio* in the miniature of Heinrich von der Mure (75v). In her studies of poet images in troubadour and *trouvère* chansonniers, Huot notes how the scroll (which appears similar to the roll in the *Codex*, with a vertical orientation) is associated with both oral performance and lyric composition, even as it also represents a written text.[98]

The roll in author portraits similar to that of Emperor Henry, like those of Heinrich von Veldeke and Walther von der Vogelweide (30r and 124r), figures prominently as a symbol of poetic production in the *Codex*. Curschmann compares the rolls of the *Codex Manesse* to the convention of Christian iconography as indicated by a cleric such as Guillaume Durant (d. 1296) in his *Rationale divinorum officiorum*: the empty rolls in the *Codex* indicate the dynamic process of word to writing. Similarly, the rolls of the patriarchs symbolize their "imperfecta cognitio" as the process of their revelation, whereas the written word as "perfecta cognitio" is represented by the books held by the Apostles.[99] The *Codex* rolls represent not only the process of poetic production but, for the reader, the activation of memory through a symbol that is ultimately an empty—and thus potential—signifying frame. As a poetic attribute, the empty roll signifies a canonized tradition, yet requires the viewer to imagine, through the *Codex*'s words and text, the lyric performance. This process of memory relates to what Richart de Fournival, canon of Amiens Cathedral in 1240 and later chancellor, describes in the preface to his picture book *Li Bestiares d'Amours* as the two gates with equal access to memory: *painture* and *parole*. As Carruthers points out, both verbal and visual texts produce mental images that one sees in the present (*veir*).[100] The empty roll of Emperor Henry affirms the prestige of the *Minnesang* tradition through its citation of sacred and secular iconography, while also provoking the image of a temporal poetic performance of a lyric text.[101]

By serving as a space and sign for a developing secular and vernacular iconography of oral and written production, the multifunctional roll facilitates a dynamic process of memory. It acts as an instrument for readers to imagine poetry and poets in different ways, while also creating a hermeneutic of the *Codex*. In keeping with the lay and municipal environment of the *Codex*, the roll also coincides with images of charters or scrolls traditionally serving as emblems of legal transactions. For example, the Henry image, Ewald Vetter observes, may have a direct connection to contemporary images in privilege collections of the thirteenth to fourteenth centuries, such as the *Kopialbuch* of Saint Florian.[102] Such privileges, in which images of seated kings with documents act as official records of legal transactions or feudal protection, converge with twelfth-century images of Cicero seated with a scroll and the title "Orator" indicated below him.[103] These images also contain attributes of office or rank, such as classical architectural surroundings, and often have a person of smaller size, symbolizing his lower social standing, receiving the written scroll. The illustrative strategies of official legal bulletins and authors involving scrolls in privilege collections or legal documents of ranked noblemen may often overlap with the *rex et propheta / princeps litteratus* traditions.[104]

Like the immediate communicative function of these official bulletins or the heraldic arts, Henry's portrait grants a visual stamp of authority to the book without subscribing to a strict social or sacred hierarchical order of signified meanings or allegory. The first lines of the first lyric of the entire *Codex*, "Ich grüeze mit gesange die süezen / die ich vermîden niht wil noch enmac" (I greet with song the sweet one whom I will not and cannot let go), conform to the portrait of the emperor as a courtly lover, "Mir sind diu

19. Walther von der Vogelweide miniature from Codex Palatinus Germanicus 848, f. 124 (*Codex Manesse*) (ca. 1300–1340). Photograph: Universitätsbibliothek Heidelberg.

20. Privilege image from *Kopialbuch* (Ms. 101b, f. 18v) (1276–79). Photograph: Stiftsarchiv, Saint Florian, Austria.

rîche und diu lant undertân / swenne ich bî der minneclîchen bin" (Riches and lands are my subjects, whenever I am by my loved one).[105] Like Frederick in the Bassano fresco, he depicts himself in these lines as a troubadour-king who submits to the code of love. Yet the effect of this miniature is much different from the monumental fresco in the baronial house, for it is not a mise-en-scène involving members of the court but an official portrait. Performance, as signified by the empty roll rather than ideally represented on

21. Privilege image from *Kopialbuch* (Ms. 101b, f. 18v) (1276–79). Photograph: Stiftsarchiv, Sankt Florian, Austria.

a wall in situ, or technically depicted in the *Cantigas*, acts upon the memory of the reader through reflection of the poet's texts and image in the portrait. Finally, the emblematic mode of the opening image allows a flexible framework for authoritative citation and abstraction of these visual traditions. This efficacious style of the *Codex* communicates poetic worthiness by deploying a plurality of traditions and poets.

22. Privilege image from *Kopialbuch* (Ms. 101b, f. 39v) (ca. 1310). Photograph: Stiftsarchiv, Sankt Florian, Austria.

The Rhetoric of the Miniatures: Topoi *and* Figurae

How did people read the *Codex*'s lyrics and texts, and how is reading this songbook different from reading other illustrated vernacular texts? In her discussion of Gregory the Great's letter to Serenus (ca. 600) on how one should learn from images, Carruthers astutely points out that according to Gregory, "picturing" is a rhetorical activity in that the reader must "internalize," "familiarize," and "domesticate" the picture in order to understand a *historia* (the text or story worth venerating, in Gregory's view) to which it refers. This rhetorical activity involves committing images to an activity of both *lectio* and *meditatio*—reading and meditation—in order to compose a *historia* that will be remembered.[106] This theory applies to picturing as a rhetorical activity in the *Codex*, because its miniatures allegorize or gloss lyric texts and cite both sacred texts and local works. If we compare the prominence of the full-page miniatures to the illustrations in troubadour songbooks, it is evident that images play a greater role in shaping the reader's interpretation and memorialization of *Minnesang*. Perhaps a distinct product of the social and historical environment from which the *Codex* emerges, this rhetorical conception of *picturae*—the performance of the *Codex*—makes present the absent voices and ideas of *Minnesang* in a manner that reflects an increasing desire in the late Middle Ages of *repraesentare* (in the original Latin sense of

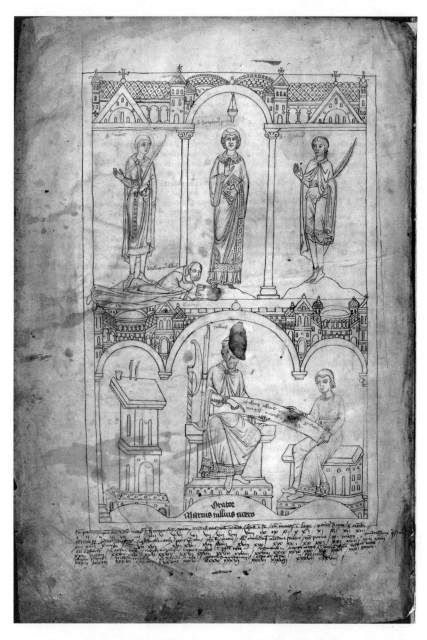

23. Cicero as "Orator" (Ms. Lat. f. 252, f. 1v) (ca. 1150–58). Photograph: Staatsbibliothek Preußischer Kulturbesitz.

the derived term *praesens*): remembering *Minnesang* by making it present in time through both word and picture.[107] In other words, the songbook commemorates *Minnesang* by asking the reader to reproduce lyric poetry through his own rhetorical construction of verbal and visual texts. We can assume that the *Codex*'s artists, compilers, and readers employed classical and medieval rhetorical practices of both verbal composition and reading to the miniatures and lyric texts. Repeated images and gestures constitute a vernacular consisting of *topoi* and *figurae* in visual terms. Silhouette-type figures in the miniatures allow for a visual *ars dictandi*, the composition of similar poses within a consistently delineated frame, producing a heraldic visual system that contains variety within a stable overarching framework. Such heraldic authority through a uniform style is encapsulated in the portrait of Henry.

In addition to Gregory's theory of visualizing *picturae*, the theorization of rhetoric in the twelfth century also serves as a foundation for adapting rhetorical principles to the *Codex*'s program of images. For example, Thierry of Chartres develops Cicero's conjunction of wisdom and eloquence by emphasizing the ethical role of rhetoric in civil affairs.[108] Wisdom and rhetoric bind communities together as a civil science ("scientia civilis"), or the science of both speaking and acting according to reason ("civilis ratio"). This ethical application of rhetoric may have influenced later artists and readers: they visualized the eloquence of the *Minnesang* as a visual and verbal art of speaking well that brings a community together — the songbook as a product of a "civil science." Keeping in mind Gregory's spiritual idea of picturing as a rhetorical activity, and the ethical application of rhetoric in civic affairs, let us now look at some examples.

Figurae

In considering grammar, the first of the seven *artes* and the foundation for all of them, Quintilian tells us that it has two parts, "scientia recte loquendi," the science of correct speech, and "enarratio poetarum," the study of the poets (*Institutio oratoria* I.4.2).[109] Grammar concerns language as an instrument of discourse, and rhetoric comprises the entire effect of forms of language, audience, and meaning. Figures or *figurae* were considered part of grammar: for figures of language, these included anaphora (repetition of words at the beginning of clauses) and homeoteleuton (similarity of endings); and for figures of thought, they included litotes, metonymy, and allegory.[110] What are the visual *figurae* in the *Codex* that serve as translations or glosses of lyric texts, or *enarratio poetarum*? How do these *figurae* achieve the overall rhetorical effect of attributing cultural value to the *Minnesang* tradition?

First, we have already considered how the roll acts as a visual metonymy for the poet and his works. Affirming Curschmann's analysis that the empty roll, as attribute, poetic exchange, or official bulletin may encompass a range between oral and written communication, we might say that the metonymic roll stands in for the prestige of the poet and his production.

Second, as pointed out by Kurt Martin, the ubiquitous coats of arms, shields, and crests as heraldic signs signify much more than the features of a face in the miniature of Wolfram von Eschenbach (149v).[111] Their formulaic articulation connects the persona to a greater social order or courtly imaginary. For example, a visual anaphora occurs in the miniatures where the same heads appear in the coat of arms and crest, such as the Lady in Frauenlob (399), or the priest's head in Herr Pfeffel (302). These recurring faces are positioned in the same upper quadrants of the frame, within the repeating attributes of shield and crest.

Inspiring knights to embark on virtuous quests of honor or symbolizing the art of courtship between a man and a woman mediated by a lyric text,[112] Love in its various guises collectively constitutes a visual grammar of *figurae*. The shield in the miniature of Alram von Gresten (311) and the crested helmet of Ulrich von Lichtenstein (237) allude to Love in its various disguises as emblem or allegorical figure; in the former the word "Amor" is inscribed on a silver shield on a blue band between a knight and lady. The lady reads a book with the first lines of Ulrich von Zazikhoven's "Lanzelet," "Who is skilled at remembering words, think wisely."[113] Behind the couple a tree fills the background, its branches forming a heart around the shield, which is not a personal shield but the shield of Love. The centrally positioned shield and the heart-shaped branches incorporate the lovers, becoming a figure through which to read the couple's interactions, just as the couple try to 'read' each other's thoughts as characters in a romance. Although verbal *figurae*, such as the shield in the miniature of von Buchein (271) that contains an inscription on an open book, "MINNE / SINNE / TWINGET / STRALE / QVALE / BRINGET" (Love compels the senses; his dart brings anguish), also evoke the metaphor of Love as wounding the lover, such *figurae* are categorically different from the symbolic centrality of the *Amor* shield in the miniature of Alram von Gresten enclosed within a heart.

For composing their miniatures, artists of the *Codex* also drew from heraldic description, *topoi* from antiquity, vernacular texts, and media

24. Frauenlob miniature from Codex Palatinus Germanicus 848, f. 399 (*Codex Manesse*) (ca. 1300–1340). Photograph: Universitätsbibliothek Heidelberg.

25. Pfeffel miniature from Codex Palatinus Germanicus 848, f. 302 (*Codex Manesse*) (ca. 1300–1340). Photograph: Universitätsbibliothek Heidelberg.

26. Alram von Gresten miniature from Codex Palatinus Germanicus 848, f. 311 (*Codex Manesse*) (ca. 1300–1340). Photograph: Universitätsbibliothek Heidelberg.

27. Ulrich von Lichtenstein miniature from Codex Palatinus Germanicus 848, f. 237 (*Codex Manesse*) (ca. 1300–1340). Photograph: Universitätsbibliothek Heidelberg.

1. (left) Historiated initial showing face of Christ from *Chansonnier R* (Bibl. Nat. fr. 22543, f. 5) (fourteenth century). Photograph: Bibliothèque nationale de France.

2. (right) Historiated initial showing Peire Cardenal/Saint James/ pilgrim from *Chansonnier R* (Bibl. Nat. fr. 22543, f. 67) (fourteenth century). Photograph: Bibliothèque nationale de France.

3. (right) Historiated initial showing Crowned Mary from *Chansonnier R* (Bibl. Nat. fr. 22543, f. 103v) (fourteenth century). Photograph: Bibliothèque nationale de France.

4. (top) Marginalia from *Chansonnier N* (Ms. 819, f. 56r) (late thirteenth century). Photograph: The Pierpont Morgan Library, New York.

5. Christ's Capture from the *Donaueschinger Psalter* (Cod. Don. 186, f. 11)
(ca. 1260–70). Photograph: Württembergische Landesbibliothek, Stuttgart.

28. von Buchein miniature from Codex Palatinus Germanicus 848, f. 271 (*Codex Manesse*) (ca. 1300–1340). Photograph: Universitätsbibliothek Heidelberg.

such as ivory caskets dealing with courtly love and illuminated psalters. For example, miniatures of war and knights on horseback recall epic ekphrasis from antiquity to medieval times.[114] The clearest visual adaptation of formulaic style seen in medieval poetry consists of the heraldic signs and emblematic character of the *Codex*. Finally, many miniatures contain images of courtly love motifs: love service toward women; falconry; animals of love such as squirrels, rabbits, and lapdogs; and flowering trees associated with springtime love. We also see conventional interactions between couples, such as ritualized clasped hands in a formal ceremony of union, or a game of chess signifying the game of courtship.[115]

Rhetorical Composition in the Codex

Employing visual *figurae* drawn from the *topoi* and metaphors of courtly love, the artists of the *Codex* used the rhetorical techniques of *inventio, elocutio,* and *dispositio,* adapted to a particular visual vernacular. Starting with an existing lyric, they probably devised a general conception (invention), arranged it in the space of the page (disposition), and devised a unified visual style (elocution). In analyzing their outcomes, however, I will address these terms not as part of a process but as heuristic aspects of the *Codex* that enable us to see a visual vernacular under construction. While isolating these aspects for the purpose of analysis, I do not imply that certain rhetorical techniques were functional to the exclusion of others. Accordingly, in discussing how the artists deploy these procedures throughout the *Codex* to unify the collection, and to create correspondences between text and image, I will first describe disposition and elocution, since in visual terms these techniques are most apparent when the miniatures are consulted side by side, and most significant when the book is interpreted as an overall corpus with a heraldic style. In a close analysis of a few key miniatures, I will then discuss invention, the most important technique, for it concerns how the artists visualize lyric texts in terms of subject matter and treatment and thus encompasses the other two techniques. By using these terms to describe the *Codex* as a rhetorical text, I intend to show how it represents a communal engagement involving both artists and public, who compose in different ways. The artists, who read the lyric texts rhetorically, compose visual texts; likewise their public, readers of the *Codex*'s texts and images, read images rhetorically. Thus my analysis of the rhetoric of the *Codex* accounts for a text that involves its creators and its public at different points in time and according to different contextual situations.

Dispositio

Originally in antique rhetoric, "disposition" was part of invention in that it was related to the five sections of the oratory. In the *Codex Manesse*, the artists of the miniatures arranged and ordered images according to poet and limitations of the frame, just as a medieval speaker or writer ordered his text according to subject matter and occasion. In classical oratory, one began with an exordium or introduction, and then moved to the narrative or exposition of the facts. In troubadour love lyric, a *canso* should open with a springtime description, rather than end with it. As noted previously, a shield and a crested helmet, when included, are usually placed in the upper quadrants of the frame. Deliberate placement of images within the frame was likely facilitated by the fact that, in the process of creating the miniature in the workshop, a master artist oversaw the heraldic unity between figures and attributes.[116] A pair of figures often occupies a balanced division of space, emphasized by the shield and crest that hangs above them, such as the couple in the portrait of Burkhart von Hohenfels (110r) or Reinmar der Alte (98r). Artists also used space to intensify the tension between lovers, such as the chess scene of Göli (262v) and the "Liebestrank" (love potion) of von Buchein (271r).[117] The use of empty parchment space is striking compared to the likely pictorial influences of the *Codex*, in which we see the background consistently filled with architectural details or other figures (see, for example, the Donaueschinger Psalter, ca. 1260–70 [plate 5]). The frontal position of the knight Wachsmut von Künzigen (160v) is an arresting adaptation of the knight on horse conventionally seen from the side, as in the portrait of Heinrich von Rugge (122r) for example, or the historiated initial of Bertran de Born in the troubadour chansonnier A, f. 189 in the Vatican.

Diverse frontal positions emphasize the emblematic character of the images. The frontality of Wachsmut, seeming to come forward out of the frame, is accentuated by the identical dogs at his sides, their noses pointing in the direction of the knight's sharply pointed boots. Arthur Haseloff notes that this frontal image may have been influenced by similar images in liturgical manuscripts, such as the frontal image of Saint George on horseback in an initial of the fifty-first Psalm.[118] While Wachsmut, either menacing or foreboding, is the embodiment of knighthood, Tannhäuser (264), who wears the garb of the Order of Teutonic Knights and seems to be walking on air, with vines on each side of him, symbolizes religious veneration.[119]

29. Wachsmut von Künzigen miniature from Codex Palatinus Germanicus 848, f. 160v (*Codex Manesse*) (ca. 1300–1340). Photograph: Universitätsbibliothek Heidelberg.

30. Tannhäuser miniature from Codex Palatinus Germanicus 848, f. 264 (*Codex Manesse*) (ca. 1300–1340). Photograph: Universitätsbibliothek Heidelberg.

Diction and Relative Disposition

If as part of their rhetorical art of invention, artists chose a *topos* to treat their subject material, and composed this *topos*—theme, image, motif—into a proper order, then we can designate the application of color and decorative apparatus (*ornatus*) as the diction (*elocutio*) of their rhetorical art. Diction, in terms of speaking or writing, treats the style or decoration of discourse through choice of words and figures of speech (*Institutio oratoria*, VIII.2.1, 3.1). As the application of color to the preliminary sketchings was done in separate stages, we can assume that the ornate details of colors and decoration were applied toward a uniform heraldic style that could be amplified and abbreviated. A stylistic anaphora, as against the figural anaphora of Frauenlob or Pfeffel or the narrative anaphora that I will discuss later in relation to invention, produces a style that embodies a visual ornamentation of "cohesion and multiplicity." I take these terms from Eugène Vinaver's description of medieval vernacular epic and romance composition (works presented "like an organism that unites two seemingly contradictory principles: that of cohesion and that of multiplicity"),[120] to emphasize how these two principles can function on different textual and visual levels. Medieval literature and images draw from a common storehouse to give form to an idea under conventional rhetorical codes, but visual images in the *Codex* convey this variation and invention of *topoi* using a grammar specific to the material framework of the songbook and available references. For instance, in the images of knights such as Wachsmut, Heinrich von Rugge, Walther von Mezze, or Hartmann von Aue (184v), a vivid repetition of crest, shield, and banner exists within a unified coat of arms. In the images of Ulrich von Lichtenstein, Walther von Mezze, or Hartmann, this unified decorative element is further emphasized by the heraldic signs positioned in the same direction on a blank background, and by the frequently fanciful aspect of these signs as purely ornamental or onomastic.

This ornamental quality across different portraits also works in tandem with the relative disposition of similar meditating poet types such as Heinrich von Veldeke, Rudolf von Neuenburg (20), and Walther von der Vogelweide. All of these portraits depict the poets seated with their left hands on their knees and their heads inclined toward a roll that they either hold (Rudolf) or point to (Walther and Heinrich). Variations of the seated, meditating poet type signify an oral performance, a known lyric text, or a state of meditation. In Walther's image, the portrait depicts the first line of his famous *Spruch*, "Ich saz ûf eime steine / und dahte bein mit beine"

31. Hartmann von Aue miniature from Codex Palatinus Germanicus 848, f. 184v (*Codex Manesse*) (ca. 1300–1340). Photograph: Universitätsbibliothek Heidelberg.

(I sat on a stone, and covered one leg with the other),[121] and the empty roll symbolizes the lyric text of the meditating poet. The space in Walther's portrait intensifies his meditating act and the singularity of his poetic style and persona. In contrast to the stark, empty background surrounding Walther, flowers and birds surround Heinrich; this springtime background of love informs our interpretation of his meditating gesture, as it inspires the future lyric product that the empty roll signifies. This portrait also suggests the subject and style of an earlier poet, known to be the founder of courtly *Minnesang*. Finally, in the portrait of Rudolf, the speaking gesture of his right hand and the focus on the roll he is holding suggest a poet in the act of composing. Clearly these various treatments of similar disposition, what Hella Frühmorgen-Voss calls "Bildtypen" of author or genre portraits, function rhetorically to shape different conceptions of the poet.[122] Invention, the most important division of rhetoric, arises from a visual *topos* involving specific figures or motifs and a deliberate, formal order of disposition.

Invention: Scriptural Rhetorical Performance in the Codex

Until now I have been applying the principles of classical and medieval rhetoric to the work of the *Codex* artists: how did they provide a persuasive image that emblematized the troubadour and his texts, and how can their techniques of deploying certain figures, themes, or stylistic strategies be seen as rhetorical acts of *dispositio* and *elocutio*? In deploying an effective language of signs, what do these images actually communicate to the reader of the *Codex*? That is to say, what is the act of *inventio* for the artists as readers of the lyric texts and, on the other hand, for the readers of the images that the artists produce?

To explore this last question, one can study how artists invent a scriptural narrative from verbal material in certain miniatures. In his *De doctrina christiana*, Augustine describes this invention as finding a "res," or interpretation as discovering scriptural truths that will be expounded through preaching (1.1).[123] Although it is apparent from the *Codex* that the artists draw equally from secular (courtly) and sacred texts, a quality that in many ways draws them closer to the rhetoric of classical oratory than to Augustinian hermeneutics of the scriptures, certain images demonstrate that artists interpreted lyric texts by means of images that privilege scriptural truth. In other words, they visually invent an Augustinian *res* that ennobles secular lyric, and teaches lay readers the cultural value of *Minnesang*.

32. Rudolf von Neuenburg miniature from Codex Palatinus Germanicus 848, f. 20 (*Codex Manesse*) (ca. 1300–1340). Photograph: Universitätsbibliothek Heidelberg.

Hadlaub and Noli me tangere

The lyrics of Johannes Hadlaub, citizen of Zürich, survive only in the Manesse codex; while he was not a member of the nobility, his praise of the literary patronage of important nobles and citizens in the region is significant for understanding the *Codex* as a book of self-authorization. Due to the geographical and temporal proximity of Hadlaub to the manuscript, scholars speculate that he himself may have collaborated with the patron and artists of the *Codex*.[124] The miniature emphasizes the importance of this poet, the most prolific of the Swiss *Minnesänger*, by its unique layout and *historia*. The privileging of his work accords with striking qualities of Hadlaub's corpus: it begins with a particularly large, richly ornamented initial, appears in a unique scribal hand,[125] and leaves no space for inclusion of further poems, indicating that this corpus was perceived to be complete.[126]

Further, the Hadlaub miniature (371r) is one of only two in the entire corpus of the *Grundstock* to use a bi-zonal layout of an upper and lower zone (see plate 6).[127] The other miniature is of Klingsor von Ungerlant (219v), suggesting that the format of these miniatures was important for the use of *historia*. Not only does the bi-zonal division of space imitate the frame organization of miniatures in illustrated biblical and epic texts,[128] but the miniatures of Klingsor and Hadlaub both relate to central scenes from scripture. The miniature of Klingsor represents the legendary *Wartburgkrieg* of the court of Count Hermann I of Thuringia in the early thirteenth century. In this court *Sangspruchgedichte* were composed and collected; in his romance *Parzival*, Wolfram von Eschenbach famously describes this collection of song competitions. The artist cites the sacred iconography of the Last Judgment, Christ in Majesty, and the Crowning of the Virgin to visualize the authority of the *Landgrafen* in the contest and the mythic solemnity of the occasion.

The artist of Klingsor von Ungerlant's miniature cites a sacred *historia* to interpret (rhetorically invent in Augustinian terms) a legend of *Minnesang*. The worthiness of "Gesang" is demonstrated by visualizing this scene through Christian truth; the image of the *Wartburgkrieg* represented in the dual scenes appears as the *res* of sacred judgment. To emphasize the veracity of this image as an authentic document, moreover, the famous competing poets are identified by name: "Walther von der Vogelweide, her Wolfram von Eschenbach, her Reinmar der alte, dertugenhafte Schriber, Heinrich von Ofterdingen unt Klingesor von Ungerlant." This sacred coherence synthesizes different poetic and historical realities: while Wolfram and Walther

33. Klingsor von Ungerlant miniature from Codex Palatinus Germanicus 848, f. 219v (*Codex Manesse*) (ca. 1300–1340). Photograph: Universitätsbibliothek Heidelberg.

mention being at the court of the count of Thuringia in their lyrics, Klingsor is a character in Wolfram's *Parzival*.

The Hadlaub citation of *Noli me tangere*, or "Christ appears to Mary Magdalene," is a more complex interpretation of scenes from the first two songs of Hadlaub's corpus. The top panel, depicting a scene from the second text in the lyric corpus, depicts the fainting poet surrounded by his friends in a castle. His companions have arranged a meeting between a lady and the poet, the lady refusing her suitor despite his claiming to have loved her since they were children, "Ích diene ír sît daz wir beidiu wâren kint" (I have served her faithfully since we were both children).[129] As the rejected lover faints, his friends hold him up and place her hand in his. In the lyric, the poet refuses to let go of her hand, and she bites his hand to be released from it. The artist offered his own interpretation of this text by having the lady's spotted lapdog bite the poet's hand. The bottom scene from the opening song of the corpus, a separate scene but visually related to the first by the church tower occupying the right side of both the frames, and the aforementioned dog in the arms of the lady, shows how the poet disguised himself as a pilgrim to hide a love letter in his beloved's robes as she leaves church: "Ích nàm ir achte / in gewánde als ein pílgerîn, / so ich heinlîchste machte, / do sî gieng von mettîn" (I watched out for her, in the dress of a pilgrim so I could do it secretly as she left early Mass).[130] We see in the panel the lady reacting in a shocked manner: "ist daz ein tobig man?" (is this a madman?) The dog plays a key role in recognizing the poet, and indicates how the artist used the songbook format for his own interpretation of the lyric texts.[131]

Further, the dog plays a part in the religious citation. The bottom panel cites *Noli me tangere* but reverses the roles of Christ and Mary: instead of Christ rejecting the prostitute, it is the virtuous lady who rejects the disguised and devious suitor. By citation and reversal — the penitent Mary Magdalene now the disguised pilgrim, and the lady as the unstained Christ who must rise to his Father first after the Annunciation — the artist shows the supposed holiness of the poet's pilgrim disguise and the dog as replacing the central gesture of Christ forbidding contact. The dog may be seen as a humorous and playful interpretation as well as a practical one, placing the top and bottom scenes in interpretive relation to each other (narrative anaphora). Yet like the *Wartburgkrieg* miniature, this image persuades the reader of Hadlaub's central importance to the community of the *Manesse* — the poet proving himself as courtly lover among his peers — and signifies the worthiness of his lyric as embodying virtue. The dog functions as mediator between lady and poet to emphasize the intensity of near touch in both the scriptural and courtly stories, and directs the reader to view the scene of courtly desire as a foil for a spiritualized desire symbolized by Mary Magdalene.

Through the use of exegetical rhetorical procedure — the finding of *historiae* in the lyric texts — the artists translate the sacred idea of Christ's tangibility into a secular one. The dog is not a symbol but rather the enigmatic presence of a kiss longed for, and whose sensual presence lingers in the memory of the lover: "Ir bîzzen was so zartlich, wîblich, fîn, / des mir wê tet, daz so schiere zergangen was. / mir wart nie baz, daz muoz wâr sîn!" (Her bite was so tender, womanly, and dignified, that it pained me that it was over so soon. It was never better for me, you can take my word for it.)[132] The citation of *Noli me tangere* confronts sensuality with Christian morality: the poet's love as excessive or misguided (dressing up as a pilgrim and insulting the sanctity of his lady's piety, part of her essential worthiness). Such a reading accords with a penitent Mary Magdalene, who, despite being in the presence of risen Christ must concede to Christ's return to the Father and his role in the greater Christian worldview. The shield at the bottom left of the Hadlaub miniature, depicting the same black squirrel on the shoulder of Heinrich von Vedelke but with the addition of a red collar to match his red tongue, suggests that Hadlaub not only is at the mercy of the lady but has succumbed to earthly desires of the flesh. In the case of Heinrich, the poet's head turned away from the squirrel and his pointing gesture toward the empty roll seems to indicate that he has sublimated his desire as poiesis. In contrast, Hadlaub's head turned away from the squirrel in the context of the *Noli me tangere* suggests the unresolved struggle between spiritual and earthly concerns. Furthermore, the direction of the squirrel and his tongue mimes the direction and appearance of the dog, reinforcing the duality of the scene that plays upon courtly love, sacred iconography, and the attachment of the poet to his lady. The dog and the reversal of the *Noli me tangere* represent specific examples of invention: discovering sacred *historiae* through creative, anecdotal exposition of lyric scenes.

These scenes of pleasurable suffering, involving the lover and his unapproachable lady, are of course common to many medieval artworks that thematize carnal love. Like caskets depicting courtly scenes that were private objects of moveable property — dowry by the bride's family at marriage — the *Codex*, as lyric anthology, is a physical container of texts representing feudal transactions. For the suitor, the casket acts as a public statement about economic and erotic commitment, embodying a courtly ideal of virtue.[133] The

Hadlaub miniature in a 35 × 25 cm monumental book, depicting the *fin'amor* ideology of submission and fidelity to the lady, signifies the communal bonds of the *Manessekreis* through the local culture of *Minnesang*. In the Hadlaub scene, the artist visually interprets Hadlaub's praise of the Manesse patronage well in that the visualization of the poet's submission to his lady signifies his loyalty to his patrons and morals in the larger context of the memorial book. These courtly images within objects create unambiguous public statements of cultural value or sociopolitical obligations. We might say that the *Codex,* like caskets, established economic and social bonds among families who claimed the *Minnesänger* as their cultural heritage.

Reinmar von Brennenberg: A vida *of Christian Martyrdom*

Just as the Hadlaub and *Wartburgkrieg* miniatures use religious iconography to invest the poets of the *Minnesang* and the patrons of the *Codex* with prestige, so the miniature of Reinmar von Brennenberg (188) also cites the Passion to impress a troubadour's *vida* into the memory of the reader (see plate 7). Like the *vidas*, this miniature most likely draws from legendary accounts and the lyric texts of the troubadour. In his *Minnesinger* edition, Friedrich von der Hagen describes Regensburg documents attesting that a certain "Reimaro de Prennenberc"—perhaps the same Reinmar of the *Codex*—a troubadour active in the mid-thirteenth century in the bishopric of Regensburg, was involved in a vendetta of Regensburg citizens that resulted in his murder.[134] Whether the miniature depicts the poet's actual murder has been debated by many scholars. Joachim Bumke and Walter Koschorreck agree that von der Hagen interpreted the Regensburg documents, only vaguely referring to a certain "Reinmar," using the *Codex* miniature depicting a murder as evidence.[135] Thus they argue that a more plausible source for the miniature's subject matter is Brennenberg's lyrics about his heart not being in his body (a lyric convention of courtly love), and the late thirteenth-century "Bremberger song," which is a version of the popular medieval "eaten heart" motif found in the *vida* of the Occitan troubadour Guillem de Cabestaing, the French *Roman du castelain de Couci*, and the *Herzmaere* of Konrad von Würzburg (a version of the *Roman*). This motif concerns a cuckolded man making his wife eat the heart of her lover (such as the poet Bremberger).[136] Thus, for his depiction of the poet, the artist might have drawn from the following: legends about Reinmar's death in 1276, Reinmar's lyrics about his separated heart, and a version of the Bremberger song in which the Princess of Austria eats the heart of the poet.

On one level, the miniature depicts a creative reading of the lyrics in the *Codex* that may have combined the legend of the vendetta murder with the lyric convention of bodily separation and the eaten-heart motif. Reinmar sings of being half a person ("sô trage ich lîbeshalp den schîn," as such I carry the appearance of half a person), and his lady as a sweet murderess ("reine süeze senfte morderin," a pure sweet and gentle murderess) who has possession of his heart.[137] While Reinmar here uses the conventional motif of his heart's not being in his body as a sign for his true love for his lady, the artist interpreted these lyrics by having the poet violently pierced in the head and heart by the swords of his surrounding attackers. Reinmar's murder alludes to the bodily fragmentation and violence in those lyric texts.

On another level, in order to establish the myth surrounding this troubadour, informed by his lyrics or the legend of his murder or both, the artist drew upon a scriptural scene to translate the verbal metaphors of the lyrics into a visual image of martyrdom. He invents a murder scene from several metaphors and motifs of one lyric (KLD 44): his body being torn in two ("enzwei geteilet," divided in two; "da ich halber bin," since I am half a person), his heart in possession of his lady ("mîn herze ist doch bî ir, swâ ich der lande bin," my heart remains by her, whatever country I am in), and his lady as a sweet murderess.[138] The miniature synthesizes and concretizes these metaphors of unrequited courtly love into one of violent death and the division of the body. This image formally cites the Passion, such as the miniature of Christ's capture on f. 11 of the Donaueschinger Psalter (see plate 5), a psalter close to the *Codex* both geographically and historically.

In the *Codex* miniature, the bottom two-thirds of the frame depict the young beardless man in courtly dress and a short sword at his hip attacked by a group of men dressed in identical headwear and sword. A double red band divides this portion of the frame from the top panel of heraldic signs. Although schematic and lacking the important iconographical details such as the kiss of Judas, the image immediately evokes the scene of Christ's capture. The formal composition draws our eye to the centrality of the victim and the movement of attack surrounding him. The relative empty background of the Brennenberg miniature starkly contrasts with the fullness of the Donaueschinger Psalter, which leaves no parchment uncovered and whose figures not only fill the frame but seem to be bursting out of it with their activity. The space between swords and feet in the *Codex* miniature heightens the multiplicity of similar actions and people involved in the murder of the serene figure. One sword goes into the head and one into the chest area, creating an angle marked by gushing red blood. This diametrical opposition, the red framework drawing the eye to the center of the murder, is further drawn out by the victim's red shirtsleeves. Color and figures work differently in the Donaueschinger miniature, in that the figures crowd around him, but our gaze is likewise drawn to the central interaction of Judas and Christ, highlighted by Judas's green cloak. The blood from Peter's victim, and his drawn sword, do not play the same central role as the stylized profusion of knives and blood of the *Codex* miniature.

The subject matter of Christ's capture, Judas's kiss and betrayal, would seem to have nothing to do with the Reinmar miniature. But the legend and lyrics of Reinmar also involve a betrayal — either by the lady or by his fellow townsmen — that influenced his depiction as a martyr unjustly killed. The Passion also narrates the inevitable separation of Christ from the earthly realm and his suffering for all mankind. By citing a scene from the Passion through a schematic organization of figures drawing from psalters or illustrated Bibles, the artist foregrounded the Christian theme of explicit bodily suffering and spiritual renewal, creating a vivid emblem of the love poet — Reinmar as Christlike figure. This theme, integral to medieval Christian consciousness, constitutes the presence of this *pictura*, in the same way the eaten-heart legend was fascinating precisely because of its perversion of the *corpus domini* and transubstantiation. Reinmar's heart as separate from him, his body unwhole and fragmented, retains this provocation of metonymy or synecdoche through the power of the image. The artist of the miniature both restores a hermeneutic wholeness to the memory of Reinmar by placing this motif in relation to Christ's capture and betrayal, and retains the lyrical oscillation of heart and body through the piercing of a centralized body in two places (brought out by the ninety-degree configuration of sword angles) and the conspicuous profusion of blood. This spilled blood is already not part of the body but an ambiguous extension of the troubadour's "lîp," which is "weder dort noch hie" yet "endelîche beide hie und dâ" (body . . . that is neither there nor here . . . ultimately both here and there).[139] In summary, the image of Reinmar is a fascinating example of how the artists of the *Codex* invented an emblematic image through an engagement of the poet's lyric texts, legends, and available verbal and visual material.

CONCLUSION

The miniatures of the *Codex Manesse* demonstrate how readers applied medieval principles of rhetoric and translation to attribute value to vernacular lyric as "poetry." Within a monumental cultural book, there were many ways to read images and texts together. At the beginning of this chapter, I emphasized how images in medieval songbooks offers readers different ways to assemble concepts of poetry and the poet from lyrics before genres such as Renaissance emblems directed the interpretation of image by text: one can think of the examples in this chapter as a prehistory of the emblem as genre. For example, the *Codex* author portraits do not reflect an archival distance from classical models. In contrast, Renaissance author portraits include classical attributes and architecture that teach the viewer the direct line of imitation from antiquity to the sixteenth century in their depiction of a scholar, an author, or a poet.[140] Moreover, medieval author portraits represent the ideals of Christian truth or the art of love, unlike the subjective author, who claims his work as his own. Artists and compilers such as those involved in the *Codex* create analogs between poet and work and between poet and poetic models, employing an emblematic mode that embodies a heterogeneous plurality of visual particulars. In the *Codex*, variety and bricolage within an authoritative visual mode represent a symbolic density or condensation of references while creating a specific idiom through the organization of space and use of heraldic attributes. As we have seen, the miniatures may translate a lyric text, a *vida*, or visual and verbal references intrinsic or external to the *Codex*, in addition to authoritative traditions. Thus the courtly culture of the *Codex* combines local traditions with universal ones, but not necessarily in a way that follows a consistent set of hierarchical values, such as the scriptural *historiae* over secular courtly love. The opening miniature of Emperor Henry and the *Wartburgkrieg* miniature depict recognizable iconographical traditions in the particular idiom of the *Codex*; yet the sword oddly placed in the frame of the Henry miniature and the particular combination of historical and literary figures of the *Wartburgkrieg* reveal attention to local sources and visual composition, as well as pragmatic concerns of balancing out the frame with all the required attributes.

For the artists and readers of the *Codex*, then, interpreting meaning from lyric texts and images tended to be an ad hoc process, culling from different sources to set up an idealized monumental figure of *auctoritas* and mediated by the practice of a visual rhetoric that I have described. The rules for envisioning the *poeta* were not yet as codified as they would become in the Renaissance, in which parameters would be set by classical models and applied to the Christian cosmological view. Rather, the medieval troubadour is an exemplar of virtue depicted in a fluid variety of forms and poses, citing a variety of authorities. The depiction of his poetic product is also informed by vernacular oral traditions, the growth of a lay literacy, and written traditions of poets as symbolized by the multifunctional roll. Furthermore, the poet may be depicted through an image exemplifying his social rank, or as a figure in a typical courtly topic, as in a hunting scene. The portrait of a Renaissance poet, imitating his ancient predecessors and alone at his desk in the study with writing tool in hand, is quite different from Walther von der Vogelweide's portrait, which, while appearing to be a sincere rendering of a reflective poet, could equally function as either a literal translation of his lyric text or an official bulletin in the manner of legal privileges (see figs. 20–22). Indeed, Renaissance portraits, in their depiction of authors as writers, are closer iconographically to the evangelist portraits or the medieval portraits of Saint Jerome or Saint Augustine than are the *Codex* miniatures. The images analyzed from songbooks suggest that the memorialization of troubadour lyric through images was conventional and ideological, but open to creative interpretation in its synthesis of references. Most important, compilers and artists of songbooks sought to memorialize this lyric in a way that would be meaningful for each songbook's public.

Chapter Four

CANCIONEROS AND
THE ART OF THE SONGBOOK

A MODERN READER who compares the Castilian cancioneros of the fifteenth and sixteenth centuries with the earlier vernacular songbooks might suppose a linear historical development. Like the Italian troubadour chansonniers that contain Occitan poets and their lyric works, the Castilian cancioneros transmit a variety of vernacular metered verse destined for public performance as song or recitation. Like the chansonniers, cancioneros are ordered by genres and authors, and contain verse of different forms and thematic content. Songbooks of both kinds reflect the tastes of their compilers or the courts in which they were compiled, as well as the often diverse linguistic backgrounds of the scribes, compilers, and poets. Also like the Italian chansonniers, many cancioneros conserve lyrics rather than melodies. Yet given these similarities, if we compare the quantitative production of verse and the numbers of poets, the differences are startling — and prompt some urgent questions about the production and reception of Castilian lyric. Consider the numbers: there are 40 extant chansonniers, 2,542 compositions, and 350 known troubadours, in addition to anonymous works.[1] The five Galician-Portuguese *cancioneiros* conserve even less lyric material; an estimated 1,679 *testi*.[2] Then consider the situation in Castilian Spain. From the final years of the fourteenth century to the first years of the sixteenth, the production of poetry conserved in lyric anthologies flourished, at least in quantity, throughout Europe but especially in the kingdoms of Aragon and Castile. More than 7,000 poems of more than 700 poets are conserved in 190 manuscripts and 221 printed anthologies.[3] How should we view the prolific production of poetry and the obsession with preserving this poetry in the cancioneros? If this is not a natural progression of the earlier troubadour chansonniers, what new episode in the life of the medieval songbook does it tell? In what terms should we view this newly self-conscious production, and how should we describe the emergence of what appears here as a full-fledged genre?

In shifting the emphasis from discrete poets and poems to the cancionero as a literary object in its own right, I argue in this chapter that the emergence of the cancionero as a genre in the Castilian tradition reflects a fundamental shift in the phenomenon of the songbook. Certainly the self-conscious publication and preservation of poetry during the fifteenth and sixteenth centuries relates to the development of composing poetry and cancioneros as an important ritual among coteries of different social classes associated with the Castilian and Aragonese courts. Unlike the traditions I have already examined, cancioneros not only serve to transmit and memorialize poetry but are literary objects with immediate relations to their social contexts.[4] I seek to explain how the cancionero, as a genre, became a form of communal production and shaped the transformation of lyric forms. In the particular sociohistorical contexts that I treat here, cancioneros comprise at once literary artifact, poetic genre, and phenomenological situation.

From the perspective of comparative songbook traditions, it becomes apparent that, unlike the troubadours, the poets of the cancioneros were acutely aware of the symbolic importance of preserving and publishing poetry in a new way.[5] When Santillana, one of the most central poets of the cancioneros, speaks of his grandmother's Galician-Portuguese "volumen"—whose contents he can explicitly recall, including poets and lyric genres—and refers to other "cançioneros,"[6] these words by a poet and owner of cancioneros represent a significant change from the Italian chansonnier tradition. In the Italian tradition, compilers and, possibly, would-be poets made anthologies of a mostly historically distant, nonnative lyric tradition, in part to associate the cultural prestige of the troubadours with their own vernacular tradition. While Santillana seems to have had access to his grandmother's Galician-Portuguese *cancioneiro* in a similar situation, it is clear from his prolific presence in the Castilian cancioneros that his coterie of poets circulated, compiled, and published lyric anthologies that included their own poetry in addition to that of poets of an older generation composing in Galician-Portuguese or Castilian. Indeed, Santillana's use of the word *cancionero* as separate from *libro* in his letter to Don Pedro demonstrates that the preservation and composition of vernacular lyric in a cancionero was a distinct literary practice.[7] As we will see in the *Prologus Baenensis* to the

Cancionero de Baena (ca. 1435–45, *Prologus* ca. 1450), the first attested cancionero, poetic treatises and cancionero rubrics represent poets' awareness of building a literary tradition by means of a book: not only compiling older vernacular poetry but consciously composing poetry for such songbooks. Moreover, the fifteenth-century genre of cancioneros and cancionero poetry reflects mainly a communal production of coteries, rather than the single-author songbook tradition seen in the Italian context following the model of Petrarch's *Rime sparse* or *Canzoniere*.

Drawing from recent scholarship that considers the cancioneros as a kind of literary production related to a distinct social context during the late medieval period,[8] I place the cancionero as genre in the context of songbook traditions. In the first part of the chapter, I compare *vidas* and *razos* of the chansonniers to the organization and the rubrics of cancioneros. The makeup of cancioneros establishes a different kind of relation between the songbook and its public, and signifies how the cancionero differs as a phenomenon. I then describe the literary and court culture of late medieval Castile to explain how cancioneros contributed to a ritualistic production of poetic knowledge and social order that involved its own forms of literary invention. In the last part of the chapter I consider how texts are grouped in cancioneros according to varying principles. These principles demonstrate how poets made sociopoetic distinctions even as they maintained memberships in their coteries and followed contemporary poetic conventions.

In the courts of Aragon and Castile between the reigns of Juan II and the Catholic Monarchs, the songbook, now as literary object and genre, functions as a site of both fluidity and stability. By fluidity I mean that the songbook expresses intertextual dialogue among poets; and by stability, that it embodies poetry as a *summa* of knowledge and as a courtly ritual. I approach this dialectic from three perspectives. First, in terms of theory and practice, Juan Alfonso de Baena, the compiler of the *Cancionero de Baena*, establishes epistemic stability through his *Prologus Baenensis* dedicated to his patron, King Juan II; his rubrics organize his songbook under certain concepts of poetic knowledge such as "graçia infusa."[9] His cancionero embodies the best art of poetry as granted by God, and he explains his reasoning in the *Prologus*. Yet while his symbolic book confers prestige and value upon the lyrics, the actual content of the *Prologus* and the poems show these concepts to be ambiguous and shifting under changing sociocultural conditions: for example, are the courtiers of cancioneros primarily lettered men (*letrados*) or aristocrats? Efforts to define the value of poetry work in tandem with efforts to justify the social status of various courtiers.

In using the word *ritual* to describe both court festivities and literary activity such as cancionero production, I depend upon Le Goff's argument that a ritual is a system that "functions only if all the essential elements are present and is significant and effective only by virtue of each one of those elements, whose meaning individually can be made clear only by reference to the whole."[10] Compiling or composing poetry for a cancionero takes place in the context of ritual activity. The material product, in turn, is the outcome of a "ritual purification of art."[11] Further, the quest for symbolic unity and hierarchical order in a range of social practices from tournaments to the publication of cancioneros emphasizes the extent to which these activities belong to a common political discourse.

Second, the cancionero represents stability by maintaining diverse content within shifting constellations of poets, topics, and formal genres. Aside from the courtly activity out of which this poetry emerged, we can assume that poets read series of dialogic poems in early circulating versions of cancioneros, which in turn shaped their mode of address as well as their lyric forms and content. As a symbolic book, the cancionero authorizes the convergence of multiple vernacular traditions and lyric forms in Castilian: *serranillas* by Caravajal (mid-fifteenth century) with shifting female personae from peasant girls to royal patrons; the *dezir* or *decir* (learned composition or recitation) that treats subject matters from astronomy to love; the inheritance of troubadour lyric, the Galician-Portuguese *cantiga*, and the *serranilla* from *the Libro de buen amor*; and the early influences of Dante and Petrarch as well as the French narrative *dit*.

Although cancioneros transmit self-defining gestures, they ultimately encourage a synthesis of views. They cultivate a decorum of cultural and social adherence that in the end displays a tissue of communal poetry, marked by what Hans Ulrich Gumbrecht would call *Assimilationsstrukturen*,[12] that is, the fluidity of "textual configurations" in a corpus of individual texts and the application of these configurations to different occasional or literary situations. The cancioneros represent poetry as a self-perpetuating mechanism of variations made paratextually rather than hierarchically. For example, Baena and Santillana are highly familiar with the circulating poetry of their contemporary peers and patrons, but their knowledge of *auctores* is often secondhand rather than from primary sources.[13] In collective poetry based on a topic or lyric form, such as a series of *serranillas* begun by Santillana, or the *Dezir a las siete virtudes* by Francisco Imperial (ca. 1350–1408), poets extend available models rather than trying to outdo or undo them.[14] This process of extension belongs to a notion of imitation that is particular to the culture of the cancionero. Such a culture promotes poetry as a communal act and as a branch of knowledge. This culture is hardly derivative or inferior but involves an awareness or mentality with certain material and humanistic horizons specific to late medieval Castile.

"LOCAL" AND "DISTANT" READINGS: FROM CHANSONNIER *VIDAS/RAZOS* TO CANCIONERO RUBRICS

From previous chapters we know that rubrics can indicate how compilers and their public conceived of poetry and the memorial function of the songbook. Given the elevated status of vernacular literature in the fifteenth century, and the social and cultural environment of Castile, do cancionero rubrics represent a memorial function of songbooks and aesthetic values different from earlier traditions? Let us start with the similarities. Julian Weiss and Garcia have argued, using Huot's and Poe's fundamental scholarship on chansonniers,[15] that the rubrics of the *Cancionero de Baena* correspond to the *vidas* and *razos* in the sense that they represent the interest of compilers in promoting the merits of the poetry for their patrons.[16] Yet both Weiss and Garcia have been careful to point out that the rubrics reflect Castilian literary models, such as the *mester de clerecía* works of the fourteenth century and the scholastic *accessus*. Further, although influenced by chansonniers or *cancioneiros* in the way that they organize lyrics by genre and poets, the compilers of the cancioneros are more directly concerned with promoting certain social coteries of lettered men and aristocratic patrons. In the *Baena*, for example, the role of Baena as compiler ("escrivano e servidor del . . . Rey de Castilla"),[17] dedicating and confirming the value of poetry to his patron in an academic prologue represents a significant development in the vernacular lyric anthology tradition.

The *vidas* and *razos* create an extralyrical fictional reality around the lyrics to produce a stabilizing image of the lyric persona. Indeed, more important than their historical accuracy as sources of information (which at times is verifiable) about the troubadour world is the way they function in relation to lyric texts, performing what Alfred Jeanroy first described as "metaphor giving rise to anecdote"; they tell us much about how medieval readers of troubadour poetry "transformed the lyric experience into prose."[18] In explaining the identity of the troubadour and the origins of love and song production, *vidas* and *razos* supply for the reader a hermeneutic framework from which to understand the troubadours and songs, thus giving these texts an archival life outside of the original performance environment through a structure of consistent qualities (birthplace, station in life, unattainable woman). For example, through Jaufre Rudel's *vida* one reads his lyrics with the image of his dying in the Countess of Tripoli's arms. The portrait of the poet accompanying the *vida* underscores this dominant image. In their supplementation of the lyric "I,"[19] these rubrics establish a permanent ideology of *fin' amor*.

In contrast, cancionero rubrics function more pragmatically, as they assume their intended audience's knowledge of the poetry and poets that they frame. Rather than reading these lyrics from a historical distance (with the notable exception of the *Prologus*, which I will discuss later), they provide the most cursory information, assuming that the reader not only recognizes but identifies with a more contemporary context of poetic production. The rubrics in the *Cancionero de Baena* possess some qualities of *vidas* and *razos* but do not seek to create an extralyrical reality for the benefit of the reader. Even when introducing a poet in the manner of the *vidas*, the rubrics do not supply an image of the poet through descriptive qualities of origin, social status, or patron. Instead, they emphasize the poet's competence:

> Aquí se comiençan las cantigas muy escandidas e graçiosamente asonadas, las preguntas e respuestas sotiles e bien ordenadas e los dezires muy limados e bien fechos e de infinitas invençiones que fizo e ordenó en su tiempo el muy sabio e discreto varón e muy singular componedor en esta muy graçiosa arte de la poetría e gaya çiençia, Alfonso Álvarez de Villasandino, el qual, por graçia infusa que Dios en él puso, fue esmalte e luz e espejo e corona e monarca de todos los poetas e trobadores que fasta oy fueron en toda España.[20]

> Here begin the well scanned and gracious sounding *cantigas*, subtle and well ordered *preguntas* and *respuestas*, and very polished and well made *dezires*, and infinite *invençiones* that Alfonso Álvarez de Villasandino made and arranged in his time, the wise and modest man and very singular composer in that gracious art of poetry and gay knowledge, and who by the *graçia infusa* that God placed in him, was the polish and light and mirror and crown and king of all the poets and troubadours that until today were in all of Spain.

Before even stating Villasandino's name, Baena describes the quality of the lyric production we are about to read (*cantigas, preguntas e respuestas, dezires*);

the poetry is qualified by a plethora of adjectives and adverbs (*muy escandidas e graçiosamente asonadas, muy limados*), certifying that the poet, as a "muy singular componedor," composes "la poetría" and "gaya çiençia": key words that the compiler has already defined and explained to his patron, Juan II, in his *Prologus*. Baena is concerned hère with using a vocabulary discussed by his literary coterie represented in the cancionero. As commentary, these rubrics do not explain lyric material as lives or events prompting a song's composition; rather, they justify the value of a poet and his works through developing contemporary concepts of "poetría": the art of composition that qualifies as a branch of knowledge or science, and a necessary skill of courtiers.

Further, cancionero rubrics often simply state the circumstance of a poem or the addressee, and thus serve an occasional, curatorial function. For example, the rubrics that continuously precede poems in the *Baena* simply identify addresser, addressee, and occasion, collectively creating a contextual tissue of close relations of repeated poet and patrons within a certain cancionero. Thus both chansonnier and cancionero rubrics reflect the social and cultural aspirations of their readers, but the cancionero compilers apply scholastic and intellectual concepts to lyrics (as a specific case in the *Baena*) or communicate practical information related above all to a contemporary social context. Another rubric of Villasandino in the *Baena* states:

> Esta cantiga fizo el dicho Alfonso Álvarez en loores del Rey don Juan, fijo del Rey don Enrique el viejo, quando reinó nuevamente.[21]

> The said Alfonso Álvarez made this *cantiga* in praise of King John, son of King Henry the elder, when he newly reigned.

Like the first rubric, the mentions of "España" and the "Rey don Juan" no longer serve as permanent reference points in the life of a poet, as they do in earlier *vidas*. Rather, they indicate one particular occasion of poetic activity: "Quando reinó nuevamente." Thus these rubrics form a different "historical" (extralyrical) picture from those of the *vidas*, and serve a different curatorial function. Rubrics express contemporary social activities of the court and a new diversity of poetic material. In general the fifteenth century sees a proliferation of various kinds of lyric forms applied to different subject matters such as the *dezir, serranilla*, and *pregunta/respuesta*.

Even in the rubrics introducing *cantigas* dedicated to a certain woman, the dynamic of courtly love changes once a poet writes a poem to his "esposa." The rubric that introduces Villasandino's *cantiga* made for his wife, stating that she has the name "Mayor,"[22] well represents the kind of amatory poetry in the cancioneros and the rubrics related to it: a socially legitimate love expressed through what is now the self-conscious literary activity of the cancionero poet replaces the secret longing for a certain "domna" in troubadour *cansos*. Here Villasandino plays with his wife's name as he reflects on his love for her: "Mayor alegría estraña / tengo agora enteramente" (Greater, strange happiness I now have entirely; lines 5–6), using the word "Mayor" to begin every *copla*. The rubric affirms this stylized literary gesture of an established tradition of love poetry by simply stating: "Esta cantiga fizo el dicho Alfonso Álvarez por amor e loores de su esposa, la postrimera que ovo, que avía nombre Mayor" (The said Alfonso Álvarez made this *cantiga* for the love and praise of his wife, the last one he had, who had the name "Mayor").

A brief glance at the most common rubrics in cancioneros such as the *Baena*, *Palacio* (ca. 1439), *Estúñiga* (ca. 1462), and *General* (1511) gives one a sense of what I call the "distant" memorial function of the *vidas* and *razos* compared to the "local" memorial function of the cancionero rubrics.[23] The regularity of the rubrics in style and function maintains common references and citations, collectively forming a corpus of a community of poets in a curatorial manner. Often they state simply poet and genre: "Cancíon de Costana,"[24] or an occasion, such as this petition by Baena: "Petiçión que fizo e ordenó el dicho Johan Alfonso para el Conde don Fadrique e Álvaro de Luna" (Request made and arranged by the said Juan Alfonso for Count Fadrique and Álvaro de Luna).[25] By contrast, although the *vidas* and *razos* use common rhetorical formulas, they reinforce the singularity of each troubadour and his or her corpus of production. A reader consulting chansonniers I and A, for example, gets a sense of a collection of poets who, while representative of courtly culture, retain their individuality rather than forming a social collective or school. The chansonniers preserve a distant phenomenological situation by means of these specific literary-historical apparatuses.

In summary, cancionero rubrics demonstrate the more self-conscious literary environment of fifteenth-century Castile because they relate the poetic activity of a close social group. Although cancionero rubrics certainly share with these chansonnier prose texts the function of preserving a body of poetry, unlike their earlier counterparts they read like a transcription of courtly activity and are rooted in a more narrowly circumscribed range of goals—whether rhetorical concepts, or the adherence to a certain court or poetic coterie. They thus describe what often appears to be a local, social situation of correspondence and dialogue among poets. While the chansonnier texts supply a historical and explanatory context for the reader, the cancioneros assume more knowledge of local politics, poets, and circulating poems from their audience.

FROM "LA MENGUA SCIENÇIA" TO "GAYA ÇIENÇIA": THE DESIRE FOR DISTINCTION AND GESTURES OF ORDER

In cancioneros we see two preoccupations of late medieval society: an interest in theorizing poetry as a form of knowledge, and the physical and material practice of poetry as part of courtly rituals, including elaborate pastimes such as jousting tournaments and hunting. Efforts to define the roles of poet and poetry in society both drive and complement the ritual display of communal ideals by aspiring courtiers and royalty. What José María Aguirre has characterized as the cancionero poets' "intellectual delight taken in the code of courtliness" relates to the practiced rituals and elaborate pageantry of the time in a manner that is more than historical. A comparison of the *Prologus* to the *Cancionero de Baena*, Enrique de Villena's *Arte de trovar* (ca. 1427–33),[26] and the chronicle of the 1428 Fiesta at Valladolid that naturalized the rise to power of the king's valet, Álvaro de Luna, suggests common underlying principles behind the theory and practice of the age. The procedural application and self-conscious display of poetic and ritual conventions prove membership in a courtly community. A courtier's competence arises despite contingent notions of social and intellectual worthiness, thus allowing poets such as Baena, Villasandino, and Luna to be competent through an application of conventions suited to their different aesthetic, social, or political interests. This generative application of conventions may seem an irrational or curiously "medieval" (in the romanticized sense of 'primitive') obsession with courtly ritual. But understanding it is essential to understanding the cancionero as a culture, a mentality, and a social phenomenon.

The Prologus Baenensis: *"graçia infusa" and the Making of a Courtier*

For Baena, *graçia infusa* occurs once the poet has mastered the art or technique of poetry, as the art

es avida e reçebida e alcançada por graçia infusa del Señor Dios, que la da e la embía e influye en aquel o aquellos que bien e sabya e

sotyl e derechamente la saben fazer e ordenar e componer e limar
e escandir e medir pos sus pies e pausas, e por sus consonates e
sílabas e açentos, e por artes sotiles e de muy diversas e singulares
nombranças.[27]

is thirsty for and ready and attainable by the *graçia infusa* of Lord
God, that gives and sends it, and influences that or those things
that well and wisely and subtly and justly know it to make and order and compose and polish and scan and regulate by its feet and
pauses, and by its consonants and syllables and accents, and by
subtle arts and very diverse and singular numbers.

Weiss argues that Baena's definition of *graçia* "amounts to little more than
a divine sanction, allowing the poet to practice what he has already learnt
after serious and dedicated study."[28] According to Baena, the causal relation
between craft and grace (*ars/ingenium*) is that grace will result from following
certain rules of versification ("fazer e ordenar e componer . . ."). In contrast,
the troubadours and Dante explain in their works how craft is inspired by
God or *Amor*—the virtuosity of *trobar* equals the intensity of their desire for
salvation or the Lady's favor and erotic consummation. One thinks of the
beginning of Bernart de Ventadorn's "Can vei la lauzeta mover," in which a
soaring bird reminds him of his longing for his lady, moving him to sing; or
Dante's "I' mi son un che, quando / Amor mi spira, noto, e a quel modo / che'
e' ditta dentro vo significando" (I in myself am one who, when Love breathes
within me, take note, and to that measure which he dictates within, I go signifying, *Purg.* 24.52–54).[29] What makes a competent poet in Baena's view is
the cultivation of a courtliness that combines the study of letters, a wisdom
acquired from an active courtly life ("aya visto e platicado muchos fechos del
mundo," has seen and told of many worldly deeds),[30] and an eloquence that
is self-consciously and explicitly performed through ritual procedures of
pretending ("que sea amador e que siempre se preçie e se finja de ser enamorado, porque es opinión de muchos sabios que todo omne que sea enamorado, conviene a saber," that one would be a lover and always pride oneself
and pretend to be in love, because it is the opinion of many wise ones that all
who are in love are agreeable to knowledge).[31] Thus eliding the true cause or
definition of poetry for its justification (*graçia*), Baena concludes his *Prologus*
describing the kind of qualities one should possess as an ideal poet, many
of them the familiar profile of the model courtier in Europe at this time.[32]

Baena's argumentative ambivalence is also clear in his *Prologus* when he

frames his defense of poetry only after describing the importance of studying history and the necessity for rulers to encourage the study and writing
of all kinds of books. He compares the benefit of "leer e saber e entender
todas las cosas de los grandes fechos" (reading and knowing and understanding everything of great deeds),[33] with other courtly pastimes (*juegos*) such as
hunting and jousting.[34] Most of this is based almost word for word on the
prologues to Alfonso X's *General estoria* and *Estoria de España*,[35] and is com-
monplace. When Baena finally gets to praising poetry, he simply adds poetry
to these other worthy activities of the court, without arguing for its virtue
on its own terms or as of greater value than the others:

> el arte de la poetría e gaya çiençia es una escriptura e conpusiçión
> muy sotil e bien graçiosa, e es dulçe e muy agradable a todos los
> oponientes e rrespondientes d'ella e componedores e oyentes.[36]

> the art of poetry and gay knowledge is a very subtle and gracious
> doctrine and composition, and it is sweet and very agreeable to all
> opponents and respondents of it and composers and listeners.

Weiss perceptively observes that Baena only implies that poetry shares the
function and effects of the previously discussed letters and courtly pastimes.[37]
Furthermore, Baena uses the term "gaya çiençia," meaning here a branch of
knowledge with its own set of rules, to lend authority to the rather weak description of poetry as "muy sotil e byen graçiosa . . . dulçe e muy agradable."
This rhetorical strategy of lateral addition and implication or *insinuatio*,[38]
rather than analytical justification and definition of poetry, underlies the
logic of cancionero production. This rhetorical turn is crucial, because it
transforms the focus of poetry from its creation to its production as a social
phenomenon. In the *Prologus*, Baena essentially says that one can be a good
poet if one is a model courtier, not that a good courtier cultivates a certain
kind of poetry, or—what we might expect—that in order to be a courtier
one must be a good poet who is inspired in a certain way. Baena's *Prologus* is
a prescriptive poetics in the sense that he lists personal conditions in which
one can achieve "gaya çiençia." But from describing why poetry is worthy
like other courtly activities, Baena goes directly to the idea that one can
have poetic grace by virtue of being a proper courtier. He emphasizes a kind
of competence defined by socially and culturally prestigious qualifications
(*graçia infusa, gaya çiençia*) ambiguously defined. These qualifications are
nevertheless achieved by playing out certain approved courtly conventions,

such as "se finja de ser enamorado." Thus we can see how a whole range of socially ambitious courtiers, from *letrados* such as Villasandino to aristocrats such as Santillana, have the theoretical space to define their poetry as they please in the cancioneros but must follow (or, in the cancionero, are placed under certain rubrics as if they were following) certain basic rules of social convention and terms of production. This may explain why love lyric becomes only one poetic mode among others, and why the content of the *dezir* may range from amatory to scholastic. What is most evident, however, is the extreme productivity of a coterie of poets at this time, demonstrating poetry to be a required courtly exercise.

Baena also stresses the symbolic significance of poetic activity through the material existence of his *libro*. By gathering lyrics into his "muy notable e famoso libro,"[39] and supplying a theoretical justification in his *Prologus*, Baena ensures the virtue and prestige of his collection before his patron. The poet is associated with the exercise of courtly behavior, and the cancionero's virtue lies in the organization and compilation of what is labeled as poetic knowledge: the *Prologue* dictates that the poetry that follows, and what the cancionero as compilation contains, is a branch of knowledge. Emphasizing that the cancionero has pleasurable, educational, and therapeutic benefits, and blurring the distinction between cause and effect, Baena ensures that the poetry and poets in his *libro* fulfill his nebulous conditions of *gaya çiençia*, and that the cancionero affirms their cultural prestige.

Rules, Ritual, and the Book: Villena's Institution of Poetic Activity in Arte de trovar *and the* Ritual Purification of Poetry

Baena's defense of poetry as *gaya çiençia* is by no means exceptional for the time. In Villena's description of the Barcelona Consistory in the *Arte de trovar*, three ideas shaping poetic activity emerge as integral to the *Prologus* and the social production of poetry during the fifteenth century: the lapsed state of contemporary poetry and the need for an order embodied in the past; faith in an intellectual hierarchy and the need of institutions such as the Consistory that guarantee observance of immutable rules; and the symbolic importance of preserving such rules in books that represent the permanence and regeneration of wisdom.[40] The ritualistic features contained in Villena's description of the prize-giving ceremonies of the Consistory correlate with the cancionero's embodiment of poetic order and wisdom. Furthermore, Villena's description of the contest links the concept of poetic knowledge with social rituals of public institutions and the preservation of rules and poetry in books. The prolific production of cancioneros and poetry during the fifteenth century, an activity character-ized by José Antonio Maravall as a ritualistic purification of art entailing staged, almost theatrical procedures, results in poetry as institutionally sanctioned wisdom. Thus the activity of the Consistory informs our under-standing of cancionero poetry in its adherence to poetic rules and, perhaps more important, its promotion of ritualistic display. This ritual aspect sanc-tifies poetry and maintains its wisdom from a diminished state, "la mengua de la sciençia" (the decline of knowledge).[41]

Similar to Baena's elision of craftsmanship and poetic grace in a can-cionero that guarantees poetry's prestige, Villena's hierarchy of order de-pends upon the ritualistic competition of the Consistory, which requires would-be poets to follow the rules of art. The Consistory distinguishes the "claros ingenios" from "los oscuros" (bright wits from the benighted).[42] In Villena's image of the Consistory, the ideal poet emerges only through the process of social activity and the evaluation of a governing body whose role is to establish and maintain these rules. Like earlier writers of vernacular *artes*, Villena scorns contemporary poetry because too many would-be poets fail to practice "la gaya dotrina";[43] it has become difficult to distinguish the most excellent poets who communicate divine wisdom from "los oscuros":

> Por la mengua de la sciençia todos se atreven a hazer ditados, sola-mente guardada la igualdad de las syllabas, y concordançia de los bordones, según el compás tomado, cuydando que otra cosa no sea cumplidera a la rímica dotrina. E por esto no es fecha diferencia entre los claros ingenios, e los oscuros.[44]

> Because of the decline of knowledge, everyone attempts to make compositions, merely by retaining the equality of syllables, the concordance of endings, and following the given meter, taking care that anything else would not be fulfilled according to the rhythmic doctrine. And that is why there is no difference between the bright wits and the benighted.

The "mengua de la sciençia" justifies the treatise, which is to rehabilitate the rules of knowledge in today's lapsed state of poetry. Villena even tells Santil-lana, to whom the treatise is dedicated, that though nature has granted him "ingenio," "por mengua de la gaya dotrina" (because of the decline in the gay doctrine) he is unable to communicate or give concrete shape to his "es-çelentes invençiones" (excellent inventions).[45]

Although Villena's *Arte* does not stray theoretically from other vernacu-lar poetic treatises of the period,[46] it is useful for understanding how can-cionero culture can create sociopoetic distinctions (*claros/oscuros*) through institutionalized ritual activity. He describes the evolution of the Consis-tory from "França," its foundation by "Ramón Vidal de Besaldú," to the synthetic compilation of the rules of art in a "libro de las *leyes de amor*" (book of the laws of love), and finally to the development of the Catalan Consis-tories under the Kings Joan I and Martí I of Aragon.[47] While its historical veracity has been debated, this account serves to justify the Consistory and its "reglas" (rules) of "gaya sciença" through royal authority.[48] Royal patrons of the Consistory materially support not only the preservation of lyrics in songbooks but the rules of lyric composition, the "sciença" as "complida orden de cosas inmutables e verdaderas" (the complete order of immutable and true things).[49] King Martí I sponsors "la reparaçión de los libros del arte e vergas de plata de los vergueros"[50] (the repairing of vernacular treatises and the silver rods of the officials), indicating the extent to which the vernacular treatises and regalia that Villena describes are deemed essential to preserv-ing this cultural tradition.

Poetic treatises and the preservation of lyric go hand in hand with the public performance and evaluation of poetry as a manifestation of hierar-chical order. Villena describes a ritual that takes on a religious dimension. There are appointed judges of specific rank and expertise, such as theology and law ("el otro maestro en theología, el otro en leyes").[51] At the beginning of the poetic competition, troubadours, nobles, "mantenedores" (sustainers of the ritual), and "vergueros" (protectors of truth and due process) gather in the palace; the poetic treatises are placed in the center of the room upon "un bastimento cuadrado tan alto como un altar, cubierto de paños de oro, e en-çima puestos los libros del arte, e la joya" (a square pedestal as high as an altar, covered with golden cloths, and on top were placed the books of the art, and the prize). When the master of theology introduces a theme, there is silence, "fecho silencio." Each of the competitors reads a poem aloud ("publicasen") on the ordained theme, and then presents it written down "en papeles dam-asquines de diversos colores, con letras de oro, e de plata, e illuminaduras fermosas" (on paper decorated with diverse colors, with letters of gold and of silver, and beautiful illuminations). The members of the Consistory then take these works away to judge them in private according to the "reglas del arte," screening them for "vicios" of "contenidos" (flaws of content) and marking these in the margins. After deliberating and voting, the jury gives the prize to the least flawed poem. As the participants congregate after this private assessment, there again is a ceremonial "silencio" before the winner is announced. The winning poem is immediately entered in "el registro del consistorio: dando authoridat y liçençia para que se pudiese cantar e en público dezir" (the register of the consistory: giving authority and license so that it could be sung and publicly recited).[52] The procedure incorporates the act of composing, reciting, singing, and publishing an "obra"; only after being judged on its poetic merits is the work authorized to be publicly performed.[53] This "obra," institutionally sanctioned through the ritual and sacred atmosphere of the competition ("silencio," "letras de oro"), and recorded in the register of the Consistory, embodies distinguished poetry through rules and communal verification. The ritual purifies the work and the poet, who bear witness to the "sciençia" symbolized by the book on the altar. Villena concludes by stating that the Consistory demonstrates "aquel avantaje que Dios e natura fizieron, entre los claros ingenios, e los oscuros . . . e no se atrevían los ediothas" (what advantage God and nature made, between the bright wits and the benighted . . . and the idiots didn't try).[54] This last statement is telling; Villena assumes that only the most virtuous poets will even attempt to abide by such rules and to perform before such an institution. Thus the establishment of permanent rules and an institution to enforce them fulfills a "complida orden," creating a true poetic wisdom.

The symbolic position of the *libro* in the Consistory, representing the permanence of *sciençia* and facilitating the communal affirmation of an intellectual hierarchy, helps explain why cancionero poets were highly conscious of both composing poetry as a courtly ritual and compiling poetry in cancioneros.[55] Let us turn to another kind of courtly ritual during this period, the Fiesta of Valladolid in 1428, to see how ritual adherence to rules and procedural applications of conventions generates a social hierarchy of distinctions—a "complida orden de cosas immutables e verdaderas"—in another context.

THE CANCIONERO AND COMMUNAL PERFORMANCE: THE 1428 FIESTA OF VALLADOLID

So far I have discussed the culture of cancioneros in terms of its theoretical justification as a courtly activity (*Cancionero de Baena*), and in relation to poetic knowledge as ritual (Consistory). In what way was this culture implicated in paradramatic events that included *juegos* (games, entertainments) or *entremeses* (interludes) during courtly tournaments and religious celebrations? Many cancionero poets were participants in such events, and their works were a product of these various public spectacles and court activities. Poetry may have been recited during *entremeses* by costumed minstrels in courtly tournaments, or may have served as the text of allegorical *farsas* (moral plays) or other *representaciones* (representations of a dramatic nature) during Corpus Christi festivals.[56] This theatrical aspect of poetry demonstrates the extent to which the production of cancioneros was intertwined with both courtly rituals and popular spectacles. Such dramatic performances often served as an aristocratic pastime of intricately coded courtly games while also providing universal images of a pagan, Christian, or chivalric nature for a wider audience.[57] In the case of the Fiesta of 1428 held in Valladolid and chronicled by Pedro Carrillo de Huete, the royal falconer of King Juan II,[58] one also sees that such rituals served the important function of creating political stability by naturalizing turbulent changes of power among the rulers of fifteenth-century Spain.[59]

Since previous studies have discussed the relation between the poetry of the cancioneros and specific court festivities and games,[60] I will focus instead on the material and physical articulation of convention in the ceremonies of the Fiesta as they relate phenomenologically to the production of cancioneros. First, literary works and public ceremonies such as the cancioneros and the Fiesta at Valladolid promoted courtly ideals for both established and aspiring nobility. Changes in nobility at this time included new families displacing older ones, great lords who had previously resided on their estates becoming courtiers and residing with the king, and aspirants competing for the support of this new elite class. Status-seeking supporters of royal patrons, emulating the chivalric prowess embodied in romances such as *Lancelot* or *Tirant lo Blanc*, knew that by participating in the intimate life of the king and his court, they could advance their own private interests — aggrandizing their estates, forging marriage alliances, achieving knighthood and thus exemption from taxation.[61] Such tournaments fostered a pro-aristocratic ideology with practical social and economic implications: while members of a rising noble class participated to show their support of the king, magnates of vast estates and accumulated wealth most likely also supported the cultivation of the chivalric ideal as a public demonstration of their dominance in political life.

Second, the Fiesta, like the cancioneros, allowed for poetic invention through the dramatization of courtly rituals, and brought a community together through a common set of values that were explicitly manifested. If we regard the art of composing poetry and producing cancioneros as ritual activities, we can perhaps draw a parallel between the literary pursuits of these courtiers and their participation in ceremonial pageantry: both activities reflect an exuberant articulation of conventions that in turn becomes a medium for innovation. To take an example of this innovation within what were carefully scripted dramatic performances, the jousting ceremonies featured in the Fiesta and the *entremeses* surrounding these events became an opportunity to invent a more sophisticated kind of group poetry such as *invençiones,* which require a lady to interpret a verbal message (*letra*) from a knight in relation to a visual sign (*divisa*). The language used for describing these jousting tournaments became intertwined with sexual wordplay.[62] In these developments concerning the relation between poetry and courtly rituals, one can see how invention could occur within an impromptu theatricality. It is this quality that I now discuss in relation to the cancioneros.

Although it is easy to criticize Johan Huizinga's *The Autumn of the Middle Ages*[63] as a simplistic view of fifteenth-century France and Burgundy, his study of courtly rituals such as tournaments in relation to medieval mentalities are still useful for our study of cancioneros. Huizinga studies the truth value in "illusions" and rituals of medieval culture, which is different from "true facts" of political and economic life (62). He argues that "life forms" such as rituals of chivalry and love lyric are cultivated from a quotidian reality of extremes; he explores this tension in the life of medieval people through physical or religious aspects of culture, or from static ideologies of state and society (61–63, 126 ff.).

Like the extravagant activities of the Burgundian court described by Huizinga, the Fiesta at Valladolid belongs to what was already a longstanding European tradition of the knightly tournament mythologized in romances, in which knights fight each other to prove their honor. Similar to Burgundian tournaments, Castilian *pasos de armas* required that their participants understood the conditions of play. Lances tipped with coronals, elaborately decorated armor, and a central barrier (*tela*) to separate jousters and horses represent the difference between the theatrical quality of these performances and the original function of tournaments as training grounds for military combat.[64]

The manner in which Carrillo de Huete describes the activities of the Fiesta is essential for shaping our perspective of the poetry of the cancioneros. At the beginning of the chronicle, the description of the "fortaleza"— set up in the square of the city, with its multiple towers, bell, and colored griffins—constitutes a planned artifice that houses its actors like a stage. Rather than playing on the fiction of a formidable fortress that guards the ladies inside (the chronicler tells us there is a lady in every tower), Carrillo de Huete simply narrates the construction of artifice: he describes the stage, which is populated by numerous men and women and also provides dressing rooms for the prince and a stable for the horses on the ground floor. The narrator points out that the towers on the completed fortress, made of "madera e de lienço" (wood and cloth), resemble stone masonry.[65] Such details indicate that the chronicler is noting the material construction of this theatrical stage set, and admires the extent of its verisimilitude. Just as Baena insists in his *Prologus* that *gaya çiençia* requires that one "siempre se preçie e se finja de ser enamorado," the chronicler's observations suggest an awareness of the seriousness of the game but also the extent to which it is merely a spectacle.

According to Huizinga, "the entire knightly culture of the fifteenth century is dominated by a precarious balance between sentimental seriousness and easy derision," in which "the rigid face occasionally relaxes for a moment into a smile" (85). Perhaps this is too much to apply to the Fiesta. Yet the falconer's care to describe the numbers of people involved and the luxurious royal regalia of the jousting knights is noteworthy. When Prince Enrique of Aragon comes forth as defender of the lists, five named knights accompany him. During the *entremeses*, eight beautifully dressed damsels ride well-appointed chargers, followed by a goddess on a *carro*, with twelve singing damsels. In the towers over the gate to the fortress, the men are described as "muchos gentiles omes, con vnas sobrecotas de argentería, de la librea que el señor ynfante avía" (very gentle men, with surcoats of silver, of the livery that the lord prince had).[66] The numbering of the damsels and not these men seems arbitrary and is hardly systematic; however, the fact that they are numbered and the emphasis on material luxury draft these actors into an imagined romance, which acquires a symbolic aura. Just as Villena and Baena believe that poetic knowledge grows quantitatively through the history and preservation of letters, the establishment of a hierarchy and rules in which "los ingenios" would be revealed as against the "oscuros," Carrillo de Huete's articulation of a divine hierarchy consisting of numbers and self-conscious largesse demonstrates the court's faith in a regeneration of chivalric virtue through ritual practice.

Furthermore, the *entremeses* may have required this staged fiction as a pretext, for they occurred between narrative episodes and jousting and were opportunities to invent within an environment of order: that is to say,

Huizinga's "smile" here is not derisive but is part of a literary activity that reflects everyone's willing enactment of the chivalric fiction. Before the contest of the *arco del pasaje peligroso*, the prince dances and drinks at the base of the fortress, and then brings on the *entremeses*. Certainly, as Ian Macpherson notes, "the game of Courtly Love became the ideal vehicle for the literary after-dinner soirées and the post-tournament festivities: occasional poems, riddles, *motes, letras, invençiones, preguntas* and *respuestas* became the staple diet of such reunions, because they particularly lent themselves to group activity, native intelligence and quickness of wit in all its senses."[67] We cannot know for sure if it was in these breaks that the courtier devised his word/image riddles destined for his beloved, but it is safe to assume that these different modes of courtly play encouraged a creative dynamic that likely shaped the nature of cancionero poetry. As the specificity of a jousting event would have an informed an ad hoc composition immediately following it, the meaning of this poem in terms of the specificity of the situation is lost to us modern readers. We can only recreate in our minds the creative atmosphere in which the different levels of playfulness were performed with the *arco del pasaje peligroso* romance. As the chronicler recounts:

> E como venían algunos cavalleros, venían al *arco del pasaje peligroso* . . . E salían luego de la fortaleza vna dama . . . e dezía:
> —Cavalleros, ¿qué ventura vos traxo a este tan peligroso passo, que se llama de la fuerte ventura? Cúnplevos que vos volbades, sinon no podredes pasar syn justa.
> E luego ellos rrespondían que para ello eran prestos. De los quales salío el señor Rey de Castilla, e veynte e quatro cavalleros . . . e el señor Rey con vnos paramientos de argentería dorada, con vna cortapisa de armiños muy rrica, e vn plumón e diademas de mariposas.
> E quebró el dicho señor Rey dos varas muy fuertes, e andovo tal cavallero que fué maravilla, que nenguno andaba tal. E despúes salió el rrey de Navarra, con doze cavalleros, todos como molinos de viento.[68]

And as some knights approached, they came to the *Arch of the Dangerous Passage* . . . and afterwards leaving from the fortress . . . a lady said:
Knights, what fortune draws you to this very dangerous pass, called of the strong fortune? You are obliged to turn back, for you will not be able to pass without a trial.

And then they responded that they were prepared for it. From their group came the lord king of Castile, and twenty-four knights . . . and the lord king with armor of gilded silver, and a rich ermine hem-band, a quilted jacket, and a butterfly crown.

And the said lord king broke two very strong lances, and he went like a knight who was marvelous, no one went like him. And afterward came the king of Navarre, with twelve knights, all like windmills.

In the case of cancionero poetry, the lack of historical documentation from which to interpret this chronicle calls upon the modern reader to imagine the range of invention that the participants and audience could undertake. If this test is done in complete seriousness, did the king's squire really die afterward, as the chronicler recounts, from bile bursting in his body? How far did the theatrical performance go, and was it always the case that the lances were then tipped? If the test was performed with a hint of derision, in Huizinga's "smile" mode, did the twelve knights perform in a farcical manner? In this instance it is more interesting to imagine this ritual as taken very seriously indeed, and the description of windmills as emphasizing the grandiose and menacing stature of the knights. However, this scenario could serve as the prehistory of Don Quixote's encounter with windmills, that famous parable that encapsulates the emergence of modern consciousness by reinterpreting medieval romance. At the very least, the chronicler's mention of the *entremeses* surrounding these courtly jousts (rather than describe them, he simply indicates when they occurred) suggests the extent in which the performance of chivalry had become self-reflexive in fifteenth-century Castile: as such, the space for invention and modulation multiplies through different potential levels of play and seriousness given to the theatrical costumes and personnel involved (*molinos*; the royal *cortapisa de armiños*; *diademas de mariposas*; numbers — *veynte e quatro cavalleros*), and the oscillation between serious play and the *entremeses* that are part of the Fiesta. Maybe the invention happens because of the enforcement of hierarchies. Insofar as they belong to the same culture, the Fiesta and the cancionero promote play within accepted parameters (the book, the tournament) as a way of affirming social consensus. This similarity is one reason the cancionero may be seen as a productive genre of literary invention even as it reinforces hierarchies of poetic and social distinctions.

RETHINKING *LA POESÍA CANCIONERIL*:
THE POETRY OF THE CANCIONEROS

In this final section, I will describe how the cancionero as genre cultivates various sophisticated forms of intertextuality.[69] In the cancioneros, intertextuality appears in the formal interdependence between two or more texts, which can include a dialogue among poets on a specific topic, such as the praise for a woman, or different poets contributing a *copla* (stanza) to a *serranilla*, for example. Already drawing from a common stock of *topoi* and metrical forms, poets increasingly rely on a reader's knowledge of contemporary social or political situations for their citations and references. On the one hand, these poets compose poetry for literary self-validation as part of being a model courtier; on the other, the poetic culture requires new kinds of competitive gestures that either formally or thematically challenge another poet's work. As a result, while various cancioneros, such as the *Palacio* or *Estúñiga*, seem loosely ordered by poet and genre, within these categories one sees groups of texts that carry their own particular dynamic dialogue or stage a particular narrative. Although this intertextuality is present in the earlier works of the troubadours, the proliferation and circulation of cancioneros cultivate a keen awareness of literary publication among patrons and courts. This awareness may in turn result in the competitive posturing memorialized in cancionero poetry and in the high expectation of a response that poets encode into their works.

More than earlier songbooks and despite being chronologically closer to us, the cancionero represents poetry as a social activity challenging our modern conceptions of an autonomous lyric "work" or "poet." While we modern readers must reconstruct the context, the cancionero provides loose transcriptions of series such as the *dezir*, *réplica*, and *contrarréplica*, occasional poetry based on certain events, and communally composed *serranillas*. Compilers of cancioneros pragmatically order poetry by author, but an author corpus may contain a series of poems consisting of different poets. Indeed, in Hernando del Castillo's *Cancionero general*, an entire section is devoted to *letras* and *invenciones*, which are the best example of group activity since their interpretation depended on a courtly context and visual cues. Poetry of this kind in a cancionero forces us to reconsider where a "work" or a "poet" ends and begins. The ordering and rubrics of most cancioneros do not represent a clear narrative intent of the compiler or a specific use of commentary and lyric such as we see in Dante's *Vita Nuova* or Guillaume de Machaut's fourteenth-century *Voir-Dit*. Instead, compilers express an argument by means of the anthology genre, whether in prologues, such as those of Baena, Santillana, and Juan del Encina that discuss the role and practice of poetry, or by the compilation of cancioneros that consciously build a literary canon based on a region, a historical tradition, or coterie.[70] Even in these latter cases, in which the cancionero embodies a unified narrative or is placed under the auspices of a poet, the cancionero maintains the heterogeneity of lyric anthologies like the chansonniers, where rubrics and ordering retain shifting relations between works and poets.

Several examples of intertextuality show how the order of a certain dialogue series required the specialized knowledge of the readers. Even with conventional categories such as *topoi* and lyric form in mind, poets cultivated their own distinctiveness in collective poetry in increasingly nuanced ways, including references to family members, compact and arcane citations of *auctores*, and, in the case of Francisco Imperial, his own translation of Dante, which became his trademark. In the *Estúñiga*, the order of several works of the poet Caravajal allows readers to construct their own romances among historical personages of Alfonso V's court. Thus the cancionero here becomes a work space different from the *Carmina Burana* or *Libro de buen amor*. The songbook is a textual space for romantic intrigue, where Caravajal uses lyric forms such as the *epístola* and the *romançe* to compose in innovative ways and in the personae of his patrons. Finally, by their very use of the words *libro* and *cancionero,* poets and compilers reveal the extent to which songbooks influence their perception of themselves and their works.

In my attempt to explain how the cancionero as genre shaped the poetry of this period, I will address the following questions: In what way is collective poetic activity displayed in cancioneros? How can their organization help us imagine how the cancionero became an important medium for poetry as a social activity? Keeping in mind that other European courts cultivated similar kinds of sophisticated courtly games, the production of cancioneros alongside these court activities qualifies as a uniquely Iberian situation. In the *Cancionero general,* an essential aspect of a witty performance was indeed the recording of such accomplishments in a cancionero representing the best of courtly society. The more hermetic quality of the poetry contained in the *Cancionero general*, and the preference for more compact lyric forms such as the octosyllabic *canción*—a quatrain followed by an eight-line *copla de arte menor* whose last four lines are identical to the initial quatrain— reflect the newly gained prestige of Castilian and the desire to promote the language through the production of cancioneros. This quality also speaks to a cultlike literary activity that drives both the formal condensation of poetry and the theatrical nature of poetic compositions. Group compositions of a serial type, poetry that arises from performance situations, and the compilation of such poetry into a book that may include prologue, ranking, and emendations — these activities define the genre but pertain to different points in the practice of cancionero production. Let us now look at some examples to understand how seriality and condensation build on each other and interact to form the genre.

Structural Tendencies in the Cancioneros: Apparent but Flexible

In most cases, compilers organize texts under poets and lyric genres. But even in the most representative cancioneros such as the *Estúñiga* or the *Palacio*, there is no consistent application of these organizing principles. Within these categories, different lyric forms are often grouped under one poet, such as the *pregunta/respuesta*,[71] which may include a series of poets or several lyric forms under one poet. These principles of organization represent an important change in the memorial aspect of the songbook tradition: the compilers of the cancioneros must collate more heterogeneous lyric forms than the *canso*, such as the *dezir,* which could be narrative, didactic, or satirical, and include multiple poets and different poems based on one occasion (*serranillas, preguntas/respuestas*). Cancioneros transmit a more complex situation of collective poetic activity than earlier songbook traditions and reflect the efforts of compilers to create loose constellations of topics, themes, and genres.

Two examples of complex organization occur in the *Cancionero de Baena*. Although the *Baena* is known for being eccentric in that it represents the moralizing verse of bourgeois clerks rather than the aristocratic love poetry of the Aragonese court,[72] being the earliest cancionero it nonetheless shows various processes of compilation.[73] Judging from the *Tabla* that Baena included, the cancionero appears to organize poems by authors. In the section on Francisco Imperial, however, poems are grouped thematically as *dezires* dedicated to the birth of Juan II. Following *dezires* by Imperial, the series includes those by Fray Diego de Valencia, Fray Bartolomé de Córdoba, Anónimo, and Mosé, the latter a surgeon to Enrique III. This series also occurs in the *Cancionero de San Román* (ca. 1454) in the same order, except that it lacks the *respuesta* of Fray Diego de Valencia.[74] After this thematic series in the *Baena*, the section continues with a *dezir* and a *respuesta* by Fernán Pérez de Guzmán, a *contrarréplica* by Imperial, and a *respuesta* by

Diego Martínez de Medina.[75] Yet this *pregunta/respuesta/contrarréplica* is just one section within a larger thematic group of poems concerning "Estrella Diana" (nos. 231–36).[76] In the *pregunta/respuesta* subgroup, Baena organizes these *dezires* together because they correspond thematically and formally: the *respuesta dezires* by Guzmán, Imperial, and Martínez de Medina match in rhyme and meter (the *arte mayor* typically used for the *dezir* with matching *coplas*), and the poets respond precisely to each other by arguing over Imperial's treatment of the "Estrella Diana" (see, for example, Guzmán accusing Imperial of attributing improper value to his subject, "quien lo*a* infintoso por codiçia vana," who falsely praises with vain greed," 232.4). Another element that may bind the texts together is the reference to family members or personal acquaintances as provocative gestures. Imperial makes a point of invoking a cousin of Guzmán's in his *contrarréplica* as a higher authority: "E de lo judgado de aquestos errores/declina, amigo, ante el Almirante" (And of being judged of those errors, move aside, friend, before the Almirante, 232bis.17–18), the "Almirante" being Diego Hurtado de Mendoza. Such correspondences — Francisco Imperial, occasional theme, *Estrella Diana*, series of *pregunta/respuesta*—are representative of the complex intertextuality upon which a compiler such as Baena must impose a loose order that allows for such constellations of text and references.

Another example of this complexity is the representation of Alfonso Álvarez de Villasandino in the *Baena*.[77] On the one hand, the compiler emphasizes Villasandino, as he appears as the basis of the compilation. Yet if we examine the poet's section that opens the *Baena* after the *Prologus*, the texts suggest other interests of the compiler: the first three songs are *cantigas* dedicated to the Virgin Mary and King Juan, perhaps reflecting Baena's interest in linking Castilian poetry to the literary heritage of Alfonso X, including the *Cantigas de Santa María*. (This is not surprising, given that Baena's *Prologus* is based substantially on Alfonso X's *General estoria* and *Estoria de España*.) In addition to acknowledging the Galician-Portuguese poetic tradition, Baena's prologue and opening texts grant authority to his cancionero since the order of the contents reflects the principles he sets down in his *Prologus*: the recognition of "grandes fechos passados"[78] (great past deeds) embodied in the Castilian monarchs, and the morally uplifting role of poetry exemplified by Alfonso's *Cantigas* and his efforts to unify a cult of the Virgin Mary with the Castilian monarchy. The poems proceed to *dezires* dedicated to the Infante (no. 4 [ID1150]), and to Villasandino's *esposa* with the name "Mayor" [ID1151]. Villasandino is honored as "el muy esmerado e famoso poeta, maestro e patrón de la dicha arte" (the very careful and famous poet, master and exemplar of the said art) in the *Preprólogo*,[79] but the texts that begin his corpus first honor the Virgin Mary and the monarchs. Only when that obligation is fulfilled do the *cantigas* pass on to the poet's song dedicated to his "esposa." Just from this small section of the poet's works, one sees how the notion of an author corpus has become more complex in this songbook tradition, as the compiler must negotiate historical circumstances, the value of poetry, and his position as clerk for Juan II. By way of contrast, Garcia has noted how Fernán Pérez de Guzmán is the authoritative figure in the *Cancionero de Oñate-Castañeda* (ca. 1485 [HH1]), which features all of his religious poetry with a distinct structure, and within a literary history of fifteenth-century poetry.[80] Perhaps because of the later date, this compiler felt more at liberty to follow his aesthetic tastes.

A series of *serranillas* in the *Cancionero de Palacio* offer another example of the flexibility of text groups in the cancionero.[81] The *Palacio* is well known for showing the tastes of the courts of Aragon and Castile during the fifteenth century, including the works of King Juan II, Condestable don Álvaro de Luna, the Infante don Pedro of Portugal, the Mendoza family, and other nobles. Lacking the explicit intellectual interests reflected in the *Baena Prologus* and in poetry treating scholastic and moral issues, the *Palacio* gathers mostly love poetry, which would have held the greatest interest for its aristocratic audience. While some texts are organized according to poets, the diversity of forms, themes, and authors suggests that there was no overarching tendency to organize texts by author as in the *Baena*. Two groups of *serranillas* (more precisely, octosyllabic *serranas*, or *cantigas de serrana*) show how texts were organized by lyric genre. In the first group of *cantigas de serrana* (nos. 28–30 [ID2424–26]), which include Santillana and García de Pedraza responding to a *serrana* by the Comendador de Segura or Rodrigo Manrique (nephew of Santillana), the responding poets continue the original text by adding an eight-line *copla* in the same meter and rhyme. The last four lines recall the initial *copla* using the same rhyme scheme, an extended version of the refrain we first saw in the *troba caçurra estribillo* of the *Libro de buen amor serranas*. Although the unity of these three texts is formally clear, in the next group of *serranillas*, numbers 33–34 [ID2428–29], one by Mendo de Campo (34) responds to another by Francisco Bocanegra (33), but de Campo's *serranilla* appears more autonomous because of its separate rhyme scheme and refrain. The Galician inflections ("m'engan," line 4; "geytossa," line 9; "condana," line 12) reinforce this impression. These texts test the assumption of what is a work: rather than appearing as a unified work by several poets under the same metrical scheme, these texts appear as multiple works organized by genre. Such variations of text groups from one cancionero to the next demonstrate how concepts such as work, genre, and theme were flexible as structuring principles for the compilers. Even when dealing with forms that by nature are intertextual and dialogic (*serranas* and *pregunta/respuesta*), the compiler may have found other principles more compelling. This open structure recalls the tendencies we have seen in the dance songs with German refrains in the *Carmina Burana*, where relations between lyric texts may be made metrically or thematically.

Fluidity within the Cancionero: Caravajal in the Cancionero de Estúñiga

Clearly the medium of the cancionero facilitates dynamic convergences of subject matter, poets, and historical actors. The corpus of Caravajal, well represented in the *Estúñiga*, shows how a fluid experimentation with lyric genres and poetic address confounds historical reality and the lyric world. Caravajal takes on the personae of his patrons, and in a series of his texts he stages a narrative romance among Alfonso V, his lover Lucrecia d'Alagno, and Queen María of Aragon, who was never with the king during his long stays in Italy. This romance occurs as a result of the anthology: the juxtaposition of the *romançe* and *epístola* stages the narrative. The compilation of the *epístola* and *romançe* [IDo612, IDo613] in three cancioneros and in the same order (MN, RC, and VM1) indicate that these two texts were supposed to be read together as a sort of narrative romance. In the letter, Caravajal writes to Alfonso V in the voice of Queen María of Aragon; she calls her husband "César" and, despite lamenting his long absence, admires his "grandes fechos" (great deeds) in his military expeditions.[82] In the following "Romance por la sennora Reyna de Aragón," composed of continuous octosyllabic verse with even, assonating lines, he fills out this image of the queen by making her a model of chastity and virtue ("la muy casta donna María," the chaste lady Maria; line 2), the queen suffering as a result of the heroic "César."[83] In other poems, Caravajal assumes the voice of the king in a poem addressed to Lucrecia in her absence from Naples. In the *Estúñiga*, the rubric that heads this poem reads "Por mandado del sennor Rey, fabblando en propia persona, siendo mal contento de amor, mientra madama Lucrecia fue a Roma" (By the order of the King, narrated in his own person, being saddened in love, while lady Lucrecia was at Rome).[84] This rubric indicates that Caravajal or the compiler plays with different levels of feigning: at times Caravajal assumes the voice of the king or queen, or in the case of this rubric he sends a poem by the order of the king. We cannot know why there are such discrepancies of impersonation, but they attest to the different modes of theatricality that *Estúñiga*'s public enjoyed. In a more conventional mode, Caravajal, as himself, addresses the king or queen; in *Estúñiga* number 126 he praises the queen for her "virtud" (virtue),[85] while in number 55 he praises Lucrecia for her "beldat" (beauty) and refers directly to Alfonso's *lema*, "Sití Perillós."[86] This gesture is provocative, as it refers to Alfonso's emblem and reinforces his political exploits (the emblem represents the conquest of Pizzafalcone in 1442), while his audience would have known that Lucrecia was in a dangerous position, from a social and political standpoint, as the king's lover.[87] In another poem dedicated to the king and related to the "sitio peligroso" (dangerous seat) poem, number 102,[88] Caravajal employs an *invençion cortesana* that appears in the *Cancionero general* [ID6400]: Alfonso V got "el sitio peligroso y dixo: Seguidores vencen" (the dangerous seat and said: Followers conquer). In this poem Caravajal invokes the emblem explicitly: "Oíd qué dize mi mote: / "Siempre vencen seguidores, / no puedo vencer amores" (Listen to what my motto says: Followers always conquer, I cannot conquer love; lines 1–3).[89]

In summary, Caravajal uses lyric forms and personae to dramatize the relationship between King Alfonso, Lucrecia, and Queen Maria. A cancionero associated with Alfonso's court during his reign over Naples, the *Estúñiga* displays Caravajal's appropriation of a courtly intrigue into a narrative of romance and epistle, and his creative use of the king's emblem. As a cultural monument of Alfonso's Neopolitan court, the cancionero blurs literary, political, and social realities for courtly entertainment and aristocratic prestige.

Courtly Entertainment and Competence: Citation and Serialism

In contrast to the example of Caravajal, who inhabits different personae, and a cancionero that displays his different lyric and prose forms as a political love narrative, a poet may come to embody a certain form or topic, as does Pedro Torrella in his *Coplas de maldecir de las mujeres, Calidades de las donas* (Stanzas of insults against women, qualities of ladies [ID0043]), which provoked a large number of responses by other poets. Perhaps the enormous proliferation of poetry, poets, and cancioneros during the fifteenth century may be attributed to self-sustaining topics that poets could respond to and reinterpret in endless ways. The *Maldecir* of Torrella, a poet who wrote in Catalan and Castilian in the court of Alfonso V, became a favorite pretext for poets to argue in defense of women. The misogynistic satire, composed of a long series of novenas, attacks the hypocrisy and false virtue of women, comparing them among other things to "lobas" (wolves, line 19).[90] The *Maldecir* became so well known as a topic that poets referred to it as an authority; a rubric that begins a poem by Hernán Mejía refers to some *coplas* that he found in "un cancionero de mal dezir de las mugeres" (a *cancionero* of insult songs against women), and Lucena composes a "repetición de amores" and cites the "libro del pensamiento de Torrellas" (the *libro* of Torrella's thought).[91] This literary exercise of citing poets and their major works develops into a common practice among cancionero poets. For example, in one poem Torrella manifests his views of love by quoting certain "trobadors" such as Lope de Estúñiga, Villasandino, and Santillana.[92] He defends his *Maldecir* from his attackers by glossing the last *copla* for Juana of Aragon, sister of Fernando the Catholic and the second wife of Ferrante the King of Naples.[93] And he defends himself by composing the prose "Razonamiento en defension de las donas" (Reasons in defense of ladies [ID2146]).

While Torrella's *Maldecir* is an example of a certain topic merging with the identity of a poet, and shows how a topic inspires competitive and citational activity among a close group of poets to make it self-sustaining, the "Misa de amor" and "Regla del galán" genres [ID0034, ID0141] — parodies of the Mass made popular by Suero de Ribera and Juan de Dueñas, and by Ribera's *coplas* on the "galán" — allow for an endless serial citation of references in another way. In Ribera's "Misa de amor" (Mass of love), a classic example of fifteenth-century "hipérbole sagrada" or sacred hyperbole,[94] the profane glossing of the Mass reminds us of the range of citation and *auctores* that the poets had at their disposal. The sacroprofane practice of glossing religious texts as secular love treatises is common in medieval literature, but what is new in the cancionero is the leveling and proliferation of citational authorities: *auctores* such as Ovid but also fellow poets such as Torrella.

Parallel to ironic forms of textual authority — religious texts and scholastic judicial models such as the "repetitio" of Lucena[95] — is the development of compositions for secular virtue that aim to be authoritative in their thoroughness, such as Suero de Ribera's "galán" *coplas*. In the "Regla del galán" (Rules of courtliness), as the composition is called in one manuscript, or "la regla galana," as the poet refers to it in another composition in which he extends the original *coplas* [ID0517], Ribera outlines the qualities that a model courtier should have: he must be honest and without quarrel ("el galán persona honesta / ha de ser y sin renzilla" lines 9–10), cunning and informed ("e ser de buena respuesta, / tener la malicia presta / por fingir de avisado," lines 12–14), gifted in imagination and words ("ha de ser magina-tivo ... donoso motejador ... disimulador en risa," lines 17–22), and must carry himself appropriately in light dress and bearing — not eating stew and speaking effectively, pretending to be grander than the Duke of Milan ("vestido siempre liviano," line 36, "non deve comer cozido," line 50, "deve fablar poderoso, / enfingir de grandioso / más que el Duque de Milán; lines 65–68).[96] In this last quality especially, one sees how this serious handbook of social decorum and behavior for would-be model courtiers easily finds its way to parody and hyperbole. In another example of citation as parody, Ribera composes an "otro dezir," which supplements his *Regla* by applying the concept of *galán* to Jews.[97] The poem reads as a caricature of the courtier Jew during Castile's transitional period of three religions: "El gálan convien que tena / la nariz luenga e bermeja" (A courtly man requires a long and vermillion nose; lines 17–19).[98] Like the *Ubi sunt*, the Dance of Death, and *De Casibus*, this genre of serial compositions and variations on a single topic invoke a Christian sense of the unknowable workings of God. One approaches this sense through an increasing citation of the unknowable, a *horror vacui*. Yet unlike these moralizing genres, in late medieval Castile such examples of serial lists become intertwined with the playful activity of the courts as well as the serious reflection of rulers or laypersons. Finally, the serial topic also relates to Juan de Baena's "imaginary reading list" of *auctores* in a *dezir*, in which a listing of *exempla* proves his craft of "fingir" or courtly play and liter-ary pretending; in this case serial citation serves his scholastic and courtly aspirations as a poet. The desire to display competence in a serial, citational form, later replaced by the translation of classical *auctores* through primary sources, became in itself a form that could be parodied and manipulated in the same manner in which Ribera composed a *Misa de amor*.[99] Thus the formal link between the ostentatious seriality that poets use to prove they are proper courtiers (a requirement of *galán*) and the involution of that se-riality into parody (also a requirement of *galán*, to show one's witty *ingenio*) constitutes an important quality, and perhaps limit, of the cancionero genre. The cancioneros become an ideal medium for this Janus-like model (compe-tence/parody) of serial form.

THE CONDENSATION OF POETRY AND THE LIMIT OF THE GENRE?

The citational and serial aspects of the above examples show how the cancionero as genre made material the adherence of courtiers to Ribera's

Regla and received notions of conduct and behavior. The craft of composing poetry as a "cortesano exerçiçio" (courtly exercise, to take a term from
Santillana's *Prohemio*)[100] became self-sustaining as the impulse of invention
arrived from extending certain topics or lyric texts (Torrella's *Maldecir* or
collective *serranillas*, for example) and organizing them in relation to different text groups. However, in the *Cancionero general de Hernando del Castillo*, containing the poets and poetry most representative of the period of
the Catholic Monarchs, *invençiones* and *canciones* appeared that reflected
new attitudes toward poetic composition at court. The restriction of the
octosyllabic *canción* and the typical lexicon led to semantic enrichment.[101]
Invençiones, composed of one to three octosyllabic lines, sometimes with a
pie quebrado, or half-line, emerged from the combination of visual *divisa* and
verbal *letra* in tournaments such as the one in Valladolid.[102] The *Cancionero
general* records 113 *invençiones*. Such works, playing with the relation between
image and word, and taking a more sexually explicit attitude toward love
by experimenting with content and form, represent a new development of
Baena's maxim for courtiers in his *Prologus* that one should "always pretend
to be in love."

The growing popularity of *invençiones* and *canciones* among the courtiers
of the last two decades of the century indicate how poetry had gone the
other direction from the more fluid *dezir*: both lyric forms flourished as art
forms because of the formal tautness and concision of what they do not
say—the semantic and metrical restrictions of the *canción* ultimately play
on the suggestive ambiguity of abstract words such as "perdición" that can
be interpreted on many levels, and the metrical economy of two lines such
as the following by Costana: "Justa fue mi perdicíon / de mis males soy contento" (Justa was my ruin, of my sorrows I am content). These lines resound
with such a grace and impact that the poem became one of the most popular
pieces of the period and the *lema* of the Bishop of Guarda, who had an affair
with a woman named Justa Rodrigues Pereira.[103] The reduction of poetic
form suggests that in this period of the cancioneros, the collective poetic
activity that had always been part of the production of cancioneros became
even more circumscribed and cultish, resulting in an extreme version of a
poetry of the initiated. Instead of compositions that applied certain lyric
forms to different occasions, this poetry was characterized by ambiguous
euphemisms, the use of *annominatio*, in which the poet supplies the listener/
reader with one of two possible significations and leaves him or her to find
the other one, as well as a smaller network of references and internal formal
restrictions that often play on sexual innuendo.[104] Here the pleasure of in-

tertextuality begins to arrive less from the responding in kind to a text or poet using an accepted paradigm (form or theme), than from an ambiguity that depends on a situational interpretation.[105]

A comparison of Santillana's *Prohemio* (ca. 1445–49) and Juan del Encina's *El Arte de poesía castellana* (1496)[106] discloses a trend toward a poetry that values the secret rather than the explicit, material display of competence. While one might characterize the poetry of the *Cancionero general* as merely a concentrated version of game-playing or pretending ("fingir"), the differences between Santillana and Encina as theorists on Castilian poetry point to the changing intellectual outlook of poets during the course of the fifteenth century. The *Prohemio* is a prologue and letter addressed to the young Don Pedro (1429–66), son of Prince Pedro of Portugal, treating his knowledge and judgment concerning poetry, while Encina's is a treatise and prescriptive poetics dedicated to Prince Juan, son of Fernando and Isabel. Both works introduce personal cancioneros of their authors as dedicatory prologues. Santillana's letter, written in the last years of his life, is accompanied by "obretas" or small works of his youth,[107] and in his effort to establish a literary tradition for Castilian poetry he traces a development that includes the troubadours, the Galician-Portuguese tradition, the *Cantigas* of Alfonso X, and the *Libro del Arçipreste de Hita*. In citing Arnaut Daniel and Guido Guinizelli, Santillana distinguishes between what Weiss paraphrases as "those who first practise the art, and those who later achieve mastery of it," when he writes: "E así commo dize el philósofo, de los primeros, primera es la especulación" (And it is as the philosopher says, of the first ones, first was speculation),[108] a reference to the Aristotelian theory of "potentiality and act, a process of 'becoming' which entailed the gradual elimination of an inherent shortage."[109] This Aristotelian maxim of growth and becoming corresponds to the cancionero, a collection that shows the precedents of contemporary poetic achievements. (We also saw this phenomenon in Villena's account of vernacular poetics.) Further, as a model courtier in his late years who considers Castilian poetry to be at the peak of its development, Santillana implies, by sending the *Prohemio* with his youthful cancionero, that his own life is a model of the history and progress of Castilian verse.

In contrast, Encina's *Arte* and cancionero is a work of youth (he was eighteen when he dedicated his cancionero to the young Prince Juan),[110] and although his summary of the development of Castilian poetry is cursory by comparison to Santillana's, his more technical, prescriptive poetics indicates a change in priorities and, more important, several conscious breaks with the past. First, he privileges the Italian tradition as the immediate forebear of Castilian verse. He does not mention the troubadours or the Galician-Portuguese tradition, emphasizing the new centrality of the Italian influence. Moreover, he clarifies the difference between a "poeta" and a "trobador" (the poet "contempla en los géneros de los versos," reflects on the genres of the verses).[111] Encina is concerned not only with the study of verse and the Castilian literary tradition but with the practice of poetic composition: he gives a more technical account of prosody by using contemporary classics as examples (such as the *Coronación* of Juan de Mena). He establishes the two major kinds of verse meters as the *arte real* and the *arte mayor*, and describes how a *pie* may be *consonante* or *assonante*. Believing that the Castilian literary tradition was at its height, poetry having spread from Italy to Spain,[112] Encina is also wary of its corruption; thus he calls for laws because "nuestra lengua estar agora más empinada y polida que jamás estuvo . . . parecióme ser cosa muy provechosa ponerla en arte y encerrarla debaxo de ciertas leyes y reglas, porque ninguna antigüedad de tiempos le pueda traer olvido" (our tongue is now fully at its height and more polished than it has ever been . . . it seems to me a prudent thing to treat it as an art and protect it behind sure laws and rules, so that no great length of time can drag it into oblivion).[113] Thus in a theoretical and practical sense, Encina places stricter standards on Castilian poetry by his application of rules and theoretical distinctions (poet versus troubadour, leaving out troubadours from the Castilian literary tradition).

Compared to its precursors the *Prohemio* and the *Arte de trovar*, Encina's *Arte* presents poetry—its study and composition—as a humanistic enterprise requiring natural predisposition (*ingenio*) but also learned craftsmanship. Encina approaches literary history less as an aggregation of knowledge or an emerging hierarchy (the Aristotelian principle, Villena's *los claros*) than as past models that must be mastered in the present. He describes how one can master lyric forms as a craft and how it is essential to understand older traditions firsthand. By contrast, Santillana's *Prohemio,* as the work of a lettered aristocrat, simply assumes these principles. An example of this difference is evident when Santillana admits he has no personal knowledge of the *Cantigas* of Alfonso X but acknowledges their historical importance ("yo vi quien vio dezires suyos," I saw someone who saw his compositions),[114] while Encina recommends studying Latin works thoroughly in order to compose poetry: "come dize Quintiliano, mas discutirlos en los estilos y sentencias y en las licencias, que no leerá cosa el poeta en ninguna facultad de que no se aproveche para la copia que le es muy necessaria" (as Quintilian says, one can further discuss styles, sentences, and licenses of these works, but if one doesn't read anything of the poet in any faculty, one will not attain the copiousness that is most necessary).[115] A young and ambitious poet, musician, and dramatist, the son of a shoemaker from Salamanca and perhaps of Jewish descent, Encina composed the *Arte* as the work of a professional eager to gain a post under Prince Juan, son and heir of Fernando and Isabel.

Thus, while aspects of the cancionero genre remain constant throughout the course of the fifteenth century, there is a gradual shift in intellectual priorities and practice. Parallel to the development of poetry as more formally concise and euphemistic, and addressing a certain audience knowledgeable of more complicated rules and courtly situations, Encina aims to describe poetic forms more precisely, using clear rules and examples from earlier in the century. Both tendencies suggest continuity and departure from the past, and they intensify even further when cancioneros begin to be printed, perhaps accelerating new developments in poetry along with the preservation of the past.[116] These developments also suggest that poetry composed during the period was becoming less self-reflexive and dialogic as poets became conscious of their place in relation to both local and distant models. When Encina publishes his cancionero, he views Santillana and Mena as classic authors of the Castilian tradition, but looks upon the Italians as the ultimate model; so the word "distant" here may be applicable to a difference of consciousness resulting not only from history but from language and aesthetic values.

As a final perspective on the limits of the cancionero genre, the works of three poets of this later period also point to the limits of the "fingir" that motivated the production of cancioneros. At the same time that poets such as Encina were publishing their own cancioneros, and compilers were producing cancioneros directed at a specific audience with aesthetic judgments, certain idiosyncratic works were hinting at the limits of this poetry by commenting ironically on the "juegos" enjoyed at the courts and the cultivation of a poetry that celebrates social adherence to a static set of courtly values. In his largely autobiographical poetry, the Cordobese *converso* Antón de Montoro occasionally betrays the fragility of the fictive reality upon which cancionero poetry depends. In his famous verses addressed to Isabel I, asking her for protection during the persecutions in Córdoba in 1473–74, Montoro depicts the difficulty of being a *converso* (one who converted or pretended to convert to Christianity) and favor-seeking courtier. Using the satire and black humor that were his stock in trade, the "ropero amargo" (bitter clothes-peddler) describes his wretched life ("Hize el *Credo* y adorar / ollas de toçino grueso, / torreznos a medio asar, oyr misas y rezar,"

I recite the credo, I worship pots full of greasy pork, I eat half-cooked bacon, listen to Mass and pray),[117] and asks the queen to halt the abuse of the *conversos* ("esta muerte sin sosiego," this death without peace) at least until Christmas, when the warmth of the fire will be appreciated ("Navidad / cuando save bien el fuego") — this conclusion alluding to the fires of religious uprisings. In fifteenth-century Castile, *conversos* could never be assimilated into the idealized world envisioned by the Catholic Monarchs.[118]

While Montoro deals with religious identity by means of irony and satire, and thus comments on the limits of following social and religious practice, the poets Pedro de Cartagena (also a *converso*) and Costana push the rhetorical boundaries of love songs by explicitly referring to the materiality of language and courtly behavior. As both of these poets belonged to the courtly circle of the Catholic Monarchs, their verses expose the liability of the courtly game as "playing as though one weren't" by associating the rhetorical artifice of language with the deception of material appearances. In one poem on folio 88r of the *Cancionero general* [IDo668], Cartagena tells ladies not to judge him and his friends by the happy colors they are wearing, for they misrepresent their deathly gloom: "No juzgueys por la color / Señoras *que* nos cobría . . . *que* de fuera esta dorado / y de dentro el cuerpo muerto" (Don't judge by the color, Ladies, that cover us . . . while the outside is gilded, a dead body lies within).[119] As Gerli comments: "In this composition, Cartagena plays not only with the idea of courtly love as a deceptive game but with the notion of the perils of interpreting texts that are seen, as well as written and spoken."[120] The poet directs his audience's attention to the various modes of textual duplicity at court—not only the feigning of love but the medium in which it is feigned — through visual, written, or spoken texts. In addition to this new development of complexity in the poetry and games of the late fifteenth century, Cartagena explicitly foregrounds the "materiales" of allegory: "Es un compuesto de males / hecho para el coraçon, / destos tres materiales; / cuydado fe y aficion" (It is a compound of bad things made by the heart, and within are three materials; care, faith, and affection [IDo897], f. 88), and he describes love in a manner that foregrounds the formal structure of desire among competing suitors, as in this poem addressed to the Visconde de Altamira: "Yo soy vos y vos soys yo / nuestros tristes coraçones / son un triste coraçon / una afeccion nos prendio" (I am you and you are I, our sad hearts are a sad heart, an affection takes us [ID1813], f. 86). In these poems, Cartagena takes the conventional concepts that belong to the topic of love, such as deception, death, and unity/separation, and uses compact, chiasmic verse to emphasize the extent to which love is crafted.

Likewise, Costana's poems treating material objects resist the common tendency of the poetry of this time toward abstraction, euphemism, and sacred hyperbole. Although the poet uses the typical love motifs, the centrality of an object of shared contact carries an erotic potential, and resists becoming an allegorical object or complete synecdoche for love or for the woman, as in this poem in which Costana addresses gloves that a lady took from him: "¿Guantes, assì me dexáis? . . . mas estaréis tan ufanos en gozar de aquellas manos / que no meresce ninguno" (Gloves, like that you leave me?. . . . you will be prouder in praise of those hands, which no one deserves).[121] The objects never assume complete personification but act as conversational interlocutor for the lover's pangs of desire for his lady: "Anillo tan desseoso / de bolver donde partiste, / ¡quánto me hallo dichoso / porque a mis manos veniste!" (Ring so diligent, to return where you left, how happy I find myself because you came to my hands!)[122] In the case of the "guantes," the poet addresses these objects in the present about a past encounter—the object becomes not a self-reflexive object of the poet but a sort of friend, offering a unique contextual space between poet and beloved. Generally, these poems are a clever rhetorical variation of the lover's lament. But by adding an autonomous addressee who resists complete allegorization, and with whom the poet actively engages in a friendly dialogue, such poems expand the dramatic element of cancionero poetry. In such literary games, courtiers participate in an increasingly heightened and nuanced drama of courtly conversation.

CONCLUSION

As a medium for the transmission and preservation of poetry, and finally as literary objects that constitute a genre, cancioneros are vital for understanding the extent to which medieval songbooks helped shape conceptions of poetry in the late medieval period. For a long time scholars have judged particular texts and authors on the basis of aesthetic value alone, obscuring what songbooks enabled: experimentation among different text groups and lyric forms, and the material display of social and intellectual competence. As such, cancioneros became a testing ground for rising notions of humanism and the social and ethical role of poetry. Furthermore, in emphasizing the relation between the ritual production of literary activities, theoretical treatises, and courtly festivals, I have argued that the cancioneros were intertwined with the daily social and cultural realities of courtiers and lettered men. All these activities, displayed in the textual mode of the cancioneros if not explicitly speaking to them, represent the sedimentary and localized transformation of literary values taking place during the fifteenth century. As a literary genre, the cancionero participated in the ideologies of ritualized court life and theories of poetic knowledge, eventually imploding through the dominance of Petrarchism and the limits of cancionero poetry. Lettered men used the cancionero to transform their lyrics into a "poetry" that articulated the social and cultural values of its readers. Thus in the can-cioneros we can see readers' awareness of the songbook as a work space, discussed in previous chapters. This work space allowed the interaction of heterogeneous lyric forms and cultural values and their transformation into a literary tradition comprising what we accept today as "poets" and "poetry."

Conclusion

❦

SONGBOOK MEDIEVALISMS

MANUSCRIPT ARCHIVES, classificatory manuals, and critical editions have been instrumental in my study of songbooks as an emergent genre. In these remaining pages, I want to turn these instruments themselves into objects of study. Catalogue numbers and bibliographic descriptions in institutions dedicated to preserving medieval manuscripts have their own stories to tell. How does the transmission history of a medieval songbook notate modern medievalisms, that is to say, modern interpretations of the Middle Ages? Let us return to that exemplary songbook, Ms. fr. 854 in the Bibliothèque nationale, an Italian troubadour chansonnier copied in a Venetian scriptorium in the thirteenth century. Identified by Occitan scholars as chansonnier I according to a classification system established in the nineteenth century, it is well known for its luxurious quality and clear organization of genres, as well as the large number of troubadour texts it contains. On the verso side of a cover page of 854, one reads in a sixteenth-century hand, "Liure des anciens poetes provençeaulx." This hand has been identified on manuscripts belonging to the library of Fontainebleau under François I, and accords with the current title on the spine: "TROBADOVRS OV ANCIENS POETES PROVENCAVX."[1] The title indicates the contents for which it is valued: texts of troubadours or old Provençal poets, rather than, as in other cases, songs or lyric texts (for instance Ms. fr. 856, chansonnier C, also in the Bibliothèque nationale, bears the title "Chansons des Poetes Provinciaux," songs of provincial poets). The manuscript's current and former presence in the national library and the library of François I signifies the membership of the troubadours and Occitan in France's cultural heritage since the Renaissance. It points to a period, the sixteenth century, when troubadours became part of the national literary canon, even as poets of a regional dialect and a historically distinct culture. It is important to recall that parts of the region where the courts of the troubadours flourished did not enter the French kingdom until after Hundred Years' War — the region of Provence, for instance, joined in 1481. The chansonnier's current catalogue number, description, and sigla as a known manuscript in an institution enables us to trace its history and cultural status, and reflects the common consensus that this object is a "chansonnier."

Yet as most scholars of medieval manuscripts know, this kind of stable identification and classification has only recently occurred. Since the rise of philology in the nineteenth century, scholars have been tracing "lost" manuscripts through the previous work of antiquarians; in the case of chansonniers, for example, they were studied as sources for regional histories. To Marc-Antoine Dominicy, a seventeenth-century lawyer from Cahors, the works of the troubadours were important in order to understand the history of France when it was still divided into regions of "langue d'ouy" and "langue d'oc." He was fortunate enough to have access to a chansonnier similar to Ms. 854 as well as other Occitan fragments for his "Histoire du païs de Quercy."[2] While manuscript culture today occurs largely under the purview of institutions that preserve these valuable artifacts, until the nineteenth century manuscripts were seen as books rather than as museum objects and could be circulated among friends, connoisseurs, and antiquarians for personal interest.

I will here focus on notions of songbook culture so as to understand how the idea of the songbook shaped private and institutional practices for social or historical purposes. I take "songbook culture" to mean postmedieval practices of scholars and amateurs, including the production of diplomatic transcriptions or critical editions in songbook format, and the edition, extraction, and translation of medieval songbooks to create modern ones. As studies in the history of the book have shown,[3] the labeling of medieval artifacts such as chansonnier I by philologists and institutions reveals how these objects — especially those labeled miscellanies, anthologies, and songbooks — have signified shifting cultural values. It has been a fundamental task of modern medievalists to use histories of books and manuscripts, especially their modes of transmission during and after the Middle Ages, to question literary histories, revered authorities, canons, and the concept of literature itself. In the case of Ms. 854, we see how the provenance, catalogue, and bindery titles of an object reflect interpretations of its contents. After the Middle Ages, the idea of the songbook conditioned philological practices through a valuation of either the songbook's contents or the songbook as container. These two modes of interpretation are especially clear in pre-nineteenth-century antiquarianism, where the publication of a medieval text often meant the transcription of a lyric text from a single source, and included its creative elaboration and translation rather than the empirical reconstruction of a phantom originary text.[4] In their production of songbooks, postmedieval readers and scholars dismantled or reinforced the medieval songbook in ways that reflect personal interests and cultural priorities of the age. The idea of the medieval songbook was essential for the cultivation of literary activity imagined within regional, intellectual and national communities. By looking at some key examples from the seventeenth to the twentieth centuries in the traditions I have treated in this book, we can see that medieval songbooks have always been interpreted within frameworks of local and cultural assumptions.

The two modes of interpretation can be seen in the following ways. First, studies and editions elaborate on an organizational principle in the manuscript (for example, the author) in order to promote historical, aesthetic, or social values in songbook form. This interpretation, in the form of transcriptions and translations of lyric texts in songbook or chronicle format, or in the form of critical author editions, neglects the medieval manuscript as a performative document that transmits contradictory or flexible guidelines, consistent with medieval poetry. An author edition replaces the nebulous idea of the "author" both as a literary persona and a material phenomenon expressed in medieval songbooks with the historical fact of a biographical canon. Second, regarding the songbook as container symbolizing a collective, editions and studies of songbooks frame their contents under a national or cultural myth. These two postmedieval songbook practices are themselves medievalisms: they reflect different forms of medieval alterity as a projection of a cultural other, and they also show the extent to which the idea of the songbook has been significant for both the undermining and the building of literary traditions.

LYRIC CONTENTS: AUTHOR, HISTORY, AND LANGUAGE

Recalling the title of chansonnier I, the idea of the poet has been one of the most operative dismantling principles of the songbook for serving the interests of postmedieval readers. It is significant that the first official introduction to the troubadours placed overwhelming emphasis on their biographies rather than their lyrics. Jean de Nostredame elaborated creatively on the compilation of Italian chansonniers keyed to authors in order to promote his native region. In his *Vies des plus celebres et anciens poetes provensaux* (1575),[5] Nostredame includes some transcriptions of lyric texts but focuses almost exclusively on translating the *vidas* of the chansonniers into French. Despite promoting the literary value of the Provençal language and the troubadours for poets such as Dante and Petrarch, and although he describes the different lyric genres, he apparently did not find it necessary to include many of the "œuvres de nos poëtes provensaux" (9). Claiming to base his publication on the study of several manuscripts (mostly invented), he translated and revised the *vidas* to grant prestige to the nobility of Provence — making all the troubadours hail from his own province and fabricating legends of the troubadours to directly connect them to the regional aristocracy.[6] Later, the seventeenth-century Dominicy viewed the *Vies* as an authoritative source for his own regional history, using Nostredame's creative versions of troubadour biographies instead of drawing on the chansonniers to which he had access ("que j'ai chez moi manuscrites"). While Dominicy did extract information from the chansonniers to create his regional history, and may have been more interested than Nostredame was in creating an accurate history, he still viewed Nostredame as a faithful transcriber of the manuscripts.

Enlightenment scholars (and, later, nineteenth-century philologists)[7] remedied what they considered amateur studies and the romanticization of the manuscript sources by producing what amounted to anti-songbooks: the eighteenth-century medievalist Jean-Baptiste de La Curne de Sainte-Palaye went about collecting versions of surviving troubadour poems from known manuscripts, but when his collaborator the Abbé Millot wrote the *Histoire littéraire des troubadours* in 1774, he presented a history containing no quotations of troubadour lyrics in Occitan. Sainte-Palaye recognized a need for a first-hand account of the troubadours — to make the public familiar with ("faire connoître") a literature clearly essential to the history of France's spiritual progress ("se faire une idée juste du progrès de l'esprit en France").[8] Yet by viewing the troubadours' work as historical documents of France's spiritual development rather than as lyric texts, Sainte-Palaye's *Histoire* fulfills a historical distance at the cost of literary sensibility. As Lionel Gossman has argued, the desire of Sainte-Palaye and Millot to demonstrate historical competence, discredit past myths, and link the troubadours to universal questions concerning French civilization ultimately consigned the troubadours to the history of ideas rather than the history of literature. Even Millot himself concludes that the goal of their work was "de faire connoître les idées plutôt que le style des Troubadours."[9] This anti-songbook as history reflected the current belief that troubadour poetry had no aesthetic value and served as a negative example of a barbaric period in a progressive history of ideas and the human spirit.

In contrast to the earlier transcriptions of lyric excerpts in the formats of *vida*-based anthology or chronicle, critical author editions and publications of generic classification in the nineteenth century represent another version of the content principle as a mode of songbook interpretation. Because the Occitan language never corresponded to any historical political unity—the Italian chansonniers themselves being compilations of nonnative (Occitan) poetry with a cultural and aesthetic status independent of an ethnic or geographic identity for their thirteenth-century Italian audience—the treatment of troubadour manuscripts during the nineteenth century reflects the romantic preoccupations with the Middle Ages in ways different from the more familiar view of medieval epics as the origin of national culture. Author editions, handbooks, and dictionaries represent how scholars valued troubadour lyric not as the origin of a national culture but as the origin of Romance language or a grammatical poetic instinct, and the troubadour as embodying "the Romantic poet-hero."[10] Songbooks contained valuable lyrics that, like objects in an archaeological dig, needed to be unearthed from their unreliable and decayed manuscript shell and reconstructed by means of statistical evidence of other witnesses and sound empirical methods. The tools required for this kind of excavation are reference manuals such as Karl Bartsch's *Grundriß zur Geschichte der provenzalischen Literatur* (1872), which classifies the troubadour manuscripts and names troubadours in alphabetical order with all attributed songs listed alphabetically by incipit. François-Juste-Marie Raynouard published the still major Occitan dictionary, the *Lexique Roman*, as a response to his view of this language as a "langue romane primitive" (*Choix des poésies littéraire*, 1816).[11] Bartsch in his 1857 edition of *Peire Vidal* (the first such edition to apply a systematic classification of troubadour manuscripts) proposes that chansonniers are composed of discrete "Liederheften" or "song-notebooks," "which recorded the songs either from a written copy or from oral delivery that they [the troubadours] had learned."[12] Bartsch's author edition distanced itself from the preoccupations of epic scholarship, such as the epic as the origin of a collective voice based on the separation of oral and written stages of transmission.

In all these cases, the extraction, generic classification, and edition of authorial and lyric content from manuscripts demonstrate that not only was the disposition of the material container insignificant, but the idea of a songbook was of little value for the new anthologies keyed to emergent conceptions and debates concerning medieval vernacular literature (oral versus written transmission, epic versus lyric). The desire to affirm or codify certain ideas of troubadour authorship, history, and language preceded the heterogeneity of the material container. As Nichols points out in examining Jeanroy's *Bibliographie sommaire des chansonniers provençaux* (1916), Jeanroy, like philologists before him, was mainly interested in the generic disposition, location, and classification of individual texts, which he considered more important than the organization of the manuscript.[13] In efforts to historicize nineteenth-century Romance philology, Nichols calls for the study of the "manuscript matrix," focusing on texts as they appear in tangible manuscripts of parchment or paper involving different artisans, from scribe to illuminator, rather than on an ideal reconstructed text.[14] In order to establish literary traditions (the troubadours as Nostredame's Provence, Sainte-Palaye and Millot's view of the troubadours as a history of ideas) or prove scientific hypotheses (Raynouard's theory of a primitive Romance language, the oral and written transmission of troubadour lyric) the songbook had to be dismantled or excavated as a medieval artifact and its lyric or authorial contents extracted, creatively translated, or philologically classified.

LYRIC CONTAINER: KINGDOM, REGION, AND NATION

In contrast to songbook contents as serving personal, individual, or aesthetic interests, the songbook as container has been a powerful symbol of a collective. In the Iberian and German traditions, the songbook has embodied a linguistic or cultural unity, and this unity has served the purpose of promoting the aesthetic heritage of a region or nation-to-be. The songbook commemorated an age that exhibited the promise of a people. The *Cantigas de Santa María* figures as a model for the symbolic potential of the songbook for promoting cultural unity and cultural literary historics; it is an important precedent for later songbook mythologies. As a troubadour serving the Virgin Mary in hopes of winning salvation, Alfonso is the troubadour-king, the compiler-poet who unites his kingdom through a songbook. As discussed in chapter three, the miniatures cultivate the idea that the songs are the work of Alfonso himself, the songs constituting a royal autobiography. One need only recall the opening miniature of the Escorial codex depicting Alfonso directing the compilation of the *Cantigas* among his court.[15] The *Cantigas* established for the Iberian tradition a distinctly performative myth of the *cancionero*, as the songbook is seen as invested with supernatural powers. In *cantiga* number 279, the king is miraculously cured of an illness when a volume containing some *cantigas* is placed on his person.[16] Given that the poems were also performed, the *Cantigas* not only preserves lyric poetry and possesses value as a cultural monument but physically united Alfonso's kingdom through music sung communally.

With this institutional model of Iberian songbooks as a significant precedent, poets like Santillana looked to the content, prestige, and flexible structure of songbooks to make their place in an Iberian literary tradition. In his *Prohemio,* Santillana mentions a *cancioneiro* that belonged to his grandmother; "aver visto un grand volumen de cantigas, serranas e dezires portugueses e gallegos; de los quales toda la mayor parte era del Rey don Donís de Portugal" (I have seen a large volume of *cantigas*, serranas and Portugese and Galician *dezires*; of which the majority are by King Dinis of Portugal).[17] As both a family heirloom and an archival object, the songbook embodies historical continuity from the Galician-Portuguese lyric under King Dinis (r. 1279–1325) to contemporary Castilian lyric. He includes with the *Prohemio* his own *volumen* of his lyrics — acknowledging the literary history that songbooks provide for composing poetry in the present. Moreover, as Dagenais has argued, in the *Prohemio* Santillana recognizes the poetic experimentation of early Castilian authors, such as Juan Ruiz, whose works may have circulated in multiauthored anthologies containing diverse lyrics.[18] By the mid-fifteenth century, cancioneros — perhaps the "Libro del Arçipreste de Hita" cited by Santillana along with the *volúmenes* of Santillana's grandmother and his own — embody vernacular lyrics from different eras while collectively inviting emendation as an Iberian tradition continuing into the present. Moreover, it is clear from the *Prohemio* that songbooks constitute a literary history both in their diverse contents and as works in themselves—for example, the "Libro" as an important document of early Castilian poetry in various forms, his grandmother's *volumen* as testimony to the Galician-Portuguese lyric tradition, and finally his *volumen* containing lyrics informed by these songbooks.

The songbook as performative myth, and as cultural monument that enables literary traditions and rejuvenates contemporary poetic production, can also be seen in Johann Jakob Breitinger and Johann Jakob Bodmer's transcription (*Abschrift*) of the main *Minnesang* songbook, the *Sammlung von Minnesingern aus dem schwäbischen Zeitpunkte* (1759), and in Bodmer's *Das Erdmännchen* story (1749),[19] which contextualized the symbolic importance of the songbook. Bodmer and Breitinger's *Sammlung* was motivated by their interest in Middle High German literature as a source for reviving literary language: German could return to its unregulated, freer state through cultivation of its dialects and study of Middle High German lyric's "noble simplicity."[20] Moreover, their naming of the large Heidelberg manuscript (Codex Palatinus Germanicus 848) as the *Codex Manesse*—based on their belief that the Manesse family of Zürich was responsible for its compilation—emphasized the historical study of their native Swabian culture (such as the Hohenstaufen dynasty) and Alemannic dialect (which Bodmer thought was closely related to Middle High German). In short, a study of medieval culture located in a linguistic region, history, and idiom could rehabilitate the language of the German people. In their preface, the editors mention how Old English anthologies have inspired modern English poets such as John Dryden, and hope this collection of medieval German lyric will have the same effect in German-speaking lands ("Deutschland," *Sammlung,* "Vorrede" IV).

In the *Sammlung* and the allegorical *Erdmännchen*, it is clear that Bodmer believed that the rehabilitation of German literary language required humanistic editorial activity, including the study of Middle High German, transcribing manuscripts, and nourishing the totemic idea of the songbook as facilitating immediate contact between medieval and contemporary poets. In *Erdmännchen*, a mysterious dwarf from the royal household of King Laurin (a famous court around 1200), bestows "die manneßische Sammlung von Minneliedern" (Manesse's collection of *Minnesang* lyric) on a modern admirer of medieval poetry.[21] A *Wettgesang* or singing contest occurs between the narrator and the dwarf, as stanzas from Friedrich von Hagedorn are antiphonally juxtaposed with verses from the Manesse songbook. The dwarf gives the *Sammlung* to the narrator because the poet, proving himself worthy of the collection of *Minnesang*, can now take on the duty of protecting and continuing a cultural inheritance. Bodmer develops a mythical songbook as a romantic vision of underground poetry recovered from the dust of oblivion and the dangers of historical circumstances, staging a lyric immediacy between past and present through a magical book, as the details of the luxurious quality and magical aura of the "Buch" attest.[22] As both a philological and mythological object belonging to the occult world, the *Co-*

dex Manesse enables poiesis by symbolizing a cultural heritage and providing models of ancient poetic forms for inspiring poets.[23] Indeed, like the *Codex* poet Hadlaub, who expressed his admiration for the Manesses's patronage of *Minnesang* by compiling songbooks in Zürich, Bodmer continued the Manesse tradition through the combination of his scholarship and mythologization of the songbook (the *Codex* as vehicle for and object of poetry). *Erdmännchen* explains how the *Codex Manesse* contains the origin of German letters by preserving the spirit of the High Middle Ages through a specific dialect and poetry that retains the original force of German's diction. In Bodmer's *Codex* imaginary, a Swabian songbook becomes a cultural monument of German literary language by embodying the "age of golden lovesong" ("der Alter des güldenen Liebesgesanges").[24]

Finally, the drive to create a cultural monument of German *Volk* through the idea of the songbook in the nineteenth century is reflected in Karl Lachmann's foundational edition of Middle High German lyric, *Des Minnesangs Frühling*, completed by his student Moriz Haupt in 1857. Lachmann and Haupt established a chronological canon of poets and their works from the early to high periods of *Minnesang*. During a century of the institutionalization of *Germanistik*—the romantic project of imagining a German nation or people through a unified German language and literature following the theories and work of the Grimm brothers, Friedrich Schlegel, and others[25]—Lachmann's edition represented the historical fascination with seeing the monumental songbook as the collected work of whole generations and as establishing a literary canon. It continued Bodmer's idea of a songbook as the golden age of German culture, but now a positivistic critical edition embodied this idea rather than diplomatic transcription contextualized by the allegory of a *Sammlung*. Similar to Lachmann's view articulated in his 1826 edition of the *Nibelungenlied*, in which he follows the hypothesis of Ferdinand Wolf, Schlegel, and others that the song had been gradually assembled rather than composed by a single author,[26] *Des Minnesangs Frühling* substantiated *Minnesang* as a collection of different works and poets over time. In giving priority to the idea of an age of poetic flowering rather than individual authors, this critical edition in songbook format constitutes a monument of German culture. Meanwhile, the author editions of troubadours such as Bartsch's *Peire Vidal* and Lachmann's own *Die Gedichte Walthers von der Vogelweide* (1827) continued the biographical principle built into the songbooks and the lyric itself while incorporating new methods of textual criticism into the construction of an author.

Later editors responded to Lachmann and Haupt's textual criticism in successive editions. An examination of the various *Frühling* editions represents how different editorial methods and philological viewpoints work within an ideological songbook framework or challenge that hermeneutic container: at first the monumental *Frühling* represents the romantic desire, not only to preserve a lyric tradition from the contingency of time, but to create a perfect songbook out of the imperfect reality of manuscript transmission. The Lachmannian system of mechanical transmission and closed recension presupposes written transmission, since any oral transmission must assume variants that escape stemmatic control. As William Paden comments concerning the chansonniers, "the ideal manuscript for Lachmannian analysis is a passive replica of its original; the chansonniers, with their elaborate evidence of philological effort of many kinds on the part of their producers, complicate the notion of error beyond any possibility of unraveling it."[27] Many chansonniers and *Liederhandschriften* show evidence of using various sources, perhaps one main source shared among different collections combined with favorite local poets, or inflected with the regional language of the copyist. In the case of the latest texts, some would be actively revised at the time of compilation by contemporary troubadours. In such conditions, variants should be seen not as a deviation from an *Urtext* but, as Zumthor theorizes *mouvance*, an innovative creative process of participatory reproduction from an oral and written perspective.[28]

In contrast to a songbook monument built on Lachmann's system, and converging with recent troubadour scholarship, contemporary *Minnesang* editors call the most recent editions of *Frühling* an "Arbeitsausgabe mit 'offenem' Text" (a work edition with an open text): a more transparent, critical edition whose apparatus and commentary make historical documentation of variants available for its readers.[29] This edition documents what Nichols, following Zumthor, has called "le dire": performative acts and contexts of speaking present in a "manuscript matrix," aspects of oral performance, and interactions between written and oral phenomena, recoverable only obliquely in the manuscripts as multiple insertions. "Le dire" is opposed to "le dit": "communication as fact and artifact."[30] In the second half of the twentieth century a new generation of editors—among them Kuhn, Hugo Moser, Helmut Teervoren, and Günther Schweikle[31]—strove to establish different editorial principles from their predecessors, incorporating new theories of song performance and written transmission. Increasingly dubious of Lachmann's conjectural principles, they produced diplomatic editions and editions based on the "Leithandschriftenprinzip" first established by Joseph Bédier. This approach, favored by the most recent editors of

Frühling, Moser and Teervoren, conservatively edits from one manuscript (*Leithandschrift*) and, if necessary, considers variant versions from more than one manuscript. Unlike the Lachmannian method, which seeks to reconstruct the original text from all available manuscripts, the *Leithandschrift* method presupposes the disturbance of the original song unity, given the oral-to-written transmission history. Thus one has to negotiate a level of unity restricted to a strophe or *Lied*. In the most recent edition of *Frühling*, the base manuscript may vary from strophe to strophe, while Schweilke in his editions chooses a base manuscript for an entire poem.[32] In their prefaces, these editors stress the subjectivity that goes into editorial judgment in an effort to make their choices transparent to the reader. The reader understands how the editor constructs a *Lied* from the corpus of manuscripts (or one manuscript) and, when unsatisfied with the editor's text, may freely choose other variants made apparent to him. The editors emphasize the agency of text interpretation over the imposition of an editor's judgment. In short, the editorial history of the *Frühling* constitutes a history of *Minnesang* editions as the affirmation and dismantling of the German songbook as cultural monument.

Finally, in the modern scholarship of late medieval cancioneros we see the persistence of the songbook container as cultural practice and national mythology. Given the precedent of the *Cantigas*, and the prolific production of cancioneros in the fifteenth and sixteenth centuries, it is notable that despite a few nineteenth-century editions,[33] and other "modest and less systematic" work of other scholars,[34] it was not until the twentieth century that Raymond Foulché-Delbosc published an anthology and useful bibliography of the cancionero corpus.[35] On the one hand, the editing of that corpus suffered from a lack of interest as scholars viewed its contents as mostly mediocre poetry before the Golden Age. On the other, when critical editions and bibliographies were produced, post–Civil War scholarship focused on the editing of single cancioneros. As Beltran Pepió states, "from the 1940s through the early 1970s it [was] thought that each cancionero represented a particular school, period, or compiler, and research was redirected into editing them as an organic whole." Although these editions made the texts available, Spanish philology focused solely on this kind of research; until recently there has been a striking lack of literary study on individual cancionero poets.[36]

Why do we see this combination of editorial neglect and the privileging of the manuscript container? One possible answer is that while the collaboration of nationalist theories of culture and philology shaped continental textual criticism in its pursuit of the phantom archetype, motivating the analysis of a songbook's contents into linguistic reference manuals, or author or epoch editions, the cancionero was perceived as both archival object and embodiment of a cultural tradition continuing in the present. This persistence of the cancionero as an inviolable container from the late nineteenth to the mid-twentieth centuries may be attributed to a growing nationalistic purpose guiding the understanding of Spanish literary history. Beginning in 1836, a few years after the death of Fernando VII, the National Library (formerly the Royal Library) began acquiring books in a conscious attempt to provide the nation with a patrimony; a Royal Decree declared Spanish literature a university discipline. In addition to these important institutional developments, native historians such as José Amador de los Ríos wrote a history of Spanish literature (*Historia crítica de la literatura española*, 1861) characterized by a unified language, "lengua castellana" or "español," and a unified religious ideology, Catholicism. According to Amador de los Ríos, the idea of Catholicism was "grounded in the medieval period, and crystallized in the Castilian tongue."[37] With such ideas of cultural, religious, and linguistic continuity, medieval traditions function in the present to fulfill their divinely ordained promise. This image of an ideologically unified Spain as simultaneously ancient, medieval, and modern perpetuated the paradoxical nonalterity of cancioneros as objects of study.

Contributing to this paradoxical quality of the cancionero, scholars at this time encouraged the idea of Spanish literature as a communal project of the people rather than as a canon of authors. While criticizing cancionero lyric as artificial and of little aesthetic worth, Marcelino Menéndez y Pelayo and Ramón Menéndez Pidal, arguably the most influential Hispanists of the late nineteenth and twentieth centuries, articulated a national literary traditionalism that buttressed the sociological phenomenon of a cancionero as an inviolable communal book. For example, Menéndez Pelayo encouraged the view of cancioneros as representative of a continuing Spanish medieval tradition in the present. In the prologue to the first volume of *Antología de poetas líricos castellanos*, he explains the value of the cancionero tradition as a literary archive that testifies to "todas las transformaciones del arte" (all the transformations of art); he further emphasizes that a single poet cannot give a good account of the aesthetic culture of an era like a *Cancionero*.[38] Menéndez Pelayo both places his anthology ("esta colección") within the continuing cancionero tradition (recalling Santillana), and emphasizes the cultural value of the cancionero as an archival object. Such collections are greater than the work of a single poet, for they

give us, at a glance, the production of an entire period. Likewise, Menéndez Pidal, expounding a version of the German romantic ideal of *Volksgeist*,
views Spanish epics and ballads as living organisms that have evolved over
time, becoming traditional literature as they come to represent the total of
several authors collaborating with one another, the Spanish people as the
author of a work.[39]

Thus, while the contents of late medieval cancioneros are generally ex-
empt from the national works that embody the Spanish spirit, both Menéndez Pelayo and Menéndez Pidal set the tone for cancioneros to be viewed
as a living tradition (Menéndez Pelayo) and as a work representing the collaboration of Spaniards over time (Menéndez Pidal). Their legitimizing language confirms the importance of a unified literary tradition, and within
this traditional rhetoric the cancionero represents a patrimony of "el pueblo
español," despite containing middling verse.[40]

The insistence on a medieval Spanish character, combined with the
condemnation of cancionero poetry, helps us to imagine a scenario where
cancioneros are at once valued as traditional cultural objects and neglected
as philological artifacts — the result being the lack of author editions and
the view of each book as representative of a social group or literary coterie.
From this perspective, the material and historical reality of the cancionero
container has dominated the philological instinct that we have seen in the
other traditions: to dissect and systematize its contents, or to recreate a
stable literary canon through a definitive critical edition in songbook format
such as *Des Minnesangs Frühling*. In contrast to this latter situation, Spain's
first decades of the twentieth century see a humanistic spirit akin to the per-
sonality of Miguel de Unamuno, a contemporary of Menéndez Pidal (both
of the generation of 1898) and cited by the latter, who wrote about the persistent spirit of a people: "Siéntome con un alma medieval, y se me antoja
que es medieval el alma de mi patria; que ha atravesado ésta, a la fuerza, por
el Renacimiento, la Reforma y la Revolución, aprendiendo, si, de ellas, pero
sin dejarse tocar al alma . . . y el quijotismo no es sino lo más desesperado
de la lucha de la Edad Media contra el Renacimiento" (I feel that my soul
is medieval, and it strikes me that the soul of my country is medieval: I feel
that it has passed perforce through the Renaissance, the Reformation, the
Revolution, indeed learning from them but never letting its soul be touched;
and Quixotism is nothing but the despairing struggle of the Middle Ages
against the Renaissance).[41] This cultural attachment to the eternal Middle
Ages of Spanish identity informed the manner in which the cancionero was
at once elided as a philological object of study and yet held up as a testimony

of the contemporary soul — a document of the Spanish people and its surviving medieval traditions despite periods and fashions imposed from the
outside.

I end with the cancionero because in many ways it demonstrates the
two poles of what a songbook can mean as a source of valuable contents or
as an ideological container. It shows the complex ways in which the idea of
the Middle Ages, as mirror of national or cultural identity, can permeate
and condition editorial practices. The medieval songbook or the idea of the
songbook at once affects and is affected by narratives of ethnic, linguistic,
or cultural identity. As my study has argued all along, we can think of songbooks as becoming alive in the various hermeneutic interactions between
reader and object, including the various postmedieval afterlives of these
interactions. The cancionero is a paradigmatic example: on the one hand,
current cancionero scholarship reflects an awareness of the cancionero as an
important literary object and phenomenon in the history of Iberian letters;
on the other, cancioneros are sources of lyric texts whose aesthetic value is
being reassessed. Critical editions of authors and poems, reference works,
and book-length studies of cancionero verse have revised the negative judgments of earlier critics.[42] The focus has shifted back to the cancionero, not
as an unreliable manuscript container, nor as an inviolable medieval phenomenon, but as an embodiment of the sociological functions of cancionero
verse during a period in which *el arte de trovar* was a practice that Menéndez
Pelayo describes as a "*sport* más refinado."[43] Although cancionero scholarship has benefited from comparisons with other vernacular songbook traditions, it has also been considered on its own performative terms — the
songbook as genre of self-representation.[44] While scholars work from the
familiar position of songbooks and their memorial functions, they look at
texts within the context (social, literary, cultural, material) of a cancionero,
and regard the placement and ordering of text groups as frames that shape
the hermeneutic reception of individual texts.

Can the medieval songbook help us understand modern "songbooks"
of all sorts? This book has sought to present the medieval songbook as
both physical artifact and generic concept, this duality challenging unified narratives of poetry. I have also ventured to show how the medieval
songbook is both a communal object and a discourse reinterpreted by different readers over time, its works and authors placed in new collections
even as we become more aware of the physical contexts in which they first
appeared.[45] It emblematizes what has been seen as the postmodern quality
of medieval textuality — work, author, and literature seen as anthology, as-

sembly, or pastiche constantly in process of formation, quotation, and deformation. Modern songbooks represent both an audience's expectations and an editor-compiler's intentionality; they reflect modes of transmission and reception that shape the contents and principles of lyric collocation (public concerts, personal listening devices, record, cassette, iPod). Since medieval songbooks translate performative, oral, and auditory experiences of lyric poetry, they are useful for thinking about how archival objects relate to the medium and social conditions in which the lyrics are performed, just as modern poetry continues to be anthologized, and literary traditions are made and unmade through the practice of the songbook — the very process of making lyric poetry.

Notes

INTRODUCTION

1. Seth Lerer, "Medieval English Literature and the Idea of the Anthology" *PMLA* 118 (2003): 1255.

2. See Hans Robert Jauss, *Alterität und Modernität der mittelalterlichen Literatur: Gesammelte Aufsätze 1956–1976* (Munich: Wilhelm Fink, 1977), and its translation, with corresponding articles, in *New Literary History* (1979): 181–227, esp. 185, 187–94.

3. Hugo Kuhn, *Entwürfe zur einer Literatursystematik des Spätmittelalters* (Tübingen: Max Niemeyer, 1980).

4. Previous studies over the terms that have been traditionally attributed to manuscript collections of lyric texts (anthology, miscellany, *chansonnier*, *Liederhandschriften*, *cancionero*) include Elizabeth W. Poe, *Compilatio: Lyric Texts and Prose Commentaries in Troubadour Manuscript H (Vat. Lat. 3207)* (Lexington, KY: French Forum, 2000); essays in *The Whole Book: Cultural Perspectives on the Medieval Miscellany*, ed. Stephen G. Nichols and Siegfried Wenzel (Ann Arbor: University of Michigan Press, 1996) [Nichols and Wenzel], and in Susanna Fein, *Studies in the Harley Manuscript* (Kalamazoo: TEAMS, 2000). See also Lerer's significant discussion about concepts of "literature" as it pertains to the anthology, in "Medieval English Literature."

5. Examples of important philological theses and work on manuscripts include D'Arco Silvio Avalle, *I manoscritti della letteratura in lingua d'oc,* revised edition of Lino Leonardi (1961; Turin: Einaudi, 1993); the series *Intavulare: tavole di canzonieri,* ed. Anna Ferrari et al. (Vatican City: Biblioteca Apostolica Vaticana, 1998–); and individual songbook studies such as those of chansonnier H by Maria Careri, *Il canzoniere provenzale H (Vat. Lat. 3207): struttura, contenuto e fonti* (Modena: Mucchi editore, 1990), and Poe, *Compilatio.*

6. One can chart a revision — or "renovatio" as Nichols states in his introduction to "The New Philology," special issue of *Speculum* 65 (1990): 1 — of medieval studies, from the 1979 special issue of *New Literary History,* "Medieval Literature and Contemporary Theory," featuring a translation of Jauss's introduction to *Alterität,* and influenced by debates concerning Paul Zumthor's *Essai de poétique médiévale* (Paris: Seuil, 1972); to the 1988 special issue of *Romanic Review,* the "Legitimacy of the Middle Ages," which considers theoretical issues of orality and ideologies of text editing (essays reprinted in *The New Medievalism,* ed. Marina S. Brownlee, et al. [Baltimore: Johns Hopkins University Press, 1991]); and to the 1990 special issue of *Speculum* (see above). One sees the influence of Kuhn/Jauss historical typologies and genre perspective in the ambitions of the

unfinished *Grundriß der romanischen Literaturen des Mittelalters* (Heidelberg: C. Winter, 1968–) [*GRLM*]. *Medievalism and the Modernist Temper*, ed. R. Howard Bloch and Nichols (Baltimore: Johns Hopkins University Press, 1996) [Bloch and Nichols] is just one representative example of the study of medieval literature seen from the history of scholarship, institutions, and national ideologies.

7. Stephen G. Nichols, "'Art' and 'Nature' Looking for (Medieval) Principles of Order in Occitan *Chansonnier* N (Morgan 819)," in Nichols and Wenzel 83–121, and "The Early Troubadours: Guilhem IX to Bernart de Ventadorn," in *The Troubadours: An Introduction*, ed. Simon Gaunt and Sarah Kay (Cambridge: Cambridge University Press, 1999) 66–82 [Gaunt and Kay]; Sylvia Huot, *From Song to Book: The Poetics of Writing in Old French Lyric and Lyrical Narrative Poetry* (Ithaca: Cornell University Press, 1987) 11.

8. Vincenç Beltran Pepió, "The Typology and Genesis of the *Cancioneros*," and Michel Garcia, "In Praise of the *Cancionero*: Considerations on the Social Meaning of the Castilian *Cancioneros*," in *Poetry at Court in Trastamaran Spain: From the* Cancionero de Baena *to the* Cancionero General, ed. E. Michael Gerli and Julian Weiss (Tempe, Arizona: Medieval and Renaissance Texts and Studies, 1998) 19–46, 47–56 [Gerli and Weiss]; Brian Dutton et al., *Catálogo-índice de la poesía cancioneril del siglo XV* (Madison: Hispanic Seminary of Medieval Studies, 1982); Brian Dutton and Jineen Krogstad, eds., *El cancionero del siglo XV, c. 1360–1520*, 7 vols. (Salamanca: University Press and Biblioteca Española del Siglo XV, 1990–91).

9. Jan-Dirk Müller, *Rules for the Endgame: The World of the Nibelungenlied*, trans. William T. Whobrey (Baltimore: Johns Hopkins University Press, 2007); Horst Wenzel, *Spiegelungen: zur Kultur der Visualität im Mittelalter* (Berlin: Erich Schmidt, 2009); Kathryn Starkey, *Reading the Medieval Book: Word, Image, and Performance in Wolfram von Eschenbach's Willehalm* (Notre Dame: University of Notre Dame Press, 2004).

10. Aurelio Roncaglia, "Rétrospectives et perspectives dans l'étude des chansonniers d'oc," in *Lyrique romane médiévale: La tradition des chansonniers. Actes du Colloque du Liège, 1989*, ed. Madeleine Tyssens (Liège: Bibliothèque de la Faculté de Philosophie et Lettres de l'Université de Liège, 1991) 19–38 [Tyssens, *Lyrique romane*], esp. 41.

11. John Dagenais, *The Ethics of Reading in Manuscript Culture: Glossing the* Libro de Buen Amor (Princeton: Princeton University Press, 1994).

12. *Cancioneiro da Ajuda*, ed. Carolina Michaëlis de Vasconcellos, 2 vols. (Halle: Niemeyer, 1904); see also diplomatic edition of Henry H. Carter, *Cancioneiro da Ajuda* (New York, London: MLA, Oxford University Press, 1941).

13. I use the conventional *sigla* to designate the chansonniers: see Alfred Pillet and Henry Carstens, *Bibliographie der Troubadours* (1933; New York: Burt Franklin, 1968), x–xliv [Pillet and Carstens].

14. Dante Alighieri, *De vulgari eloquentia*, ed. Pier Vincenzo Mengaldo, *Opere minori*, ed. Mengaldo et al., 2 vols. (Milan: Ricciardi [1979–]) 2: 187 (Bk. II, 6, 7).

15. See Sylvia Huot on the Old French chansonniers (*Song to Book*) and Olivia Holmes in *Assembling the Lyric Self: Authorship from Troubadour Song to Italian Poetry Book* (Minneapolis: University of Minnesota Press, 2000). While agreeing with Huot and Holmes's

findings on the emergence of single-author compilations, my study attempts to expand our understanding of the songbook as a genre and phenomenon through an interdisciplinary, comparative (building hermeneutic relations beyond national literary traditions), and transhistorical methodology. My study also aims to complement Jane H. M. Taylor's *The Making of Poetry: Late-Medieval French Poetic Anthologies* (Turnhout: Brepols, 2007), which examines the compilation and reception of late medieval French codices, such as the authorized manuscripts of Christine de Pizan, Eustache Deschamps, and Charles d'Orléans.

16. John Freccero, "The Fig Tree and the Laurel: Petrarch's Poetics," *Diacritics* 5 (1975): 34–40. The fact that the *Rime sparse* has been traditionally entitled *Canzoniere*, or songbook, demonstrates the foundational aspect of songbooks for the Italian Renaissance. The first recorded use of this title was in 1516; see Guglielmo Gorni, "Le forme primarie del testo poetico," *Letteratura italiana* 3.1 (Turin: Einaudi, 1984) 509.

17. Laura Kendrick, *The Game of Love: Troubadour Wordplay* (Berkeley and Los Angeles: University of California Press, 1988); Amelia E. Van Vleck, *Memory and Re-creation in Troubadour Lyric* (Berkeley and Los Angeles: University of California Press, 1991); and Müller, *Rules for the Endgame.*

18. Jacques Le Goff, *My Quest for the Middle Ages*, trans. Richard Veasey (New York: Palgrave Macmillan, 2005) 89.

19. See Nichols, "Introduction" 8; and "The Early Troubadours," in Gaunt and Kay 75.

20. In *Subjectivity in Troubadour Poetry* (Cambridge: Cambridge University Press, 1990), Sarah Kay contests Zumthor's "I" as purely situated in language and in formal and musical conventions by arguing for elements of historical and temporal selfhood. All troubadour songs are identified by first line and by number from Pillet and Carstens.

21. Jacques Derrida, *Archive Fever: A Freudian Impression*, trans. Eric Prenowitz (Chicago: University of Chicago Press, 1996) 11.

22. Of the major Italian manuscripts compiled in this period, many of the owners were Italian nobility or aristocrats; see William D. Paden, "Manuscripts," in *A Handbook of the Troubadours*, ed. F. R. P. Akehurst and Judith M. Davis (Berkeley: University of California Press, 1995) 307–33, esp. 309 [Akehurst and Davis]; see also Avalle, *I manoscritti.* That most chansonniers were compiled in Italy testifies to the interest during the thirteenth to sixteenth centuries in claiming the troubadours for an Italian literary tradition. François Zufferey, *Recherches linguistiques sur les chansonniers provençaux* (Geneva: Droz, 1987), relates how out of forty chansonniers extant, those compiled in northern Italy number twenty-six and include AIKDDªHST (316).

23. According to Angelica Rieger, out of the forty-six main Occitan chansonniers, nine out of the thirty parchment chansonniers contain illumination: AIKNEMHCR. AIKHN are from Italian ateliers compiled during the thirteenth century. See Rieger, "Ins e.l cor port, dona, vostra faisso: Image et imaginaire de la femme à travers l'enluminure dans les chansonniers de troubadours," *Cahiers de civilisation médiévale* 28 (1985): 385–415; especially 386–87; Maria Luisa Meneghetti, *Il pubblico dei trovatori* (Turin: Einaudi, 1992)

245-76. In addition to the references of Pillet and Carstens, I will also refer to the edition and notes of Martín de Riquer, *Los trovadores: Historia literaria y textos*, 3 vols. (Barcelona: Ariel, 2001) 1: 12-14 [Riquer], and Zufferey 4-6.

24. See Holmes's discussion of the transmission of vernacular poetry through a written medium, especially the passage on the "massive variability of the manuscript tradition" (*Assembling* 4-6, esp. 5), and Gustav Gröber's hypotheses discussed in chapter two.

25. Van Vleck, *Memory and Re-creation* 66-68.

26. "Erec et Enide," ed. Jean-Marie Fritz, in Chrétien de Troyes, *Romans* (Paris: Librairie Générale Française, 1994) line 14.

27. See Müller's critical analysis of these concepts in his study of the *Nibelungenlied*, *Rules for the Endgame* 18.

28. See Ana María Gómez-Bravo, "*Decir canciones*: The Question of Genre in *Cancionero* Poetry," in *Medieval Lyric: Genres in Historical Context*, ed. Paden (Urbana: University of Illinois Press, 2000) 158-87.

CHAPTER ONE

1. Malcolm B. Parkes, "The Influence of the Concepts of *Ordinatio* and *Compilatio* on the Development of the Book," in *Medieval Learning and Literature: Essays Presented to Richard William Hunt*, ed. J. J. G. Alexander and M. T. Gibson (Oxford: Oxford University Press, 1976) 115-41. See also Richard Hunter Rouse and Mary Ames Rouse's discussion on the *florilegium,* which bears on *Carmina*'s aspect as a collection of extracts that would have been disseminated in a clerical environment, "The *Florilegium Angelicum*: Its Origins, Content, and Influence," 66-114 in this collection.

2. I refer to the facsimile edition, *Carmina Burana: Facsimile Reproduction of the Manuscript Clm 4660 and Clm 4660a*, ed. Bernhard Bischoff, Publication of Medieval Manuscripts 9 (Brooklyn: Institute of Mediaeval Music, 1967); and the critical edition, *Carmina Burana*, ed. Alfons Hilka, Otto Schumann, and Bernhard Bischoff, 2 vols. (Heidelberg: Carl Winter, 1930-78). All citations are from this critical edition (*Carmina* or CB, and Schumann's introduction in vol. 2, part I, Schumann), with reference to the Bischoff facsimile and his introduction [*Carmina Burana*, ed. Bischoff]. I also consult the *Carmina Burana: Texte und Übersetzungen,* ed. Benedikt Konrad Vollmann (Frankfurt: Deutscher Klassiker Verlag, 1987). Schumann dates the emergence of the manuscript at the end of the thirteenth century (Schumann 2: I, 71* and 81*), stating that a definite *terminus a quo* is 1219 (no. 168a, the strophe by Neidhart). Peter Dronke, "A Critical Note on Schumann's Dating of the Codex Buranus," *Beiträge zur Geschichte der deutschen Sprache und Literatur* 84 (1962): 173-83, argues that the manuscript must be earlier, and the dating of the paleography and the illustrations evidences the main part of the collection cannot be later than 1250. Walther von der Vogelweide's *Palästinalied* (*Carmina* no. 211) further delimits the compilation to the early twenties of the thirteenth century (Vollmann, 899-900).

3. The *Libro de buen amor* is preserved in three extant manuscripts and a Portuguese fragment: the manuscripts are S (University of Salamanca), G (Gayoso, Spanish Academy), and T (Toledo, National Library of Madrid). Unless otherwise noted, I cite G. B.

Gybbon-Monypenny's edition, *Libro de buen amor* (Madrid: Clásicos Castalia, 1988). The S manuscript is believed to be the most complete and latest of the extant versions as indicated by the S *explicit* of 1343 (S, st. 1634ab), the 1330 *explicit* of T, and similar lacunae of G and T, compared to S. For both the *Carmina* and the *Libro*, all English translations are my own, unless otherwise noted.

4. On Augustinian hermeneutics see Marina S. Brownlee, *The Status of the Reading Subject in the* Libro de Buen Amor (Chapel Hill: University of North Carolina Press, 1985); Laurence De Looze, *Pseudo-Autobiography in the Fourteenth Century* (Gainesville: University Press of Florida, 1997); and E. Michael E. Gerli, "The Greeks, the Romans, and the Ambiguity of Signs: *De doctrina christiana*, the Fall, and the Hermeneutics of the *Libro de buen amor*," *Bulletin of Spanish Studies: Hispanic Studies and Researches on Spain, Portugal, and Latin America* 79 (2002): 411–28. For the influence of Arabic and Hebrew traditions, see Francisco Márquez Villanueva, *Orígenes y sociología del tema celestinesco* (Barcelona: Anthropos, 1993); and Michelle Hamilton, "The Musical Book: Judeo-Andalusi Hermeneutics in the *Libro de buen amor*," *La Corónica* 37.2 (2009): 33–59. Ramón Menéndez Pidal and Leo Spitzer have described the *Libro* as a "Cancionero." Emending the former's definition of a humorous biography with elements intended for public performance by a minstrel, Leo Spitzer qualified the *Libro* as a primarily didactic work; see Menéndez Pidal, *Poesía juglaresca y orígenes de la literatura románica*, 6th ed. (Madrid: Instituto de Estudios Políticos, 1957) 211; Leo Spitzer, "En torno al arte del Arcipreste de Hita," in *Lingüística e historia literaria* (Madrid: Gredos, 1955) 138–42. Gybbon-Monypenny argues that the *Libro* was intended for an individual reader in "The Spanish *Mester de Clerecía* and Its Intended Public: Concerning the Validity as Evidence of Passages of Direct Address to the Audience," *Medieval Miscellany Presented to Eugène Vinaver*, ed. Frederick Whitehead, A. H. Diverres, and F. E. Sutcliffe (Manchester: Manchester University Press, 1965) 230–44.

5. The term "protean text" is from Raymond S. Willis, "Two Trotaconventos," *Romance Philology* 17 (1963–64): 362. See also R. B. Tate, "Adventures in the 'sierra,'" in *"Libro de buen amor" Studies*, ed. G. B. Gybbon-Monypenny (London: Tamesis, 1970) 228 [*LBAS*]. Willis characterizes the Archpriest's poetry as "protean" while Tate sees the "author" as a "protean figure."

6. Middle Latin poets such as Hugo Primas (fl. twelfth century), Archipoeta (ca. 1160), Peter of Blois (d. ca. 1200), and the master of sequence, Walther of Chatillon (ca. 1135–1200).

7. See Helen Waddell, *The Wandering Scholars* (London: Constable, 1949), for the European medieval tradition of satirical Latin verse, characterized by the student enjoyment of worldly pleasures or satires against the corruption of the church.

8. See Gordon A. Anderson and Thomas B. Payne, "Early Latin Secular Song," in *Grove Music Online*, ed. L. Macy (Accessed March 7, 2005), <http://www.grovemusic.com>.

9. See *Carmina Burana*, ed. Bischoff 27 (citing Schumann 2: I, 71*); Olive Sayce, *Plurilingualism in the Carmina Burana: A Study of the Linguistic and Literary Influences on the Codex*, Göppinger Arbeiten zur Germanistik 556, ed. Ulrich Müller, Franz Hundsnurscher, and Cornelius Sommer (Göppingen: Kümmerle, 1992) 199; Kuhn, "Die Liedersammlung," in

Codex Manesse: Die Große Heidelberger Liederhandschrift: Kommentar zum Faksimile des Codex Palatinus Germanicus 848 der Universitätsbibliothek Heidelberg, ed. Walter Koschorreck and Wilfried Werner (Kassel: Ganymed, 1981) 131–44 [Koschorreck and Werner].

10. For a thorough discussion of the manuscripts, including their dating and scribal tendencies, see Dagenais 118–21.

11. "por ende yo, Joan Roíz, / açipreste de Fita, della primero fiz / cantar . . ." 19b–d; and "Yo Johan Ruiz" 575a.

12. For a good summary of the period see Joseph F. O'Callaghan, *A History of Medieval Spain* (Ithaca: Cornell University Press, 1975) 459–86.

13. Félix Lecoy makes a strong argument for the Goliard influence in the *Libro* in "L'inspiration goliardique," in *Recherches sur le Libro de buen amor de Juan Ruiz, Archiprêtre de Hita,* Introd. A. D. Deyermond (1938; Farnborough: Gregg International, 1974) 213–37.

14. Hans Spanke, "Der Codex Buranus als Liederbuch," *Zeitschrift für Musikwissenschaft* 13 (1930–31): 246.

15. C. S. Lewis, *The Discarded Image* (Cambridge: Cambridge University Press, 1964) 10.

16. See *Histoire de l'édition française: Le livre conquérant, du Moyen Âge au milieu du XVIIe siècle,* ed. Roger Chartier and Henri-Jean Martin (Paris: Fayard/Promodis, 1989) 97.

17. *Patrologiae Cursus Completus,* Series Latina, ed. J.-P. Migne (Paris: Garnier, 1844–1905) [PL].

18. *Carmina Burana,* ed. Bischoff 13.

19. Vollmann 911.

20. The *Fragmenta* stand in close connection to the main manuscript in their format (line number and ruling), and it is supposed that they were inserted into the text not long after the volume had been completed. The fact that these *Fragmenta* contain similar material, formatted according to the earlier codex, is significant insofar as it reflects the fact that the later compilers understood the *Carmina* as a songbook (*Carmina Burana,* ed. Bischoff 20).

21. Both Meyer and Schumann have reconstructed the original order of the more than 250 works to determine the lacunae. See *Carmina Burana,* ed. Bischoff 19–20 for a description of how they went about reconstructing the order of poems. I use the numbering of the critical edition.

22. The main part of the manuscript consists of fols. 1–106, written by two scribes designated by Schumann as h^1 and h^2, with possible interventions of a third, h^{1a}. All three hands are of a German character, but h^1 and h^2 betray Italian influence. See *Carmina Burana,* ed. Bischoff 27–28, Sayce, *Plurilingualism* 25–29.

23. See Bischoff introduction 22–23; for Bernt, see *Die Gedichte des Codex Buranus lateinisch und deutsch,* ed. Carl Fischer, trans. Hugo Kuhn, annotations by Günther Bernt (Zürich and Munich: Artemis, 1974). (Text of Hilka/Schumann/Bischoff with minor changes)]; for Wachinger, see Ernst Martin, "Die Carmina Burana und die Anfänge des deutschen Minnesangs," *Zeitschrift für deutsches Alterthum und deutsche Literatur* 20 (1876): 46–99.

24. See *Carmina Burana*, ed. Bischoff 9, and Vollmann 910 in the *Carmina*'s aspect as encyclopedia and moral guide.

25. Hans Spanke, "Ein lateinisches Liederbuch des 11. Jahrhunderts," *Studi Medievali* 2nd ser. 15 (1942): 111–42.

26. Vollmann suggests reading the collection under the rubrics of the seven deadly sins (912).

27. Nos. 135–48, 150–53, 155, 161–75, 179–83; Bischoff, in his edition (27 n. 1), notes that most of these stanzas are *unica*. Martin and Spanke consider it a possibility that "the German added strophes were intended to arouse interest among or to make possible the active participation of an audience not capable of understanding Latin"; see Spanke, "Der Codex Buranus als Liederbuch" 246; Martin, "Die Carmina Burana" 68.

28. John Stevens, *Words and Music in the Middle Ages: Song, Narrative, Dance and Drama, 1050–1350* (Cambridge: Cambridge University Press, 1986) 65, referencing Stevens, *Cambridge Music Manuscripts 900–1700*, ed. I. Fenlon (Cambridge: Cambridge University Press, 1982) 43, and Otto Schumann, "Die jüngere Cambridger Liedersammlung," *Studi Medievali* 16 (1943–50): 45–85. Stevens suggests that the *Carmina* was compiled for a particular kind of clerical milieu similar to the one of the *Later Cambridge Songs* (Cambridge University Library, MS Ff.I.17, thirteenth century), an anthology which he uses to reconstruct some of the pitchless neumes of the *Carmina*: "the presence of numerous text scribes [in a collection of 16 pages only] argues a community at work, a community of clerics, perhaps the teachers or students of a cathedral or monastery school. The interlarding of a mainly sacred repertory with lively, though never gross, secular songs supports this opinion."

29. Sources for the *Carmina* probably include the Notre-Dame repertory found in Mediceus 29. I (F) and Ms. Oxford, Bodleian, Rawlinson C 510, *Carmina Burana*, ed. Bischoff 26.

30. For example, 151a and 169a belong to no. 51 of Walther von der Vogelweide (based on numbering by Lachmann), *Walthers von der Vogelweide Gedichte*, ed. Hermann Paul, Altdeutsche Textbibliothek 1 (Tübingen: Max Niemeyer, 1965). No. 151a is stanza 3 and 169a is stanza 4 of no. 51.

31. See Spanke, "Der Codex Buranus als Liederbuch" 241–51, for a description of the different kinds of music in the *Carmina*; and Walther Lipphardt, "Unbekannte Weisen zu den Carmina Burana," *Archiv für Musikwissenschaft* 12 (1955): 122–42 [3 facs.].

32. Saint Augustine, *On Music*, trans. Robert Catesby Taliaferro, The Fathers of the Church, ed. Roy Joseph Deferrari, vol. 4. (New York: Fathers of the Church, 1947).

33. Richard L. Crocker, "Versus," in *Grove Music Online*, ed. L. Macy (Accessed March 7, 2005), <http://www.grovemusic.com>.

34. Ibid.

35. Folios 432r1–443r2 of MS UL Gg.5.35, Cambridge University Library. *The Cambridge Songs (Carmina Cantabrigiensia)*, ed. and trans. Jan M. Ziolkowski, Medieval and Renaissance Texts and Studies 192 (Tempe, Arizona: Medieval and Renaissance Texts and Studies, 1998).

36. Ziolkowski xxxix–xliv.

37. Ernst Robert Curtius, *European Literature and the Latin Middle Ages,* trans. Willard R. Trask, Bollingen Ser. 36 (1953; Princeton: Princeton University Press, 1990) 490: "For Latin poetic theory ca. 1200, then, the situation is as follows: The art of the poet has first and foremost to prove itself in the rhetorical treatment of the material; for this he can choose between two procedures — either he ingeniously draws out his subject, or he dispatches it as briefly as possible."

38. Curtius 57, 59, "technical authorities before modern science," and "a treasury of worldly wisdom and general philosophy . . . . Quintilian called them "sententiae" (literally: judgments) because they resembled the decisions of public bodies. Such lines are 'mnemonic verses.' They are learned by heart; they are collected; they are arranged in alphabetical order that they may be ready to hand."

39. Lynn Thorndike, "Unde Versus," *Traditio* 11 (1955): 163–93.

40. Bernt, in *Carmina Burana. Die Gedichte* 875.

41. In considering how visual and verbal texts interact in medieval manuscripts, one might compare the *versus* with the marginalia studied by Michael Camille; see Camille, *Image on the Edge: The Margins of Medieval Art* (1992; London: Reaktion, 2006).

42. Translations from *The Love Songs of the Carmina Burana*, trans. E. D. Blodgett and Roy Arthur Swanson, Garland Library of Medieval Literature 49B (New York: Garland, 1987). Although CB 103 was likely under CB 100 on f. 75v (see Schumann 2: I, 36* and 1: I, 168), we can assume the scribe considered its placement directly under the Aeneas and Dido miniature that groups the Dido and Troy poems.

43. Julia Walworth, "Earthly Delights: The Pictorial Images of the *Carmina Burana* Manuscript," in *The* Carmina Burana*: Four Essays*, ed. Martin H. Jones, King's College Medieval Studies 18 (London: King's College London Centre for Late Antique and Medieval Studies, 2000) 76.

44. In addition to one stanza of a dawn song by Otto von Botenlouben (CB 48a) attached to a Latin crusading song with a similar refrain, and three unattached stanzas that are later additions on 54v–55r, there are forty-nine German stanzas on fols. 56v–62v, 65r–72r, and 81r–82r. See Olive Sayce, *The Medieval German Lyric 1150–1300: The Development of Its Themes and Forms in Their European Context* (Oxford: Clarendon Press, 1982) 135 [*MGL*].

45. Often initial stanzas, *Minnesänger* such as Reinmar 147a, Heinrich von Morungen 150a, the first stanza of Walther's crusading poem, 211a, Neidhart, 168a, to name a few attested examples.

46. Only ten of the German stanzas are independently attested; Sayce (*MGL* 235–36) finds that these stanzas show a close structural and metrical similarity to the Latin to which the poems are attached to, and in the case of the strophes not attested to elsewhere the similarities are even greater (such as identity of rhyme scheme). For bidirectional contrafacta scenarios see Burghart Wachinger, "Deutsche und lateinische Liebeslieder: Zu den deutschen Strophen der Carmina Burana," in *From Symbol to Mimesis: The Generation of Walther von der Vogelweide*, ed. F. H. Bäuml (Göppingen: Kümmerle, 1984) 1–34, esp. 3. Schumann argues that nos. 151, 165, 168, and 169 are by the same composer (the *Hebetsidus* Group); except for 165, this group is accompanied by attested *Minnesänger* strophes,

see Schumann, "Die deutschen Strophen der Carmina Burana," *Germanisch-Romanische Monatsschrift* 14 (1926): 418-37 (esp. 434-35).

47. Schumann, "Die Deutschen Strophen" and Schumann, 2: I, 92.* He regards 149, 167a and the German refrain of 180 as original.

48. Such as 141a. See Martin, "Die Carmina Burana," 46-99; Richard M. Meyer, "Alte deutsche Volksliedchen," *Zeitschrift für deutsches Alterthum und deutsche Litteratur* 29 (1885): 121-236; Vollmann 1134.

49. See Schumann, "Die Deutschen Strophen."

50. Wachinger, "Deutsche und lateinische Liebeslieder" 3.

51. *Carmina Burana*, ed. Bischoff 27.

52. Wachinger, "Deutsche und lateinische Liebeslieder" 4.

53. Schumann 2: I, 118.

54. See Bernt, in *Carmina Burana. Die Gedichte* 899.

55. Curtius 493.

56. Gerli , "The Greeks, the Romans, and the Ambiguity of Signs" 411.

57. Anthony N. Zahareas, *The Art of Juan Ruiz: Archpriest of Hita* (Madrid: Estudios de Literatura Española, 1965).

58. Dagenais xiv. See also Alan Deyermond's introduction to the latest edition of Lecoy's *Recherches*, ix-xxxvii. Deyermond summarizes scholarship up to Dagenais's *Ethics*. For another review of *Libro* scholarship, see Margherita Morreale, "El Libro de buen amor, de Juan Ruiz, Arcipreste de Hita," *GRLM* 9 (1985): 2.4, 53-73, and Brownlee, *Status of the Reading Subject*, "Critical Perspectives," 12-22.

59. Gybbon-Monypenny, "Autobiography in the *Libro de buen amor* in the Light of Some Literary Comparisons," *Bulletin of Hispanic Studies* 34 (1957): 63-78, views the *Libro* in the same "erotic pseudo-autobiography" genre as Dante's *Vita Nuova*, Ulrich von Lichtenstein's *Frauendienst*, and Guillaume de Machaut's *Voir-Dit* among others, 70-78. See also De Looze's account (*Pseudo-Autobiography*).

60. Dagenais 142-43.

61. Lecoy, *Recherches* 361; Alan D. Deyermond, "Some Aspects of Parody in the *Libro de buen amor*," *LBAS* 53-78; Otis H. Green, *Spain and the Western Tradition: The Castilian Mind in Literature from El Cid to Calderón* (Madison: University of Wisconsin Press, 1963-66) 1: 46-47; Janet Chapman, "Juan Ruiz's 'Learned Sermon,'" *LBAS* 29-51, 46.

62. Dagenais 141-42.

63. See Morreale 72-73; Dagenais 185-89.

64. Dagenais 189.

65. Iñigo López de Mendoza, Marqués de Santillana, *Poesías completas*, ed. M. P. A. M. Kerkhof and A. Gómez Moreno (Madrid: Castalia, 2003) 653 [López de Mendoza].

66. John K. Walsh, "Juan Ruiz and the *mester de clerezía*: Lost Context and Lost Parody in the *Libro de buen amor*," *Romance Philology* 33 (1979-80): 62-86.

67. See Dagenais 153-70.

68. For a discussion of the term *comunal* in the troubadour context, see Catherine Léglu, "A Reading of Troubadour Insult Songs: The *Comunals* Cycle," *Reading Medieval Studies* 22 (1996): 63-83.

69. See Menéndez Pidal's study on the *serranillas, Estudios literarios,* 5th ed. (Buenos Aires: Espasa-Calpe, 1942) 195–264, esp. 218–19.

70. César Real de la Riva, "El *Libro de buen amor,* de Juan Ruiz, Arcipreste de Hita," *GRLM* 9 (1985): 1.4, 89, sees the interaction between audience and Archpriest as one of literary grafting in a "régimen de convivencia."

71. Walsh 86. See also Menendéz Pidal's view of the *Libro* as a narrative text with lyric interpolations, similar to the chantefable in *Poesía juglaresca* (212).

72. See Tate's interpretation of the *Libro* as a "transcript," *LBAS* 228–29.

73. In two articles, "Two Trotaconventos," and "Thirteen Years: Seedbed of Riddles in the *Libro de Buen Amor,*" *Kentucky Romance Quarterly* 21 (1974): 215–27, Willis argues for the "public" and "entertainment" quality of the *Libro* by studying the interpolations added to what he calls Version I of the *Libro* (MSS G and T, 1330, and fragments of the Portuguese version P) to make Version II (MS S 1343).

74. Willis, "Thirteen Years" 225, 227; María Rosa Lida de Malkiel, *Two Spanish Masterpieces: The "Book of Good Love" and "The Celestina,"* Illinois Studies in Language and Literature 49 (Urbana: University of Illinois Press, 1961).

75. Américo Castro, *Obra Reunida. España en su historia: Ensayos sobre historia y literatura,* ed. José Miranda (Madrid: Editorial Trotta, 2004) 3: 494.

76. Oleg Grabar, *The Formation of Islamic Art* (New Haven: Yale University Press, 1973) 171.

77. For a recent reading of this passage see Hamilton, "The Musical Book." Hamilton argues that the metaphor of the book as a stringed instrument played by its readers is possibly indebted to Franco-Iberian copies of Maimonides's *Guide of the Perplexed.* Past scholarship has seen the terms *puntar* and *instrumentos* as relating to musical and scribal practices, and *puntar* and *puntos* as sexually suggestive. All agree that the *copla* foregrounds the problem of interpretation in the *Libro.*

78. Tate, in *LBAS* 226–27.

79. Tate (219–21) understands the prologue narratives and lyrics as having varying relationships and, most importantly, takes the lyrics as separate from the narrative verse; Menéndez Pidal argues that the *cuaderna vía* possesses "colores realistas y caricaturescos" followed by a *canción* "de tonos idealistas" while Lida de Malkiel does not see a contrast (219). See Menéndez Pidal, *Poesía juglaresca* 212, and Lida de Malkiel, "Nuevas notas para la interpretación del *Libro de buen amor,*" *Nueva revista de filología hispánica* 13 (1959): 45.

80. The *estribillo,* as the introductory stanza that states the theme (*cabeza* or *texto*) of the *estribote,* is repeated after a sequence of couplets and a *vuelta.* Musically the *estribote* is divisible into three parts, two "*mundanzas*" and the *vuelta,* like the courtly *chanson* and as Pierre Le Gentil has pointed out, *le virelai*:

AA ‖ b b ǀ b a ‖ AA (rhymes)
αβ γ γ αβ α (melodies)
Estribillo Mundanzas Vuelta Estribillo
Refrain Couplet Reprise after couplet (Chorus).

The first datable use of the term is in Gonzalo Correas' *Gramática griega* (1627) where it appears meaning "refrains of old songs." Pierre Le Gentil discusses the *estribote/villancico*, in particular the origins in *distique de carole* and *muwashshah* in *Le virelai et le villancico: Le problème des origines arabes* (Paris: Société d'éditions "Les Belles Lettres," 1954) 212. See also Le Gentil, *La poésie lyrique espagnole et portugaise à la fin du moyen âge* (Rennes: Plihon, 1949–52) 2: 212, where he suggests the possibility that the *estribote* was sung to only two melodies, like the rondeau: $\alpha\beta$ /$\alpha\alpha\alpha\beta$ $\alpha\beta$, 229 n. 42.

81. The *Gozos de Santa María* (20–32), *Troba caçurra* (115–20), *Canticas de serrana* (987–92, 1022–42), the student begging songs (1650–55, 1656–60), the *De la pasión de nuestro señor Jhesú Christo* (1046–58, 1059–66), and the *Ave María* songs (1661–67, 1673–77), as identified by Le Gentil, *La poésie lyrique* 2: 219–24. The *Libro* is an important document of early Castilian, containing for example the earliest religious lyrics, the *Gozos de Santa María*. Scholars usually agree that the lyrics in manuscripts S and G are a part of the "Book of the Archpriest of Hita" due to the Archpriest's statement in stanza 1514 that he has written such songs. G is the only manuscript to be written in the Castilian dialect of the narrator.

82. D. McMillan, "Juan Ruiz's Use of the 'Estribote,'" in *Hispanic Studies in Honour of I. González Llubera*, ed. Frank Pierce (London: Dolphin Books, 1959) 189–93, discusses the variation of the *estribote* throughout the *Libro*; Le Gentil, *La poésie lyrique* 2: 227, tracks the *estribote* to fifteenth-century cancioneros.

83. *De vulgari eloquentia* 2: 204 (Bk. II, 8, 8).

84. The *"Razos de Trobar" of Raimon Vidal and Associated Texts*, ed. John Henry Marshall (London: Oxford University Press, 1972) 98.

85. *Zéjel* texts by Ibn Quzman (d. 1160) originating in Muslim Spain, for example.

86. See Le Gentil, *La poésie lyrique* 2: 209–18.

87. Such as the ones mentioned in stanzas 1513–14. Many of the missing lyrics fall into a distinct genre: six of them are love songs (after stanzas 80, 171, 915, 918, 1625) and four of mixed types—probably an additional *troba caçurra* about Ferrand García mentioned in 122; a satirical verse about an old woman in 947; and a dirge about Garoça in 1507. (These omissions occur only in S.) Finally, in 1021, three *serranillas* are promised but there is only one. Perhaps love lyrics were out of place in a book with burlesque and religious songs—all of which could function as light entertainment. Random songs were added to the end of manuscript G, making it likely that there was a supply of pieces on hand, added as Willis says "ad libitum." See *Libro de buen amor*, ed. Raymond S. Willis (Princeton: Princeton University Press, 1972) xlii.

88. See Lecoy, *Recherches* 83.

89. G contains evidence of songbook emendation in the secular *estribillo* at the head of the first of the *Gozos de Santa María*: *Quan[d]o los lobos preso lo an / a don Juan -en el canpo* (stanza 20), *Libro de buen amor*, ed. Manuel Criado de Val and Eric W. Naylor (Madrid: Consejo Superior de Investigaciones Científicas, 1965) 11. See also the note of Joan Corominas, ed., *Libro de Buen Amor* (Madrid: Biblioteca Románica Hispánica, 1967) 80.

90. Gybbon-Monypenny, "Autobiography" 77.

91. Ardis Butterfield, *Poetry and Music in Medieval France: From Jean Renart to Guillaume de Machaut* (Cambridge: Cambridge University Press, 2002) 55–56.

92. Although the word is commonly believed to be diminutive of Spanish *estribo* (stirrup, support), Yakov Malkiel, "Spanish *Estribillo* 'Refrain': Its Proximal and Distal Etymologies," in *Florilegium Hispanicum: Medieval and Golden Age Studies Presented to Dorothy Clotelle Clarke*, ed. John S. Geary (Madison: Hispanic Seminary of Medieval Studies, 1983) 29–43, suggests that the word may be related to the old Spanish words *trebejo* (diversion, play), *trebejar* (to play, to frolic) and their Galician-Portuguese counterparts *trebelho* and *trebelhar* (to leap, to dance). Such an etymology, if true, suggests a repeated dance pattern connected to the vocal and musical refrains. There is evidence to support this hypothesis: in a manuscript describing the ceremonial crowning of the kings of Castile (manuscript E-E X.iii.3, copied before 1248) in church after the Alleluia "virgins who knew how to sing came, sang a cantiga and made its *trebejos.*" There are two accompanying illuminations depicting virgins playing instruments. In another example, a Galician-Portuguese poem by Macías (fl. 1340–70) in the *Cancionero de Baena* uses the term *trebello* in the last verse of a strophe to indicate the refrain that follows. See Isabel Pope and Emilio Ros-Fábregas, "Estribillo," *Grove Music Online*, ed. L. Macy (Accessed January 3, 2006), <http://www.grovemusic.com>.

93. McMillan 85.

94. Tate, in *LBAS* 220 n. 1

95. As McMillan summarizes: $a_6 a_6\ a_6 a_6$ // $b_6\ b_6\ c_6\ c_6$ / $a_6 \ldots$ x 20, musically, $\alpha\beta$ $\gamma\gamma\alpha\beta$ (following the scheme of the *Cantigas*) 187.

96. Sayce, *MGL* 241.

97. Vollman 1147.

98. See for example 167a, 174a I.

CHAPTER TWO

1. Other versions of this rubric in this chansonnier's index use the verb form "trobadas." In this chapter, I use italics within manuscript citations (e.g., "Bernart de Ventedor") to indicate abbreviations in the original text.

2. The earliest dated chansonnier is D, compiled according to a colophon at the head of the index by an anonymous compiler in 1254. Those that include *vidas,* such as AHIK, date from the thirteenth century.

3. See, for example, Huot, *Song to Book*; Kay, *Subjectivity in Troubadour Poetry*; and Michel Zink, *La Subjectivité littéraire autour du siècle de Saint Louis* (Paris: Presses Universitaires de France, 1985).

4. Holmes, *Assembling the Lyric Self* 1.

5. Gustav Gröber, "Die Liedersammlungen der Troubadours," *Romanische Studien* 2 (1875–77): 337–670; Poe, *Compilatio* 14–15. Poe discusses evidence of source collections such as the *Liber Alberici* of chansonnier D, the lost anthology produced by Bernart Amoros, and Uc de Saint Circ's annotated edition of Bertran de Born.

6. See Introduction.

7. See Nichols, "'Art' and 'Nature'" 83–86.

8. William Burgwinkle, "The *chansonniers* as books," in Gaunt and Kay 247.

9. See Kendrick, "L'image du troubadour comme auteur dans les chansonniers," in *Auctor et auctoritas: Invention et conformisme dans l'écriture médiévale. Actes du colloque tenu à l'Université de Versailles-Saint-Quentin-en-Yvelines (14–16 juin 1999),* ed. Michel Zimmerman (Paris: École des Chartes, 2001) 507–19, who discusses how the compilers of the Italian chansonniers authorize the troubadours as poets using bibliographic strategies (visual apparatus of an "auteur" as scribe or cleric) borrowed from biblical and classical traditions, in effect "individualizing" the troubadours (514) and "subjecting the texts to an author as Foucault defines it" (519).

10. For recent scholarship on troubadour names and naming see *Tenso* 22 (2007), especially Matilda Tomaryn Bruckner's introduction, "Acts of Nomination: Naming Names and Troubadour Poetry, Introduction" (1–8) and Michelle Bolduc's "Naming Names: Matfre Ermengaud's Use of Troubadour Quotations" (41–74).

11. Acts of self-naming and signature have been generally linked to discussions of poststructuralist notions of discursive authority (Barthes, Foucault); by examining the chansonnier as an emergent genre that mediates the reception and appropriation of lyric texts and authors, I am building on the work of Burgwinkle, Huot, Nichols, Poe, and others. Articles by Poe, "'No Volc Aver Nom Raÿmbaut!': Names and Naming in *So Fo El Tems,*" *Tenso* 22, and Léglu, "Languages in Conflict in Toulouse: *Las Leys d'Amors,*" *Modern Language Review* 103 (2008): 383–96, examine interesting cases of troubadour names in Occitan prose texts serving as substitutions for lyric texts. In the *Leys d'Amors*, the section on proper names indicates three kinds of proper names: "propri nom, sobre nom, e nom daventura" (proper name, surname, and the name of adventure or occasion). The proper name is associated with the baptismal name, the surname is the name of the family, and a given name such as "majordome" indicates a specific social relation. [Adolphe-Félix] Gatien-Arnoult, ed., *Monumens de la littérature romane depuis le quatorzième siècle: Las Flors del Gay Saber, estier dichas las Leys d'Amors,* 3 vols. (Paris: Silvestre; Toulouse: Bon and Privat [1841–43]) 2: 32.

12. For a discussion of the troubadour song as a "tension between the voice and the letter" (151) based on a theoretical discussion of Augustine's interpretation of the voice and the letter (or writing), see Nichols, "Voice and Writing in Augustine and in the Troubadour Lyric," in *Vox intexta: Orality and Textuality in the Middle Ages,* ed. A. N. Doane and Carol Braun Pasternack (Madison: University of Wisconsin Press, 1991) 137–61, esp. 153.

13. See Van Vleck, *Memory and Re-Creation,* especially her statistical evidence of stanzaic and line variations (76), and Zumthor, *Essai de poétique médiévale.*

14. *Peire d'Alvernha: Liriche,* ed. Alberto Del Monte (Turin: Loescher-Chiantore, 1955) 119–20, lines 1–18. Unless otherwise noted, all page numbers and verse lines are indicated from cited editions and appear in text parenthetically. Where not indicated, translations are my own. For discussion of the different theories surrounding the dating of this song, see Riquer 1: 332–33.

15. Translation (with minor change) is from *Lyrics of the Troubadours and Trouvères: An*

Anthology and a History, ed. and trans. Frederick Goldin (Gloucester, MA: Peter Smith, 1983) 171.

16. See Frank Chambers's catalogue of troubadour names that occur in lyric poems, in *Proper Names in the Lyrics of the Troubadours* (Chapel Hill: University of North Carolina Press, 1971).

17. *The Life and Works of the Troubadour Raimbaut d'Orange*, ed. Walter T. Pattison (Minneapolis: University of Minnesota Press, 1952) 24.

18. *Biographies des troubadours: Textes provençaux des XIIIe et XIVe siècles*, ed. Jean Boutière and A.-H. Schutz (Paris: Nizet, 1964) 263 [Boutière and Schutz].

19. Chansonnier D is conventionally divided into five sections: index, D, D^a, D^b, D^c. D^a contains folios 153–211. See Burgwinkle's summary of chansonnier D, "The *chansonniers* as books" 254–56.

20. This substitution is transmitted in AD^{a}IKN^{2}z, Riquer 1: 340.

21. Pillet and Carstens 281 and Riquer 1: 335.

22. In the *vidas* (Boutière and Schutz 7, 441), their names appear as variations of "Lo Coms de Peitieus" and "Roembauz d'Aurenga." When Guilhem's lyrics are attributed, his name appears in the chansonniers and *vidas* as "Lo coms de Peit[i]eus," whereas Raimbaut's attributions generally do not include a title (except in the indexes of *tensos*). In his *vida* he is named "lo seingner d'Aurenga."

23. See Gerald Bond's images of charters, letters, and seals that signify Guilhem's lordship over Poitiers and much of Aquitaine: *The Poetry of William VII, Count of Poitiers, IX Duke of Aquitaine*, ed. Gerald A. Bond, Garland Library of Medieval Literature 4A (New York: Garland, 1982). As count of Aquitaine, Guilhem retains the title of the duchy in the name of William/Guilhem ("Guillelmus Aquitanorum dux" 102), and the title count of Poitiers ("Comes Pictaviensium" 100). See especially the reproduction of official Poitevin coinage minted by Count Guilhem: it bears the name of "Carlus" or Charlemagne on the penny, and "Wuililmo" on the half-penny, indicating the continuity of the Carolingian lineage (xii). See Pattison's introduction to *The Life and Works of the Troubadour Raimbaut d'Orange* 3–27, on Raimbaut's family alliances to the two powers of southern France at the time — the count of Toulouse and the king of Aragon (until 1164 the count of Barcelona) — who figure importantly in his lyrics. Raimbaut's name indicates his inheritance of Orange from his mother, Tiburge d'Orange; "Raimbaut" is the name of Tiburge's father.

24. See "Companho farai un vers [qu'er] covinen," in Guglielmo IX, *Poesie*, ed. Nicolò Pasero (Modena: STEM Mucchi, 1973) 16–35. For a discussion of Guilhem's poetic voice as thematizing "the emotional range of desire as a correlative of political and secular power," see Nichols, "Voice and Writing" 153–57.

25. Bond, *The Poetry of William VII* 98–99 (letter to Count William from the abbot of Vendôme). I use Bond's translations of these documents.

26. Ibid., 100–101 (letter to Count William from Pope Urban II).

27. William D. Paden, *An Introduction to Old Occitan* (New York: MLA, 1998) 94–99. Even though the paraphrase is earlier than the count's documented life, the manuscript is speculated to have been written down in the late eleventh century in the Benedictine

abbey of Saint Martial of Limoges. As feudal overlord of the abbey's holdings, Guilhem would have been familiar with the liturgical culture there, and it has been proposed that many of his songs are formally similar to the music developed at Saint Martial.

28. See Kurt Lewent, "*Lo vers de la Terra de Preste Johan* by Cerveri de Girona," *Romance Philology* 2 (1948–49): 22–24.

29. Poe, "'No Volc Aver Nom'" 34. *The Life and Works of the Troubadour Raimbaut d'Orange*, ed. Pattison 88, lines 22–23 (I use Pattison's translations).

30. See note of Pattison, *Raimbaut d'Orange* 141. Such as this rubric in the index of *tensos* in chansonnier I: "En Blancat et en Raimbaut."

31. In contrast to the *Codex Manesse* or chansonnier W (Paris, Bibl. Nat. fr. 844), the latter of which contains French and Occitan lyrics; in both these examples we can perceive a loose ranking of poets by social status.

32. Zufferey, "A propos du chansonnier M (Paris, Bibl. Nat., fr. 12474)," in *Lyrique romane* 221–42. Thus Marcabru's songs are attributed to "Raymbaud Dorenia" (221).

33. See Riquer's summary of this song, I: 139.

34. Paden 84.

35. Pasero 269.

36. Pattison, *Raimbaut d'Orange* 36, dates this song to 1162 due to the historical referent to the Count of Barcelona.

37. See Pattison, *Raimbaut d'Orange* 67, for variants. This stanza is missing in manuscripts IKN^2.

38. See Zufferey, "A propos."

39. On the variant, see Pattison, *Raimbaut d'Orange* 155.

40. Editions and translations from *Marcabru: A Critical Edition*, ed. Simon Gaunt, Ruth Harvey, and Linda Paterson (Cambridge: D. S. Brewer, 2000), and *The Songs of Bernart de Ventadorn*, ed. and trans. Stephen G. Nichols et al. (Chapel Hill: University of North Carolina Press, 1962), 11 (I have lightly altered some translations for emphasis). For a discussion of this aspect of Marcabru, see Gaunt, Harvey, and Paterson 221–24.

41. Boutière and Schutz 20–21, 10–13.

42. Curtius 515–18; Mary J. Carruthers, *The Book of Memory: A Study of Memory in Medieval Culture* (Cambridge: Cambridge University Press, 1990) 216.

43. *Medieval Europe: A Short History*, ed. Judith M. Bennett and C. Warren Hollister, 9th ed. (Boston: McGraw-Hill, 2002) 248. See also M. T. Clanchy, *From Memory to Written Record: England 1066–1307*, 2nd ed. (Cambridge, MA: Blackwell, 1993) 328–34. Of particular interest is the comparison of English lawyers' manuals with Occitan chansonniers. Like chansonniers, these manuals range in format from plainer working copies to ones designed for presentation (280–81).

44. Roman Jakobson, *On Language*, ed. Linda R. Waugh and Monique Monville-Burston (Cambridge, MA: Harvard University Press, 1990) 387.

45. Peggy Kamuf's work on the signature of post-Enlightenment authors is useful here: "as a piece of a proper name, the signature points, at one extremity, to a properly unnameable singularity; as a piece of language, the signature touches, at its other extremity,

on the space of free substitution without proper reference," *Signature Pieces: On the Institution of Authorship* (Ithaca: Cornell University Press, 1988) 12. One can perhaps consider proper names in songbooks as the prehistory of the persistent presence of "the body writing" as described by Kamuf: the remains of the troubadour voice and bodily performance translated to discrete moments of a scribal act, embodied within a manuscript codex (the tactile experience of a proper name rendered on remains of the body of an animal skin).

46. See Bolduc's discussion of how vernacular authors translate and appropriate sacred Latin *auctoritas*: "appropriation of authority takes place at the junction of such contraries of sacred and secular," *The Medieval Poetics of Contraries* (Gainesville: University Press of Florida, 2006) 34.

47. François Pirot, "Ce n'était point le troubadour Marcabru . . . ," *Annales du Midi* 78 (1966): 538.

48. For example, PC 293.12a, 168, lines 31–36, 176; see Ruth E. Harvey, *The Troubadour Marcabru and Love*, Westfield Publications in Medieval Studies 3 (London: University of London, 1989) 141–42.

49. Paraphrase from "Lo vers comens cant vei del fau" (I begin the *vers* when I see the top [PC 293.33]) 420, lines 49–54.

50. See Nichols's discussion of this phenomenon in reference to Guillaume IX's lyrics, "Voice and Writing" 153.

51. See Suzanne Thiolier-Méjean, *Les poésies satiriques et morales des troubadours* (Paris: Nizet, 1978) 541.

52. For a discussion of Occitan nonlyric texts that are placed under the authority of God through these kinds of invocations, see Françoise Vielliard, "Auteur et autorité dans la littérature occitane médiévale non lyrique," in *Auctor et auctoritas* 375–89.

53. Bolduc, *Medieval Poetics* 43.

54. *Le Breviari d'amor de Matfre Ermengaud*, ed. Peter T. Ricketts (tome 5; Leiden: Brill, 1976–) 5:78. The translation is from Harvey, *The Troubadour Marcabru and Love* 20.

55. Bolduc, "Naming Names" 42.

56. See *Lexique roman*, ed. François Raynouard (Paris, 1838–44), continued by Emil Levy, ed., *Provenzalisches Supplement-Wörterbuch, Berichtigungen und Ergänzungen zu Raynouards "Lexique Roman,"* (Leipzig: O. R. Reisland, 1894–1924), especially Levy's entry on "legir" 4:353–54.

57. *Les poésies de Bernart Marti*, ed. Ernest Hoepffner (Paris: Honoré Champion, 1929). Harvey, *The Troubadour Marcabru and Love* 4.

58. Riquer 2: 924, lines 8–9; Harvey, *The Troubadour Marcabru and Love* 5.

59. *Le Roman de Flamenca*, ed. Ulrich Gschwind (Bern: A. Francke, 1976) I, line 702.

60. Arnaut Daniel, *Canzoni*, ed. Gianluigi Toja (Florence: Sansoni, 1960). All citations are from this edition. Translations are my own unless otherwise noted.

61. Curtius 97 n. 27.

62. See Toja 39.

63. For example see Riquer 3: 1315, l. 45, and 1400, l. 45.

64. Riquer 2: 914.

65. Bloch, *Etymologies and Genealogies: A Literary Anthropology of the French Middle Ages* (Chicago: University of Chicago Press, 1983) 37.

66. Tertullianus, *Opera Omnia Tertulliani* 2 c. 3, PL 1156A.

67. See Arnaut's *vida* and comments by Benvenuto d'Imola and Raimon de Durfort (Toja 11–14).

68. *The Holy Bible* (Douay-Rheims), (London: Baronius Press, 2005) 744. See *The Divine Comedy of Dante Alighieri*, ed. and trans. Robert M. Durling (Oxford: Oxford University Press, 1996–2011) 2 [*Purgatorio*]: 454. All references to the *Commedia* are from this edition. For similar proverbs in troubadour lyrics, see Eugen Cnyrim, *Sprichwörter, sprichwörtliche Redensarten und Sentenzen bei den provenzalischen Lyrikern*, Ausgaben und Anhadlungen aus dem Gebiete der romanischen Philologie 71 (Marburg: N. G. Elwert, 1888) 38, under "Redensarten und Sprichwörter, die vergebliches Hoffen . . . oder unnütz verschwendete Mühe und Arbeit bezeichnen."

69. Freccero 35.

70. Boutière and Schutz 59, line 3.

71. Similar to *trobar car, trobar ric* means to "exhibit an abundance of poetic resources" (see Gaunt and Kay's appendix of Occitan terms, 294). See also Frank M. Chambers, *An Introduction to Old Provençal Versification* (Philadelphia: American Philosophical Society, 1985) 117.

72. See Gianfranco Contini, "Préhistoire de l'*aura* de Pétrarque," *Varianti e altra linguistica: Una raccolta di saggi* (Turin: Einaudi, 1970) 195.

73. As Toja notes, Ugo Angelo Canello was the first to recognize how Arnaut uses these techniques to great effect. The *rimas dissolutas*, in their spreading out of the rhyme scheme to successive stanzas, reinforce the feeling of desire and expectation (Toja 40 n. 1).

74. Goldin 211.

75. Canello suggests that that the *l'aura/laura/laurs* in these three pieces are an allusion to a certain Laura and was thus an inspiration for Petrarch to create a *senhal* Laura. While it is right to point out the connection of these three words, the common rhyme and sonority of -*aura* could scarcely be more different from a Petrarchan Laura, see Contini, "Préhistoire" 195.

76. Goldin 217.

77. As Toja (280) points out in his commentary on "taverna," Dante employs similar language in speaking of the need to 'unlock the workshop of that art [of vernacular poetry],' "artis ergasterium" in *De vulgari eloquentia* 2: 160 (Bk. II, 4, 1).

78. Boutière and Schutz 58.

79. Toja suggests this is merely one possibility for one of Arnaut's ladies, as his lyrics suggest a handful of *senhals*, 18–19.

80. From Riquer's edition of "Pois Peire d'Alvernh'a chantat" (Riquer 2: 1042, lines 43–48). This is the Monk's imitation of the Peire d'Alvernhe gallery song discussed at the beginning of chapter two.

81. Toja 9.

82. There have been various studies concerning Arnaut Daniel's influence on Dante

(namely in *De vulgari eloquentia*, the *Rime Petrose*, and the *Commedia*) and on Petrarch (*Triumphis cupidinis*); for a good summary see Toja's introduction 65–113 and Pier Vincenzo Mengaldo, "Oc (oco)," *Enciclopedia dantesca* 4 (1973): 111–17. Maurizio Perugi, "Dante e Arnaut Daniel," *Studi danteschi* 51 (1978): 59–152, revises Salvatore Santangelo's thesis that Dante had scarce knowledge of the troubadours, *Dante e i trovatori provenzali* (Catania: Giannotta, 1921): Dante most likely had access to at least one chansonnier and some kind of Old Occitan grammar; see also Marshall's discussion of Santangelo's hypotheses in relation to Raimon Vidal's *Razos de Trobar* and Dante's knowledge of Occitan texts and culture in *The "Razos de Trobar"* 161–66.

83. See Contini's introduction in Toja's edition, xii; for Dante, Arnaut is the culmination of troubadour lyric, and to show his admiration he redirects Arnaut's desire into one that will achieve a celestial joy.

84. James Nohrnberg, "The Autobiographical Imperative and the Necessity of 'Dante': *Purgatorio* 30.55," *Modern Philology* 101 (2003): 1–47.

85. Sordello: "Tan m'abelis lo terminis novels" [P.C. 437.35]; Folquet: "Tan m'abelis l'amoros pensamens" [P.C. 155.22]; *De vulgari eloquentia* 2: 185 (Bk. II, 6, 6).

86. Freccero 37.

87. *Petrarch's Lyric Poems: The* Rime sparse *and Other Lyrics*, ed. and trans. Robert M. Durling (Cambridge, MA: Harvard University Press, 1976) 366–67, 398–99.

88. See Toja's comment on Arnaut's signature, 281.

89. See Margaret Spanos, "The Sestina: An Exploration of the Dynamics of Poetic Structure," *Speculum* 53 (1978): 545–57; and Marianne Shapiro, *Hieroglyph of Time: The Petrarchan Sestina* (Minneapolis: University of Minnesota Press, 1980) 44–48.

90. See Introduction.

CHAPTER THREE

1. I use the word "emblem" or "emblematic" in the sense of a typical representation, unless otherwise specified. I am aware that the word has specific meanings in medieval and Renaissance contexts, such as a figured object of symbolic meaning—examples of this include a heraldic device or object accompanying the image of a saint. During the Renaissance, the emblem is a specific type of poetry, often a visual symbol with an accompanying gloss or motto. I address this phenomenon in chapter four in relation to the poetry of cancioneros. I am primarily interested in the "emblematic mode" of certain songbook images accompanying lyric texts that form their own typical representation as a kind of pictorial condensation and matrix of visual and vernacular cultures. I also separate the use of this term from "iconography," which traditionally refers to the study of the development of themes used by artists.

2. See Barbara Newman, "Love's Arrows: Christ as Cupid in Late Medieval Art and Devotion," in *The Mind's Eye: Art and Theological Argument in the Middle Ages*, ed. Jeffrey F. Hamburger and Anne-Marie Bouché (Princeton: Department of Art and Archaeology of Princeton University, 2006) 263–86, esp. 263 [Hamburger and Bouché].

3. In his letter to Serenus, bishop of Marseilles (ca. 600), Gregory the Great states

NOTES TO PAGES 100–104 : 237

that images should be neither venerated nor forbidden, as they can serve as instruments of salvation for the faithful. See Herbert L. Kessler, "Gregory the Great and Image Theory in Northern Europe during the Twelfth and Thirteenth Centuries," in *A Companion to Medieval Art*, ed. Conrad Rudolph (Malden, MA: Blackwell, 2006), Blackwell Reference Online, 28 July 2009, reference to the *Registrum epistularum*, Letter IX, 209 and XI, 10.

4. See Kessler, "Gregory the Great."

5. Kessler cites this useful passage from Augustine's treatise; see *Spiritual Seeing: Picturing God's Invisibility in Medieval Art* (Philadelphia: University of Pennsylvania Press, 2000) 118.

6. Camille, *Gothic Art: Visions and Revelations of the Medieval World* (London: Everyman Art Library, 1996) 12–25, passim.

7. In addition to the illustrations in this book, readers are urged to consult the *Codex Manesse* portraits available on line through the Universitätsbibliothek Heidelberg, and *Portraits de troubadours: Initiales du chansonnier provençal A (Biblioteca Apostolica Vaticana, Vat. lat. 5232)*, ed. Jean-Loup Lemaitre and Françoise Vielliard (Vatican City: Biblioteca Apostolica Vaticana, 2008).

8. De Looze, "Signing Off in the Middle Ages: Medieval Textuality and Strategies of Authorial Self-Naming," in *Vox Intexta* 165, and Alistair J. Minnis, *Medieval Theory of Authorship: Scholastic Literary Attitudes in the Later Middle Ages* (London: Scolar, 1984). See Minnis's discussion of the Aristotelian prologue as developing the idea of the human *auctor*, chapters 3 and 4.

9. See Kendrick, "L'image du troubadour" 514–18.

10. Ibid., 516.

11. Camille, *Gothic Art* 14.

12. See Huot, "Visualization and Memory: The Illustration of Troubadour Lyric in a Thirteenth-Century Manuscript," *Gesta* 31 (1992): 3–14; Nichols, "'Art' and 'Nature'"; Rieger, "'Ins e.l cor port, dona, vostra faisso'"; Meneghetti, *Il pubblico*; Geneviève Brunel-Lobrichon, "L'iconographie du chansonnier provençal *R*: essai d'interpretation," *Tyssens, Lyrique romane* 245–71.

13. See Newman, "Love's Arrows" 277, citing Jacobus de Voragine's *Sermo* 264: "Jacobus de Voragine explained the miracle [Saint Francis receiving the stigmata from Christ as *vulnera amoris*] by speculating that, through the power of the imagination—the *vis imaginativa* of medieval psychology—the image of the wounded Christ impressed itself so forcefully on the mind's eye that it was subsequently able to imprint itself on the saint's very flesh."

14. Zufferey, "La partie non-lyrique du chansonnier d'Urfé," in *Revue des Langues Romanes* 98 (1994): 1–25 ["La partie non-lyrique"].

15. Zufferey, "La partie non-lyrique" 24; for a table of contents, see Brunel-Lobrichon, in *Tyssens, Lyrique romane* 249–54.

16. Brunel-Lobrichon 270; Zufferey, "La partie non-lyrique" 25.

17. See Marisa Galvez, "From the *Costuma d'Agen* to the *Leys d'Amors*: A Reflec-

tion on Customary Law, the University of Toulouse, and the *Consistori de la sobregaia companhia del gay saber," Tenso* 26 (2011): 30–51.

18. The artist of the chansonnier responsible for the main historiated initials was of northern origin and was influenced by the Parisian Gothic style of illumination common at the end of the thirteenth century; see Robert Branner, *Manuscript Painting in Paris during the Age of Saint Louis: A Study of Styles* (Berkeley: University of California Press, 1977), black and white figures 6 and 7, and color figure IV. One also sees the dominance of "la culture d'oïl" in the intended conservation of melodies (many staves are empty), as R is the only chansonnier of the Midi to preserve the melodies, a common practice of French chansonniers.

19. See commentary on this metaphor by Gaunt, Harvey, and Paterson 436–37, and historical analysis of this song by Paterson, "Syria, Poitou and the Reconquista (or: Tales of the Undead): Who Was the Count in Marcabru's *Vers del lavador?*" in *The Second Crusade: Scope and Consequences*, ed. Jonathan Phillips and Martin Hoch (Manchester: Manchester University Press, 2001) 133–49.

20. See David Freedberg, *Power of Images: Studies in the History and Theory of Response* (Chicago: University of Chicago Press, 1989) 206.

21. Hamburger, "The Place of Theology in Medieval Art History: Problems, Positions, Possibilities," in Hamburger and Bouché 17: "in comparison with the East, images were theologically less burdened with being vehicles, let alone embodiments, of Truth . . . ; images developed in a myriad of ways, not only because they met essential human needs, but also because the relative absence of prescriptive legislation and liturgical strictures created by default a variety of imaginative spaces in which they could flourish."

22. Hamburger, *The Visual and the Visionary* 317, 321.

23. Ibid. 372–73. In the indulgence, Christ's upraised arms present him as the Judge in Matthew 25, as Hamburger describes it, "extending his right hand to those who repent and denying his blessing to those who do not."

24. Brunel-Lobrichon 258, 268, n. 84; Rieger 388.

25. Even if this initial does not depict Saint James, the theme of pilgrimage is clear; see, for example 224r, where a pilgrim in a red hat appears in the narrative of Rocamadour, a famous medieval pilgrimage site.

26. Riquer 3: 1484.

27. Léglu, "Vernacular Poems and Inquisitors in Languedoc and Champagne, ca. 1242–1249," *Viator* 33 (2002): 119.

28. Léglu, "Defamation in the Troubadour Sirventes: Legislation and Lyric Poetry," *Medium Ævum* 66.1 (1997): 33–34.

29. Version of R, with reference to René Lavaud's edition, *Poésies complètes du troubadour Peire Cardenal: 1180–1278* (Toulouse: Privat, 1957) 144, lines 8–16.

30. Zufferey, "La partie non-lyrique" 3.

31. Lavaud 366, lines 33–42.

32. "Una cuitatz fo, no sai cals" (There was a city, I can't say its name), Lavaud 530–39, lines 65 and 69.

33. See "Clergue si fan pastór / E son aucizedór" (Clergy pretend to be shepherds / but they are murderers [PC 335.31]), Lavaud 170–77.

34. Lavaud 302.

35. Lavaud 232–38.

36. Lavaud 232, lines 2–3.

37. Lavaud 666 (citing Karl Vossler).

38. Lavaud 232, lines 3–14.

39. See Jean-Claude Schmitt, *Le corps des images: Essais sur la culture visuelle au Moyen Âge* (Paris: Gallimard, 2002) 236.

40. Suzanne Thiolier-Mejean, *L'archet et le lutrin: Enseignement et foi dans la poésie médiévale d'Oc* (Paris: L'Harmattan, 2008) 329.

41. Chansonnier C, Paris, Bibl. Nat. fr. 856, transmits the autographed songbook of the troubadour; see Guiraut Riquier, *Las cansos: Kritischer Text und Kommentar*, ed. Ulrich Mölk (Heidelberg: Carl Winter, 1962) 19.

42. Monica Longobardi, "I vers del trovatore Guiraut Riquier," *Studi mediolatini e volgari* 29 (1982–83): 158–59, lines 16, 18–19.

43. The supplication occurs in R on 116v, col. 6–117v, col. 5.

44. Joseph Linskill ed., *Les épitres de Guiraut Riquier, troubadour du XIIIe siècle: Edition critique avec traduction et notes* (Liège: Association internationale d'études occitanes, 1985) 218.

45. [PC 248.44], Longobardi 50.

46. See Michael Routledge, "The Later Troubadours . . . *noels digs de nova maestria* . . . ," in Gaunt and Kay 99–112.

47. Hamburger, "Introduction," in Hamburger and Bouché 6.

48. Folquet's poems from *Le troubadour Folquet de Marseille: Édition critique*, ed. Stanislaw Stronski (1910; Geneva: Slatkine, 1968).

49. In addition to Newman, "Love's Arrows," see Huot, "Visualization and Memory" 3–14, 8; Carruthers, "Moving Images in the Mind's Eye," in Hamburger and Bouché 287–305; Nichols, "'Art' and 'Nature,'" in Nichols and Wenzel.

50. See Huot, "Visualization and Memory"; Nichols, "'Art' and 'Nature,'" in Nichols and Wenzel 108–9.

51. See Huot, "Visualization and Memory" 8.

52. Nichols, "'Art' and 'Nature,'" in Nichols and Wenzel 107–8.

53. Newman observes that Love's lance on folio 64 is the same weapon linked with the amorous wounding of Christ ("Love's Arrows," in Hamburger and Bouché 276).

54. Maria Elisa Avagnina, "Un inedito affresco di soggetto cortese a Bassano del Grappa: Federico II e la corte dei da Romano," in *Federico II: Immagine e potere*, ed. Maria Stella Calò Mariani and Raffaella Cassano (Venice: Marsilio, 1995) 108–9 [Calò Mariani and Cassano].

55. Alfonso's portrait would have been informed by Frederick's imperial *renovatio* portraiture; see Rafael Cómez Ramos "El retrato de Alfonso X, el Sabio en la primera *Cantiga de Santa María*," in *Studies on the* Cantigas de Santa Maria: *Art, Music, and Poetry,*

ed. Israel J. Katz and John E. Keller (Madison: Hispanic Seminary of Medieval Studies, 1987) 34–52; 38 [Katz and Keller].

56. Existing depictions of Frederick II as classical Roman emperor date from his reign over Sicily after 1231: the headless statue of Frederick from the Gateway of Capua, dated between 1234 and 1247, and imperial coins. Other images include the fresco of *Omaggio dei popoli della terra a Federico II* in the Palazzo Abbaziale of San Zeno (dated after 1238); the portrait of Frederick on f. 144 of the *Chronica Regia Coloniensis*, ms. 476, Bibliothèque Royale de Belgique (dated around 1238); Frederick II *in maestà* (the frontal image of the crowned Roman emperor seated on a throne holding scepter and orb) of f. IV of *De arte venandi cum avibus*, Ms. 1071 Biblioteca apostolica Vaticana di Roma (dated between 1258 and 1266); and the *Exultet* miniature in the Museo Diocesano in Salerno (dated between 1220 and 1227); see Mirko Vagnoni, "Il significato politico delle caratteristiche iconografiche di Federick II di Svevia," *Iconographica* 5 (2006): 67. In the case of Alfonso, the *Cantigas* depict the king as classical Roman emperor in the image of the frontal throned king that opens the collection, as well as a troubadour interacting with the Virgin Mary and his people. Other images of Alfonso outside of the *Cantigas* include his portraits in the *Libro de ajedrez*, the *Lapidario*, the *Grande y general estoria*, the central nave of León Cathedral, and a statue in the Toledo Cathedral. See Cómez Ramos, in Katz and Keller 34–52.

57. See Vagnoni, "Il significato politico," and Cómez Ramos, in Katz and Keller 34–52, for more details about cultural projects and laws passed by these two emperors. Vagnoni, 69, discusses the *Dictatus papae* of Gregory VII, in which the emperor is defined as an executive organ of the pope.

58. Avagnina, "Bassano, Ezzelino e Federico: Il misterioso affresco 'cortese' di casa Finco," in *Federico II e la civiltà comunale nell'Italia del Nord*, ed. Cosimo Damiano Fonseca and Renato Crotti (Rome: Luca, 1999) 525–47, 534 [Fonseca and Crotti]; and "Un inedito affresco," in Calò Mariani and Cassano 107.

59. Vagnoni, 67, believes the style similar to the Barletta bust of Frederick, which is why he dates this fresco to a later period of 1245–50.

60. In her comparison of this "cantore-suonatore" to chansonnier portraits of Bartolomeo Zorzi in Italian chansonniers ms. fr. 854 and ms. lat. 5232 (I and A), Meneghetti, "Federico II e la poesia trobadorica alla luce di un nuovo reperto iconografico," in Fonseca and Crotti 515–16, argues convincingly that this is a troubadour of a high level, not merely a goliard, citing the portrait of accomplished minstrel Perdigo in MS I, folio 49.

61. See Avagnina, "Un inedito affresco," 105–12, and Meneghetti, "Federico II e la poesia," 507–23.

62. Vagnoni 71.

63. See Camille, *The Medieval Art of Love: Objects and Subjects of Desire* (New York: Harry N. Abrams, 1998) 94–107, for a general discussion of this love motif.

64. Avagnina ("Bassano" 539–40) has in particular pointed out the intimate details of the falconry book and fresco compared with the more monumental and official homage fresco at San Zeno, Verona, and the neoclassical portrait of Frederick at the beginning of *De arte venandi*.

65. Avagnina ("Bassano" 541) sees many convergences in the natural style of *De arte venandi* and the Bassano fresco: "l'identità dell'afflato laico e naturalistico che pervade le illustrazioni del codice vaticano e ispira il realismo pungente e cordiale dei personaggi del dipinto de Bassano."

66. Meneghetti, "Federico II e la poesia" 512. For the possibility of Frederick's exposure to chansonniers through Alberico da Romano, see Stefano Asperti, "Le chansonnier provençal T et l'École Poétique sicilienne," *Revue des Langues Romanes* 98 (1994): 49–77.

67. See David Abulafia, "The Kingdom of Sicily under the Hohenstaufen and Angevins," in *The New Cambridge Medieval History: c. 1198–1300,* ed. David Abulafia (Cambridge: Cambridge University Press, 1995–2005) 5: 497–521.

68. See Martinez, "Italy," in Akehurst and Davis 280.

69. Meneghetti, "Federico II e la poesia" 513; Meneghetti, *Il pubblico* 158–61.

70. C. Jean Campbell, *The Game of Courting and the Art of the Commune of San Gimignano 1290–1320* (Princeton: Princeton University Press, 1997) 65–66 n. 37.

71. Other manuscripts state several times that Alfonso "made" certain *cantigas*, and in some (e.g., nos. 1, 347, 400, and 401) he speaks in the first person; see Jack Sage, "Cantiga," in *Grove Music Online*, ed. L. Macy (Accessed May 25, 2007), <http://www.grovemusic .com>.

72. Maricel Presilla, "The Image of Death and Political Ideology in the *Cantigas de Santa María,*" in Katz and Keller 428–89.

73. Joseph T. Snow, "Current Status of *Cantigas* Studies," in Katz and Keller 482.

74. "A vigia de Santa Maria d'Agosto será dita *Des quando Deus sa Madr' aos ceos levou* e no dia será dita a precisson *Bẽeita es, Maria Filla, Madr' e criada*" (cantiga 420); see *Cantigas de Santa María,* ed. Walter Mettman (Madrid: Clásicos Castalia, 1986–89) 1: 16.

75. Ernst H. Kantorowicz, "Kingship under the Impact of Scientific Jurisprudence," in *Twelfth-Century Europe and the Foundations of Modern Society*, ed. Marshall Clagett et al. (Madison: University of Wisconsin Press, 1980) 89–111, 101. See also Kantorowicz, "Frederick the Second," in *The King's Two Bodies: A Study in Mediaeval Political Theology* (Princeton: Princeton University Press, 1957) 97–143.

76. The eighteenth-century Swiss critics Johann Jakob Bodmer and Johann Jakob Breitinger first attributed the Heidelberg manuscript to the Manesse in their *Proben der alten schwäbischen Poesie des Dreyzehnten Jahrhunderts, aus der Maneßischen Sammlung* (Zürich, 1748). For further discussion see my "Conclusion: Songbook Medievalisms."

77. For an overview see Herta-Elisabeth Renk, *Der Manessekreis: Seine Dichter und die Manessische Handschrift* (Stuttgart: W. Kohlhammer, 1974).

78. Eva Moser, "Historische Landschaft und Buchkultur," in *Buchmalerei im Bodenseeraum: 13. Bis 16. Jahrhundert* (Friedrichshaften: Robert Gessler, 1997), ed. Eva Moser, 7–22; Cordula M. Kessler, "Gotische Buchmalerei des Bodenseeraumes aus der Zeit von 1260 bis um 1340/50" in *Buchmalerei* 70–96.

79. The three later artists follow the "architectonic" elements of the *Grundstock;* Ewald M. Vetter, "Die Bilder," in Koschorreck and Werner 43–44; Gisela Kornrumpf sees the *Codex* produced in different stages, *Vom Codex Manesse zur Kolmarer Liederhand-*

schrift: Aspekte der Überlieferung, Formtraditionen, Texte (Tübingen: Max Niemeyer, 2008) 1–31 ("Die Anfänge der manessischen Liederhandschrift").

80. *Die Schweizer Minnesänger*, ed. Max Schiendorfer and Karl Bartsch, vol. 1 (Tübingen: Max Niemeyer, 1990–) 30, 8, line 6 [SMS].

81. For an overview of pattern books, see Robert W. Scheller, *Exemplum: Model-Book Drawings and the Practice of Artistic Transmission in the Middle Ages (ca. 900-ca. 1450)* (Amsterdam: Amsterdam University Press, 1995).

82. Ursula Peters, *Das Ich im Bild* (Cologne: Böhlau, 2008).

83. See *Codex Manesse: Katalog zur Ausstellung vom 12. Juni bis 2. Oktober 1988 Üniversitätsbibliothek Heidelberg*, ed. Elmar Mittler and Wilfried Werner (Heidelberg: Braus, 1988) for artworks related to the world of the *Codex*, such as house frescoes, *Wappenrolle*, plastic arts, and illuminated books.

84. Such as the *Wappenbalken* in the Haus zum Loch (1306) and *Wappenfriese* in the Haus "zum langen Keller," (ca. 1320), both in Zürich; the Schöne Haus in Basel (ca. late thirteenth century).

85. See Haiko Wandhoff, "The Shield as a Poetic Screen: Early Blazon and the Visualization of Medieval German Literature," in *Visual Culture and the German Middle Ages*, ed. Kathryn Starkey and Horst Wenzel (New York: Palgrave Macmillan, 2005).

86. See Karl Clausberg's summary "Das Heraldische und Wohlgeordnete," in *Die Manessische Liederhandschrift* (Cologne: DuMont, 1978) 64–72; Hella Frühmorgen-Voss, *Text und Illustration im Mittelalter: Aufsätze zu den Wechselbeziehungen zwischen Literatur und bildender Kunst* (Munich: Oscar Beck, 1975), and Gisela Siebert-Hotz's dissertation "Das Bild des Minnesängers: Motivgeschichtliche Untersuchungen zur Dichterdarstellung in den Miniaturen der Großen Heidelberger Liederhandschrift" (diss., University of Marburg, 1964).

87. Nichols, "Picture, Image, and Subjectivity in Medieval Culture," *MLN* 108 (1993): 621.

88. See Hugo Steger, *David rex et propheta* (Nuremberg: Hans Carl, 1961) 121 ff.

89. Ewald Jammers, *Das Königliche Liederbuch des deutschen Minnesangs: Eine Einführung in die sogenannte Manessiche Handschrift* (Heidelberg: Lambert Schneider, 1965) 85 ff.

90. See Calò Mariani, "Immagine e potere" and Valentino Pace, "Miniatura di testi sacri nell'Italia meridionale al tempo di Federico II," in Calò Mariani and Cassano.

91. See Joachim Bumke, "Die Ständeordnung und die Reihenfolge der Dichter in der Heidelberger Handschrift," in *Ministerialität und Ritterdichtung* (Munich: Beck, 1976) 31 ff.

92. Kornrumpf (*Vom Codex Manesse*) argues for an original anthology that favored social rank; while I agree with her findings, the additions to the original core group still prioritizes a songbook that accommodates a diversity of poets rather than strict feudal hierarchy.

93. See Bumke 14–21.

94. See Vetter, "Die Bilder," in Koschorreck and Werner 45–46.

95. Kurt Martin, ed., *Minnesänger: Vierundzwanzig farbige Wiedergaben aus der Manessischen Liederhandschrift* (Baden-Baden: Woldemar, 1960–64) 1: 11.

96. Michael Curschmann, *"Pictura laicororum litteratura?* Überlegungen zum Ver-hältnis von Bild und volkssprachlicher Schriftlichkeit im Hoch- und Spätmittelalter bis zum Codex Manesse," in *Pragmatische Schriftlichkeit im Mittelalter: Erscheinungsformen und Entwicklungsstufen*, ed. Hagen Keller, Klaus Grubmüller, and Nikolaus Staubach (Munich: Wilhelm Fink, 1992) 221-23.

97. Curschmann 222. In the *Weingartner*, the empty roll as attribute of poets plays a more dominant role in the more archaic-seeming portraits.

98. Huot, *Song to Book* 246-47.

99. Curschmann 224.

100. Richard de Fournival, *Li Bestiaires d'amours di Maistre Richart de Fornival et Li Response du Bestiaire*, ed. Cesare Segre (Milan: Ricardo Ricciardi, 1957) 5: "Car quant on ot .i. romans lire, on entent les aventures, ausi com on les veïst en present." Carruthers, *Memory* 223.

101. See Curschmann's discussion of the rolls of singers, 225.

102. See Vetter, "Die Bilder," in Koschorreck and Werner 45-46.

103. Ibid. 69.

104. Different theories exist concerning the formal qualities of Henry: Jammers (*Das Königliche Liederbuch*, 170-78) argues that the *Codex Manesse* is a Habsburg songbook made under the patronage of either Konradin, his wife Elizabeth, or their daughter Agnes von Ungarn, in the area of Zürich after the Habsburg loss of Sicily. In producing a songbook representative of the Habsburg legacy, they would have been aware, through family con-nections, of the Alfonso's *Cantigas*, and competitive with Charles of Anjou's production of *Chansonnier du Roi* (176-77).

105. *Des Minnesangs Frühling*, ed. Hugo Moser and Helmut Tervooren et al., 37th and 38th ed. (Stuttgart: S. Hirzel, 1977-88) [MFMT] 1: 71, 3, lines 1, 1-2; 72, 2, lines 1-2.

106. Carruthers, *Memory* 222.

107. Ibid., 222, 224.

108. Thierry of Chartres, prologue to the *Commentaries on the* De Inventione and Rhetorica ad Herennium, ca. 1130-40, in *The Latin Rhetorical Commentaries by Thierry of Chartres*, ed. Karin Margareta Fredborg (Toronto: Pontifical Institute of Mediaeval Stud-ies, 1988).

109. Quintilian, *Institutio Oratoria*, ed. and trans. H. E. Butler (Cambridge, MA: Har-vard University Press, 1920).

110. Curtius 44-45.

111. Martin, vol.1, commentary to *Tafel* 9.

112. For further discussion see Curschmann 225, and Koschorreck, "Die Bildmotive," in Koschorreck and Werner 109. [Koschorreck, "Die Bildmotive"]

113. Martin vol. 1, commentary to *Tafel* 21; see also Koschorreck, "Die Bildmotive" 109.

114. Vetter, "Die Bilder," in Koschorreck and Werner 62 ff.

115. Camille, *The Medieval Art of Love* 95 and passim.

116. See Vetter, "Werkstattstruktur und Arbeitsvorgang" and "Unterzeichnung und Ausführung," in "Die Bilder" Koschorreck and Werner 56 ff.

117. Vetter, "Die Bilder," in Koschorreck and Werner 71.

118. Ibid. 65.

119. Martin vol. 1, commentary to *Tafel* 18. Richard Meyer finds this frontal image similar to the gravestone image of Count Conrad of Thuringia (d. 1241) in the Elisabeth-kirche in Marburg. Such similarities accord with his *vida*, which states that this holy knight-poet was granted the grace of God; see Koschorreck, "Die Bildmotive" 118.

120. Eugène Vinaver, *À la recherche d'une poétique médiévale* (Paris: Nizet, 1970) 44–45.

121. *Walthers von der Vogelweide Gedichte* 69.

122. Frühmorgen-Voss 57–88.

123. Augustine, *De doctrina christiana*, ed. William M. Green, *CSEL* 80 (Vienna: Hoelder-Pichler-Tempsky, 1963).

124. Schiendorfer, in Johannes Hadlaub, *Die Gedichte des Zürcher Minnesängers,* ed. Max Schiendorfer (Zürich: Artemis, 1986) 194.

125. Werner, "Die Handschrift und ihre Geschichte," in Koschorreck and Werner 19–20.

126. Schiendorfer 195.

127. Vetter, "Die Bilder," in Koschorreck and Werner 46.

128. Vetter, ibid. 66, points to the illustrated "Willehalm von Orlens" (ca. 1270).

129. SMS 316 line 1, 8.

130. SMS 313 lines 5–8.

131. SMS 313 2, line 2; see Koschorreck, "Die Bildmotive" 110.

132. SMS 317 lines 33–35. For an extended discussion of the significance of the lapdog in this scene see Andrea Rapp, "*Ir bîzzen was so zartlich, wîblich, fin*: Zur Deutung des Hundes in Hadlaubs Autorbild im *Codex Manesse*," in *Tiere und Fabelwesen im Mittelalter*, ed. Sabine Obermaier (New York: Walter De Gruyter, 2009) 207–32. Rapp insists on merely the appearance of a bite from the lapdog, and that this apparent bite represents the holy presence of the kiss from the Lady (the salvatory pain of true *Minne*).

133. Camille, *Medieval Art of Love* 12; see casket from the Upper Rhine, ca. 1320 from the Cloisters Collection of the Metropolitan Museum of Art in New York. There is a similar emblem of a squirrel within scenes representing the game of courtship on the underside cover.

134. See Friedrich von der Hagen, ed, *Minnesinger: Deutsche Liederdichter des zwölften, dreizehnten und vierzehnten Jahrhunderts* (1838–61; Aalen: O. Zeller, 1962–63) 4: 279 ff.; and Carl von Kraus and Gisela Kornrumpf, eds., *Deutsche Liederdichter des 13. Jahrhunderts*, 2nd ed. (Tübingen: Max Niemeyer, 1978) 2: 386 [KLD].

135. Koschorreck, "Die Bildmotive" 107; Frühmorgen-Voss 78.

136. KLD 2: 385–86, and Koschorreck, "Die Bildmotive" 107; for further discussion of the "Bremberger song" and "Bremberger" material for *Meistergesang,* see Arthur Kopp, *Bremberger-Gedichte: Ein Beitrag zur Brembergersage*, Quellen und Forschungen zur deutschen Volkskunde 2 (Vienna: Dr. Rud. Ludwig, 1908), and John Meier, "Drei alte deutsche Balladen: 3. Das Brembergerlied," *Jahrbuch für Volksliedforschung* 4 (1934): 56–65.

For an overview of the eaten-heart motif and the Brennenberg/Bremberger tradition, see Vilmos Voigt, "The Woman Who Destroys Life—*La Belle Dame Sans Merci*," *Folkloristika Svetur* 21.28 (2004): 165–86, esp. 170–77.

137. Koschorreck, "Die Bildmotive" 107; KLD 1: 330 (strophes 9 line 7, 7 line 9).

138. KLD 1: 330 (strophes 9 lines 2–3, 7 line 10); f. 189r.

139. KLD 1: 328 and 331 (strophes 4 line 10, 9 lines 10–11).

140. For images and discussion, see Ruth Mortimer, "The Author's Image: Italian Sixteenth-Century Printed Portraits," *Harvard Library Bulletin* n.s. 7.2 (1996): 7–87.

CHAPTER FOUR

1. Zufferey, *Recherches* 316; István Frank, *Répertoire métrique de la poésie des troubadours.* (Paris: Honoré Champion, 1953–57) 1: xvi n. 1; Riquer 1: 9.

2. The Galician-Portuguese lyric corpus, transmitted relatively uniformly, survives in just three major collections without music (apart from Martin Codax's individual anthology, the so-called *Vindel* manuscript dating from about 1300, and the fragmentary folio of Dom Dinis, both of which include music): the *Cancioneiro da Vaticana*, the *Cancioneiro Colocci-Brancuti* (two early sixteenth-century Italian collections copied for and by Angelo Colucci), and the *Cancioneiro da Ajuda*, probably copied before 1300 and never completed. There is also the *Cantigas de Santa María* of Alfonso X's court, which includes music (ca. 1270–90). See Giuseppe Tavani "La poesia lirica galego-portoghese," *GRLM* 2 (1980): 1.6, 25–28.

3. Brian Dutton and Victoriano Roncero López, eds., *La poesía cancioneril del siglo XV: Antología y estudio* (Madrid: Iberoamericana, 2004) 14 [Dutton and Roncero López] 5.

4. See Garcia, "In Praise of the *Cancionero*," in *Gerli and Weiss* 51.

5. See Jeremy N. H. Lawrance, "The Spread of Lay Literacy in Late Medieval Castile," *Bulletin of Hispanic Studies* 62 (1985): 79–94.

6. López de Mendoza 642; for further discussion, see my "Conclusion: Songbook Medievalisms."

7. Santillana's use of the word "cancionero" for lyric anthologies emphasizes Dutton's point that the *cuatrocentistas* themselves used this term for their lyric anthologies. See Dorothy Severin, "'Cancionero': un género mal-nombrado,'" *Cultura Neolatina* 54 (1994): 98–99, and Dutton's response, Dutton and Roncero López 19 (citing López de Mendoza 642).

8. See Garcia, "In Praise of the *Cancionero*"; Roncaglia, "Rétrospectives et perspectives" 19–38; and Hans Ulrich Gumbrecht, *Eine Geschichte der spanischen Literatur* (Frankfurt: Suhrkamp, 1990) 1: 126–46.

9. *Cancionero de Juan Alfonso de Baena*, ed. Brian Dutton and Joaquín González Cuenca (Madrid: Visor Libros, 1993) 7.

10. Jacques Le Goff, *Time, Work, and Culture in the Middle Ages*, trans. Arthur Goldhammer (Chicago: University of Chicago Press, 1980) 250.

11. See José Antonio Maravall, "La concepción del saber en una sociedad tradicional," in id., *Estudios de Historia del Pensamiento Español: Serie Primera, Edad Media*, 3rd ed. (Madrid: Ediciones Cultura Hispánica, 1983) 203–54.

246 : NOTES TO PAGES 170-177

12. See Gumbrecht, *Geschichte* 1: 129; as well as "Intertextuality and Autumn/Autumn and the Modern Reception of the Middle Ages," in *The New Medievalism* 301–30.

13. See Lawrance, "Juan Alfonso de Baena's Versified Reading List: A Note on the Aspirations and the Reality of Fifteenth-Century Castilian Culture," *Journal of Hispanic Philology* 5 (1981): 101–22, as well as Julian Weiss's discussion of Santillana in *The Poet's Art: Literary Theory in Castile* c. *1400–60*, Medium Aevum Monographs New Series 14 (Oxford: Society for the Study of Mediaeval Languages and Literature, 1990) 165–228.

14. Such a series of *cantigas de serrana* occurs in the *Cancionero de Palacio*. See Brownlee, "Francisco Imperial and the Issue of Poetic Genealogy," in *Gerli and Weiss* 71–73.

15. Weiss, *Poet's Art* 42, Garcia, in *Gerli and Weiss* 49, Huot, *Song to Book*; Poe, "Old Provençal *Vidas* as Literary Commentary," *Romance Philology* 33 (1979–80): 510–18; id., "The *Vidas* and *Razos*," in Akehurst and Davis 185–97; and id., *From Poetry to Prose in Old Provençal: The Emergence of the* Vidas, *the* Razos, *and the* Razos de trobar (Birmingham, AL: Summa, 1984).

16. Weiss, *Poet's Art* 42.

17. *Canc. de Baena* 1.

18. Poe, in Akehurst and Davis 190. Alfred Jeanroy, ed., *La poésie lyrique des troubadours* (1934; New York: AMS, 1974) 1: 112; see also Meneghetti, *Il pubblico* 209–44.

19. For an analysis of the chansonnier reception of the lyric "je," see, for example, Paul Zumthor's description of the "je" becoming "objective" and "figurative" in *Langue, texte, énigme* (Paris: Seuil, 1975) 178; and Jauss's "abstraction of the lyrical 'I'" in *Alterität und Modernität* 418.

20. *Canc. de Baena*, 11 [ID1147], [PN1]. I follow the system of classification of the cancioneros and their contents (poets, works) in Brian Dutton et al., *Catálogo-índice*. However, while citing individual works by the catalogue's ID, I will generally refer to the designated names of the cancioneros. Translations are my own.

21. *Canc. de Baena* 14 [ID1149].

22. *Canc. de Baena* 17 [ID1151].

23. *Palacio*: [SA7], *Estúñiga* [MN54], *General* [11CG].

24. Dutton and Roncero López 519 [ID1955].

25. *Canc. de Baena* 638 [ID1483].

26. F. J. Sánchez Cantón, ed., "El 'Arte de trovar' de Don Enrique de Villena," *Revista de Filología Española* 6 (1919): 158–80. Citations from *Enrique de Villena: Obras completas*, ed. Pedro M. Cátedra (Madrid: Turner, 1994) 1: 355–70.

27. *Canc. de Baena* 7.

28. Weiss, *Poet's Art* 51.

29. Ibid. 52.

30. *Canc. de Baena* 8.

31. Ibid.

32. See Weiss, *Poet's Art* 49 on this point about the anticlimatic ending of the *Prologus*.

33. *Canc. de Baena* 5.

34. *Canc. de Baena* 6.

35. Weiss, *Poet's Art* 48.

36. *Canc. de Baena* 7.

37. Weiss, *Poet's Art* 49.

38. Weiss, *Poet's Art* 49.

39. *Canc. de Baena* 1.

40. See Weiss's analysis of Villena's "gaya ciencia," *Poet's Art* 55–83.

41. Cátedra 355.

42. Ibid.

43. Ibid.

44. Ibid.

45. Ibid.

46. Such as the *Leys d'amors* of Guilhem Molinier, who would have been the authoritative source for participants of the Consistory (Weiss, *Poet's Art* 70).

47. Cátedra 355–57.

48. Weiss, *Poet's Art* 66.

49. Cátedra 359.

50. Ibid. 357.

51. Ibid. 356.

52. Ibid. 358

53. Gómez-Bravo, *"Decir canciones,"* 160.

54. Cátedra 359.

55. See my "Conclusion: Songbook Medievalisms" on the symbolism of the book in relation to Bodmer and Alfonso X.

56. Angus MacKay, "Ritual and Propaganda in Fifteenth-Century Castile," *Past and Present* 107 (1985): 33.

57. Teófilo F. Ruiz, "Fiestas, torneos y símbolos de realeza en la Castilla del siglo XV. Las fiestas de Valladolid de 1428," in Adeline Rucquoi, ed., *Realidad e imagenes del poder: España a fines de la Edad Media* (Valladolid: Ambito, 1988) 249.

58. Pedro Carrillo de Huete, *Crónica del Halconero de Juan II*, ed. Juan de Mata Carriazo (Madrid: Espasa-Calpe, 1946) 21–26.

59. See Francisco Rico, "Unas coplas de Jorge Manrique y las fiestas de Valladolid en 1428," *Anuario de Estudios Medievales* 2 (1965): 515–24; and MacKay "Ritual and Propaganda."

60. See Ian Macpherson, "The Game of Courtly Love: *Letra, Divisa* and *Invençión* at the Court of the Catholic Monarchs," in Gerli and Weiss 95–110; Rico, "Unas coplas"; MacKay, "Ritual and Propaganda"; articles of Macpherson and MacKay reprinted in Ian Macpherson and Angus MacKay, *Love, Religion and Politics in Fifteenth Century Spain*, Medieval Iberian Peninsula Texts and Studies 13 (Boston: Brill, 1998).

61. See O'Callaghan 610–12.

62. See especially Macpherson and MacKay, "'*Manteniendo la tela*': el erotismo del vocabulario caballeresco-textil en la época de los Reyes Católicos," in *Actas del Primer*

Congreso Anglo-Hispano, Vol. I: Lingüística, ed. Ralph Penny (Madrid: Castalia, 1993) 1: 25–36.

63. Johan Huizinga, *The Autumn of the Middle Ages*, trans. Rodney J. Payton and Ulrich Mammitzsch (1921; Chicago: University of Chicago Press, 1996).

64. Macpherson, "The Game of Courtly Love" 100–101.

65. Mata Carriazo, in Carrillo de Huete 21.

66. Ibid.

67. Macpherson, "The Game of Courtly Love" 101.

68. Mata Carriazo, in Carrillo de Huete 21–22.

69. For a good overview of intertexuality see Meneghetti, "Intertextuality and Dialogism in the Troubadours," in Gaunt and Kay 181–96.

70. See Garcia, in *Gerli and Weiss,* passim.

71. As Weiss points out (*Poet's Art* 32), the *pregunta/respuesta* goes back to the troubadour tradition of the *tenso* and *joc-partit*, but in fifteenth-century Castile this genre treats astrological or theological topics such as the ones in the *Baena*.

72. For example, the *Cancionero de Estúñiga,* ed. Nicasio Salvador Miguel (Madrid: Alhambra, 1987).

73. See Dutton, "Spanish Fifteenth-Century *Cancioneros*: A General Survey to 1465," *Kentucky Romance Quarterly* 27 (1979): 445–60. See also introduction of the *Canc. de Baena* for differences between original compilation and copy ([PNI]).

74. *Canc. de Baena,* 255n. *San Román*: [MH1].

75. [IDs 1366, 1367, 1368, 1369]. For a discussion of this series, see María Rosa Lida de Malkiel, "Un decir más de Francisco Imperial: Respuesta a Fernán Pérez de Guzmán," in id., *Estudios sobre la literatura española del siglo XV* (Madrid: Ediciones Porrúa Turanzas, [1976]) 311–24.

76. [IDs 1366–69, ID0539, ID1370, ID1371], *Canc. de Baena* 280–89.

77. Garcia, in *Gerli and Weiss* 52.

78. *Canc. de Baena* 3.

79. *Canc. de Baena* 1.

80. Garcia, in *Gerli and Weiss* 54–56.

81. *Cancionero de Palacio,* ed. Ana M. Álvarez Pellitero (Salamanca: Junta de Castilla y León, 1993).

82. *Canc. de Estúñiga* 530–31.

83. *Canc. de Estúñiga* 535, 539.

84. *Canc. de Estúñiga* 559 [ID0623].

85. *Canc. de Estúñiga* 544 [ID0615].

86. Refers to the "dangerous seat" of the Arthurian round table reserved for the noblest knight, *Canc. de Estúñiga* 515, n. 34 [ID0604].

87. See *Canc. de Estúñiga* 515, n. 34 and Dutton and Roncero López 423 n. 550.

88. *Canc. de Estúñiga* 508 [ID0601].

89. This poem is actually the *glosa* of the *mote,* ""Siempre vencen seguidores" [ID3646].

90. Dutton and Roncero López 327.

91. Dutton and Roncero López 336, 341.

92. [ID3068], Dutton and Roncero López 324–26.

93. [ID2390], Dutton and Roncero López 331.

94. See Lida de Malkiel, ""La hipérbole sagrada en la poesía castellana del siglo XV," in id., *Estudios* 291, who discusses the oldest Castilian example in the *Libro de buen amor*, 308.

95. See Fernando Gómez Redondo, "Lucena, *Repetición de amores*: sentido y estructura," in Ana Menéndez Collera and Victoriano Roncero López, eds., *Nunca fue pena amor (Estudios de literatura española en homenaje a Brian Dutton)* (Cuenca: Ediciones de la Universidad de Castilla-La Mancha, 1996) 293–304.

96. Dutton and Roncero López 349–52.

97. [ID0517], Dutton and Roncero López 353–54.

98. Dutton and Roncero López 353.

99. Lawrance argues that the list in ID0285 contains *exempla* rather than the first-hand knowledge of primary sources, "Juan Alfonso de Baena's Versified Reading List" 101–22.

100. López de Mendoza 642.

101. See Keith Whinnom's systematic study of the *canciones* of the *Cancionero general*, "Towards the Interpretation and Appreciation of the *Canciones* of the *Cancionero general* of 1511," in *Medieval and Renaissance Spanish Literature: Selected Essays by Keith Whinnom*, ed. Alan Deyermond et al. (Exeter: University of Exeter Press, 1994) 114–32.

102. See Macpherson, "The Game of Courtly Love" 103–4.

103. Dutton and Roncero López 518 [ID1955]; Macpherson, "Secret Language in the *Cancioneros*: Some Courtly Codes," *Bulletin of Hispanic Studies* 62 (1985): 51–56.

104. See Dutton and Roncero López 44–45, Whinnom "Towards the Interpretation," and Macpherson, "Secret Language in the *Cancioneros*."

105. For thorough descriptions of how *invenciones* functioned, see Macpherson, "The Game of Courtly Love" 103, and "Secret Language."

106. Francisco López Estrada, ed., *Las poéticas castellanas de la Edad Media* (Madrid: Taurus Ediciones, 1984) 67–133.

107. López de Mendoza 642.

108. Ibid. 649.

109. Weiss, *Poet's Art* 220.

110. López Estrada 67–71.

111. López Estrada 83.

112. López Estrada 82.

113. López Estrada 78.

114. López de Mendoza 655.

115. Ibid. 655; López Estrada 85.

116. The *Cancionero general* had many reprints after its first appearance in 1511 [11CG]. See introduction to the facsimile edition: Antonio Rodríguez-Moñino, ed., *Cancionero General: recopilado por Hernando del Castillo (Valencia, 1511)* (Madrid: Real Academia Española, 1958).

117. Marcella Ciceri and Julio Rodríguez Puértolas, eds., *Antón de Montoro: Cancionero* (Salamanca: Ediciones de la Universidad de Salamanca, 1990) 292. See also Kenneth R. Scholberg, *Sátira e invectiva en la España medieval* (Madrid: Gredos, 1971) 315–16; Ciceri and Puértolas 75.

118. See Scholberg 310–27.

119. Citations from *Cancionero general* [11CG] from Rodríguez-Moñino.

120. E. Michael Gerli, "Reading Cartagena: Blindness, Insight and Modernity in a *Cancionero* Poet," in *Gerli and Weiss* 174.

121. [ID6876]; these poems of Costana appear in the 1514 edition of *Cancionero general*, cited from Dutton and Roncero López 519.

122. [ID6879], Dutton and Roncero López 521.

CONCLUSION

1. See A. Thomas, "Les manuscrits provençaux et français de Dominicy," *Romania* 17 (1888): 401–16.

2. Thomas 402.

3. For a sense of the scholarship in the English and Romance traditions, see Lerer, "Medieval English Literature," and the collection of essays in Nichols and Wenzel.

4. See for instance Kendrick's discussion of Nostredame in "The Science of Imposture," in Bloch and Nichols 95–126, esp. 100.

5. Jehan de Nostredame, *Les vies des plus célèbres et anciens poètes provençaux*, ed. Camille Chabaneau, introd. Joseph Anglade (1575; Paris: Honoré Champion, 1913). Although Nostredame claims to use authentic manuscript sources according to the sixteenth-century Italian humanist practice, Anglade (citing the studies of Paul Meyer and Karl Bartsch) points out the invention of most of his sources ("Les Sources"); Nostredame did use three chansonniers as sources (121).

6. In addition to Kendrick, "Science of Imposture," see Nathan Edelman, *Attitudes of Seventeenth-Century France toward the Middle Ages* (New York: King's Crown Press, 1946) 343.

7. Kendrick, "Science of Imposture."

8. Lionel Gossman, *Medievalism and the Ideologies of the Enlightenment: The World and Work of La Curne de Sainte-Palaye* (Baltimore: Johns Hopkins University Press, 1968) 303. He refers to Sainte-Palaye's "Projet d'étude sur l'histoire de France."

9. Jean Baptiste de La Curne Sainte-Palaye and Claude Millot, *Histoire littéraire des Troubadours* (Paris, 1774) 2: 309; Gossman 317–18.

10. See John M. Graham, "National Identity and the Politics of Publishing the Troubadours," in Bloch and Nichols 72.

11. Karl Bartsch, ed., *Grundriß zur Geschichte der provenzalischen Literatur* (Eberfeld, 1872); Raynouard and Levy, *Lexique Roman* and *Provenzalisches Supplement-Wörterbuch*.

12. These comments anticipate transmission theories discussed in chapter two. Graham, in Bloch and Nichols 71, citing *Peire Vidal's Lieder*, ed. Karl Bartsch (Berlin, 1857) foreword, second and third unnumbered pages; see also Bartsch's *Grundriß* 27.

13. Nichols, "'Art' and 'Nature'" in Nichols and Wenzel 86.

14. Nichols, "Introduction" 8: "Recalling that almost all manuscripts postdate the life of the author by decades or even centuries, one recognizes the manuscript matrix as a place of radical contingencies: of chronology, of anachronism, of conflicting subjects, of representation."

15. See chapter three.

16. Sage, "Cantiga."

17. López de Mendoza 654. Dutton states that this songbook has since been lost, and that it dates from the "post-dionisíaca" years of Galician-Portuguese poetry, between 1300–1350. In the decade of 1340, el Conde de Barcelos recopied a *Livro das cantigas*, the same book owned by Santillana's grandmother doña Mencía de Cisneros, which records the lyric production of King Dinis's court (Dutton and Roncero López 14).

18. Although the works mentioned by Santillana, including the *Libro*, are primarily in *cuaderna vía*, I agree with Dagenais that Santillana is making a point about the various poetic forms used by early Castilian poets, *Ethics* 174.

19. Bodmer, *Neue critische Briefe über gantz verschiedene Sachen, von verschiedenen Verfassern* (Zürich, 1749) 474 ff. [NCB].

20. See Eric A. Blackall's discussion of Bodmer and Breitinger, *The Emergence of German as a Literary Language: 1700–1775* (Ithaca: Cornell University Press, 1959) 276–313, esp. 310; and Peter Hans Reill, *The German Enlightenment and the Rise of Historicism* (Berkeley: University of California Press, 1975) 199 ff.

21. NCB 481; the narrator does not intuitively identify with the dwarf's song, but has studied it, since he refers to Goldast von Haiminsfeld (1578–1646), Bodmer and Breitinger's predecessor, who had studied and published excerpts from *die Große Heidelberger Liederhandschrift*.

22. NCB 497–98.

23. See Jan-Dirk Müller, "J.J. Bodmers Poetik und die Wiederentdeckung mittelhochdeutscher Epen," *Euphorion* 71 (1977): 336–52.

24. NCB 495.

25. See Jeffrey M. Peck, "'In the Beginning Was the Word': Germany and the Origins of German Studies," in Bloch and Nichols 127–47, and Gumbrecht, "Un souffle d'Allemagne ayant passé: Friedrich Diez, Gaston Paris, and the Genesis of National Philologies," *Romance Philology* 40.1 (1986): 1–37.

26. As Graham comments: "He based his text on the oldest but most poorly written text, while assuming that the other manuscripts had descended from it in a straight line, which meant that they could not be used to reconstruct the archetype" (70).

27. Paden, "Manuscripts" 316.

28. Zumthor, *Essai de poétique médiévale*.

29. See MFMT "Vorwort zur 38. Auflage."

30. Nichols, "Modernism and the Politics of Medieval Studies," in Bloch and Nichols 31.

31. See Günther Schweikle, *Minnesang* (Stuttgart: Metzler, 1995); Walther von der Vogelweide, *Die Gedichte Walthers von der Vogelweide*, ed. Karl Lachmann and Hugo Kuhn (Berlin: Walter de Gruyter, 1965); and MFMT 2: 7–24.

32. For a discussion see Sayce, *MGL* 3.

33. Dutton and Roncero López 6; see also Jules Piccus, "The Nineteenth-Century *Cancionero general del siglo XV*," *Kentucky Foreign Language Quarterly* 6 (1959): 121–25; *El Cancionero de Juan Alfonso de Baena*, ed. P[edro] J[osé] Pidal (Madrid, 1851); *Cancionero de Lope de Stúñiga, códice del siglo XV*, ed. F[uensanta] del V[alle] and J[osé] S[ancho] R[ayón] (Madrid, 1872).

34. Dutton and Roncero López 6.

35. *Cancionero castellano del siglo XV*, ed. R. Foulché-Delbosc, Nueva Biblioteca de Autores Españoles (Madrid: Bailly-Baillière, 1912–15); R. Foulché-Delbosc and L. Barrau-Dihigo, *Manuel de l'hispanisant* (New York: Putnam, 1920).

36. Beltran Pepió, in *Gerli and Weiss* 20 nn. 3 and 4, mentions some key studies on individual authors, such as Lida de Malkiel on Juan de Mena (1950) and Lapesa on Santillana (1957) among others.

37. See Wadda C. Ríos-Font, "Literary History and Canon Formation," in David T. Gies, ed., *The Cambridge History of Spanish Literature* (Cambridge: Cambridge University Press, 2004) 28–29; José Amador de los Ríos, *Historia crítica de la literatura española* (Madrid: Imprenta de José Rodríguez, 1861–65) 1: n.p.

38. D. Marcelino Menéndez y Pelayo and Rogerio Sánchez, eds., *Antología de poetas líricos castellanos*, Biblioteca Clásica 136 (Madrid: Viuda de Hernando and Cia., 1890–1916) 1: v–vi [Menéndez Pelayo].

39. Menéndez Pidal, *Los españoles en su historia* 9–10, 159–161; see also Nelson R. Orringer, "Ideas, Aesthetics, Historical Studies," in Gies 539–40.

40. Menéndez Pelayo 1: xi.

41. Miguel de Unamuno, *Del sentimiento trágico de la vida en los hombres y en los pueblos* (Madrid: Renacimiento, [1912]) 313.

42. Dutton et al., *Catálogo-índice* (1982); Dutton and Krogstad, *Cancionero del siglo XV* (1990–91); Beltrán Pepió, *La canción de amor en el otoño de la Edad Media* (Barcelona: Promociones y Publicaciones Universitarias, 1988); Juan Casas Rigall, *Agudeza y retórica en la poesía amorosa de cancionero* (Santiago de Compostela: Universidade, 1995); Francisco Crosas López, *La materia clásica en la poesía de Cancionero* (Kassel: Reichenberger, 1995).

43. Menéndez Pelayo 5: xxii–xxiii.

44. See Garcia's discussion of how the *Cancionero de Oñate-Castañeda* reflects the aesthetic tastes of a compiler creating his own literary canon, and how the compiler creates not only an anthology but "a real historical manual" in that he organizes his cancionero in a way that helps the reader to understand poetic trends and developments of the fifteenth century (in *Gerli and Weiss* 54–56); Gumbrecht's phenomenological notion of the "intertextuality" of fifteenth-century cancioneros describes "textual configuration types" as having certain recurring semantic or rhetorical structures, enabling them to be "adapted" to specific situations; see "Intertextuality and Autumn."

45. See Riquer's comprehensive anthology (now in a single volume) and Robert Kehew's recent bilingual anthology of troubadour poetry, *Lark in the Morning: The Verses of the Troubadours* (Chicago: University of Chicago Press, 2005), which includes the translations of Ezra Pound, W. D. Snodgrass, and Robert Kehew.

Bibliography

༄ ༄

MANUSCRIPTS

Heidelberg. Universitätsbibliothek. Codex Palatinus Germanicus 848 [*Codex Manesse*].

Modena. Biblioteca Estense e Universitaria. α.R.4.4 [troub. Ms. D].

New York. Pierpont Morgan Library. Ms. 819 [troub. N].

Paris. Bibliothèque Nationale. Française 854 [troub. I]; Fr. 856 [troub. C]; Fr. 15211; [troub. T]; Fr. 22543 [troub. R]; Fr. 12474 [troub. M].

Rome. Biblioteca Vaticana. Latino 5232 [troub. A]

PRIMARY SOURCES

Alfonso X, el Sabio. *Cantigas de Santa María*. Ed. Walter Mettman. 3 vols. Madrid: Clásicos Castalia, 1986–89.

———. *Cantigas de Santa María*. Edición facsímil del Códice T.I.1 de la Biblioteca de San Lorenzo el Real de El Escorial. Siglo XIII. 2 vols. Madrid: Edilán, 1979.

Arnaut Daniel. *Canzoni*. Ed. Gianluigi Toja. Florence: Sansoni, 1960.

Augustine. *De doctrina christiana*. Ed. William M. Green. *Corpus scriptorum ecclesiasticorum latinorum* 80. Vienna: Hoelder-Pichler-Tempsky, 1963.

———. *On Music*. Trans. Robert Catesby Taliaferro. The Fathers of the Church, ed. Roy Joseph Deferrari. Vol. 4. New York: Fathers of the Church 1947.

Bernart Marti. *Les poésies de Bernart Marti*. Ed. Ernest Hoepffner. Paris: Honoré Champion, 1929.

Bernart de Ventadorn. *Seine Lieder*. Ed. Carl Appel. Halle: Niemeyer, 1915.

———. *The Songs of Bernart de Ventadorn*. Ed. and trans. Stephen G. Nichols Jr. et al. Chapel Hill: University of North Carolina Press, 1962.

Bodmer, Jakob. *Neue critische Briefe über gantz verschiedene Sachen, von verschiedenen Verfassern*. Zurich: Orell, 1749.

Boutière, Jean, and A.-H. Schutz, eds. *Biographies des troubadours: Textes provençaux des XIIIe et XIVe siècles*. Paris: Nizet, 1964.

Breitinger, Johann Jakob, and Johann Jakob Bodmer, eds. *Critische Briefe*. 1746. Hildesheim: G. Olms, 1969.

———, eds. *Proben der alten schwäbischen Poesie des Dreyzehnten Jahrhunderts, aus der Maneßischen Sammlung*. Zurich, 1748.

———, eds. *Sammlung von Minnesingern aus dem schwäbischen Zeitpunkte, CXL Dichter enthaltend; durch Ruedger Manessen*. 2 vols. Zurich: Orell, 1758–59.

The Cambridge Songs (Carmina Cantabrigiensia). Ed. and trans. Jan M. Ziolkowski. Medieval and Renaissance Texts and Studies 192. Tempe, Arizona: Medieval and Renaissance Texts and Studies, 1998.

Cancioneiro da Ajuda. Ed. Carolina Michaëlis de Vasconcellos. 2 vols. Halle: Niemeyer, 1904.

Cancionero de Juan Alfonso de Baena. Ed. P[edro] J[osé] Pidal. Madrid, 1851.

Cancionero de Juan Alfonso de Baena. Ed. Brian Dutton and Joaquín González Cuenca. Madrid: Visor Libros, 1993.

Cancionero castellano del siglo XV. Ed. R. Foulché-Delbosc. Nueva Biblioteca de Autores Españoles. 2 vols. Madrid: Bailly-Baillière, 1912–15.

Cancionero de Lope de Stúñiga, códice del siglo XV. Ed. F[uensanta] del V[alle] and J[osé] S[ancho] R[ayón]. Madrid, 1872.

Cancionero de Estúñiga. Ed. Nicasio Salvador Miguel. Madrid: Alhambra, 1987.

Cancionero General: Recopilado por Hernando del Castillo (Valencia, 1511) [facsimile]. Ed. Antonio Rodríguez-Moñino. Madrid: Real Academia Española, 1958.

Cancionero de Palacio. Ed. Ana M. Álvarez Pellitero. Salamanca: Junta de Castilla y León, 1993.

Il Canzoniere Provenzale Estense [facsimile]. 2 vols. Introd. D'Arco Silvio Avalle and Emanuele Casamassima. Modena: STEM-Mucchi, 1979–82.

Carmina Burana. Ed. Alfons Hilka, Otto Schumann, and Bernhard Bischoff. 2 vols. Heidelberg: Carl Winter, 1930–78.

Carmina Burana: Facsimile Reproduction of the Manuscript Clm 4660 and Clm 4660a. Ed. Bernhard Bischoff. Publication of Medieval Manuscripts 9. Brooklyn: Institute of Mediaeval Music, 1967.

Carmina Burana: Texte und Übersetzungen. Ed. Benedikt Konrad Vollmann. Frankfurt: Deutscher Klassiker Verlag, 1987.

Carmina Burana. Die Gedichte des Codex Buranus lateinisch und deutsch. Ed. Carl Fischer. Trans. Hugo Kuhn. Annotations by Günther Bernt. Zurich and Munich: Artemis, 1974.

Carmina Burana. The Love Songs of the Carmina Burana. Trans. E. D. Blodgett and Roy Arthur Swanson. Garland Library of Medieval Literature 49B. New York: Garland, 1987.

Carrillo de Huete, Pedro. *Crónica del Halconero de Juan II.* Ed. Juan de Mata Carriazo. Madrid: Espasa-Calpe, 1946.

Chrétien de Troyes. *Romans.* Ed. Michel Zink, Jean-Marie Fritz et al. Paris: Librairie Générale Française, 1994.

Codex Manesse: Die Miniaturen der Großen Heidelberger Liederhandschrift. Ed. Ingo F. Walther and Gisela Siebert. Frankfurt: Insel, 1988.

Dante Alighieri. *De vulgari eloquentia.* Ed. Pier Vincenzo Mengaldo. *Opere minori.* Ed. Mengaldo et al. 2 vols. Milan: Ricciardi [1979–].

———. *The Divine Comedy of Dante Alighieri.* Ed. and Trans. Robert M. Durling. Introd. Ronald L. Martinez and Robert M. Durling. 3 vols. Oxford: Oxford University Press, 1996 [*Inferno*] , 2003 [*Purgatorio*], and 2011 [*Paradiso*].

Enrique de Villena. *Obras completas de Enrique de Villena*. Ed. and introd. Pedro M. Cátedra. 3 vols. Madrid: Turner, 1994.

Folquet de Marseille. *Le troubadour Folquet de Marseille: Édition critique*. Ed. Stanislaw Stronski. 1910. Geneva: Slatkine, 1968.

Gatien-Arnoult, [Adolphe-Félix], ed. *Monumens de la littérature romane depuis le quatorzième siècle: Las Flors del Gay Saber, estier dichas las Leys d'Amors*, 3 vols. Paris: Silvestre; Toulouse: Bon and Privat, [1841–43].

Guglielmo IX. *Poesie*. Ed. Nicolò Pasero. Modena: STEM Mucchi, 1973.

———. *The Poetry of William VII, Count of Poitiers, IX Duke of Aquitaine*. Ed. Gerald A. Bond. Garland Library of Medieval Literature 4A. New York: Garland, 1982.

Guiraut Riquier. *Las cansos: Kritischer Text und Kommentar*. Ed. Ulrich Mölk. Heidelberg: Carl Winter, 1962.

———. "I vers del trovatore Guiraut Riquier." Ed. Monica Longobardi. *Studi mediolatini e volgari* 29 (1982–83): 17–163.

———. *Les épitres de Guiraut Riquier, troubadour du XIIIe siècle: Édition critique avec traduction et notes*. Ed. Joseph Linskill. Liège: Association internationale d'études occitanes, 1985.

The Holy Bible. Douay-Rheims. London: Baronius Press, 2005.

Kraus, Carl von, and Gisela Kornrumpf, eds. *Deutsche Liederdichter des 13. Jahrhunderts*. 2nd ed. 2 vols. Tübingen: Max Niemeyer, 1978.

Libro de buen amor. Ed. Manuel Criado de Val and Eric W. Naylor. Madrid: Consejo Superior de Investigaciones Científicas, 1965.

Libro de buen amor. Ed. Joan Corominas. Madrid: Biblioteca Románica Hispánica, 1967.

Libro de buen amor. Ed. Raymond S. Willis. Princeton: Princeton University Press, 1972.

Libro de buen amor. Ed. G. B. Gybbon-Monypenny. Madrid: Clásicos Castalia, 1988.

López Estrada, Francisco, ed. *Las poéticas castellanas de la Edad Media*. Madrid: Taurus Ediciones, 1984.

López de Mendoza, Iñigo, Marqués de Santillana. *Poesías completas*. Ed. M. P. A. M. Kerkhof and A. Gómez Moreno. Madrid: Castalia, 2003.

Marcabru. *Marcabru: A Critical Edition*. Ed. Simon Gaunt, Ruth Harvey, and Linda Paterson. Cambridge: D. S. Brewer, 2000.

Matfre Ermegnaud. *Le Breviari d'amor de Matfre Ermengaud*. Ed. Peter T. Ricketts. 4 vols. Tome 5: vv. 27252T–34597. Leiden: Brill, 1976– .

Menéndez y Pelayo, D. Marcelino, and Rogerio Sánchez, eds. *Antología de poetas líricos castellanos*. Biblioteca Clásica 136. 14 vols. Madrid: Viuda de Hernando and Cia., 1890–1916.

Menéndez Pidal, Ramón. *Estudios literarios*. 5th ed. Buenos Aires: Espasa-Calpe, 1942.

———. *Los españoles en su historia y los españoles en la literatura*. Buenos Aires: Espasa-Calpe, 1951.

———. *Poesía juglaresca y orígenes de la literatura románica*. 6th ed. Madrid: Instituto de Estudios Políticos, 1957.

Migne, J.-P., ed. *Patrologiae Cursus Completus*. Series Latina. 221 vols. Paris: Garnier, 1844–1905.

Des Minnesangs Frühling. Ed. Hugo Moser and Helmut Tervooren et al. 37th and 38th ed. 3 vols. Stuttgart: S. Hirzel, 1977–88 (using edition of Karl Lachmann, Moriz Haupt et al.).

Montoro, Antón de. *Cancionero*. Ed. Marcella Ciceri and Julio Rodríguez Puértolas. Salamanca: Ediciones de la Universidad de Salamanca, 1990.

Nostredame, Jehan de. *Les vies des plus célèbres et anciens poètes provençaux*. Ed. Camille Chabeneau. Introd. Joseph Anglade. 1575. Paris: Honoré Champion, 1913.

Peire d'Alvernhe. *Peire d'Alvernha: Liriche*. Ed. Alberto Del Monte. Turin: Loescher-Chiantore, 1955.

Peire Cardenal. *Poésies complètes du troubadour Peire Cardenal: 1180–1278*. Ed. and trans. René Lavaud. Toulouse: Privat, 1957.

Peire Vidal. *Peire Vidal's Lieder*. Ed. Karl Bartsch. Berlin: Dümmler, 1857.

Petrarca, Francesco. *Petrarch's Lyric Poems: The* Rime sparse *and Other Lyrics*. Ed. and trans. Robert M. Durling. Cambridge, MA: Harvard University Press, 1976.

Quintilian. *Institutio Oratoria*. Ed. and trans. H. E. Butler. 4 vols. Cambridge, MA: Harvard University Press, 1920.

Raimbaut D'Aurenga. *The Life and Works of the Troubadour Raimbaut d'Orange*. Ed. Walter T. Pattison. Minneapolis: University of Minnesota Press, 1952.

Raimon Vidal. *The "Razos de Trobar" of Raimon Vidal and Associated Texts*. Ed. John Henry Marshall. London: Oxford University Press, 1972.

Richard de Fournival. *Li Bestiaires d'amours di Maistre Richart de Fornival et Li Response du Bestiaire*. Ed. Cesare Segre. Milan: Ricardo Ricciardi, 1957.

Riquer, Martín de, ed. *Los trovadores: Historia literaria y textos*. 3 vols. 1975. Rpt. in single volume, Barcelona: Ariel, 2011.

Le Roman de Flamenca: Nouvelle occitane du 13e siècle. Ed. Ulrich Gschwind. 2 vols. Bern: Francke, 1976.

Sainte-Palaye, Jean Baptiste de La Curne, and Claude Millot. *Histoire littéraire des Troubadours*. 3 vols. Paris, 1774.

Schiendorfer, Max, and Karl Bartsch, eds. *Die Schweizer Minnesänger*. Vol. 1. Tubingen: Max Niemeyer, 1990– .

Thierry of Chartres. Ed. Karin Margareta Fredborg. *The Latin Rhetorical Commentaries by Thierry of Chartres*. Toronto: Pontifical Institute of Mediaeval Studies, 1988.

Walther von der Vogelweide. *Walthers von der Vogelweide Gedichte*. Ed. Hermann Paul. Altdeutsche Textbiliothek 1. Tübingen: Max Niemeyer, 1965.

———. *Die Gedichte Walthers von der Vogelweide*. Ed. Karl Lachmann and Hugo Kuhn. Berlin: Walter de Gruyter, 1965.

WORKS CITED

Abulafia, David, ed. *The New Cambridge Medieval History, c. 1198–1300*. Vol. 5. Cambridge: Cambridge University Press, 1999.

Akehurst, F. R. P., and Judith M. Davis, eds. *A Handbook of the Troubadours*. Berkeley: University of California Press, 1995.

Amador de los Ríos, José. *Historia crítica de la literatura española*. 7 vols. Madrid: Imprenta de José Rodríguez, 1861–65.

Anderson, Gordon A., and Thomas B. Payne. "Early Latin Secular Song." In *Grove Music Online*, ed. L. Macy. <http://www.grovemusic.com>. Accessed March 7, 2005.

Asperti, Stefano. "Le chansonnier provençal T et l'École Poétique sicilienne." *Revue des Langues Romanes* 98 (1994): 49–77.

Avagnina, Maria Elisa. "Un inedito affresco di soggetto cortese a Bassano del Grappa: Federico II e la corte dei da Romano." In *Federico II: Immagine e potere*, ed. Calò Mariani and Cassano (see entry below), 105-111.

———. "Bassano, Ezzelino e Federico: Il misterioso affresco 'cortese' di casa Finco." In *Federico II e la civiltà comunale*, ed. Fonseca and Crotti, 525-47.

Avalle, D'Arco Silvio. *I manoscritti della letteratura in lingua d'oc*. Rev. ed. of: *La letteratura medievale in lingua d'oc nella sua tradizione manoscritta: Problemi di critica testuale*. 1961. Rpt., ed. Lino Leonardi. Turin: Einaudi, 1993.

Bartsch, Karl, ed. *Grundriß zur Geschichte der provenzalischen Literatur*. Elberfeld, 1872.

Beltrán Pepió, Vicente. *La canción de amor en el otoño de la Edad Media*. Barcelona: Promociones y Publicaciones Universitarias, 1988.

Bennett, Judith M., and C. Warren Hollister, eds. *Medieval Europe: A Short History*. 9th ed. Boston: McGraw-Hill, 2002.

Blackall, Eric A. *The Emergence of German as a Literary Language: 1700–1775*. Ithaca: Cornell University Press, 1959.

Bloch, R. Howard. *Etymologies and Genealogies: A Literary Anthropology of the French Middle Ages*. Chicago: University of Chicago Press, 1983.

Bloch, R. Howard, and Stephen G. Nichols, eds. *Medievalism and the Modernist Temper*. Baltimore: Johns Hopkins University Press, 1996.

Bolduc, Michelle. *The Medieval Poetics of Contraries*. Gainesville: University Press of Florida, 2006.

———. "Naming Names: Matfre Ermengaud's Use of Troubadour Quotations." *Tenso* 22 (2007): 41–74.

Branner, Robert. *Manuscript Painting in Paris during the Age of Saint Louis: A Study of Styles*. Berkeley: University of California Press, 1977.

Brownlee, Marina Scordilis. *The Status of the Reading Subject in the* Libro de Buen Amor. Chapel Hill: University of North Carolina Press, 1985.

Brownlee, Marina S., Kevin Brownlee, and Stephen G. Nichols, eds. *The New Medievalism*. Baltimore: Johns Hopkins University Press, 1991.

Brunel-Lobrichon, Geneviève. "L'iconographie du chansonnier provençal *R*: essai d'interpretation." In Tyssens, ed., *Lyrique romane médiévale*, 245–71.

Bumke, Joachim. *Ministerialität und Ritterdichtung*. Munich: Beck, 1976.

Burgwinkle, William. "The *Chansonniers* as Books." In Gaunt and Kay, *The Troubadours*, 246-62.

Butterfield, Ardis. *Poetry and Music in Medieval France: From Jean Renart to Guillaume de Machaut.* Cambridge: Cambridge University Press, 2002.

Calò Mariani, Maria Stella, and Raffaella Cassano, eds. *Federico II: Immagine e potere.* Venice: Marsilio, 1995.

Camille, Michael. *Gothic Art: Visions and Revelations of the Medieval World.* London: Everyman Art Library, 1996.

———. *The Medieval Art of Love: Objects and Subjects of Desire.* New York: Harry N. Abrams, 1998.

———. *Image on the Edge: The Margins of Medieval Art.* 1992. London: Reaktion, 2006.

Campbell, C. Jean. *The Game of Courting and the Art of the Commune of San Gimignano 1290–1320.* Princeton: Princeton University Press, 1997.

Careri, Maria. *Il canzoniere provenzale H (Vat. Lat. 3207): Struttura, contenuto e fonti.* Modena: Mucchi editore, 1990.

Carruthers, Mary J. *The Book of Memory: A Study of Memory in Medieval Culture.* Cambridge: Cambridge University Press, 1990.

———. "Moving Images in the Mind's Eye." In Hamburger and Bouché, eds., *The Mind's Eye,* 287–305.

Casas Rigall, Juan. *Agudeza y retórica en la poesía amorosa de cancionero.* Santiago de Compostela: Universidade, 1995.

Castro, Américo. *Obra Reunida. España en su historia: Ensayos sobre historia y literatura.* Ed. José Miranda. 3 vols. Madrid: Editorial Trotta, 2004.

Chambers, Frank M. *Proper Names in the Lyrics of the Troubadours.* Chapel Hill: University of North Carolina Press, 1971.

———. *An Introduction to Old Provençal Versification.* Philadelphia: American Philosophical Society, 1985.

Chartier, Roger, and Henri-Jean Martin, eds. *Histoire de l'édition française: Le livre conquérant, du Moyen Âge au milieu du XVIIe siècle.* Paris: Fayard/Promodis, 1989.

Clanchy, M. T. *From Memory to Written Record: England 1066–1307.* 2nd ed. Cambridge, MA: Blackwell, 1993.

Clausberg, Karl. *Die Manessische Liederhandschrift.* Cologne: DuMont, 1978.

Codex Manesse: Katalog zur Ausstellung vom 12. Juni bis 2. Oktober 1988 Üniversitätsbibliothek Heidelberg. Ed. Elmar Mittler and Wilfried Werner. Heidelberg: Braus, 1988.

Cnyrim, Eugen. *Sprichwörter, sprichwörtliche Redensarten und Sentenzen bei den provenzalischen Lyrikern.* Ausgaben und Abhandlungen aus dem Gebiete der romanischen Philologie 71. Marburg: N. G. Elwert, 1888.

Contini, Gianfranco. *Varianti e altra linguistica: Una raccolta di saggi.* Turin: Einaudi, 1970.

Copeland, Rita. *Rhetoric, Hermeneutics, and Translation in the Middle Ages: Academic Traditions and Vernacular Texts.* Cambridge: Cambridge University Press, 1991.

Crocker, Richard L. "Versus." *Grove Music Online.* Ed. L. Macy. <http://www.grovemusic.com>. Accessed March 7, 2005.

Crosas López, Francisco. *La materia clásica en la poesía de Cancionero*. Kassel: Reichenberger, 1995.

Curschmann, Michael. *"Pictura laicororum litteratura?* Überlegungen zum Verhältnis von Bild und volkssprachlicher Schriftlichkeit im Hoch- und Spätmittelalter bis zum Codex Manesse." In *Pragmatische Schriftlichkeit im Mittelalter: Erscheinungsformen und Entwicklungsstufen*, ed. Hagen Keller, Klaus Grubmüller, and Nikolaus Staubach, Munich: Wilhelm Fink, 1992, 211–19.

Curtius, Ernst Robert. *European Literature and the Latin Middle Ages*. Trans. Willard R. Trask. Bollingen Ser. 36. 1953. Princeton: Princeton University Press, 1990.

Dagenais, John. *The Ethics of Reading in Manuscript Culture: Glossing the* Libro de Buen Amor. Princeton: Princeton University Press, 1994.

De Looze, Laurence. *Pseudo-Autobiography in the Fourteenth Century*. Gainesville: University Press of Florida, 1997.

Derrida, Jacques. *Archive Fever: A Freudian Impression*. Trans. Eric Prenowitz. Chicago: University of Chicago Press, 1996. Originally published as *Mal d'Archive: Une impression freudienne*. [Paris]: Galilée, 1995.

Doane, A. N., and Carol Braune Pasternack, eds. *Vox Intexta: Orality and Textuality in the Middle Ages*. Madison: University of Wisconsin Press, 1991.

Dronke, Peter. "A Critical Note on Schumann's Dating of the Codex Buranus." *Beiträge zur Geschichte der deutschen Sprache und Literatur* 84 (1962): 173–83.

Dutton, Brian. "Spanish Fifteenth-Century *Cancioneros*: A General Survey to 1465." *Kentucky Romance Quarterly* 27 (1979): 445–60.

———, et al. *Catálogo-índice de la poesía cancioneril del siglo XV*. 2 vols. in 1. Madison: Hispanic Seminary of Medieval Studies, 1982.

———, and Jineen Krogstad, eds. *El cancionero del siglo XV, c. 1360–1520*. 7 vols. Salamanca: University Press and Biblioteca Española del Siglo XV, 1990–91.

Dutton, Brian, and Victoriano Roncero López, eds. *La poesía cancioneril del siglo XV: Antología y estudio*. Madrid: Iberoamericana, 2004.

Dvořáková, Vlasta, et al. *Gothic Mural Painting in Bohemia and Moravia: 1300–1378*. London: Oxford University Press, 1964.

Edelman, Nathan. *Attitudes of Seventeenth-Century France toward the Middle Ages*. New York: King's Crown Press, 1946.

Fein, Susanna. *Studies in the Harley Manuscript*. Kalamazoo: TEAMS, 2000.

Fonseca, Cosimo Damiano, and Renato Crotti, eds. *Federico II e la civiltà comunale nell'Italia del Nord*. Rome: Luca, 1999.

Foulché-Delbosc, R., and L. Barrau-Dihigo. *Manuel de l'hispanisant*. 2 vols. New York: Putnam, 1920.

Frank, István. *Répertoire métrique de la poésie des troubadours*. 2 vols. Paris: Honoré Champion, 1953–57.

Freccero, John. "The Fig Tree and the Laurel: Petrarch's Poetics." *Diacritics* 5 (1975): 34–40.

Freedberg, David. *Power of Images: Studies in the History and Theory of Response*. Chicago: University of Chicago Press, 1989.

Frühmorgen-Voss, Hella. *Text und Illustration im Mittelalter: Aufsätze zu den Wechselbeziehungen zwischen Literatur und bildender Kunst.* Munich: Oscar Beck, 1975.

Galvez, Marisa. "From the *Costuma d'Agen* to the *Leys d'Amors*: A Reflection on Customary Law, the University of Toulouse, and the *Consistori de la sobregaia companhia del gay saber.*" *Tenso* 26 (2011): 30–51.

Gaunt, Simon, and Sarah Kay, eds. *The Troubadours: An Introduction.* Cambridge: Cambridge University Press, 1999.

Gerli, E. Michael. "The Greeks, the Romans, and the Ambiguity of Signs: *De doctrina christiana*, the Fall, and the Hermeneutics of the *Libro de buen amor.*" *Bulletin of Spanish Studies: Hispanic Studies and Researches on Spain, Portugal, and Latin America* 79 (2002): 411–28.

Gerli, E. Michael, and Julian Weiss, eds. *Poetry at Court in Trastamaran Spain: From the* Cancionero de Baena *to the* Cancionero General. Tempe, Arizona: Medieval and Renaissance Texts and Studies, 1998.

Gies, David T, ed. *The Cambridge History of Spanish Literature.* 2004. Cambridge: Cambridge University Press, 2009.

Goldin, Frederick, ed. and trans. *Lyrics of the Troubadours and Trouvères: An Anthology and a History.* 1973. Gloucester, MA: Peter Smith, 1983.

Gómez-Bravo, Ana María. "*Decir canciones*: The Question of Genre in *Cancionero* Poetry." In *Medieval Lyric: Genres in Historical Context*, ed. William D. Paden, 158–87. Urbana: University of Illinois Press, 2000.

Gorni, Guglielmo. "Le forme primarie del testo poetico." In *Letteratura italiana*, vol. 3.1: "Teoria e poesia." Turin: Einaudi, 1984.

Gossman, Lionel. *Medievalism and the Ideologies of the Enlightenment: The World and Work of La Curne de Sainte-Palaye.* Baltimore: Johns Hopkins University Press, 1968.

Grabar, Oleg. *The Formation of Islamic Art.* New Haven: Yale University Press, 1973.

Green, Otis H. *Spain and the Western Tradition: The Castilian Mind in Literature from* El Cid *to* Calderón. 4 vols. Madison: University of Wisconsin Press, 1963–66.

Gröber, Gustav. "Die Liedersammlungen der Troubadours." *Romanische Studien* 2 (1875–77): 337–670.

Grundriß der Romanischen Literaturen des Mittelalters. Ed. Hans Robert Jauss, Erich Köhler, et al. Heidelberg: Carl Winter, 1968– .

Gumbrecht, Hans Ulrich. "Un souffle d'Allemagne ayant passé: Friedrich Diez, Gaston Paris, and the Genesis of National Philologies." *Romance Philology* 40.1 (1986): 1–37.

——. *Eine Geschichte der spanischen Literatur.* 2 vols. Frankfurt: Suhrkamp, 1990.

——. "Intertextuality and Autumn/Autumn and the Modern Reception of the Middle Ages." In *The New Medievalism*, ed. Marina S. Brownlee et al., 301–30. Baltimore: Johns Hopkins University Press, 1991.

Gybbon-Monypenny, G. B. "Autobiography in the *Libro de buen amor* in the Light of Some Literary Comparisons." *Bulletin of Hispanic Studies* 34 (1957): 63–78.

——. "The Spanish *Mester de Clerecía* and Its Intended Public: Concerning the Validity As Evidence of Passages of Direct Address to the Audience." In *Medieval Miscellany*

Presented to Eugène Vinaver, ed. Frederick Whitehead, A. H. Diverres and F. E. Sutcliffe, 230-44. Manchester: Manchester University Press, 1965.

———, ed. *"Libro de buen amor" Studies*. London: Tamesis, 1970.

Hamburger, Jeffrey F. *The Visual and the Visionary: Art and Female Spirituality in Late Medieval Germany*. New York: Zone Books, 1998.

Hamburger, Jeffrey F., and Anne-Marie Bouché, eds. *The Mind's Eye: Art and Theological Argument in the Middle Ages*. Princeton: Department of Art and Archaeology of Princeton University, 2006.

Hamilton, Michelle. "The Musical Book: Judeo-Andalusi Hermeneutics in the *Libro de buen amor*." *La Corónica* 37.2 (2009): 33–59.

Harvey, Ruth E. "The Troubadour Marcabru and his Public." *Reading Medieval Studies* 14 (1988): 47–76.

———. *The Troubadour Marcabru and Love*. Westfield Publications in Medieval Studies 3. London: University of London, 1989.

Hadlaub, Johannes. *Die Gedichte des Zürcher Minnesängers*. Ed. Max Schiendorfer. Zürich: Artemis, 1986.

Holmes, Olivia. *Assembling the Lyric Self: Authorship from Troubadour Song to Italian Poetry Book*. Minneapolis: University of Minnesota Press, 2000.

Huizinga, Johan. *The Autumn of the Middle Ages*. Trans. Rodney J. Payton and Ulrich Mammitzsch. 1921. Chicago: University of Chicago Press, 1996.

Huot, Sylvia. *From Song to Book: The Poetics of Writing in Old French Lyric and Lyrical Narrative Poetry*. Ithaca: Cornell University Press, 1987.

———. "Visualization and Memory: The Illustration of Troubadour Lyric in a Thirteenth-Century Manuscript." *Gesta* 31 (1992): 3–14.

Intavulare: Tavole di canzonieri romanzi. Ed. Anna Ferrari et al. 8 vols. Vatican City: Biblioteca Apostolica Vaticana, 1998– .

Jakobson, Roman. *On Language*. Ed. Linda R. Waugh and Monique Monville-Burston. Cambridge, MA: Harvard University Press, 1990.

Jammers, Ewald. *Das Königliche Liederbuch des deutschen Minnesangs: Eine Einführung in die sogenannte Manessiche Handschrift*. Heidelberg: Lambert Schneider, 1965.

Jauss, Hans Robert. *Alterität und Modernität der mittelalterlichen Literatur: Gesammelte Aufsätze 1956–1976*. Munich: Wilhelm Fink, 1977.

Jeanroy, Alfred, ed. *La poésie lyrique des troubadours*. 2 vols. 1934. New York: AMS Press, 1974.

Jones, Martin H., ed. *The* Carmina Burana: *Four Essays*. King's College Medieval Studies 18. London: King's College London Centre for Late Antique and Medieval Studies, 2000.

Kamuf, Peggy. *Signature Pieces: On the Institution of Authorship*. Ithaca: Cornell University Press, 1988.

Kantorowicz, Ernst H. *The King's Two Bodies: A Study in Mediaeval Political Theology*. Princeton: Princeton University Press, 1957.

———. "Kingship under the Impact of Scientific Jurisprudence." In *Twelfth-Century Eu-*

rope and the Foundations of Modern Society, ed. Marshall Clagett et al., 89–111. 1957. Madison: University of Wisconsin Press, 1980.

Katz, Israel J., and John E. Keller, eds. *Studies on the* Cantigas de Santa Maria*: Art, Music, and Poetry*. Madison: Hispanic Seminary of Medieval Studies, 1987.

Kay, Sarah. *Subjectivity in Troubadour Poetry*. Cambridge: Cambridge University Press, 1990.

Kehew, Robert, ed. *Lark in the Morning: The Verses of the Troubadours*. Chicago: University of Chicago Press, 2005.

Kendrick, Laura. *The Game of Love: Troubadour Wordplay*. Berkeley: University of California Press, 1988.

———. "L'image du troubadour comme auteur dans les chansonniers." In *Auctor et auctoritas*, ed. Zimmerman, 507-519.

Kessler, Herbert L. *Spiritual Seeing: Picturing God's Invisibility in Medieval Art*. Philadelphia: University of Pennsylvania Press, 2000.

———. "Gregory the Great and Image Theory in Northern Europe during the Twelfth and Thirteenth Centuries." In *A Companion to Medieval Art*, ed. Conrad Rudolph. Malden, MA: Blackwell, 2006. Blackwell Reference Online. Accessed July 28, 2009.

Kopp, Arthur. *Bremberger-Gedichte: Ein Beitrag zur Brembergersage*. Quellen und Forschungen zur deutschen Volkskunde 2. Vienna: Dr. Rud. Ludwig, 1908.

Kornrumpf, Gisela. *Vom Codex Manesse zur Kolmarer Liederhandschrift: Aspekte der Überlieferung, Formtraditionen, Texte*. Tübingen: Max Niemeyer, 2008.

Koschorreck, Walter, and Wilfried Werner, eds. *Codex Manesse: Die Große Heidelberger Liederhandschrift: Kommentar zum Faksimile des Codex Palatinus Germanicus 848 der Universitätsbibliothek Heidelberg*. Kassel: Ganymed, 1981.

Kuhn, Hugo. *Entwürfe zur einer Literatursystematik des Spätmittelalters.* Tübingen: Max Niemeyer, 1980.

Lawrance, Jeremy N. H. "Juan Alfonso de Baena's Versified Reading List: A Note on the Aspirations and the Reality of Fifteenth-Century Castilian Culture." *Journal of Hispanic Philology* 5 (1981): 101–22.

———. "The Spread of Lay Literacy in Late Medieval Castile." *Bulletin of Hispanic Studies* 62 (1985): 79–94.

Le Gentil, Pierre. *La poésie lyrique espagnole et portugaise à la fin du moyen âge*. 2 vols. Rennes: Plihon, 1949–52.

———. *Le virelai et le villancico: Le problème des origines arabes*. Paris: Société d'éditions "Les Belles Lettres," 1954.

Le Goff, Jacques. *Time, Work, and Culture in the Middle Ages*. Trans. Arthur Goldhammer. Chicago: University of Chicago Press, 1980.

———. *My Quest for the Middle Ages*. Trans. Richard Veasey. New York: Palgrave Macmillan, 2005.

Lecoy, Félix. *Recherches sur le Libro de buen amor de Juan Ruiz, Archiprêtre de Hita*. Introd. A. D. Deyermond. 1938. Farnborough: Gregg International, 1974.

Léglu, Catherine. "A Reading of Troubadour Insult Songs: The *Comunals* Cycle." *Reading Medieval Studies* 22 (1996): 63–83.

———. "Defamation in the Troubadour Sirventes: Legislation and Lyric Poetry." *Medium Ævum* 66 (1997): 28–41.

———. "Vernacular Poems and Inquisitors in Languedoc and Champagne, Ca. 1242–1249." *Viator* 33 (2002): 117–32.

———. "Languages in Conflict in Toulouse: *Las Leys d'Amors*." *Modern Language Review* 103 (2008): 383–96.

Lemaitre, Jean-Loup, and Françoise Vielliard, eds. *Portraits de troubadours: Initiales du chansonnier provençal A* (*Biblioteca Apostolica Vaticana, Vat. lat. 5232*). Vatican City: Biblioteca Apostolica Vaticana, 2008.

Lerer, Seth. "Medieval English Literature and the Idea of the Anthology." *PMLA* 118: 1251–67.

Lewent, Kurt. "*Lo vers de la Terra de Preste Johan* by Cerveri de Girona." *Romance Philology* 2 (1948–49): 1–32.

Lewis, C. S. *The Discarded Image*. Cambridge: Cambridge University Press, 1964.

Lida de Malkiel, María Rosa. "Nuevas notas para la interpretación del *Libro de buen amor*." *Nueva revista de filología hispánica* 13 (1959): 17–82.

———. *Two Spanish Masterpieces: The "Book of Good Love" and "The Celestina."* Illinois Studies in Language and Literature 49. Urbana: University of Illinois Press, 1961.

———. *Estudios sobre la literatura española del siglo XV*. Madrid: Ediciones Porrúa Turanzas, [1976].

Lipphardt, Walther. "Unbekannte Weisen zu den Carmina Burana." *Archiv für Musikwissenschaft* 12 (1955): 122–42.

MacKay, Angus. "Ritual and Propaganda in Fifteenth-Century Castile." *Past and Present* 107 (1985): 3–43.

Macpherson, Ian. "Secret Language in the *Cancioneros*: Some Courtly Codes." *Bulletin of Hispanic Studies* 62 (1985): 51–56.

Macpherson, Ian, and Angus MacKay. "'*Manteniendo la tela*': El erotismo del vocabulario caballeresco-textil en la época de los Reyes Católicos." In *Actas del Primer Congreso Anglo-Hispano, vol. I: Lingüística*, ed. Ralph Penny, 25–36. Madrid: Castalia, 1993.

Macpherson, Ian, and Angus MacKay. *Love, Religion and Politics in Fifteenth Century Spain*. Medieval Iberian Peninsula Texts and Studies 13. Boston: Brill, 1998.

Malkiel, Yakov. "Spanish *Estribillo* 'Refrain': Its Proximal and Distal Etymologies." In *Florilegium Hispanicum: Medieval and Golden Age Studies Presented to Dorothy Clotelle Clarke*, ed. John S. Geary, 29–43. Madison: Hispanic Seminary of Medieval Studies, 1983.

Maravall, José Antonio. *Estudios de Historia del Pensamiento Español: Serie Primera, Edad Media*. 3rd ed. Madrid: Ediciones Cultura Hispánica, 1983.

Márquez Villanueva, Francisco. *Orígenes y sociología del tema celestinesco*. Barcelona: Anthropos, 1993.

Martin, Ernst. "Die Carmina Burana und die Anfänge des deutschen Minnesangs." *Zeitschrift für deutsches Alterthum und deutsche Litteratur* 20 (1876): 46–99.

Martin, Kurt, ed. *Minnesänger: Vierundzwanzig farbige Wiedergaben aus der Manessischen Liederhandschrift.* 2 vols. Baden-Baden: Woldemar, 1960–64.

McMillan, D. "Juan Ruiz's Use of the 'Estribote.'" In *Hispanic Studies in Honour of I. González Llubera,* ed. Frank Pierce, 189–93. London: Dolphin Books, 1959.

Meier, John. "Drei alte deutsche Balladen: 3. Das Brembergerlied." *Jahrbuch für Volksliedforschung* 4 (1934): 56–65.

Meneghetti, Maria Luisa. *Il pubblico dei trovatori.* Turin: Einaudi, 1992.

———. "Federico II e la poesia trobadorica alla luce di un nuovo reperto iconografico." In *Federico II e la civiltà comunale,* ed. Fonseca and Crotti, 507-23.

Menéndez Collera, Ana, and Victoriano Roncero López, eds. *Nunca fue pena amor (Estudios de literatura española en homenaje a Brian Dutton).* Cuenca: Ediciones de la Universidad de Castilla-La Mancha, 1996.

Mengaldo, Pier Vincenzo. "Oc (oco)." *Enciclopedia dantesca* 4 (1973): 111–17.

Meyer, Richard M. "Alte deutsche Volksliedchen." *Zeitschrift für deutsches Alterthum und deutsche Litteratur* 29 (1885): 121–236.

Minnis, Alistair J. *Medieval Theory of Authorship: Scholastic Literary Attitudes in the Later Middle Ages.* London: Scolar, 1984.

Morreale, Margherita. "El Libro de buen amor, de Juan Ruiz, Arcipreste de Hita." *GRLM* 9 (1985): 2.4, 53–73.

Mortimer, Ruth. "The Author's Image: Italian Sixteenth-Century Printed Portraits." *Harvard Library Bulletin* n.s. 7.2 (1996): 7–87.

Moser, Eva, ed. *Buchmalerei im Bodenseeraum: 13. Bis 16. Jahrhundert.* Friedrichshaften: Robert Gessler, 1997.

Müller, Jan-Dirk. "J. J. Bodmers Poetik und die Wiederentdeckung mittelhochdeutscher Epen." *Euphorion* 71 (1977): 336–52.

———. *Rules for the Endgame: The World of the Nibelungenlied.* Trans. William T. Whobrey. Baltimore: Johns Hopkins University Press, 2007. Originally published as *Spielregeln für den Untergang: Die Welt des Nibelungenlieds.* Tubingen: Max Niemeyer, 1998.

Newman, Barbara, "Love's Arrows: Christ as Cupid in Late Medieval Art and Devotion." In *The Mind's Eye,* ed. Hamburger and Bouché, 263–86.

Nichols, Stephen G. "Introduction: Philology in a Manuscript Culture." *Speculum* 65 (1990): 1–10.

———. "Voice and Writing in Augustine and in the Troubadour Lyric." In *Vox intexta,* ed. Doane, 137-61.

———. "Picture, Image, and Subjectivity in Medieval Culture." *MLN* 108 (1993): 617–37.

———. "'Art' and 'Nature': Looking for (Medieval) Principles of Order in Occitan Chansonnier N (Morgan 819)." In *The Whole Book,* 83–121.

Nichols, Stephen G., and Siegfried Wenzel, eds. *The Whole Book: Cultural Perspectives on the Medieval Miscellany.* Ann Arbor: University of Michigan Press, 1996.

Nohrnberg, James. "The Autobiographical Imperative and the Necessity of 'Dante': *Purgatorio* 30.55." *Modern Philology* 101 (2003): 1–47.

O'Callaghan, Joseph F. *A History of Medieval Spain*. Ithaca: Cornell University Press, 1975.

Paden, William D. *An Introduction to Old Occitan*. New York: MLA, 1998.

Parkes, Malcolm B. "The Influence of the Concepts of *Ordinatio* and *Compilatio* on the Development of the Book." In *Medieval Learning and Literature: Essays Presented to Richard William Hunt*, ed. J. J. G. Alexander and M. T. Gibson, 115–41. Oxford: Oxford University Press, 1976.

Paterson, Linda M. "Syria, Poitou and the Reconquista (or: Tales of the Undead): Who Was the Count in Marcabru's *Vers del lavador*?)" In *The Second Crusade: Scope and Consequences*, ed. Jonathan Phillips and Martin Hoch, 133–49. New York: Manchester University Press, 2001.

Perugi, Maurizio. "Dante e Arnaut Daniel." *Studi danteschi* 51 (1978): 59–152.

Peters, Ursula. *Das Ich im Bild*. Cologne: Böhlau, 2008.

Piccus, Jules. "The Nineteenth-Century *Cancionero general del siglo XV*." *Kentucky Foreign Language Quarterly* 6 (1959): 121–25.

Pillet, Alfred, and Henry Carstens. *Bibliographie der Troubadours*. 1933. New York: Burt Franklin, 1968.

Pirot, François. "Ce n'était point le troubadour Marcabru . . ." *Annales du Midi* 78 (1966): 537–41.

Poe, Elizabeth Wilson. "Old Provençal *Vidas* as Literary Commentary." *Romance Philology* 33 (1979–80): 510–18.

———. *From Poetry to Prose in Old Provençal: The Emergence of the* Vidas, *the* Razos, *and the* Razos de trobar. Birmingham, AL: Summa, 1984.

———. *Compilatio: Lyric Texts and Prose Commentaries in Troubadour Manuscript H (Vat. Lat. 3207)*. Lexington, KY: French Forum, 2000.

Pope, Isabel, and Emilio Ros-Fábregas. 'Estribillo.' *Grove Music Online*. Ed. L. Macy. <http://www.grovemusic.com>. Accessed January 3, 2006.

Rapp, Andrea. "*Ir bîzzen was so zartlich, wîblich, fîn*: Zur Deutung des Hundes in Hadlaubs Autorbild im *Codex Manesse*." In *Tiere und Fabelwesen im Mittelalter*, ed. Sabine Obermaier, 207-232. New York: Walter De Gruyter, 2009.

Raynouard, François, ed. *Lexique roman*. 6 vols. Paris, 1838–44. With *Provenzalisches Supplement-Wörterbuch, Berichtigungen und Ergänzungen zu Raynouards "Lexique Roman."* Ed. Emil Levy. 8 vols. Leipzig: O. R. Reisland, 1894–1924.

Real de la Riva, César. "El *Libro de buen amor*, de Juan Ruiz, Arcipreste de Hita." *GRLM* 9 (1985): 1.4, 59-90.

Reill, Peter Hanns. *The German Enlightenment and the Rise of Historicism*. Berkeley: University of California Press, 1975.

Renk, Herta-Elisabeth. *Der Manessekreis: Seine Dichter und die Manessische Handschrift*. Stuttgart: W. Kohlhammer, 1974.

Rico, Francisco. "Unas coplas de Jorge Manrique y las fiestas de Valladolid en 1428." *Anuario de Estudios Medievales* 2 (1965): 515–24.

Rieger, Angelica. "Ins e.1 cor port, dona, vostra faisso: Image et imaginaire de la femme à travers l'enluminure dans les chansonniers de troubadours." *Cahiers de civilisation médiévale* 28 (1985): 385–415.

Roncaglia, Aurelio. "Rétrospectives et perspectives dans l'étude des chansonniers d'oc." In Tyssens, ed., *Lyrique romane médiévale*, 19–38.

Rouse, Richard Hunter, and Mary Ames Rouse. "The *Florilegium Angelicum*: Its Origins, Content, and Influence." In *Medieval Learning and Literature: Essays Presented to Richard William Hunt*, ed. J. J. G. Alexander and M. T. Gibson, 66–114. Oxford: Oxford University Press, 1976.

Rucquoi, Adeline, ed. *Realidad e imagenes del poder: España a fines de la Edad Media*. Valladolid: Ambito, 1988.

Sage, Jack. "Alfonso el Sabio," and "Cantiga." *Grove Music Online*. Ed. L. Macy. <http://www.grovemusic.com> Accessed May 25, 2007.

Sánchez Cantón, F. J., ed. "El 'Arte de trovar' de Don Enrique de Villena." *Revista de Filología Española* 6 (1919): 158–80.

Santangelo, Salvatore. *Dante e i trovatori provenzali*. 1921. 2nd ed. Catania: Facoltà di Lettere e Filosofia, 1959.

Sayce, Olive. *The Medieval German Lyric 1150–1300: The Development of Its Themes and Forms in Their European Context*. Oxford: Clarendon Press, 1982.

———. *Plurilingualism in the Carmina Burana: A Study of the Linguistic and Literary Influences on the Codex*. Göppinger Arbeiten zur Germanistik 556. Göppingen: Kümmerle, 1992.

Scheller, Robert W. *Exemplum: Model-Book Drawings and the Practice of Artistic Transmission in the Middle Ages (ca. 900–ca. 1450)*. Amsterdam: Amsterdam University Press, 1995.

Schmitt, Jean-Claude. *Le corps des images: Essais sur la culture visuelle au Moyen Âge*. Paris: Gallimard, 2002.

Scholberg, Kenneth R. *Sátira e invectiva en la España medieval*. Madrid: Gredos, 1971.

Schumann, Otto. "Die deutschen Strophen der Carmina Burana." *Germanisch-Romanische Monatsschrift* 14 (1926): 418–37.

——— "Die jüngere Cambridger Liedersammlung," *Studi Medievali* 16 (1943–50): 45–85.

Schweikle, Günther. *Minnesang*. Stuttgart: Metzler, 1995.

Siebert-Hotz, Gisela. "Das Bild des Minnesängers: Motivgeschichtliche Untersuchungen zur Dichterdarstellung in den Miniaturen der Großen Heidelberger Liederhandschrift." Diss., University of Marburg, 1964.

Severin, Dorothy. "'Cancionero': Un género mal-nombrado.'" *Cultura Neolatina* 54 (1994): 95–105.

Shapiro, Marianne. *Hieroglyph of Time: The Petrarchan Sestina*. Minneapolis: University of Minnesota Press, 1980.

Spanke, Hans. "Der Codex Buranus als Liederbuch." *Zeitschrift für Musikwissenschaft* 13 (1930–31): 241–51.

———. "Ein lateinisches Liederbuch des 11. Jahrhunderts." *Studi Medievali*. 2nd ser. 15 (1942): 111–42.

Spanos, Margaret. "The Sestina: An Exploration of the Dynamics of Poetic Structure." *Speculum* 53 (1978): 545–57.

Spitzer, Leo. *Lingüística e historia literaria*. Madrid: Gredos, 1955.

Starkey, Kathryn. *Reading the Medieval Book: Word, Image, and Performance in Wolfram von Eschenbach's* Willehalm. Notre Dame: University of Notre Dame Press, 2004.

Starkey, Kathryn, and Horst Wenzel, eds. *Visual Culture and the German Middle Ages*. New York: Palgrave Macmillan, 2005.

Steger, Hugo. *David rex et propheta*. Nuremberg: Hans Carl, 1961.

Stevens, John. *Words and Music in the Middle Ages: Song, Narrative, Dance and Drama, 1050–1350*. Cambridge: Cambridge University Press, 1986.

———. *Cambridge Music Manuscripts, 900–1700*. Ed. Iain Fenlon. Cambridge: Cambridge University Press, 1982.

Tate, R. B. "Adventures in the 'sierra.'" In *"Libro de buen amor" Studies*, ed. Gybbon-Monypenny (see entry above), 219-29.

Tavani, Giuseppe. "La poesia lirica galego-portoghese," *GRLM* 2 (1980): 1.6, 6–28.

Taylor, Jane H. M. *The Making of Poetry: Late-Medieval French Poetic Anthologies*. Texts and Transitions 1. Turnhout: Brepols, 2007.

Thiolier-Méjean, Suzanne. *Les poésies satiriques et morales des troubadours*. Paris: Nizet, 1978.

———. *L'archet et le lutrin: Enseignement et foi dans la poésie médiévale d'Oc*. Paris: L'Harmattan, 2008.

Thomas, A. "Les manuscrits provençaux et français de Dominicy." *Romania* 17 (1888): 401–16.

Thorndike, Lynn. "Unde Versus." *Traditio* 11 (1955): 163–93.

Tyssens, Madeleine, ed. *Lyrique romane médiévale: La tradition des chansonniers. Actes du Colloque du Liège, 1989*. Liège: Bibliothèque de la Faculté de Philosophie et Lettres de l'Université de Liège, 1991.

Unamuno, Miguel de. *Del sentimiento trágico de la vida en los hombres y en los pueblos*. Madrid: Renacimiento, [1912].

Vagnoni, Mirko. "Il significato politico delle caratteristiche iconografiche di Federick II di Svevia." *Iconographica* 5 (2006): 64–75.

Van Vleck, Amelia E. *Memory and Re-creation in Troubadour Lyric*. Berkeley: University of California Press, 1991.

Vielliard, Françoise "Auteur et autorité dans la littérature occitane médiévale non lyrique." In *Auctor et auctoritas*, ed. Zimmerman, 375–89.

Vinaver, Eugène. *A la recherche d'une poétique médiévale*. Paris: Nizet, 1970.

Voigt, Vilmos. "The Woman Who Destroys Life–*La Belle Dame Sans Merci*." *Folkloristika Svetur* 21.28 (2004): 165–86.

von der Hagen, Friedrich Heinrich, ed. *Minnesinger: Deutsche Liederdichter des zwölften, dreizehnten und vierzehnten Jahrhunderts*. 5 vols. 1838–61. Aalen: O. Zeller, 1962–63.

Wachinger, Burghart. "Deutsche und lateinische Liebeslieder: Zu den deutschen Strophen der Carmina Burana." In *From Symbol to Mimesis: The Generation of Walther von der Vogelweide,* ed. F. H. Bäuml, 1–34. Göppingen: Kümmerle, 1984.

Waddell, Helen. *The Wandering Scholars*. London: Constable, 1949.

Walsh, John K. "Juan Ruiz and the *mester de clerezía*: Lost Context and Lost Parody in the *Libro de buen amor*." *Romance Philology* 33 (1979–80): 62–86.

Walworth, Julia, "Earthly Delights: The Pictorial Images of the *Carmina Burana* Manuscript." In *The* Carmina Burana: *Four Essays*, ed. Martin H. Jones. King's College Medieval Studies 18. London: King's College London Centre for Late Antique and Medieval Studies, 2000.

Weiss, Julian. *The Poet's Art: Literary Theory in Castile c. 1400–60*. Medium Aevum Monographs, New Series 14. Oxford: Society for the Study of Mediaeval Languages and Literature, 1990.

Wenzel, Horst. *Spiegelungen: Zur Kultur der Visualität im Mittelalter*. Berlin: Erich Schmidt, 2009.

Whinnom, Keith. "Towards the Interpretation and Appreciation of the *Canciones* of the *Cancionero general* of 1511." In *Medieval and Renaissance Spanish Literature: Selected Essays by Keith Whinnom*, ed. Alan Deyermond, W. F. Hunter, and Joseph T. Snow, 114–32. Exeter: University of Exeter Press, 1994.

Willis, Raymond S. "Two Trotaconventos." *Romance Philology* 17 (1963–64): 353–62.

———. "Thirteen Years: Seedbed of Riddles in the *Libro de Buen Amor*." *Kentucky Romance Quarterly* 21 (1974): 215–27.

Zahareas, Anthony. *The Art of Juan Ruiz: Archpriest of Hita*. Madrid: Estudios de Literatura Española, 1965.

Zimmerman, Michael, ed. *Auctor et auctoritas: Invention et conformisme dans l'écriture médiévale, Actes du colloque tenu à l'Université de Versailles-Saint-Quentin-en-Yvelines* (14–16 June 1999). Paris: École des Chartes, 2001.

Zink, Michel. *La subjectivité littéraire autour du siècle de Saint Louis*. Paris: Presses Universitaires de France, 1985.

Zufferey, François. *Recherches linguistiques sur les chansonniers provençaux*. Geneva: Droz, 1987.

———. "La partie non-lyrique du chansonnier d'Urfé." *Revue des Langues Romanes* 98 (1994): 1–25.

Zumthor, Paul. *Essai de poétique médiévale*. Paris: Seuil, 1972.

———. *Langue, texte, énigme*. Paris: Seuil, 1975.

Index

❧ ❧

Page numbers in italics refer to illustrations and color plates.

Abbot of Vendôme, 68
accessus, 171
adynaton/adynata, 85, 91, 95
Aguirre, José María, 175
Alberico da Romano, Lord of Treviso, 62, 65–66, 78, 121, 122–23
Albigensian Crusade, 104, 111
Alemannic, 210
Alfonso V, 188, 192, 193
Alfonso X: and *Cantigas de Santa María*, 47, 116, *117–19*, *120–21*, 209; as classical emperor, 130, 239n55, 240n56; *General estoria* and *Estoria de España*, 177, 190; and Guiraut Riquier, 112–13; imperial portrait of, 130; in Santillana's *Prohemio*, 197–98; as troubadour-king, 7, 12, 123–25, 208
Alfonso XI, 21
Alhambra, 44
Amalric I, Vicomte, 112
alterity, 3, 205
Álvaro de Luna, 174, 175, 191
Amador de los Ríos, José, 214
analogs: in *Codex Manesse*, 127, 165; images as, 14, 99, 102; in troubadour chansonniers, 103, 105, 107, 108, 113, 116, 120
anaphora, visual, 144, 154
Andalusia, 49, 124
annominatio, 196
antiquarianism, 205
anti-songbook, as history of ideas, 206–7

apostles, 136
Aragon and Castile: courts of, 168–69, 191; kingdoms of, 14, 167
archival knowledge, 61
archive, 8–9, 23; manuscript archives, 203; name as, 59
Archpriest of Hita, 19, 21–22, 38–45, 54; as commentator, 45; like compilers of *Carmina Burana*, 45; *Libro del*, 41. See also *Libro de buen amor*
Aristotle, in Santillana's *Prohemio*, 197–98. See also Santillana, Marqués de (Iñigo López de Mendoza)
Arnaut Daniel, 66, 85–97; "Amors e iois e liocsc e tems," 91; "Ans qe·l cim reston de branchas," 91; "L'aur'amara," 88–90, 94; "En cest sonet coind'e leri" 85, 88–89; and phrase "q'amas l'aura," 88, 90; in Santillana's *Prohemio*, 197; sestina, 95; signature as metonymy for lyric corpus, 91
Arnaut de Maruelh, 65, 91, 114
ars: ars dicendi, 14; *ars dictandi*, 143; *ars/ingenium*, 176; *ars poetria*, 60, 104; lyric as, 6; storing poetry as, 15
arte/artes: arte de trovar, 216; *arte mayor*, 190, 198; *arte real*, 198; *artes praedicandi*, 81; seven, 143; vernacular *artes* (treatises), 179
Assimilationsstrukturen. See Gumbrecht, Hans Ulrich
auctor/auctores: Archpriest as, 19, 41; in

Carmina Burana, 27; citation of in cancionero, 188, 194–95; *Libro de buen amor* as, 41; Marcabru's name as, 80, 83; medieval signature as, 77; proper name as, 60; secondhand knowledge of *auctores*, 170; troubadour portrait as, 100

auctoritas, 100, 102, 165

Augustine, Saint: *De doctrina christiana* and *res*, 156, 158; *De genesi ad litteram*, 100; *De musica*, 26; on erotic love, 95; and hermeneutics, 18, 82, 223n4; interpretation of voice and letter, 231n12; on names, 87; portrait of, 166

aura, as word and rhyme sound, 85, 88–90, 93–96. *See also* Arnaut Daniel; Petrarch

aureate, 90–91

authentin, 102

author portraits: evangelist, 100; idealized and individual, 14, 60; from Renaissance, 165–66; in songbooks, 6, 10, 13, 99; of vernacular authors, 82; vernacular/secular vs. sacred, 102. See also Alfonso X; *Codex Manesse* (Codex Palatinus Germanicus 848, Manuscript C); Frederick II (Hohenstaufen)

autobiography: *Cantigas de Santa María* as royal, 209; *Libro de buen amor* as, 21, 223n4, 227n59

Avagnina, Maria Elisa, 122

Avignon, 106, 112

Baena, Juan Alfonso de: as compiler of *Cancionero de Baena*, 169, 170–75, 189, 190; knowledge of *auctores*, 170, 195; *Prologus Baenensis*, 175–79, 184, 188, 196

Barcelona Consistory, 178–81

Bartolomé, Fray de Córdoba, 189

Bartsch, Karl, 207, 211

Bassano del Grappa, fresco of. *See under* Frederick II (Hohenstaufen)

Bédier, Joseph, 212

Beltran Pepió, Vincenç, 5, 213

Benedictbeuern, abbey of, 20

Bernard Marti, 83

Bernart de Ventadorn, 1, 61, 64, 66, 74; "Can vei la lauzeta," 176; "Chantars no pot gaire valer," 75–78

Bertran de Born, 151

Bible: as codex, 22; illustrated, 164; moralized, 100

Bischoff, Bernhard, 24

Bloch, R. Howard, 87

Bocanegra, Francisco, 191

Bodmer, Johann Jakob, 16, 210–11; *Das Erdmännchen*, 210–11; and Johann Jakob Breitinger's *Sammlung von Minnesingern aus dem schwäbischen Zeitpunkte*, 210

Boethius, *Boeci* fragment in Occitan, 69

Bolduc, Michelle: *auctoritas*, 234n46; medieval author portraits, 82

Books of Hours, 13, 100

Bremberger song, 162, 244n136

Brunel-Lobrichon, Geneviève, 104

buen amor, 18, 19, 41, 59

bulletins, as influence on *Codex Manesse*, 137, 144, 166

Bumke, Joachim, 162

Burgundian court, 183

Butterfield, Ardis, 48

Bynum, Caroline Walker, 114

Cambridge Songs: eleventh-century, 26; thirteenth-century, 225n28

Camille, Michael, 102

Campbell, C. Jean, 123

canción, 15, 188, 196

cancioneiro, 167, 171, 209; content of Santillana's grandmother, 209

Cancioneiro da Ajuda, 7

cancioneros: *Cancionero de Baena*, 169, 171–73, 175, 181, 189, 190–91 (*see also* Baena, Juan Alfonso de); *Cancionero de Estúniga*, 174, 187–89, 192 (*see also* Caravajal); *Cancionero de Oñate-Castañeda*, 191, 252n44; *Cancionero de Palacio*, 174, 187, 189, 191; *Cancionero de San Román*, 189; *Cancionero general de Hernando del Castillo*, 15, 174, 187–88, 193, 196–97, 200. See also *Prologus Baenensis*

canso, 6, 8, 10, 14, 46–47, 57–58, 61, 64, 75–79, 85, 87–88, 113–14, 151

cantiga, 46, 170, 172–74, 190, 209; *de serrana* in *Cancionero de Baena*, 191, 192

Cantigas de Santa María: Alfonso X miniatures in Escorial codex, 116, *117–19*, 120–21; and Baena's *Prologus*, 190; *cantiga 279* in, 209; *cantiga 418* in, 125; *Cantigas de loor* 1, 110, 120 in, *117–19*, 124–25; *cantigas de miagre* in, 47; iconography in, 127; influence on *Libro de buen amor*, 47, 50; and opening miniature of the Escorial codex, 130, 209; as performative myth, 209; pilgrims in Escorial codex, 108, *109*; as precedent of scholarship on cancioneros, 213; as promoting cultural unity, 208–09; in Santillana's *Prohemio*, 197, 198; technical depictions of performance in, 140; and Toledo codex, 125

canzone, 46

canzoniere, 6, 95–96, 221n16

Caravajal, 15, 170, 188, 192–93

Carmina Burana (*Codex Buranus*), 6, 11, 18–38 passim, 39, 41–43, 45–48 passim, 53–54, 99; antique material in, 36–37; content and structure of, 23–25; Dido in, *32*, 37; *Fragmenta* as part of, 224n20; German lyrics in, 25, 31; German refrain stanzas in, 10, 46, 48, 53–54, 55, 192; German supplemental stanzas in, 24, 25, 31, 34–36, 38, 39, 46, 54, 226n46; historical and social context of, 20–21; nature landscape miniature in, 31, *33*, 99; *planctus* series in, 25; scenarios of compilation for refrain series in, 53; springtime songs in, 31, 40; as student anthology, 36–38; texts of black magic in, 36–37; Troy in, 37; *Vagantenstrophe* in, 35, 36; as workspace, 54, 188. See also *versus*

Carrillo de Huete, Pedro, 14; Fiesta of 1428, 182–86

Carruthers, Mary, 77, 114, 141

Cartagena, Pedro de, 200

Castile, 169, 171, 174, 185, 186, 195

Castilian, 188, 193; and cancioneros, 14, 188; in the *Libro de buen amor*, 46; literary models, 171; lyric, 167, 170, 190, 197, 198; *pasos de armas*, 183; tongue and Catholicism, 214; tradition, 198, 199

Castilian monarchy, 190

Castro, Américo, 44

Catalan, 193

catalogue numbers, 203, 204; titles, 204

Catholicism, 214

Catholic Monarchs, 15, 169, 196, 197, 199, 200; Fernando II, 194; Isabel I, 199

chansonniers, Italian, 3, 7, 10, 16, 57, 78, 102, 122, 167, 207, 221n22; illuminated, 231n9; sigla ADIK, 65

chansonniers, Occitan, illuminated, 221n23

chansonniers, Occitan, manuscripts (by sigla): A, 102, 151; D, 62, 64, 65, 77, 78, 230n2, 232n19; Da, 64–66, 77–79, 123; C, 72, 78–79, 112–13, 203; I, 57, 59, 78, 79, 103, 174, 203–5; K, 103; N, 103, 114–16, 120; R, 7, 62, 71, 81, 82, 84, 103–8, 110–16, 120, 238n18; W, 233n31

Charles d'Anjou II, 73

Chrétien de Troyes, 3, 13
Christ, 50, 82, 102, 104, 105, 106, 108,
    113, 160, 161; amorous wounding of,
    239n53; face of, 11, 62, 81, 105–8, *106*,
    107, 110–12, *plate 1*
Christic frontal gaze, 102
Christic image, 99, 104
Christ in Majesty, 130, 158
Christ's capture, 163–64, *plate 5*
Cicero, 14, 137, *142*
civilis ratio, 143
Clanchy, M. T., 233n43
coblas, 114; *unissonans, 88*
Codex Manesse (Codex Palatinus Ger-
    manicus 848, Manuscript C), 10,
    12, 164–66; Alram von Gresten in,
    144, *147*; and Bodmer's *Sammlung*,
    210, 211; dertugenhafte Schriber
    in, 158; Dietmar von Aist in, 34;
    Frauenlob in, 144, *145*, 154; Göli in,
    151; and *Grundstock*, 158; as Habsburg
    songbook, 243n104; Hadlaub in, 126,
    158, 160–62, 211, *plate 6*; Hartmann
    von Aue in, 154, *155*; Heinrich von der
    Mure in, 136; Heinrich von Veldeke
    in, 136, 154, 156, 161; Henry VI in,
    128–30, *131*, 132, 135–37, 139–40, 143,
    165; and heraldry, 128–29; Hohenfels
    in, 151; illuminators of, 126; inven-
    tion in, 156, 158, 160–64; Klingsor
    von Ungerlant in, 158, *159*; Konrad
    von Kirchberg in, 136; naming of,
    210; Ofterdingen in, 158; Pfeffel in,
    144, *146*, 154; and ranking of poets,
    242n92; Reinmar der Alte in, 151, 158;
    Reinmar von Brennenberg in, 13,
    162–64, *plate 7*; Reinmar von Zweter
    in, 136; rhetorical composition in,
    150, 151, 154, 156; rhetoric of, 141, 143,
    144, 150; Rudolf von Neuenburg in,
    154, 156, *157*; Rugge in, 151, 154; as
    songbook, 125–26; Tannhäuser in, 151,
    153; Ulrich von Lichtenstein in, 144,
    148; Ulrich von Zazikhoven's *Lanzelet*
    in, 144; von Buchein in, 144, *149*, 151;
    Wachsmut von Künzigen in, 151,
    152, 154; Walther von der Vogelweide
    in, 128, 136, *138*, 154, 156, 158, 166;
    Walther von Mezze in, 154
cognitio, imperfecta and *perfecta*, 136
compilatio, 5, 59; and *ordinatio*, 18, 19, 222n1
compiler-poet: Alfonso X as, 208; Uc de
    Saint Circ as, 65
comunal, 42, 43
comunaus, 76
conductus, 21
Conrad of Thuringia, Count, 244n119
Consistori de la sobregaia companhia del
    gai saber (Jeux Floraux), 104
"constitutive verisimilitude." *See* Freed-
    berg, David
container: cancioneros as, 213, 214, 215,
    216; songbook as, 205, 208, 213, 214
contents, of songbooks, 205, 207, 208,
    215
contrafactum, 99
conversio, 136
converso, 199, 200
copla, 187, 190, 191, 194; *de arte menor*, 188
Corpus Christi festivals, 182
Costana, 15, 174, 196, 201
critical editions: of cancioneros, 216; as
    embodying a culture, 211; as instru-
    ments of study, 203; as postmedieval
    practice, 204; songbook as sources
    for, 16; in songbook format, 215
Crocker, Richard, 26, 38
"crossover" phenomenon, 99, 114. *See also*
    Newman, Barbara
crusade, 49, 67, 81, 102, 104, 105, 107, 112,
    113, 124
cuaderna vía, 18, 21, 43
Curschmann, Michael, 136, 144
Curtius, Ernst Robert, 77, 85, 226nn37–38

Dagenais, John, 5, 22, 41, 42
Dance of Death, 195
dance songs, 22, 34, 35, 54
dansa, 46
Dante, 6, 8, 176, 206; Arnaut's influence
  on, 235n81; *De vulgari eloquentia*, 8,
  66; Imperial's translation of, 188;
  Paradiso, 93; *Purgatorio*, 46, 85, 86,
  93–94; *Vita Nuova*, 39, 187
David, King, 120, 129, 130, *132*; Alfonso
  X as, 7
Day of Judgment, 105
de Campo, Mendo, 191
De Casibus, 195
decir/dezir/decires, 14, 170, 172, 173, 178, 187,
  189, 190, 195, 196, 206
Derrida, Jacques, 9
Deutschland, 210
Dinis (king of Portugal), 209
dispositio, 150, 151, 156
dit, 2, 170
divisa, 183, 196
Doctrina de compondre dictats, 46
Dominican debate, 104
Dominicy, Marc-Antoine, 204, 206
domna, 113, 116, 123
Donaueschinger Psalter, 151, 163, 164,
  plate 5
Dryden, John, 210
Dueñas, Juan de, 194

early modern (period), 3, 16; humanism, 7;
  and Italian tradition, 15
eaten-heart legend, 162–64
Eble, Lord, 75
Ecclesiastes, 87
eighteenth-century studies of songbooks,
  16, 206–7, 210–11
ekphrasis, 150
elocutio, 150, 154, 156
emblematic, 128, 150; *Codex* miniatures
  as, 12

emblematic mode, 127, 136, 140, 150, 165,
  236n1
emblems, Renaissance, 99, 165, 236n1
emendation, 18; Archpriest as inviting, 39,
  43, 48, 54, 57; evidence of, in *Libro de
  buen amor*, 229n89
Encina, Juan del, 188; *El arte de poesía castellana*, 197–99
encyclopedia: *Carmina* as lyric collection
  and, 27, 36; *De viris illustribus*, 59;
  Distinctiones monasticae et morales, 24;
  Summa recreatorum, 24. See also *Libro
  de buen amor*
endline configuration, in *Carmina*, 30
Enlightenment, 16, 206
enarratio poetarum, 144
Enrique, Prince of Aragon, 184, 189
entremeses, 182, 183, 184, 185
epics, 13; versus lyric, 208; material in
  Carmina, 37; as origins of national
  culture, 207; scholarship, 207
epístola, 188, 192
epoch editions, 214
Esteve de Belmon, 108. See also Peire
  Cardenal
estribote, 22, 70. See also *Libro de buen amor*
Estúñiga, Lope de, 194
evangelist, 59, 100, *101*, 126, 166
exemplum/exempla, 18, 21, 27, 41, 195
Ezzelino da Romano, 121

falconry, 100, 122
farsas, 182
Fernando II. *See* Catholic Monarchs
Fernando VIII, 214
Ferrante I (king of Naples), 194
Fiesta at Valladolid in 1428, 175, 181–86,
  196
figurae, 143, 144, 150
fin' amor, 88, 91, 122, 123, 162, 172
fingir, 194, 195, 197, 199
florilegia, 23

Folquet de Marseille, 93, 115–16, 123; "Ben an mort mi e lor," 114
Fontainebleau, library of, 203
Foulche-Delbosc, Raymond, 213
Francis, Saint, 115–16, 237n13
François I, 203
Freccero, John, 8
Frederick I (Barbarossa), 129
Frederick II (Hohenstaufen), 123, 125, 129, 130, 134, 135, 139, 240n56; as classical emperor, 240n56; *De arte venandi cum avibus*, 120, 122, 130, *134*, 240n64; *Exultet*, 120, *135*; fresco, Bassano del Grappa, 116, *120*, 121–23, 124, 125, 127, 139, 240n60, 240n64, 241n65; imperial portrait of, 130; as troubadour-king, 12, 120, 123
Freedberg, David, 105
French poetic anthologies, 221n15
fresco. *See under* Frederick II (Hohenstaufen)
Frühmorgen-Voss, Hella, 156

Galician-Portuguese / Galician, 7, 47, 52, 111, 124, 168, 191; lyric corpus, 245n2; lyric traditions, 190, 197, 198, 209
gap, 68, 73, 74
Garcia, Michel, 5, 171, 191
gaya çiencia, 172, 177, 178, 180, 184
Generation of 1898, 215
genre studies, 219n6
George, Saint, 151
Gerli, E. Michael, 38, 200
Germanistik, 211
German language, 211
Ghibelline culture, 122, 123
Glosa Ordinaria, 22
Golden Age, 16, 213
goliard/Goliardic, 6, 18, 20, 21, 24, 36, 50, 224n13
Gospels of Saint Médard of Soissons, 101
Gossman, Lionel, 206

Gothic style, 111, 121
graçia infusa, 172, 175, 176, 177
Gratian, *Decretum*, 22
Great Schism, 104
Gregory the Great, 143, 236n3; *Letter to Serenus*, 141
Grimm brothers, 211
Gröber, Gustav, 58
Guilhem IX (Guilhem de Peitieu), 41, 66–69, 71, 75, 84; "Ben vueill que sapchon," 68, 75, 84; "Companho, farai un vers," 68; "Farai un vers," 68, 72; "Pos de chantar," 67, 72; and Saint Martial, 232n27; title, 232n23
Guillaume de Machaut, 6; *Voir-Dit*, 39, 188
Guillaume Durant, *Rationale divinorum officiorum*, 136
Guillem de Cabestaing, 162
Guillem Magret, 84
Guinizelli, Guido, 197
Giraut de Bornelh, 63, 64, 65
Guiraut Riquier, 104, 112, 113; "Be·m degra de chantar," 112; "Humils, forfaitz, repres," 113; *supplicatio* written to Alfonso X, 112
Gumbrecht, Hans Ulrich, *Assimilationsstrukturen*, 170, 252n44
Guzmán, Fernán Pérez de, 189; "Estrella Diana," 190

Hagedorn, Friedrich von, 210
Hagen, Friedrich Heinrich von der, 162
Hamburger, Jeffrey, 105, 238n21
handbooks, modern, of lyric poetry, 207
Haseloff, Arthur, 151
Haupt, Moriz, 211
heraldry/heraldic: and local visual media, 12, 13, 126–27, 135, 150; plastic arts, 128–29, 137; as rhetoric, 10; style, 135; visual system, 143
Hermann I, Count of Thuringia, 158, 160. See also *Wartburgkrieg*

hermeneutic opacity, 12, 57, 61–62, 64, 67, 74, 79, 82, 84, 91, 97
historia, 141, 158, 161, 165
Hohenstaufen dynasty, 123, 124, 210. *See also* Frederick I (Barbarossa); Frederick II (Hohenstaufen)
Holmes, Olivia, 58, 222n24
horror vacui, 195
Huizinga, Johan, 183–86; *The Autumn of the Middle Ages*, 183
Hundred Years' War, 204
Huot, Sylvia, 5, 114, 136, 171

iconography, 13, 82, 100, 104, 120, 125, 126, 127, 130, 132, 136, 137
Imperial, Francisco, 188, 189; *Dezir a las siete virtudes*, 170; "Estrella Diana," 190
imperial program/agendas: of Alfonso and Frederick II, 12; of secular rulers, 127
imperial ruler, Emperor Henry portrait as, 130
Incarnation, 87, 88
indulgence, *106*, 107
ingenio/ingenium, 176, 179, 181, 184, 195
initials, historiated, 11, 12, 13, 31, 81, 99, 104–5, 107–8, 110–15, 120
intertextuality in cancioneros, 14, 15, 187, 197
invençiones, 15, 172, 180, 183, 185, 187, 193, 196
inventio, 150, 156
involution, of cancionero poetry, 7, 195
Isabel I. *See under* Catholic Monarchs
Isabella (sister of Henry III of England), 121–23
Isidore of Seville, 60, 87
ivory caskets, 150, 161–62

Jakobson, Roman, 79
James, Saint, 103, 108, 110–12; initial related to pilgrims in *Cantigas de Santa María*, 238n25, *plate 2*

Jammers, Ewald, 130
Jaufre Rudel, 172
Jauss, Hans Robert, 3
Jean Renart, *Roman de la rose ou de Guillaume de la Dole*, 129
Jeanroy, Alfred, 171; *Bibliographie sommaire des chansonniers provençaux*, 208
Jerome, Saint, 87, 166; *De viris illustribus*, 59
Jeu de sainte Agnès, 72
Jews / Jewish literary tradition: caricatures in cancionero poetry, 195; as milieu of *Libro de buen amor*, 21
joglar/joglaría/jongleurs, 42, 50, 59, 112
Juan II, 169, 173, 182, 189, 190, 191, 197, 199
Juana of Aragon, 194
Judas, 163–64
juegos, 177, 182, 199

Kamuf, Peggy, 233n45
Kendrick, Laura, 102
Kopialbuch, 137. *See also* privilege images
Konrad von Würzburg, 162
Koschorreck, Walter, 162
Kuhn, Hugo, 3, 212
Kunstlandschaft, 126

Lachmann, Karl, 211; and system of mechanical transmission, 212, 213
Lancelot, 182
Landgrafen, 158
langue d'ouy / langue d'oc, 204
lapdog, in Hadlaub miniature, 160, 161, 244n132
lauda, 46
Laura, 8, 94–96. *See also* Petrarch
Lauro, 93–94
lauzengier, 83
lavador, 83–84, 105, 107–8, 112–13. *See also* Marcabru
lectio, 141
Le Gentil, Pierre, 49

legir, 83
Le Goff, Jacques, 9, 170
lema: of Alfonso V, 193; of Bishop of
  Guarda, 196
Lentini, Giacomo da, 123
Lerer, Seth, 2
letra, 183, 185, 187, 196
letrados, 169, 178
Leys d'Amors, 60, 104
Libro de buen amor: as autobiography/au-
  tobiographical in nature, 7, 18,
  21, 227n59; *Ave María* in, 50; as
  cancionero, 18–23, 38–44; *Cantica de
  loores de Santa María* in, 50; *canticas
  de serrana*, 41, 42, 44–45, 48, 50–52;
  as communal text, 44; content and
  manuscripts of, 18; *cuaderna vía*
  in, 18, 21, 43, 45, 47, 48, 228n79; *De
  commo los scolares demandan por dios* in,
  50; Endrina episode in, 44; *estribillo*
  in, 46–52, 191; *estribote* in, 46–54,
  230n92; Ferret as bad messenger in,
  42; *Gozos* in, 48, 50; as instrument,
  44–45, 228n77; and lack of overarching poetic figure, 7; as "libro del
  Arçipreste de Hita," 209; lyric in,
  229n81, 229n87; Melon de la Huerta
  in, 44; minstrel introduction in, 48;
  as moral encyclopedia, 41; as *mudéjar
  puerta*, 44; *Pasión* in, 50; as performance piece, 44; as potential text,
  43–44; in *Prohemio* (Santillana), 197;
  prose prologue of, 40; refrain poetry
  in, 47–54; and Salamanca manuscript, 18, 40, 49; as songbook, 6–7;
  as transcript, 43, 48, 54; *troba caçurra*
  in, 41, 48, 49, 50, 191; as workspace,
  54, 188
Lida de Malkiel, María Rosa, 44
lingua d'oc, 93
Lucena, 194
Lucrecia d'Alagno, 192–93

lyric "je"/"I," debates concerning, 8–9, 58,
  127, 246n19

macaronic verse, 18
Macpherson, Ian, 185
mandylion, 111
Manesse: family, 126, 160; Johannes, 126;
  Kreis, 162; patronage of *Minnesang*,
  126, 210, 211; Rüdiger, 126
manicula, 79
Manrique, Rodrigo, 191
Maravall, José Antonío, 179
Marcabru: as *auctor*, 80; "Auias de chan,"
  80; authority of through rubric and
  Christ image, 62; and chansonnier R,
  71, 104–5, 107–8, 110, 113, *plates 1–3*;
  entensa pura, 80; *intentio*, 80; "Lo vers
  comenssa," 80; and name, 11, 80–84;
  "Pax in nomine Domini," 9, 81–84;
  and transmission of name, 74; and
  vida, 75
marginalia, 10, 11, 13, 41, 102, 103, 114,
  plate 4
María of Aragon, Queen, 192–93
Martí I of Aragon, 180
Martin, Kurt, 144
Martínez de Medina, Diego, 190
Mary, Virgin, 7, 103–4, 108, 111–13, 124–25,
  158, 160, 208; and *Cantigas de Santa
  María* as cult of, 190, *plate 3*; *cantigas*
  in *Cancionero de Baena* dedicated to,
  190–91
Mary Magdalene, 160–61
Matfre Ermengaud de Béziers, *Breviari
  d'amor*, 82
"matrix, manuscript," 9, 208. *See also*
  Nichols, Stephen G.
McMillan, D., 49
medievalism, 203, 205
meditatio, 141
Mejía, Hernán, 194
Mena, Juan de, *Coronación*, 198, 199

Mendoza: Diego Hurtado de, 190; family, 191
Meneghetti, Maria Luisa, 122
Menéndez Pidal, Ramón, 18, 214–15
Menéndez y Pelayo, D. Marcelino, *Antología de poetas líricos castellanas*, 214, 215–16
mengua de la sciença, 179
mester de clerecía, 171
Middle High German, 210, 211
mimetic commentary, 14
mimetic representation, marginalia as, 102
ministeriales, 121, 126
Minnesang, 1, 6, 25, 34–35, 54, 126–29, 136, 141, 143–44, 156, 158, 162, 210–13
Minnesänger, 2, 21, 158, 162
Minnesangs Frühling, Des, 16, 211–213, 215; edition as "Arbeitsausgabe," 212
Minnis, Alistair, 100
minstrel song, 21, 42
"Misa de amor," 194–95
mnemonic, 19, 29
Monk of Montaudon, 65–66, 91–92; "Pos Peire d'Alvergn'a chantat," 66, 92
Montoro, Antón, 15, 199, 200
Mosé, 189
Moses, 87
motes, 185
Mostacci, Jacopo, 123
Mozarabs/Mozarabic, 21, 41
Müller, Jan-Dirk, 5
music/musical: function of *versus*, 25; instrument, *Libro de buen amor* as, 44–45; instrument, songs for, 43; melisma, 29, 37; notation in songbooks, 4, 10, 22, 25, 82, 126; performance in *Carmina* and *Libro*, 42–43; treatment of antique material, 37
Muslim traditions, 21

names/naming: activity of, 61; as deictic particle, 61, 64; governing a corpus of texts, 2; incantatory quality of, 67, 69, 71, 74; nominal self-invocation, 11, 60, 66, 68, 72–73, 74, 75, 78–81, 85, 86; proper, 58–97 passim, 231n11; proper and hermeneutic opacity, 61, 62, 64, 67, 72, 74, 78, 79, 82, 84, 97; proper as rubric and metonymy, 11, 12, 58, 61, 79, 80, 85, 91; as signature, 77, 79, 85–86, 91, 97; as synecdoche, 75, 77, 78; voice and proper, 58
Naples (Neopolitan court), 192, 193, 194
nationalistic purpose, of Spanish literary history, 214, 215
National Library (Spain), 214
Navarre, 185, 186
New Historicism, 5
Newman, Barbara, 99, 114
New Philology, 5, 219n6
New Testament, 87
Nichols, Stephen G., 5, 9, 77, 114, 115; "manuscript matrix," 208, 212
Nohrnberg, James, 93
Noli me tangere, 160–61
nom, 70, 71
nomen, 60
Nostredame, Jean de, *Vies des plus celebres et anciens poetes provensaux*, 206, 208
nova, "So fo el tems," 69

Old English, 210
oral: circulation, 21; experiences of lyric poetry, 217; oral-musical culture, 13; performance as related to roll, 130, 136; performances of proper name, 61; social practices, 16; traditions, 23, 166; transmission, 13, 59, 60, 212; transmitted vernacular song, 23; versus written, 207–8
orality, 9, 14
Order of Teutonic Knights, 151

ordinatio, 18, 19; and *compilatio*, 18, 19, 222n1

ornatus, 154

Otloh, von Sankst Emmeram, *Liber proverbiorum*, 24, 27, 38

Ovid, 18, 21, 194

Paden, William, 212

Padua, 121

painture/parole, 137

pandect, 59

papacy, 104, 112, 121

partimens, 114

pasos de armas, 183

Passion, the, 50, 162, 163, 164

pastourelle, 42, 52

pattern or model books, 127

Pattison, Walter, 64, 73

Pedraza, García de, 191

Pedro of Portugal, Infante, 191, 197

Peire Cardenal, 104, 108, 110–13; "Las amairitz, qui encolpar las vol," 110, 111; "De sirventes faire no·m tuelh," 111; "Un sirventes trametrai per messatge," 108, 110, 111; "Vera vergena, María, 111

Peire d'Alvernhe: "Cantarai d'aquestz trobadors," 62–66; as first poet, 64–65, 71

Peire de Lunel de Montech, 104

Peire de Monzo, 66

Peire Rogier, 63, 64, 69

Peire Vidal, 87

penitence, 72, 106, 111, 113

penitent: Arnaut as, 93; Mary Magdalene as, 160–61; in Peire Cardenal's lyric, 108

Pereira, Justa Rodrigues, 196

Peter Lombard, *Sententiae*, 22–23

Peters, Ursula, 127

Petrarch, 6, 8, 61, 85, 86, 93–96, 97, 169, 206; "Beato in sogno," 95; "Là ver l'aurora," 95–96; *Rime sparse*: 8, 85, 93–96, 169

Petrarchism, 202

philologists, 59, 204, 206

philology/philological, 5, 16, 35, 204, 205, 208, 213, 215

pictura, 141, 143, 164

Pier della Vigna, *quaestio de rosa et viola*, 122–23

pilgrim, 93, 104, 108, *109*, 110–13, 124, *plate 2*

pilgrimage, 104, 105, 107, 110–13, 124

planh, 67, 72, 84

plays: liturgical, 20; religious, 24

Plotinus, 114

Poe, Elizabeth, 69, 171

poeta, 8, 165, 172, 190, 198

poetic treatises, 180

poetría, 172, 173

poiesis, 161, 211

postmedieval practices/readers, 204–6

praesens, 143

preguntas, 172, 173, 185, 189, 190, 192

Presilla, Maricel, 124

princeps litteratus, 129, 130, 136–37

privilege images, *Kopialbuch*, 137, *139–41*, 166

Prologus Baenensis, 168, 169, 172, 173, 175–78, 184, 188, 190–91, 196

provenance, 204. *See also* cancioneros: *Cancionero de Baena*

Provençal, 206

Provencaux, Poetes, 203, 206

Provence, 204, 206, 208

Proverbs, 29, 38, 39, 41

Provinciaux, Poetes, 203

psalters, 59, 100, 126, 164; illuminated, 150

publication, 6, 11, 168, 170; of generic classification, 207; of medieval text as empirical reconstruction, 205; of medieval text as transcription

quantitative verse, 19, 20, 22, 37, 38
Quintilian, 14; in Encina's *Arte de poesía*, 198; *Institutio oratoria*, 143, 154
Quixote, Don, 186

Raimbaut d'Aurenga, 67–70; "Car, douz, fenhz," 73–75; "Escotatz, mas no say que s'es," 70–74; title, 232n23
Raimon Vidal, 69, 180; *Roman de Jaufré*, 114
Ramon Berenguer IV of Barcelona, 104
Raymond, François-Juste-Marie: *Choix des poésies*, 207; *Lexique Roman*, 207–8
razos, 59, 74, 80, 169, 171, 172, 174
Reconquest, 104, 111
recueils, 59
reference manuals, 207, 214
refrain lyric. See *Carmina Burana* (*Codex Buranus*); *Libro de buen amor*
"Regla del galán," 194–95. *See also* Jews/Jewish literary tradition
remission of sins, 105–6
Renaissance, 6, 16, 99, 165, 166, 204; medieval, 20
renovatio, 113
repertory: *Carmina Burana* as compiled from preexisting, 39; *Carmina Burana* as singable, 39; Notre-Dame, 20; Saint Martial, 20
réplica/contrarréplica, 187–90
repraesentare, 141
representaciones, 182
res, 60, 82, 156, 158
respuestas, 172, 173, 185, 189, 190, 192
Rex et propheta, 137
rhythmical meters, 20
rhythmical poetry / verse, 22, 25, 27, 36–38
Ribera, Suero de: *galán coplas*, 194–96; "Misa de amor," 194–95
Richart de Fournival, *Li Bestiares d'Amours*, 137
rimas caras, 88, 90, 92

rimas dissolutas, 88, 90
ritual, 4, 7, 10, 14, 15, 170, 175, 176, 178–83, 201, 202
roll (*rotulus*), 2, 129, 130, 136, 137, 139, 144, 156, 161, 166
romance, 2, 13, 14, 21, 50, 84, 144, 154, 158, 182–86, 192–93
romançe, 188. *See also* Caravajal
Romance lyric, 8, 20, 46
Roman de Flamenca, 84
Roman de la Rose, 13, 100
Roman du castelain de Couci, 162
romantic: desire to preserve lyric, 212; discourse, 17; preoccupations, 207; romanticization of manuscript sources, 206; troubadour poet-hero, 207
Rudolf I of Habsburg, King, 128
Ruiz, Juan, 21, 38, 209

Sainte-Palaye, Jean-Baptiste de la Curne de, 16, 206; with Abbé Millot, *Histoire littéraire des troubadours*, 206, 208
saints' lives, 59
Salamanca, 199
Salazar, Lope García de, 41
Sangspruchgedichte, 158
Santiago de Compostela, 103, 108, 110
Santillana, Marqués de (Iñigo López de Mendoza), 41, 68, 168, 170, 179, 188, 191, 209; in *Maldecir* of Torrella, 194; *Prohemio e carta al Condestable de Portugal*, 41, 47, 196–99, 209, 251n17; use of word "cancioneros," 245n7
Schlegel, Friedrich, 211
Schumann, Otto, 24
Schweikle, Günther, 212, 213
scientia civilis, 143
scroll, 2, 136, 137
Second Crusade, 104
senhal, 58, 86, 112, 123

sententia, 22, 27, 38

seraph (chansonnier N), 114–16, *plate 4*

serranillas, 170, 173, 178, 187, 189, 191, 196.
See also *Libro de buen amor: canticas
de serrana*

sestina, 95

Seville, 125

shifting mediality, 102

Sicilian school, 123

"silloge," 5

single-author compilations, 220n15

sirventes, 58, 70, 108, 111, 123

Solomon, King, 130, *133*

Sordello, 93

Spanish Crusade, 105

Spanish identity, 215–16

Spanish people, 216

Spitzer, Leo, 18

Spruchband, 136

Starkey, Kathryn, 5

Steger, Hugo, 129

student, 10, 18, 20, 22–24, 29, 35–38, 41

sudarium, 111

Swabian culture / songbook, 210–11

Tate, R. B. 43

Teervoren, Helmut, 212

tensos, 58

Tertullian, 87

Thierry of Chartres, 143

Tirant lo Blanc, 182

Toja, Gianluigi, 86

topos/topoi, 85, 86, 143, 144, 154, 187, 188

tornada, 73–75, 77–80, 85–87, 123

Torrella, Pedro, *Coplas de maldecir de la
mujeres*, 193–94, 196

Toulouse, 104, 108, 113, 115

tournaments, 170, 175, 185, 186

transcription of lyric texts, 204, 205, 210,
211

translatio, 112

translatio imperii et studii, 14

trivium, 21

trobador, 5, 42, 57, 58, 62, 78, 79, 198,
203

trobar, 39, 69, 91, 92, 112; *leu*, 75; *ric*, 88, 91

troubadour-king, 12, 120, 123, 139, 208

trouvère, 6, 20

Ubi sunt, 195

Uc de Saint Circ, 65, 122

Unamuno, Miguel de, 215

university/universities, 20, 21, 22, 59

Urban II (pope), 68

Urtext, 16, 212

Valladolid, 14

Van Vleck, Amelia, 13

Veronica, 105–6, 113

vers / versi, 5, 60, 70, 81, 82, 96

versus, 22–41 passim; *28, 30*, 54; Archpriest
in *Libro de buen amor* acting as, 43;
Benedicamus-versus, 26, 38; *cum auctoritate*, 81

Vetter, Ewald, 137

vidas, 10, 11, 58–61, 65, 66, 67, 68, 71, 72,
74, 75, 83, 85, 86, 91, 92, 102, 103, 115,
126, 162, 165, 169, 171–74, 207. *See also*
Nostredame, Jean de

villancicos, 47. See also *estribote*

Villasandino, Alfonso Álvarez de, 172–75,
178, 190–91, 194

Villena, Enrique de, *Arte de trovar*, 14, 175,
178, 179, 180, 181, 184, 197, 198

Vinaver, Eugène, 154

virelai, 46

Visconde de Altamira, 200

voice / *vox corporis*, 60, 61, 63, 67, 81; of
proper name, 58

Volk, songbook as creating idea of, 211

Vollmann, Benedikt Konrad, 24

Wachinger, Burghart, 24

Wappensymbol, 136. See also *Codex Manesse*

(Codex Palatinus Germanicus 848, Manuscript C)

Wartburgkrieg, 158, 160, 165. See also *Codex Manesse* (Codex Palatinus Germanicus 848, Manuscript C)

Wechsel, 34

Weingartner Liederhandschrift, 132

Weiss, Julian, 171, 176, 177, 197

Weltchronik des Rudolf von Ems, 130, *133*

Wenzel, Horst, 5

Wettgesang, 210

Willis, Raymond, 44

Wolfram von Eschenbach, 144; *Parzival*, 158, 160

Yahweh, 87

Zahareas, Anthony N. 38

zéjel, 47

Zufferey, François, 71, 104

Zumthor, Paul: *Essai de poétique médievale*, 9; *mouvance*, 212, 221n20

Zürich, 12, 125, 126, 127, 158, 210, 211

Züricher Wappenrolle, 130